LLOYD GAINES AND THE FIGHT TO END SEGREGATION

Studies in Constitutional Democracy

Justin B. Dyer and Jeffrey L. Pasley, Series Editors

The Studies in Constitutional Democracy Series explores the origins and development of American constitutional and democratic traditions, as well as their applications and interpretations throughout the world. The often subtle interaction between constitutionalism's commitment to the rule of law and democracy's emphasis on the rule of the many lies at the heart of this enterprise. Bringing together insights from history and political theory, the series showcases interdisciplinary scholarship that traces constitutional and democratic themes in American politics, law, society, and culture, with an eye to both practical and theoretical implications.

LLOYD GAINES

and the

FIGHT TO END SEGREGATION

———

James W. Endersby and William T. Horner

UNIVERSITY OF MISSOURI PRESS
Columbia

ISBN: 978-0-8262-2085-1 (hardcover : alk. paper)
ISBN: 978-0-8262-2236-7 (paperback : alk. paper)

Library of Congress Control Number: 2015960093

∞™ This paper meets the requirements of the
American National Standard for Permanence of Paper
for Printed Library Materials, Z39.48, 1984.

Typeface: Garamond

To Linda, Jane, Kate, and Luke

and

To Heather, Tricia, and Ellie

Contents

Acknowledgments

This is the chronicle of Lloyd Gaines and the pioneering civil rights case of *Missouri ex rel. Gaines v. Canada*, decided by the US Supreme Court in 1938. As authors we were attracted by the importance of this landmark decision as well as by the story of the dedicated individuals involved in the litigation. We found it surprising that no book-length narrative had been written. Accounts of the case often contain incomplete or incorrect information. We hope to correct that by offering an interesting and accurate narrative of the *Gaines* case.

The story we will present here could not be told—or even known in detail today—were it not for the efforts of those professionals dedicated to preserving our history. We benefitted greatly from the manuscripts of the National Association for the Advancement of Colored People, now archived and released through the Library of Congress. These papers include correspondence, newspapers, and other materials from the Gaines era. In addition, we benefitted from several collections at the University of Missouri, including the University Archives, Ellis Library, the Journalism Library, and the Law School Library, and we thank the Mizzou librarians and archivists, including Cindy Bassett at the library for the School of Law. We also thank Mark Schleer and Ithaca Bryant at the Lincoln University Archives, and we appreciate the efforts of Laura Jolly and other staff members at the State Historical Society of Missouri. We accessed information from a number of other collections, including those within the Michigan Historical Center.

We thank our research assistant, Katie VanderMolen, whose tireless and flawless work on our behalf was so critical at the early stage of this project.

We are also grateful to acquisitions editor Clair Willcox, who shepherded this project along; our reviewers, who provided helpful feedback; and the staff members at the University of Missouri Press, who supported this book. We feel it most appropriate that the story of Lloyd Gaines and the "University of Missouri case" should be published by the University of Missouri Press.

We are most appreciative of the encouragement and patience of our families. This book is dedicated to them.

The story of the Gaines case is one of the courage and conviction of a few individuals who were willing to challenge injustice and discrimination. Our world is better because of their efforts.

Illustrations

1. Thurgood Marshall, Donald Gaines Murray, and Charles Houston, during litigation against the University of Maryland. Library of Congress Prints and Photographs Division.

2. Lloyd Gaines as a student. University of Missouri School of Law Digital Collection.

3. Walter White, NAACP executive secretary (left), and Charles Houston, NAACP special counsel (right). Library of Congress Prints and Photographs Division.

4. Sidney Redmond (right) with Elmer Mosee and Daisy Lampkin, supporting the NAACP anti-lynching campaign. Library of Congress Prints and Photographs Division.

5. Silas Woodson Canada, Registrar of the University of Missouri, after his retirement in 1946. *Missouri Alumnus*, June 1967, courtesy of University Archives, University of Missouri.

6. Charles Hamilton Houston, NAACP special counsel and lead counsel for Lloyd Gaines, in 1939. Library of Congress Prints and Photographs Division.

7. William Sloan Hogsett, lead counsel for the University of Missouri. Dick Fowler, *Leaders in Our Town*.

8. Attorneys Sidney R. Redmond (center, standing), Henry D. Espy (right center), and David Grant (center, sitting), and Colored Clerks Circle

LLOYD GAINES AND THE FIGHT TO END SEGREGATION

Introduction

Less than two weeks before Christmas in 1938, Supreme Court Chief Justice Charles Evans Hughes delivered a startling pronouncement. The case before the Court was *Missouri ex rel. Gaines v. Canada.* In a majority opinion, the Court ruled that the Fourteenth Amendment's equal protection clause applied to educational institutions within a state: race could not be used as a justification to deny equality of educational opportunities. The *Gaines* decision was the first of many issued by the United States Supreme Court regarding race, higher education, and equal opportunity. The Court's application of the Fourteenth Amendment's equal protection clause imposed federal authority in defining equality and countered the dominant judicial doctrine that states had the right to determine racial relations. Although racial segregation within the states would continue for decades afterward, the Hughes Court's decision was a major turning point for constitutional interpretation of equal protection. The *Gaines* case was arguably the most significant on the issue of educational equality until the decisions of *Brown v. Board of Education* (1954, 1955).

The story of the man at the center of the landmark case is largely forgotten, even though Gaines and his legal advisors played a critical role in the civil rights movement. The case, despite its significance, has received little in-depth analysis. This work strives to provide that analysis. The story behind the *Gaines* decision brings together a mix of legal, sociopolitical, and personal factors. First, the legal counsel, attorneys for the national and local organizations of the National Association for the Advancement of Colored People (NAACP), learned what would work for civil rights advocacy in the courts.

1

Second, success required support from a coalition of groups with diverse interests, including political leaders, civic organizations, the press, and the public. Third, pursuit of a constitutional ruling involved considerable personal sacrifice on the part of the attorneys and, especially, of the litigant.

The *Gaines* decision was, as Richard Kluger wrote, "an enormous milestone."[1] The case drew public attention as the first federal decision limiting the separate but equal doctrine, the legal standard that had previously sanctioned racial segregation in the United States. The goal of *Gaines* and subsequent civil rights cases was to overturn the constitutional doctrine established in 1896 by the United States Supreme Court in *Plessy v. Ferguson. Gaines* was an important first step on the long path toward acceptance of the principle that racial segregation is inherently unequal.

Contemporaries noted that the case attracted "nation-wide attention" for several months.[2] *Gaines* was the first case in which the Supreme Court confronted racial segregation in education.[3] Eminent historian John Hope Franklin deemed the *Gaines* decision "the most significant step" toward providing African Americans opportunities for advanced education.[4] Other scholars and legal observers observed that its "far-reaching significance" would "necessitate a revolution in educational practice in the southern and border states" and mark "a new milestone in the struggle of the Negro for increased educational opportunities from which all future progress and direction in this field must be measured."[5] The impact of the legal decision was felt immediately, and it provided the impetus for the NAACP and other civil rights organizations to push for racial equality. The ruling in *Gaines* was the "first important victory in this concerted strategy" to overturn segregation, and *Brown* "emerged straight from a series of cases going back to [*Gaines* in] 1938."[6] Thurgood Marshall, then the head of the NAACP's Legal Defense Fund and a future Supreme Court justice, would remember *Gaines* "as one of our greatest victories."[7]

St. Louis resident Lloyd Gaines was a college graduate with a strong academic record who applied to the all-white law school at the University of Missouri in Columbia, the state's flagship public institution of higher learning. Lloyd Gaines was black.[8] The university registrar, Silas Woodson Canada, followed the directions of the university's administrators and its legal counsel and denied Gaines's application. Missouri, like other border and southern states, provided separate schools for blacks; the University of Missouri was for whites only. Segregation and the separate but equal doctrine were entrenched in American culture. The decades after World War I, however, saw challenges to this norm. Most of these challenges were unsuccessful as establishment interests strongly defended racial separation. However, the seeds of the civil rights movement and dramatic political and social change were planted in the interwar period. Attorneys for the NAACP in New York, Washington, and St. Louis came to Gaines's assistance. They litigated on his behalf for nearly four years, and their actions established the legal precedent for judicial decisions in the decades following World War II.

In the course of the *Gaines* case, the NAACP and civil rights advocates learned many important lessons. As events unfolded, the individual, that is, the litigant, experienced enormous stress. The NAACP and its legal staff had vetted potential litigants with standing prior to filing a lawsuit and had settled on Gaines. However, Lloyd Gaines did not or could not fulfill his commitments through the conclusion of legal activity. The black community also experienced significant pressure. Popular support from the community was important to the legal effort. Decision-makers in the NAACP did not believe that a frontal assault on segregation in the Deep South would be successful. So the NAACP initially targeted racial inequality in border states such as Maryland and Missouri where black communities could more freely support its actions.

St. Louis, Missouri, was a "northern" city that experienced the effects of the first Great Migration of African Americans between the world wars. The city had remained a Union bastion during the Civil War, but St. Louis had a history of slavery followed by racial segregation. Southern blacks, however, saw the city as a haven with greater economic opportunities. African Americans comprised a little over 6 percent of the city's population from 1900 to 1910 and nearly 11.5 percent by 1940. Northern cities Chicago and Detroit recorded similar demographic trends; however, Missouri's other large urban area did not experience such dramatic ethnic change. Although Kansas City's urban population grew significantly from 1900 to 1940, African Americans comprised 10 percent of the population in each decade.[9] Missouri's statewide African American population grew from about 5 to 7 percent over the same period, but the concentration of growth was in the St. Louis area.[10]

The national office of the NAACP needed support from attorneys working within local communities. In his excellent analysis of the NAACP's strategy for educational equality, legal scholar Mark Tushnet noted that accounts of

the organization's march toward *Brown* often have not given enough credit to local attorneys who provided the impetus for the civil rights campaign
in the state and national courts.[11] Jack Greenberg, who joined the NAACP
Legal Defense and Educational Fund in 1949, recognized the role played by
local, black lawyers and acknowledged that the national legal team "could
have done nothing without the lawyers on the frontlines in the South."[12] The
NAACP leadership recognized the need for black lawyers to engender respect,
both in the courtroom and in the arena of public opinion. The NAACP had
previously used white attorneys for legal counsel.[13] In many communities, the
number of skilled black lawyers was small. St. Louis was a city with an active
NAACP branch and a cadre of professional, black lawyers willing to invest
their efforts to produce constitutional change.

Social change on this order also requires significant popular support. Mobilization of public opinion during this era depended heavily on newspapers, in particular the black press. Newspapers produced by and for African
Americans provided the rationale for the legal agenda and encouraged readers
to support the NAACP and other groups with various forms of assistance.
Mainstream or white newspapers were more divided regarding segregation.
Some mainstream newspapers offered strong support for the establishment;
others, particularly in the North, advocated political and social change.

In addition to analyzing a landmark court case, this study examines an
organization central to that case, an interest group that pursued a legal strategy to produce major political change. The NAACP created and coordinated a plan to attack racial segregation in the United States, particularly in the
border and southern states. The organization represented the African American population, though the benefits it helped produce were public goods—
equality of opportunity for all Americans. Rival organizations, such as the
Urban League, appealed to common adherents, competed for limited resources, and sought to control the political agenda. Not all African Americans were in consensus with the goals and actions of the NAACP. Many
had different views on the goals for the civil rights movement, on the appropriate tactics to elicit political change, and on the relative importance of
desegregation or racial balance (in schools, for example). By the mid-1930s,
the organization had reached a general equilibrium of legislative (passage of
an anti-lynching bill) and judicial (a series of state cases leading to US Supreme Court decisions) strategies. During the time of the *Gaines* litigation,

the NAACP pursued both agendas but achieved more success with the latter, in particular, efforts for equal opportunity in the field of education.

There can be no doubt that a few individuals were central to the judicial legacy created by the NAACP. Charles Hamilton Houston, in particular, was the underappreciated leader and coordinator of the NAACP's legal strategy. Initially brought to the NAACP as part-time counsel in 1934, Houston became special counsel in 1935 and developed the legal strategy that would guide the NAACP's efforts for several decades. Recent scholarship by Richard Kluger, Genna McNeil, Mark Tushnet, and other scholars has rightly emphasized Houston's leadership role.[14] He was the "architect and dominant force of the legal program" of the NAACP.[15] Likewise crucial in the organization's efforts during the mid- to late 1930s were Walter White, executive director of the NAACP, Roy Wilkins, communications director, and Houston's hand-picked lieutenant, Thurgood Marshall, who would later take Houston's place as special counsel. *Missouri ex rel. Gaines v. Canada* (1938), however, was Houston's case from beginning to end. From the onset, Houston viewed the litigation as significant, stating, "I firmly believe the Missouri case is going to set the pace for Negro professional and graduate education for the next generation."[16] It was the first, necessary legal challenge to educational segregation to reach the US Supreme Court.

Houston led the NAACP legal defense team in a conscious effort to establish a legal and constitutional foundation for civil rights and for equal opportunity. His emphasis was on the rule of law and full implementation of a constitutional guarantee of equal protection through the Fourteenth Amendment. Houston saw his work as a protracted campaign against entrenched interests. As Houston advised Marshall when he assumed leadership in 1938, "Shock troops don't occupy towns."[17] The goal was fundamental change rather than pyrrhic victories. Houston's strategy stretched over the longer term. He knew his goals would not be realized quickly. The Gaines case, for Houston, was "a tactical maneuver in the long-range plan to secure a favorable US Supreme Court ruling against racial discrimination,"[18] and it was Houston's first case to reach the high court. Marshall would find ultimate triumph in *Brown*, but Houston would not live to see the fruits of his legal agenda.

What is often omitted in the discussion of the civil rights cases is the role of the NAACP branch and the local attorneys who invested their own time and resources in the larger litigation agenda. Houston and Marshall received salaries from the New York office of the NAACP. The St. Louis attorneys in-volved in *Gaines,* Sidney Redmond and Henry Espy, provided their services pro bono. Redmond and Espy, like the local, black attorneys in other com-munities who assisted the NAACP in attempts to advance its legal agenda, gambled their livelihood, and perhaps even their lives, on litigation challeng-ing Jim Crow. Although the national office reimbursed for travel and some other expenses, these monies were limited (for local counsel as well as for national counsel). Near the end of the *Gaines* litigation, the NAACP had essentially run out of money for its judicial strategy. Had *Gaines* been un-successful, it is unclear how future legal action would have continued. The national agenda was fueled by the work of local counsel.

Newspaper reporters and editors, particularly those working for African American newspapers, also contributed to those efforts. The NAACP pro-vided journalists with information on its legal (and other) strategies and out-comes. For the most part, the black press supported the NAACP's agenda in the 1930s while many newspapers in the mainstream press provided justifi-cation for segregation, although some mainstream newspapers offered tenta-tive acceptance of legal and constitutional change. The black press mobilized popular support for what was, to many African Americans, a legal agenda that seemed remote from their everyday lives.

As *Gaines* proceeded through the courts, the attorneys maintained close ties with the press corps, locally and nationally. Houston provided back-ground and technical material for articles and editorials, drafted press releases for the national office, and encouraged Redmond and others to send in useful information.[19] When the Supreme Court decision was announced, Houston had copies of the opinion sent immediately to four influential black papers as well as to NAACP organizational leaders.[20] Houston was a prolific writer and authored a number of items for *The Crisis,* the official magazine of the NAACP, and other publications.

Roy Wilkins coordinated press releases on the progress of the case and ed-ited *The Crisis.* Wilkins was born in St. Louis and had honed his skills as re-porter and editor for *The Call* in Kansas City before Walter White persuaded him to work for the NAACP. When Wilkins left *The Call,* he was replaced by Lucile Bluford, who, like N. A. Sweets, answered the NAACP's call for black applicants for higher education programs (in journalism) and later became a litigant sponsored by the NAACP in a suit against the University of Missouri.

The NAACP regularly produced press releases on its litigation efforts, and Houston and Wilkins shared some responsibilities. For instance, Wilkins made certain that Houston provided information to *Time* magazine, because of the potential for wide distribution to the mainstream audience.[21] They continued to provide the press with information through the various stages of the *Gaines* case. The relationship between the NAACP and the black press was reciprocal. As Bluford noted, "Without the black press, the NAACP's message could not have gotten to the black people."[22] The NAACP relied on the black press to publicize its judicial, legislative, and grassroots activities.

Just as the efforts of attorneys Redmond and Espy were critical to the case, so, too, were those of the plaintiff, Lloyd Lionel Gaines, an intelligent young African American with few financial resources but the motivation to make something more of himself. Gaines was aware of the NAACP's legal goals, and he wanted to follow in the footsteps of black lawyers in his local community. Racial segregation in Missouri limited his educational options. To challenge segregation, the NAACP needed standing; it needed someone willing to be the face and name of the case. Gaines, at least at first, was willing to stand and participate at a time when very few would. Gaines should be viewed as a young hero. Like the local attorneys, Gaines bet everything on Houston and the NAACP's success. Too often the summary versions of the Supreme Court decision imply that, although he won his lawsuit, Gaines did not follow through and show up for classes at the University of Missouri.[23] Such implications are simply incorrect. That is not to say that the aftermath of the *Gaines* decision is not shrouded in mystery. Certainly, the NAACP learned many lessons about finding the right plaintiff for future lawsuits. *Gaines* had much to teach about the power and position of defendants. Racial segregation in the South in the early twentieth century was part of the dominant culture, and justification for it was a core belief for many Americans. It is difficult now to comprehend the motivations and actions of those defending an abhorrent system, particularly of those seeking to deny people of color equal opportunities that we now accept as constitutionally protected for all. At the time, politicians and educators defending educational segregation feared violence and unrest if restrictions were relaxed, just as they feared the personal costs of challenging the system. The state and the University of Missouri were wrong in denying admission to Lloyd Gaines, but there is value in trying to understand how and why they made mistakes. Even within the black community there was division over what should supplant segregation—full and immediate integration or improvement and parity of black educational institutions—and what values that would best advance racial equality.

The challenge confronting NAACP counsel was huge. The US Supreme Court had sanctioned racial segregation since its 1896 decision in *Plessy v. Ferguson* and the establishment of the separate but equal doctrine. The original intent of the Fourteenth Amendment had been to protect all Americans, including newly freed slaves, from state violations of "due process of law" and "equal protection of the laws," but many states, especially those in the South, enacted laws mandating racial segregation of whites and blacks. *Plessy* was, at its core, a Fourteenth Amendment test of Jim Crow laws mandating segregation that were popping up around the country. Although the Fourteenth Amendment had been referenced previously in the *Slaughterhouse Cases* (1873), *Strauder v. West Virginia* (1879), and the *Civil Rights Cases* (1883), *Plessy v. Ferguson* was the first to examine the constitutionality of segregation through the lens of the equal protection clause; thus, it was of central importance to civil rights litigation that would follow in the twentieth century.

In *Plessy*, the Court considered a Louisiana law establishing segregation on trains, "requiring railway companies carrying passengers in their coaches in that State to provide, equal, but separate, accommodations for the white and colored races."[24] By upholding this law, the Court gave birth to the legal doctrine of "separate but equal," allowing states to mandate racial segregation despite protections offered by the equal protection clause of the Fourteenth Amendment to the US Constitution.

For all its centrality to the *Gaines* case, and its substantial impact on society as a whole, the *Plessy* decision garnered little attention from either the press or the public at the time. Historian Charles Lofgren notes that "we confront an initially puzzling phenomenon: the nation's press met the decision mainly with apathy. Why? And why did *Plessy* remain nearly invisible for a long time after 1896?" When the decision was issued, there was nothing surprising, revolutionary, or newsworthy about it. It was, rather, merely judicial acquiescence to the status quo. Lofgren notes further that "within its historical period, *Plessy* perhaps was not especially controversial."[25] Four decades later, *Plessy* was the center of the legal and constitutional controversy in the *Gaines* decision. Chief Justice Hughes cited the case as an important precedent in the Court's opinion.[26] Attorneys for the plaintiff set their sights on forcing the Court to grapple with the separate but equal precedent. After their initial success with *Gaines*, attorneys from the NAACP would continue efforts to get the Supreme Court to chip away at the separate but equal doctrine.

The Court's decision in *Brown v. Board of Education* brought about the end of racial segregation in public schools, but it is important to remember that there were two *Brown* decisions. In the first, the Supreme Court declared that "in the field of public education the doctrine of 'separate but equal' has no place. Separate educational facilities are inherently unequal."[27] However, state implementation of the Court's decision lagged. In the second *Brown* decision a year later, the Supreme Court directed federal district courts to oversee the execution of its judgment "with all deliberate speed."[28]

The Supreme Court case of *Missouri ex rel. Gaines v. Canada* could also have involved two decisions. The Court in 1938 reached a landmark decision, applying the equal protection clause of the Fourteenth Amendment to the states. The Court found that white students were provided opportunities denied to black students solely because of their race. In the majority opinion, Chief Justice Hughes writes, "It is manifest that this discrimination would constitute a denial of equal protection."[29] Lloyd Gaines's right to educational opportunity "was a personal one. It was as an individual that he was entitled to the equal protection of the laws."[30] The state, however, was intransigent and created obstacles to Gaines's admission. There should have been a second Supreme Court decision regarding implementation of the original ruling that Gaines should either be admitted to University of Missouri Law School or provided "substantially equal" legal education within the state.[31] The state did neither. NAACP attorneys initiated a second case and expected to appeal; however, the subsequent case was dropped, and Gaines's rights remained unresolved. Lloyd Gaines never attended law school at the University of Missouri.

I

Lloyd Gaines and the Missouri Milieu

Lloyd Lionel Gaines aspired to be an attorney; however, as an African American of modest means in Missouri in the 1930s, he had few options to prepare him for a career in the law. Gaines had overcome educational disadvantages before. Born in 1911 and raised on a small farm near Water Valley in northern Mississippi, Lloyd was the seventh of eleven children born to Henry Richard and Callie S. Gaines.[1] His father had been a rural schoolteacher, but marriage and a family had led him to abandon teaching and devote his time to working as a tenant farmer. The farm made a profit but not enough to allow the Gaineses to buy their own productive farm. By 1915, four-year-old Lloyd had lost his father and several siblings to disease and accident. Two of his older brothers had migrated north for jobs in industry. Around March 1926, Callie moved with Lloyd and her remaining family to live with her elder son, George Gaines, a Pullman porter who had started his own family in St. Louis.

The one-room schoolhouse for African Americans in Mississippi had not provided Lloyd with a high-quality education.[2] At age fifteen, he started the fifth grade at St. Louis's Waring Elementary School.[3] Given a healthy learning environment, he progressed at an accelerated rate.[4] In 1931, Gaines graduated from Vashon High School, the newer of two black high schools in St. Louis,[5] *summa cum laude* in a class of fifty students. He was active in student affairs, including the local honor society, the school journal, and the debating team, and he served as vice president of his senior class. Gaines won an essay contest and a $250 scholarship for an essay entitled "U.S. Government Inspection of Meat." For a year, he attended Stowe Teacher's College in

St. Louis, a municipal normal school to train teachers for black schools. At Stowe, he joined the Junior NAACP. In 1933, he also received a $50 Curators Scholarship to attend Lincoln University in Jefferson City. Gaines completed his undergraduate education at Lincoln, majoring in history with minors in education and English, graduating in the summer session of 1935.

Gaines had decided on a legal career "long before finishing high school."[6] By the time of his college graduation, he had considered a range of law school options.[7] The University of Missouri was his first choice simply because he wanted to practice law within Missouri. However, the University of Missouri never had admitted an African American applicant for any program of study. One of Gaines's teachers at Vashon High School, Zaid D. Lenoir, a member of the St. Louis NAACP, encouraged him and suggested that he contact the leadership of the organization. The local NAACP was looking for qualified black applicants to the state's premier white-only public school. Gaines's forceful argument that he wanted to attend law school at the state's public university in order to practice law in St. Louis was just the motivation that the local and national NAACP needed. Why Gaines chose not to leave the state for a legal education elsewhere is less clear.[8] To be sure, Gaines had no savings, and financial pressures burdened him throughout the litigation of the case. In a brief autobiography written for the NAACP, he noted cryptically, "I don't think that I would like to practice law in a state that denies me the legal training necessary for that practice." Yet Gaines seemed determined to pursue a career in St. Louis.

St. Louis was a vibrant, cosmopolitan city located on the Mississippi River near the mouth of the Missouri. It was more progressive than much of the rest of the state, but racial relations remained tense. Issues developing within this region became central to constitutional decision-making. It was in the St. Louis Courthouse that Dred Scott had first sued for his freedom in 1846 and 1847. The St. Louis trial court ruled in favor of Scott as it had in the cases of other slaves who had taken up residences in free territories. In 1852, however, the Missouri Supreme Court reversed the trial court. The US Supreme Court went further in 1857, and Chief Justice Roger Taney wrote the majority opinion explicitly denying American citizenship to all African Americans, whether slave or free.[9] Rather than settling the slavery question, the *Dred Scott* decision arguably pushed the nation to the brink of Civil War. Notably, Missouri, and especially St. Louis, continued to be a center for political disputes over issues of race in America.

Missouri was a slave state but remained with the Union during the Civil War. Racial divisions in the state and region ran deep throughout the nineteenth and twentieth centuries, yet St. Louis and, to a lesser extent, Kansas City were urban areas that attracted southern blacks who migrated northward. St. Louis tended to draw blacks from Mississippi, Arkansas, and Tennessee.[10] This migration from the South, in St. Louis as in other cities, increased pressure on racial relations. Civic reforms, such as a provision for the initiative petition, were added to a new municipal charter in 1914. However, the first use of the initiative, a progressive reform to improve government, was a ballot proposition institutionalizing racial segregation in housing. In a February 29, 1916, special election, St. Louis voters adopted a segregation ordinance by a nearly 3-1 margin.[11] Local Republicans obtained a temporary injunction from federal Judge David P. Dyer to prevent enforcement of the ordinance, and in 1917, the US Supreme Court ruled against a similar ordinance enacted in Louisville, Kentucky, effectively voiding the St. Louis ordinance. Nevertheless, expectations of racial segregation became ingrained in white public opinion and were enforced through informal contracts, such as restrictive covenants preventing the sale of homes in white-populated areas to black buyers.[12]

Though St. Louis and the state practiced racial segregation, economic opportunities for southern refugees were good, at least compared to conditions in the Deep South and some other urban areas.[13] Across the Mississippi River, in East St. Louis, Illinois, blacks had been victims in a vicious riot on July 2, 1917. The East St. Louis Race Riot resembled a massacre more than a political or labor protest. Estimates of deaths range between 40 and 200, nearly all of black citizens. St. Louis became "a city of asylum for those that were dispossessed and burned out in East St. Louis." Refugees crossed the bridge into Missouri, where the community provided relief and organizations such as the NAACP offered legal services.[14]

Black lawyers in Missouri were admitted to the bar, though, from the beginning, the state legal community distinguished notions of political and social equality. Legal scholar J. Clay Smith Jr. noted that as early as 1871 "bitter Democrat and secessionist" attorney A. J. P. Garesche supported the admission of black lawyer John H. Johnson in 1871 for reasons of political equality while simultaneously opposing social equality.[15] As a political right, blacks could practice law as well as make and enforce contracts, and by the twentieth century, they could hold judicial and elective offices, but they were obligated to live in a segregated society. St. Louis voters chose Charles Turpin as constable in 1910, the first black elected to public office in Missouri. N. A. Mitchell became the first black attorney to represent a white client in 1925.[16] Nevertheless, a black citizen had difficulty obtaining justice in a criminal proceeding or a civil suit involving a white person.[17] In St. Louis, blacks had political rights but not social equality. But those blacks who had migrated north had left states, such as Mississippi, where they effectively had neither political nor social rights.

Black attorneys could have difficulty in Missouri trial courts. Many had limited training and lacked the resources to pursue litigation successfully.[18] Physical assaults on black lawyers were unusual, but not unheard of. In Pemiscot County, in Missouri's Bootheel, St. Louis attorney William A. Cole was beaten by a mob of angry whites for defending four African American sharecroppers who were also threatened physically. The Missouri Supreme Court granted a writ of habeas corpus to bring the defendants to Jefferson City.[19] George L. Vaughn was a prominent black attorney from St. Louis. In 1928, Vaughn narrowly escaped racial violence in Columbia, blocks away from the state university to which Gaines later would apply for admission. Vaughn requested state intervention from the governor for protection of his client being held on criminal charges, but he lost the client to a mob.[20]

Vaughn was an active leader in the local NAACP and fought for civil rights of blacks in the courts, and he was a vocal supporter of the anti-lynching movement. In 1920, he became the first African American to run for Congress from Missouri.[21] Two years later, Vaughn was selected as the first president of the Mound City Bar Association, the organization representing black attorneys in the St. Louis region (the St. Louis Bar Association admitted only white lawyers). Much later, Vaughn would represent the J. D. Shelley family of St. Louis in court and ultimately win the 1948 landmark US Supreme Court case *Shelley v. Kraemer*, in which government enforcement of racially restrictive covenants was declared unconstitutional.[22] The national NAACP office in New York assisted Vaughn with the Supreme Court case. Thurgood Marshall and Charles Houston argued companion cases from Detroit and Washington, DC, concurrently.[23] Vaughn would become nationally known when, as an alternate delegate to the 1948 Democratic Convention, he forcefully demanded the unseating of the Mississippi delegation and adoption of a civil rights report.

Homer G. Phillips was an effective lawyer, an influential civic activist, and a fiery orator who pressed for civil rights. He had graduated from the Howard University School of Law. Many considered Phillips "the most outstanding black attorney in St. Louis."[24] Phillips, George Vaughn, newspaper publisher Joseph E. Mitchell, and others formed the Citizens Liberty League to promote black citizens as candidates for election and party offices within the Republican Party and to lobby for black political issues.[25] Phillips ran for Congress in 1926 but lost in the primary (along with his former law firm partner Vaughn).[26] Phillips was one of the dozen founders of the National Bar Association and was elected its president in 1928. The organization provided support for black attorneys and featured civil rights as a priority issue. In his keynote address to the NBA conference in 1929, Phillips challenged black lawyers to, "like a conquering army, sweep away those prevalent faults of lethargy, ignorance and false notions about segregation, which faults are the besetting sins of our groups, and . . . service to the Negro community."[27] He also lobbied persuasively for many local projects to benefit the black community, including quality public schools and a hospital to serve health care needs and training of black medical staff.[28] That hospital, "the largest and finest for Negroes in the world," was completed in 1938 and named the Homer G. Phillips Hospital after the "greatest single driving force" in its creation.[29] The efforts of Phillips and the league also led to the construction of Vashon High School, the second black high school, but the largest, in St. Louis, from which Lloyd Gaines would graduate.

While waiting for a Delmar Loop streetcar on the morning of June 18, 1931, Homer G. Phillips was shot and killed by two individuals. Two young black men were arrested and indicted for murder almost immediately, but they were tried separately, and both were acquitted. The murder of Homer Phillips remains unsolved. As noted by editor and author Edward Clayton, most observers assume the motive for the crime was dissatisfaction over some legal action, perhaps a disputed legal fee for an estate case.[30]

Even under conditions of segregation, black lawyers were in demand. In 1924, there were only twenty-eight practicing attorneys in St. Louis.[31] According to figures from the 1934 U.S. Census, "[t]here are 1,230 Negro lawyers and 159,375 white lawyers. This means one Negro lawyer for every 9,667 Negroes while there is a white lawyer for each 695 of the white population."[32] Missouri beat the national average; there were 55 black lawyers in the state (one per 4,070) and 5,505 white lawyers (one per 579).[33] A white lawyer, as Charles Houston noted, "cannot be relied upon to wage an uncompromising fight for equal rights for Negroes. He has too many conflicting interests," including profit from exploitation.[34] Even so, black lawyers had a difficult time attracting clientele, not only because their efforts were not respected in the white community, but also because blacks often sought out white attorneys, even paying higher fees, because they felt this tactic was the only path to justice within the legal system.[35] Houston dared law schools and younger African Americans to take up the fight: "The great work of the Negro lawyer in the next generation must be in the South and the law schools must send their graduates there and stand squarely behind them as they wage their fight for true equality before the law."[36]

Critical legal support for the case of Lloyd Gaines would come from Charles Hamilton Houston and other African American lawyers from the national NAACP office. However, a federal case would need to rise from a state court as public educational institutions were creations of the states. Houston and the national office depended on support from black lawyers and other leaders of the black community within the state. For *Gaines* and related litigation, Houston and his colleagues relied on a group of black lawyers in Missouri, primarily in St. Louis. The lead attorney in St. Louis, mentioned earlier, was Sidney Revels Redmond, who worked with his law partner Henry D. Espy.

Redmond was born and raised in Jackson, Mississippi. His father, Sidney Dillon (S. D.) Redmond, was a physician and, after health issues prevented him from continuing in that profession, an attorney. S. D. Redmond had also been a teacher (in his youth), a business entrepreneur, and a Republican Party leader. Sidney Revels Redmond's mother, Ida, was the daughter of Hiram Revels, the first African American in the US Senate.[37] Redmond attended Harvard as an undergraduate then went on to Harvard Law School.[38] Charles Houston received his undergraduate degree from Amherst College and served in the US Army in World War I before attending Harvard Law School (LL.B. 1922, S.J.D 1923). Several other African Americans soon followed Houston. Although it is not clear whether Houston and Redmond first met at Harvard (Redmond graduated in 1927[39]), the two men knew each other before *Gaines* began. They would occasionally reminisce about earlier times.[40]

Redmond returned to Jackson, where he practiced with his father for two years. The younger Redmond left Mississippi for Missouri in 1929 because, he explained, "the opportunities in St. Louis were greater than they were there."[41] Life as a black attorney in Jackson was trying. Sidney D. Redmond was "at odds with the white establishment, and at times with his own people." He was disbarred in 1915 but reinstated in 1920. As a leader in the Mississippi Republican Party,[42] the senior Redmond was a high-profile target for those opposed to civil rights for African Americans. While practicing together, both Redmonds had been accused of misconduct, including giving false testimony. The older Redmond had stayed to fight the charges in a prolonged legal battle that lasted several years, and he had met with mixed success. The younger Redmond had accepted an offer—the charges would be dropped "on the condition that he leave Mississippi and practice elsewhere." After residing for a brief time in Illinois, Redmond moved to St. Louis and established a law practice with another transplanted southerner, Henry Espy.[43]

Born in 1903, Henry D. Espy was raised near Gifford, Florida. His father worked 160 acres of land. Espy, however, rejected farming and sought an education. He left to attend Howard University School of Law. Espy arrived in St. Louis in 1928. Both he and Redmond soon assumed leadership positions in the Mound City Bar Association, the St. Louis branch of the NAACP, and the Republican Party. Redmond also penned the column "Legal Hints" for the *St. Louis Argus*.

Before *Gaines*, Redmond and Espy had worked together on earlier civil rights cases on behalf of the local NAACP chapter. For instance, attorney Joseph P. Harris sued the city of St. Louis in order to stop segregation of public events on the basis that the taxes of African Americans were collected and used to pay for a new municipal auditorium. Some events at the Kiel Auditorium, such as prize fights and political rallies, were integrated, but others, such as the Grand Opera, were segregated (and blacks restricted to less desirable seating). Redmond represented Harris and the St. Louis NAACP in the case, and Espy assisted. After interviewing the city's witnesses, Redmond "was complimented [by Circuit Court Judge O'Neil Ryan] for his masterful manner." However, the case was lost on a technicality. The city argued that any segregation that occurred was on the part of the organization that sold the tickets. The court agreed, and the Missouri Supreme Court refused to consider the case on appeal. Subsequently, the City of St. Louis modified its position and integrated seating at events.[44]

The case serves as an example of the close relationships among black lawyers, newspapermen, and educators working for civil rights. Witnesses, in addition to Harris, were attorneys R. L. Witherspoon and Robert Owens,

St. Louis American business manager Nathaniel Sweets, and music professor J. Roy Terry. For his dissertation research at the University of Chicago, black St. Louis minister, teacher, and author Herman Dreer analyzed black leadership in St. Louis. Based on surveys of white and black opinion leaders from 1955, Dreer found that recognized black leaders came from certain professions. Leadership during the time of *Gaines* came primarily from the occupations he identified: attorneys, educators, and newspaper editors and owners.[45] Although Dreer also found that ministers were important leaders, during the *Gaines* litigation, they operated on the sidelines, mobilizing citizens for support at meetings and rallies. The two individuals ranked most influential on Dreer's index of St. Louis black leadership were attorneys Homer Phillips and Sidney Redmond. Others among the top twenty-five were attorneys George Vaughn and David Grant, newspapermen Joseph Mitchell and Nathaniel Sweets, and leaders of black educational institutions within the city.[46] Lloyd Gaines did not make Dreer's list of leaders, although respondents mentioned Redmond's handling of his case as a major accomplishment.[47]

Attorneys Redmond and Espy each served as president of the St. Louis branch of the NAACP, with one or the other in place before, during, and after the *Gaines* case. Redmond followed Joseph E. Mitchell, who is discussed later in this chapter, and presided over the group from 1933 to 1934, Espy from 1934 to 1938, and Redmond again from 1939 through 1944. Redmond and Espy "devoted the time and energy necessary to turn the St. Louis NAACP into one of the most active branches in the country."[48] During these years, the St. Louis branch successfully lobbied for removal of "Negro only" signs from facilities within Union Station, promoted an essay contest on African American history, handled cases alleging police brutality, and secured jobs for African Americans on federal work projects, in the post office, and with the St. Louis police department.[49] In 1934, the NAACP joined other groups in a lawsuit to prevent construction of a black elementary school on the same grounds as Vashon High School (which Gaines had attended). Espy was then branch president, and the action produced a rift in the organization with many black teachers resigning. George Vaughn, Sidney Redmond, and Robert Witherspoon acted as counsel, and Judge Robert J. Kirkwood granted an injunction stopping construction because "the area there was already too small to whip a cat on."[50]

The 1935 National NAACP Convention was held in St. Louis June 25–30. Espy and Redmond had organized the event from the previous year's convention. Hosting the national convention "provided the branch with what the St. Louis NAACP leadership had planned for—publicity and stimulation."[51] The advance publicity also touted the region's seventeen Negro schools: "Among these institutions is the Vashon High School, one of the largest and most modernly equipped of its kind, with a vast auditorium seating 1,552 persons."[52] Charles Houston encouraged Roy Wilkins to ensure the convention program would take a new direction and attract more public support. He felt it should "appeal directly to the mass of black people, involve them in the proceedings, and illustrate how and why they need the NAACP."[53] The St. Louis convention drew participants from across the country. Delegates from twenty-six states attended, and *The Crisis* declared the St. Louis Conference "the best annual gathering in the last six years."[54] The convention provided a forum for Houston and the NAACP to publicize its legal strategy to attack racial discrimination.[55] Coincidentally, the convention took place over the same days in which Lloyd Gaines and several other African American students were considering whether to apply for admission to the all-white University of Missouri.

St. Louis was a newspaper town, home to Joseph Pulitzer's *Post-Dispatch* and competitors the *Globe-Democrat* and the *Republic*. Two prominent black newspapers covered the news for St. Louis, the *Argus* and the *American*. The *Argus*, founded in 1912 by Joseph E. Mitchell and his brother William, had originally served to publicize the owners' insurance business. Joseph and the *Argus*, however, began covering more local and national political news, stating that the goal "to organize the Negro community for political action." Almost immediately the *Argus* began a "crusade against segregation."[56] Mitchell was an active leader among black newspaper publishers and editors as well as in community affairs. He also wielded some political influence with local members of the Republican Party.[57] He used the *Argus* as a forum to encourage NAACP membership and support.[58] Mitchell was unanimously elected president of the St. Louis branch of the NAACP during a period of low membership. He served for several months and then handed over the leadership to the "young, progressive Harvard-trained lawyer" Sidney Redmond. As previously noted, Redmond was succeeded as president by attorney Henry Espy.[59] Mitchell believed strongly that the *Argus,* and the black press in general, needed to promote a civil rights agenda.[60]

The *St. Louis American* was the other major black newspaper in the region. The weekly was founded in 1928 by Nathan B. (Ben) Young Jr. and several other investors, including Homer G. Phillips.[61] Young took over as owner after the stock market crash in 1929.[62] Young was the eldest son and namesake of the president of Lincoln University. Educated at Yale, he graduated from Yale Law School in 1918, and worked as a practicing attorney in St. Louis. N. B. Young Jr. would become first a prosecutor and then the first black judge for the city's municipal court.[63] Nathaniel Sweets, who had been raised in Jefferson City and had graduated from Lincoln University, was hired by Young as the paper's business manager. Sweets later bought the *American,* and he became publisher in 1933.[64] (Young continued to contribute editorials and other content.) Bennie G. Rodgers began as one of two working reporters;[65] later he also became editor of the *American.* The offices of the *St. Louis American* were located in the Peoples Finance Building as were the law offices of Redmond and Espy.[66] It was a hub for the black political elite. Such proximity assured close contact among the lawyers, the NAACP, and the *American* and the *Argus* throughout the period during which the Lloyd Gaines case unfolded.

The *American* and the *Argus* were not the only newspapers disseminating the NAACP's updates on *Gaines.* The *Chicago Defender,* the *New York Age,* the *Pittsburgh Courier,* the Baltimore *Afro-American,* and others were also important in informing black citizens about the NAACP's legal agenda and the progress of the case. The origins of many black newspapers were directly linked to the legal profession.[67] However, the *Kansas City Call* played a more direct role for *Gaines,* especially in the later stages and aftermath of the decision.[68] A central figure at the NAACP had himself been a reporter and an editor at the *Call.* Chester Arthur Franklin began publishing the *Call* in May 1919. His father, George F. Franklin, had founded the *Omaha Enterprise* in Nebraska and then had purchased and published the *Star* (originally, the *Colorado Statesman*) in Denver. Chester Franklin moved to Kansas City with its larger black community and established a newspaper there in 1913.[69] Among the reporters he hired was Roy Wilkins, who became assistant secretary of the NAACP and editor of *The Crisis,* the official publication of the NAACP, after the departure of W.E.B. Du Bois.[70] He was responsible for spreading the news about *Gaines,* the civil rights agenda, and other priorities of the NAACP.

Another young reporter with the *Call,* Lucile Bluford, took over Wilkins's job when he left to work for the NAACP. As was previously noted, she applied for admission to graduate study in journalism at the University of Missouri and her automatic rejection produced additional litigation. Following Franklin's death in 1948, Bluford became editor and owner of the *Call.*[71]

The fight over desegregation at institutions of higher education was about equal opportunity, but it was also about respect. This was always reflected in the black press's coverage of the desegregation battle. Articles and editorials on *Gaines* were, unsurprisingly, in favor of the NAACP's legal agenda and, until much later, supportive of Lloyd Gaines personally. In some ways, Missouri, and its state university, was considered a leader for fair treatment of African Americans. Though many state newspapers supported segregation, including the privately owned *Columbia Tribune*, news reporting in the *Columbia Missourian*, a paper owned and operated by the university, was more objective. For instance, as the *New York Amsterdam News* informed its readers on September 24, 1930, under the headline, "Columbia Missourian Adopts Capital N.": "Following the example of larger newspapers and leading magazines in the United States, the *Columbia Missourian*, laboratory publication of the School of Journalism of the University of Missouri, now advocates the spelling of the word 'Negro' with a capital 'N.'"[72] If the leading school of journalism in the country advocated such respect and acknowledgment of the humanity of "Negroes," perhaps it would have a far-reaching impact. Unfortunately, that same school would oppose the admission of African American students for another twenty years.[73] The story of the fight to break down the admission barrier at the University of Missouri and elsewhere was a major issue for the "Negro" press.

Even as the black press in Missouri and throughout the United States disseminated the message of the NAACP and its legal staff, the press struggled to overcome challenges of its own—challenges the mainstream, white press did not face. Readership for black-oriented papers was low, as blacks had lower levels of education and less disposable income for subscriptions and whites had little interest in the papers' content. As one media history commentator noted

> It was essential that black editors show some backbone in their writing to gain black respect and what little readership was available. But showing backbone meant that editors could lose their newspapers, which were essential to the survival of the black people, or even their lives. An editor had to be bold and show a position of strength, but had to be canny enough to live through the consequences.[74]

Moreover, newspapers depended on advertising revenue, but blacks owned or managed comparatively few businesses. *St. Louis American* editor and journalist Bennie G. Rodgers noted that fighting segregation could be difficult even for black newspapers. An article opposing segregation or the lack of job opportunities in a business, for instance, could result in the loss of advertising revenues from that business.[75]

The only state institution of higher education available to black Missourians was Lincoln University in the capital, Jefferson City. Soldiers from the Sixty-second Colored Infantry, stationed at Fort Macintosh (now Laredo), Texas, and composed primarily of Missourians, had contributed funds and organization to establish Lincoln Institute, an educational institution for freed African American slaves, in 1866. Additional funds had been provided by the Sixty-fifth Colored Infantry.[76] During the war, Richard Baxter Foster, the Connecticut-born lieutenant of the Sixty-second, found his calling. In March 1865, Foster wrote his wife, Lucy, of his intention to settle in Missouri, among other officers and enlisted men of his regiment, for the purpose of establishing a schoolhouse for freed slaves, his life's work.[77] After arriving in Missouri, Foster joined with other white elites who agreed to push for the establishment of a school for African Americans. Raising additional donations was difficult, but the need was great. The school was essential, in particular, to provide education for teachers who would work in new black schools in the former slave state. Baxter led Lincoln's Board of Curators and became the institute's first (and third) principal. In 1870, the State of Missouri provided funds to support teacher training, and it took over the institution in 1879. Under Missouri's strict segregationist policy, blacks could attend no other state college.[78]

Representative Walthall M. Moore, Missouri's first African American legislator, elected from St. Louis in 1920, introduced a bill to rename the institute and to provide other educational opportunities to black Missourians. The Lincoln University Act of 1921 established the first, and only, public or state-directed institution of higher education specifically for advanced learning of African Americans. Section 7 of the act included a provision granting authority to the Lincoln University Board of Curators

> to arrange for the attendance of negro residents of the state of Missouri at the university of any adjacent state to take any course or to study any subjects provided for at the state university of Missouri, and which are not taught at the Lincoln university, and to pay the reasonable tuition fees for such attendance, provided that

> whenever the Board of Curators deem it advisable they shall have
> the power to open any necessary school or department.[79]

The statute implied that black Missourians could obtain postgraduate and other degrees, even if unavailable at Lincoln University. However, comparatively few Missourians received education through this section. Beginning in 1929, the state legislature made annual appropriations for implementation of the provision; however, the amount was insufficient to cover tuition aid for all eligible applicants.[80] Both the state's flagship institution of higher education, the University of Missouri, and Lincoln qualified as land-grant colleges under the federal Morrill Act. Lincoln University had no graduate or professional programs, and the University of Missouri accepted no black applicants, sending all African Americans seeking graduate education to other states.[81]

The status of Lincoln University, the state's only black college, figured prominently in the story of the Lloyd Gaines case, from his initial application for law school until years after the Supreme Court decision was announced. The status of Lincoln University was enmeshed in politics and opportunism. Nathaniel Sweets described how politicians and local elites would use Lincoln as "a political football to pay off their political obligations."[82] In part, this was because educational opportunity for former slaves and, later, African Americans, was a partisan issue. From the end of the Civil War through the early twentieth century, Republicans favored educational opportunities for African Americans. The political nature was also institutional—half the members of Lincoln's Board of Curators were appointed for four-year terms, while all curators for the University of Missouri had six-year terms. This gave the governor, who also served a four-year term, much greater control over Lincoln. The 1921 act required that at least half of the eight appointed curators at Lincoln be black, but the state superintendent of schools was made an ex-officio member.[83] Another political influence was segregation itself. The capital was segregated, and disputes between the races in Jefferson City seemed to be resolved in the favor of whites.[84] Black legislators at the State Capitol were unwelcome in Jefferson City eating establishments and often ate at the Schweich Hall cafeteria on the Lincoln University campus.[85] Finally, it was an era of patronage, and charges of corruption were frequently levelled at administrators and those associated with Lincoln University.[86]

Some educators strived to improve educational quality at Lincoln. In particular, President Nathan B. Young, who led the university from 1923 to

1927 and 1929 to 1931, stressed the need for quality and recruited faculty members with degrees from prominent universities in the Northeast.[87] Young had a lengthy academic career, and he had left the presidency of Florida A and M College to come to Lincoln. In a letter to W.E.B. Du Bois, published in *The Crisis*, Young wrote of his intent "to help make that school what its new name prophesies, a first-class institution of *higher learning*, a Standard College for the Negroes of the Middle West."[88] Nevertheless, the University of Missouri, off limits to African Americans, was considered the preeminent public university in the state.

The state's flagship university, and the home of its only publicly funded law school, was located in Columbia, midway between St. Louis and Kansas City and about thirty miles north of Jefferson City.[89] The University of Missouri had been the first public university established west of the Mississippi River, in 1839, and the third public university founded in the Midwest.[90] In some respects, the university was progressive for the region; women were admitted as students as early as 1867. Some faculty members held progressive views on race. Sociology Professor Carl Terrence Pihlblad denounced the misuse and misinterpretation of mental tests to justify claims of racial and ethnic superiority or inferiority.[91] On the other hand, de facto racial segregation was an integral part of the regional culture. No law or regulation prevented the admission of black students to the university, but never had one been admitted.

The University of Missouri's policy was typical of white colleges in the state and throughout the South. W.E.B. Du Bois and colleagues surveyed attitudes of college officials toward black students. Responses from three Missouri colleges about black alumni and students are illustrative of the attitudes of the time. "Never a Negro graduate nor a student. Couldn't do it in Missouri if we wanted to." "We have never had any graduates of Negro descent and are not likely to ever have." "We never had any Negro or any person with Negro blood. . . . I have not found a student in the state that would tolerate a Negro in the college. And it is even worse since the Johnson-Jeffries fight." The latter comment referred to the 1910 "Battle of the Century" when Jack Johnson, the first African American heavyweight champion of the world, defeated former champion James Jeffries, the "Great White Hope," in a boxing match that produced racial violence across the country. Among white majority institutions of higher learning in Missouri, only Tarkio College, in far northwestern Missouri, acknowledged having a black student for one year "with a credit to himself and the school," but the college official also noted, "I do not suppose any other white college in the state would receive a Negro student."[92] It was in this culture that Lloyd Gaines and other applicants requested admission to the University of Missouri.

The city of Columbia, like much of Missouri, was midwestern by temperament, but southern in terms of racial relations. African Americans comprised about 15 to 20 percent of the city's population of 20,000, but residences were limited to one large and three small geographic communities within the town.[93] Occupations and businesses were segregated, although many blacks did work as janitors, laborers, cooks, maids, laundresses, or waiters in white-owned businesses, a few at the university, and some for sororities and fraternities. Columbia had no black attorney.[94] Even in this college town, black unemployment was high. Black residences were small and cramped; few had electricity or hot water.[95] The university employed some African Americans in service positions.[96] James T. Scott was one such employee. Scott worked as a janitor in the university's medical school. Scott and his wife, a teacher at Douglass—the local black school—earned good salaries, so they were reasonably well-off.

In April 1923, Scott was arrested for the alleged rape of fourteen-year-old Regina Almstedt, the daughter of a professor of German. There now seems significant evidence that Scott was innocent of the crime, but, at the time, the accusation reinforced the deep racial division in the city. Scott requested representation by George Vaughn, the lawyer and NAACP regional officer, who drove in from St. Louis on April 28. That night, a mob began to gather downtown. Mob members broke into the jail, cut open Scott's cell, and took him to Stewart Bridge, several blocks away. At times, the crowd may have grown as large as a thousand. The mob paused at the bridge as a few individuals, including Professor Hermann Almstedt, Regina's father, asked for justice and the return of Scott. Leaders in the mob would not listen. A rope was produced, and Scott was lynched as many in the crowd cheered.[97]

An unusual characteristic of the James Scott lynching was that this crime was not perpetrated principally by poor, rural whites. Economist and sociologist Gunnar Myrdal noted that "actual participants in the lynching mobs usually belong to the frustrated strata of Southern whites."[98] NAACP president Walter White observed lynching firsthand and wrote of the economic foundations of lynching, perpetrated principally by disaffected whites.[99] The Columbia mob was composed largely of middle- and upper-class residents, women, and university students. The incident occurred only a dozen years before Gaines applied for admission to the university, and would have been on the minds of many decision-makers in the subsequent court case. Attorneys for the NAACP were well aware of the lynching.[100] Charles Houston cited the incident as a cause for concern when discussing *Gaines,* and a press release reminded black readers of the Columbia lynching.[101] The NAACP had lobbied for a federal antilynching law since its first introduction by Missouri Representative Leonidas Dyer in 1918.[102] In 1922 a version of the Dyer Bill passed the House but died in the Senate following a filibuster. Scott was lynched four months later. A Boone County grand jury came back with indictments, including one for a person accused of the actual hanging. When a subsequent jury trial resulted in a not guilty verdict for the man charged with killing Scott, the charges against the others were dropped.[103]

Racial tensions in Columbia and at the University of Missouri had eased somewhat by 1935, the year Lloyd Gaines sought admission to the University's School of Law. But Columbia remained a segregated community. The university had no black students, despite the absence of either a written regulation prohibiting their admission or a state statute that clearly addressed the issue.[104] The legal and cultural assumptions were that black students would attend Lincoln, and white students would choose from among any of the other state colleges or the University of Missouri.[105] The enabling legislation for Lincoln University, sponsored by Representative Walthall Moore, had set up provisions allowing the curators to establish new degree programs and disciplines as needed. Until such new programs were available, the state, through Lincoln, was to offer scholarships so that black students could pursue otherwise unavailable courses or degrees at educational institutions outside the state.

Missouri was the first state to enact legislation creating scholarships for black students to attend graduate and professional schools in adjacent states. Moore had no doubt intended the authorizing section of the 1921 act to improve educational prospects for black Missourians by providing students with "equal" opportunities, whether at Lincoln or at out-of-state institutions. The unintended consequence of Moore's bill was that it actually limited the development of new academic programs and the learning opportunities for blacks within the state.[106] The educational foundation created by contributions from Colored Troops in the Civil War and reinvigorated by the bill sponsored by the state's first black legislator was used to segregate blacks and whites in higher education. Technically, black applicants to the University of Missouri were not denied admission but were redirected to Lincoln University per the statutory provision. By the time Houston and the NAACP challenged the constitutionality of out-of-state tuition scholarships, six other states had passed similar legislation.[107]

Charles Houston intended to challenge the constitutionality of policies such as Missouri's educational segregation: "The NAACP had informed its branches that it would finance a plaintiff fitting its needs, and the St. Louis branch let it be known that it would like to see the matter tested in Missouri."[108] According to Henry Espy, Lloyd Gaines seemed an excellent plaintiff. "Gaines' excellent scholastic record was a consideration. The fact that he was a product of Missouri's segregated schools lessened the chance that the state would argue that he was not qualified. To argue along these lines would be to admit the inequality of education provided to Negroes in Missouri."[109]

Houston, Redmond, Espy, and Gaines faced powerful opponents and significant obstacles. In southern and border states, public opinion, including elite opinion, strongly supported racial segregation. Each state could invest substantial resources to defend its policies. Moreover, authority for racial segregation extended from the constitutional interpretation of the US Supreme Court and its separate but equal doctrine.

The NAACP would spend decades trying to reverse the Court's 1896 ruling in *Plessy v. Ferguson*.[110] That decision laid the cornerstone of the separate but equal doctrine, though its significance was unrecognized at the time.[111] After *Plessy* the high court allowed states to enforce racial segregation of transportation, schools, and public accommodations. While the *Plessy* decision had not addressed educational equality in particular, the Court's reasoning was that a state could segregate public facilities on the basis of race and the state also could require private organizations, including a common carrier like the railroad, to provide segregated facilities.[112] The implications were far-reaching. The 7–1 decision in *Plessy* did feature a lively, reasoned dissent by Justice John Marshall Harlan, the former slave owner and opponent of the Reconstruction amendments. Proponents of segregation did not have to rely long on implied approval. The Court soon extended the reach of racial segregation into society, generally, and into education, specifically.

Three years after the *Plessy* decision, the Supreme Court heard a case regarding segregated public schools in Georgia. Richmond County collected taxes from its population to pay for primary and secondary public education, although the Georgia state constitution required taxation only for elementary schools. Black and white students attended different schools. However, African American students were charged a fee to attend Ware High School in Augusta, and there were three private high schools that would enroll black students for a similar fee. Only 60 students attended the public black high school, and for budgetary reasons the board of education opted to close that school in order to provide tax revenue for 300 black students attending four elementary schools. The high school for white girls remained open, though its students were charged a fee to attend, and the county provided revenue for a denominational high school for white boys. A class-action suit was brought by several African American county residents, and the case made its way to the high court. The plaintiffs did not request integration, only closing of the white high school until the black high school was reopened.

In a unanimous decision, the US Supreme Court upheld the school board's action in *Cumming v. Richmond County Board of Education*.[113] Although the plaintiffs argued for an application of the Fourteenth Amendment's equal protection clause, the Court did not decide the case on this basis. Justice John Marshall Harlan, who alone had dissented ardently in *Plessy*, wrote the opinion upholding the school board's action.[114] The opinion discusses financial reasons motivating the board and the need to provide education for black elementary students. Harlan's opinion rejects any application of the Fourteenth Amendment for lack of evidence that "the board's refusal to maintain such a school was in fact an abuse of its discretion and in hostility to the colored population because of their race."[115] On the other hand, attorneys for the NAACP later would interpret *Cumming* in a hopeful manner. The Supreme Court had not rejected application of the equal protection clause generally but had refused it in this case for which plaintiff's counsel had not articulated how equal protection should apply.

The Kentucky legislature passed a law in 1904 that required racial segregation in both public and private schools. Berea College was a religious institution that had been founded by abolitionists in Madison County, Kentucky, before the Civil War. The college had been officially reestablished in the town of Berea immediately following the war. It remained committed to integration in higher education and maintained an interracial student body that was approximately half white and half black. The enactment of the Day Law,

"An Act to Prohibit White and Colored Persons from Attending the Same School," required educational segregation of all schools, including private institutions. Berea College was the only integrated institution in the state, and a grand jury found the college guilty of violating Kentucky law. The college, in turn, initiated a legal challenge to the constitutionality of that law.

In *Berea College v. Kentucky* (1908), the Supreme Court upheld the Kentucky statute and its mandate.[116] The Court avoided any issue pertaining to individual civil rights and the application of the Fourteenth Amendment instead focusing on the state's ability to regulate corporations, ruling that state power to regulate corporations did not conflict with the federal Constitution. Justice John Harlan, a native Kentuckian, wrote in another passionate dissent that the statute was "an arbitrary invasion of the rights of liberty and property guaranteed by the 14th Amendment against hostile state action."[117] The majority opinion, however, ignored pleas for protection of civil rights, and Berea College was forced to end racial integration in education.[118]

The Supreme Court consistently, though tacitly, supported racial segregation through its separate but equal doctrine. The Court declined to consider federal constitutional protections for Americans of African descent, allowing southern and border states to limit political and social opportunities for this racial group. *Plessy v. Ferguson*, the influential case and the source of the doctrine, gave federal sanction to segregation within the states. The decision in *Berea* demonstrated, within the field of education, the need for direct attack on state governments sanctioning segregation.

Lower courts may have read a separate but equal justification for racial segregation in education from *Plessy*, *Cumming*, and *Berea*, but the Supreme Court made no definitive statement on the question.[119] The challenge faced by Charles Houston and the NAACP legal staff was how to bring segregation and its injustices to the Court's attention in order to assert civil rights for all Americans. The NAACP developed a plan of action, and that plan focused first and foremost on segregation in education. The circumstances in Missouri made it an ideal location for a test case on the Fourteenth Amendment's equal protection clause.

2

Charles Houston and the
NAACP's Legal Strategy

From the start, the NAACP had used multiple tactics to expand the rights of African Americans: mobilizing black public opinion, organizing activists at the community level by creating local chapters, lobbying Congress, and litigating. The NAACP achieved some of its greatest successes in the judicial arena. Since 1915, nearly every civil rights case involving African Americans that reached the Supreme Court had involved the NAACP. Its legal defense arm "had the good fortune to obtain outstanding counsel in the very first cases and thereby began a confident tradition based squarely on careful preparation and dignified presentation."[1] In the 1930s, under the direction of Walter White, the organization concentrated its efforts on judicial activism.

Charles Hamilton Houston, former dean of Howard University Law School and the first full-time lawyer in the NAACP legal department,[2] was named special counsel in 1935. Son of a Washington lawyer, Houston had attended segregated public schools in the District of Columbia. He matriculated at Amherst College and graduated magna cum laude at the age of nineteen.[3] Quiet and studious, Houston seemed on track to become an attorney, but the young man expressed no particular interest in combatting racism or addressing the plight of blacks in America.[4] Military service, however, changed his perspective. As a field artillery officer in the US Army, Lieutenant Houston served in France in World War I. Disgusted by racism that showed itself in mistreatment of black soldiers by their white counterparts, Houston became convinced of the need for change in America.[5] He was persuaded to take up his father's occupation, and he entered Harvard Law School in 1919. Racism was less evident at Harvard, but it lurked beneath the surface.[6]

Houston excelled academically and was elected to the editorial board of the *Harvard Law Review*. After a period in private practice with his father's firm, Houston became dean of Howard University Law School in 1924. During his tenure, he transformed it from a mediocre to a respected law school. Soon after joining the NAACP legal team in 1934, Houston began to organize and lead litigation efforts.

The NAACP began its fight for equality in education—specifically in graduate and professional education—with the case of Thomas Hocutt, a resident of Durham, North Carolina, who sued for admission to the University of North Carolina's College of Pharmacy. At the direction of Charles Houston, the organization's lead attorney in the case was William H. Hastie Jr.[7] Hastie was Houston's cousin, and he, too, had attended Harvard Law School and later become dean of Howard University Law School. Hastie was destined for a remarkable political and legal career: he would serve as the first black judge for the District Court of the Virgin Islands from 1937 to 1939, as the appointed governor of the Virgin Islands from 1946 to 1949, and as the first black appellate judge for the US Third Circuit Court of Appeals from 1949 to 1971.[8]

Thomas Hocutt lost his case at trial. His lawyers had expected to appeal, but they were forced to drop the case when James E. Shepard, president of the North Carolina College for Negroes where Hocutt had earned his bachelor's degree, refused to release Hocutt's college transcript. The transcript was required for admission to the graduate program at the University of North Carolina.[9] Since much of the NAACP's strategy was based on finding students who were eminently qualified for the programs to which they applied—save for their ethnic background—denial of access to documents that would prove Hocutt's suitability for the pharmacy school did tremendous damage to the case. However, *Hocutt* was path-breaking in the NAACP's litigation strategy.[10]

Soon the NAACP was pursuing similar cases aimed at breaching the barriers that blocked African Americans from receiving the highest level of education in the United States. The NAACP's plan for attacking segregated education drew on analysis prepared by attorney Nathan Ross Margold. Margold, a Harvard Law School graduate and a former assistant US attorney, in the words of Walter White, "did a brilliant job of research" and "mapped out a broad frontal attack on the basic causes of discrimination."[11] The Margold paper, a "powerful piece of work,"[12] provided the outline for the NAACP's plan of action—the plan its legal team would use to undermine the separate but equal doctrine.

Segregation and discrimination were monumental problems faced by the black community and other minorities in the United States in the early twentieth century. Overcoming such entrenched social and legal obstacles required not a scattershot approach but, rather, one that was precisely targeted. Nathan Margold was given the task of putting together such a plan in 1930. Margold produced a comprehensive analysis of then-current law and a strategy for attacking segregation in education in seven southern states—Alabama, Arkansas, Florida, Georgia, Louisiana, Mississippi, and South Carolina. Margold's appointment to this task was endorsed by many, including Charles Houston.[13]

In 1930, the American Fund for Public Service, also known as the Garland Fund after philanthropist Charles Garland, gave the NAACP a sizable grant to begin a legal fight against segregation.[14] Although grants from the Garland Fund had been assisting the NAACP's work since 1922, this large grant—$100,000—was specifically for starting the NAACP legal department in earnest. Taking on an array of issues and cases, even while absorbing the financial impact of the Great Depression, significantly limited the NAACP agenda. The first step in the NAACP's legal strategy was the production of a document that included information about, and legal analysis of, the status of blacks in America in several respects, including "segregation and unequal apportionment of school funds," "residential segregation," "segregation in common carriers," "disenfranchisement," and "exclusion from jury service."[15] With regard to education, following an extensive analysis, Margold came to recommend a strategy based on the Fourteenth Amendment's equal protection clause, which would attack segregation by attacking discrimination in the form of unequal funding for black and white primary and secondary schools.

Margold wrote, "We are not trying to deprive southern states of their acknowledged privilege of providing separate accommodations for the two races. We are trying only to force them to comply with their equally acknowledged duty to provide 'equal if separate' accommodations in white and colored schools."[16] This need was due to the decisions by the Supreme Court in *Plessy v. Ferguson* and subsequent cases, analyzed by Margold in his report. He continued to outline the strategy, which really was an attack on segregation *through* an attack on discriminatory funding for black schools, writing, "The state law now affords us no real opportunity to fight the disgraceful discrimination that is being practiced under it. We must attack the practice of segregation, as *now provided for and administered*, or permit the discrimination to go on for the most part unimpaired."[17]

Margold continued,

> Compulsory segregation of white and colored school children conceivably might itself have been held a form of discrimination forbidden by the Fourteenth Amendment to the Constitution of the United States. But statutes providing for such segregation were approved before the enactment of the Fourteenth Amendment, despite more or less similar limitations in state constitutions . . . and have continued to be upheld ever since, *wherever the segregation has been unaccompanied by other forms of discrimination*. The question as to the validity of such statutes did not actually arise before the Supreme Court of the United States until 1927; but by that time so extensive and uniform a body of authority had accumulated though decisions in other courts that the Supreme Court refused to consider the question an open one.[18]

The 1927 case to which Margold referred was *Gong Lum v. Rice*,[19] regarding whether Bolivar County, Mississippi, violated the rights of a Chinese American girl, Martha Lum, by not permitting her to attend the district's white-only high school.

In writing the majority opinion, former president and Chief Justice William Howard Taft equated the circumstances of Chinese Americans and African Americans. Taft wrote: "The case then reduces itself to the question whether a state can be said to afford to a child of Chinese ancestry, born in this country and a citizen of the United States, the equal protection of the laws by giving her the opportunity for a common school education in a school which receives only colored children of the brown, yellow, or black races."[20] Taft answered this question in this way:

> We think that it is the same question which has been many times decided to be within the constitutional power of the state legislature to settle, without the intervention of the federal courts under the federal constitution. . . . Most of the cases cited arose, it is true, over the establishment of separate schools as between white

pupils and black pupils, but we cannot think that the question is any different, or that any different result can be reached, assuming the cases above cited to be rightly decided, where the issue is as between white pupils and the pupils of the yellow races. The decision is within the discretion of the state in regulating its public schools, and does not conflict with the Fourteenth Amendment.[21]

The *Lum* decision was based, according to Margold's analysis, on a theory of the Fourteenth Amendment like that of a US Second Circuit Court of Appeals decision from New York in *People ex rel. King v. Gallagher*, in 1883. The circuit court's constitutional interpretation was that the Fourteenth Amendment only pertained to the rights one has as a citizen of the United States and, because education was a state responsibility, the Fourteenth Amendment did not apply. As Margold put it, "The privilege of receiving an education at public expense, the court held, being conferred only by state law, is not a privilege enjoyed by virtue of one's being a citizen of the United States and is always subject to discretionary state regulation, so far as concerns the privilege and immunity clause of the Fourteenth Amendment."[22] The judges also concluded that the equal protection clause of the Fourteenth Amendment required only that everyone have access to education of equal quality, not that the education be desegregated.[23]

The path to success, Margold argued, was not through trying to prove that state officials treated students in a discriminatory fashion with any number of decisions and policies, largely because such discrimination was often easily justified by state officials in court before sympathetic state judges. Margold cautioned,

> it is well to remember that states are required, under the Fourteenth Amendment, only to provide accommodations which are substantially equal under all the circumstances. Special factors may exist or arise to justify considerable divergence from a proportionately equal division of school funds or even limited discrimination in accommodations and facilities. States may properly allow their officers a considerable amount of leeway or discretion in the administration of their public school systems; and no court can reasonably be expected to interfere with the action of the officers unless it is shown to have been motivated by race prejudice or is so serious that it can reasonably be explained in no other way.[24]

Rather than trying to prove discrimination on the part of state and school officials, Margold charted a plan to show that, through unequal apportionment of public funds, students of different ethnicities were treated differently, in violation of the Fourteenth Amendment's equal protection clause:

> Not even the most prejudiced southern court may reasonably be expected to uphold the propriety of state action which provides educational facilities for whites while it denies them altogether to Negroes. The difference between a denial of all facilities and a denial of equal facilities is one of degree, not of kind. The Fourteenth Amendment prohibits states from denying "to any person within its jurisdiction," not *all* but "*equal* protection of the laws," and the prohibition is contravened as much by discrimination in the character and quality of education facilities afforded under state law as by denial of those facilities altogether.[25]

Charles Houston and the NAACP would use that tactic for determining venues, but not in elementary and secondary education, as Margold proposed. The first several cases attacked segregation in higher education, including *Gaines*.

Margold's optimism for this strategy came from his reading of the Supreme Court's decision in *Cumming v. Richmond County Board of Education* (1899).[26] At first glance, the majority opinion by Justice John Marshall Harlan, a ruling against the plaintiff, seemed to offer little reason for optimism. Harlan took a position similar to *King v. Gallagher* and *Lum v. Rice*. However, in Harlan's final words, Margold found hope: " . . . except in the case of a clear and unmistakable disregard of rights secured by the supreme law of the land. We have here no such case to be determined, and as this view disposes of the only question which this Court has jurisdiction to review and decide."[27] Margold intended for the Court to receive cases that showed such "clear and unmistakable disregard of rights." He planned to do this even if it was hard to define what was "clear and unmistakable," such as, Margold wrote, "[w]here the question relates to the quality of the educational facilities or instruction, or to the prudence with which educational funds are being expended. . . ."[28] In such situations, he acknowledged, " . . . great difficulty might be encountered in making out a case warranting judicial intervention."[29] But ambiguity would not always be a problem. Margold proposed, avoiding subjective questions such as *how money was spent differently* between white and black schools and focusing instead on the objective issue of *how much money* was allocated to white and black schools.

The goal was to demonstrate that separate was not equal. Margold continued,

> Even here, however, actual conditions in most any southern community should provide sufficient facts which, if expertly and comprehensively prepared and proven, would amply establish the requisite abuse of discretion. The prevailing discrimination, moreover, is due largely to a disproportionate allocation of school funds between white and colored schools, rather than to the injudicious use of such funds as are made available for the latter. The factors establishing the unfair character of this discrimination are much more tangible and susceptible of convincing demonstration than those relating to discrimination resulting from careless or unwise administration.[30]

To Margold, such disproportionate allocation for white and black education would be evidence unambiguous enough to demonstrate a clear violation of the equal protection mandated by the Fourteenth Amendment.

Margold summarized the strategy:

> It is essential to distinguish between a system of racially segregated schools which affords state officers an opportunity, through violations of their legal duties, to discriminate against Negroes, and a system which, without violation of state law, can and is uniformly employed as the means for accomplishing the discrimination. In the former situation, remedies are available under the state law for eliminating the discrimination without affecting the segregation, and if not improper, it at least is unnecessary to go beyond them. In the latter situation, no such remedies are available, and it is both necessary and proper to attack the constitutional validity of the system itself which, as administered under the sanction of state law, deprives Negroes of the rights guaranteed them under the Fourteenth Amendment.[31]

Equal and separate facilities would be unnecessarily expensive, and a costly burden that southern states and communities would be unlikely to bear.

Moreover, demonstrating budgetary inequalities is tantamount to demonstrating a violation of constitutional rights.

Margold outlined three scenarios involving school segregation in which he felt the NAACP should be able to pursue successful legal action. In each, there was an uneven allocation of funds between white and black schools. In the first scenario, he outlined a situation in which state law *mandated* that money be allocated equally between white and black schools, but the law was not followed by the officials responsible for the allocation.[32] In the second, state law *designated* someone to divide funds between black and white schools without specifying how the responsible person was to make this division.[33] In the final scenario, the state law provided guidelines for the division of money but the person responsible for carrying out the law *was given discretion* to decide how, exactly, to divide money within the spirit of the law.[34]

The first scenario, Margold argued, was not amenable to solution by a lawsuit in federal court but, rather, needed to be rectified by actions taken within the states because, in each case where he identified such discrimination, state law provided the means for rectifying imbalances of this sort. Since it was possible, in Margold's estimate, to prove that discrimination was taking place and that such discrimination was illegal according to the state statute, there was no ground for a legal suit.

The second scenario, however, provided ample ground for a legal challenge because states with such laws created a situation in which officials clearly had discretion to make decisions that had a discriminatory effect without violating the applicable statute. The action would not be taken against the officials making such discriminatory funding decisions but, rather, against the law which allowed them to do so. Margold took his legal support for this argument from a pre–*Plessy v. Ferguson* Supreme Court decision in the case of *Yick Wo v. Hopkins*.[35] In this case, Yick Wo was jailed for operating an illegal laundry in the city of San Francisco. He was denied a permit to operate a laundry legally by a board of supervisors that was clearly making discriminatory decisions about which applicants received permits and which did not receive permits based on the ethnicity of the applicants.

The San Francisco city ordinance, as written, appeared neutral. It was the discretion it gave to supervisors that made the law unconstitutional because it allowed the supervisors to behave in a discriminatory way. As Justice Thomas Matthews wrote in the majority opinion, "Though the law itself be fair on its face and impartial in appearance, yet, if it is applied and administered by public authority with an evil eye and an unequal hand, so as practically to make unjust and illegal discriminations between persons in similar circumstances, material to their rights, the denial of equal justice is still within the prohibition of the Constitution."[36] In *Yick Wo*, the Court found, the supervisors were practicing exactly this kind of discrimination. Matthews wrote,

> The fact of this discrimination is admitted. No reason for it is shown, and the conclusion cannot be resisted that no reason for it exists except hostility to the race and nationality to which the petitioners belong, and which, in the eye of the law, is not justified. The discrimination is, therefore, illegal, and the public administration which enforces it is a denial of the equal protection of the laws and a violation of the Fourteenth Amendment of the Constitution.[37]

Making the connection to *Yick Wo*, Margold argued that a law which gives an official, or officials, the discretion to divide money between white and black schools unequally is no different than a law which expressly mandates an unequal division of funds between black and white schools.[38] As Margold put it, "To vest a white officer in a southern community with wide discretion in the division of funds between white and colored schools, limited only by the vague requirement of a uniform school system, or a fair division, is bound to result in actual and extensive discrimination against the latter, and, in a properly prepared case, could be shown beyond peradventure to have done so in actual practice."[39]

The third scenario was more complex legally. Although Margold saw little difference between the second and third scenarios in practical impact, there was, he argued, an important legal distinction which made the third scenario (like the first) hard to litigate. In some cases, it might be possible to argue that not only was the law being implemented in a biased fashion but also that the law which allowed such biased decision making to take place was in violation of the Fourteenth Amendment, which would make the third situation similar to the second situation. However, in other cases, the law in question might provide tools within the state for enforcing a more equitable division of funds between black and white schools, making it more like the first scenario and, hence, not good material for a federal case.[40]

In a detailed analysis of school funding laws at both the state and local levels in seven states where previous research suggested legal action be taken—Alabama, Arkansas, Florida, Georgia, Louisiana, Mississippi, and South Carolina—Margold concluded that trying to fight legal battles in state courts, either asking for court orders (mandamus), injunctions, or trying to press claims that officials were breaching the legal requirements of their positions would be a futile fight. Difficulties included the multiplicity of jurisdictions involved, "the very multiplicity of suits which would have to be brought is itself appalling";[41] the fact that legal fights would in many cases need to be fought annually; and his belief that most southern courts would simply be hostile to such legal action. This analysis prompted Margold to conclude that it would be a waste of the organization's limited financial resources to attempt to use state laws to enforce equal funding for black and white students in elementary and secondary education.[42]

Much of the report's chapter on education focused on elementary and secondary education because the bulk of funding came from the local and state governments. There was little federal government funding for education, except for higher education. Margold identified three main sources of federal funds for education: (1) the granting of federal lands to states for the states to sell and invest the proceeds from the sales in order to use the interest to help fund "at least one state college where agriculture and mechanical arts are taught"; (2) an annual appropriation of $50,000 to states to help fund those land-grant colleges; and (3) appropriations to states to assist in the paying of the salaries of faculty who teach "agricultural and industrial subjects."[43] Because he was not focused on higher education, Margold did not conduct the same exhaustive analysis of these federal funds as of the implementation of school funding at the state and local levels, and he concluded that, without further research and data collection, it was difficult to know if there was anything to be gained by pursuing legal action with regard to the states' use of federal funds. However, Margold believed that none of the three sources of federal funding were likely to provide an opportunity for successful litigation, concluding, "The general legal situation as to all three funds, after they are paid over to the respective states, is, of course, precisely the same as the one with respect to various state funds."[44] As with primary and secondary education, he saw little opportunity for litigation filed in state courts which would be highly resistant to helping the black cause.

Margold paid little attention to college or graduate education in his report. His relative lack of interest in higher education differed significantly from what eventually became the strategy of Charles Houston and the NAACP legal defense team. Unlike Margold, Houston was primarily interested in breaking down barriers to the highest levels of education before anything else. For Houston, judges, recipients of the benefits of higher education, regardless of their stance on segregation, might be sympathetic to those seeking similar intellectual advancement.

In making suggestions for how the NAACP should begin its fight for equality in education, Margold concluded, "In none of the seven states, where litigation is recommended in the American Fund memorandum, are any direct and effective legal remedies available to enforce equal but separate educational accommodations for white and colored children."[45] The problem, Margold reiterated, was that

> only a very small part of the prevailing discrimination occurs in violation of state law and can be remedied there under. For the most part, we have a situation in which each of the seven states requires segregation of the white and colored races in its schools under conditions which enable its officers to provide accommodations in the colored schools, grossly inferior to those provided in the white schools. Coupled with this, we have the consistent, long continued practice of these officers to take ample advantage of the opportunity which the state law affords them and the complete absence of any way of stopping this practice through resort to any remedy provided by the state law. We have, in a word, a case of segregation irremediably coupled with discrimination.[46]

This combination, segregation coupled with discrimination, would allow the NAACP, in Margold's estimation, to attack the injustice of education for blacks in the South indirectly, on the issue of funding in federal court. Since the US Supreme Court had regularly supported segregation, Margold's proposal was for a legal assault through the equal protection clause of the Fourteenth Amendment, aimed at inequitable funding of schools for whites and schools for blacks, and not a frontal attack on segregation itself. Because, in his analysis, there was very little likelihood of working at the state level to pursue equal funding for black schools—thanks to the wording of state laws, the reluctance of southern courts to rule against state officials, and other factors cited in his report—Margold counseled against a piecemeal campaign of going after schools to try to force them simply to spend more money for black students on a school-by-school, or district-by-district basis. He wrote, "This vicious situation, it seems to me, represents the very heart of the evils in education against which our campaign should be directed. It would be a great mistake to fritter away our limited funds on sporadic attempts to force the making of equal divisions of school funds in the few instances where such attempts might be expected to succeed."[47]

What was needed, according to Margold, was a strategy more broadly envisioned:

> If we boldly challenge the constitutional validity of segregation if and when accompanied irremediably by discrimination, we can strike directly at the most prolific sources of discrimination. . . . [T]he threat of using this adjudication as a means of destroying segregation itself, would always exert a very real and powerful force at least to compel enormous improvement in the Negro schools through voluntary official action.[48]

Margold felt that the worst that could happen in pursuing this strategy was that black schools would dramatically improve through a well-aimed legal strategy while, in the best case, attacking the discrimination present in a segregated system could, ultimately, dismantle that segregated system.

The route to success was not to be found, Margold argued, in filing lawsuits against states, calling for injunctions to require those states to provide equal funding for black and white schools in states where there was no legal requirement for equal funding. He assessed such a strategy this way, writing of the Fourteenth Amendment, "The pertinent provision of that amendment merely prohibits the states from denying the equal protection of their laws to persons within their jurisdiction. It does not purport and cannot be construed to supply affirmative duties for state officers which the state law should, but does not, impose."[49]

Earlier US Supreme Court decisions in many ways discouraged frontal attacks on segregation, but Margold saw promise in the Supreme Court's decisions in *Cumming v. Richmond Board of Education, Yick Wo v. Hopkins* and *Gong Lum v. Rice.* Margold argued that it would be a clear case of discrimination, according to the principles expressed in *Cumming,* not if blacks and whites were required to attend separate schools, but if there was no school for blacks, or if the school for blacks was not substantively equivalent to the school for whites. He wrote, "Where a similar school is not provided, it is the exclusion of the Negroes from the white school which contravenes the Fourteenth Amendment, and it is that exclusion which can be attacked through mandamus to compel admission of colored children into the white school despite invalid provisions in the state constitution or statutes to the contrary,"[50] and he continued, making reference to *Lum*, "There is no distinction between a case where no school at all is available and one where an inferior one is provided. The Negro children are entitled to equal accommodations. Where the only way they can get such accommodations is by admission to the white school, their exclusion from that school under color of state law contravenes the Fourteenth Amendment and can be corrected by mandamus."[51] In sum, the Margold strategy was predicated upon an attack on inequitable school funding, with the objective of, at a minimum, bringing black schools up in quality and, in a best case scenario, of requiring the admission of black students to white schools where it was clearly not possible to raise black schools to the level of white schools. There is the tacit assumption that local and state governments would be unable or unwilling to pay for equal, separate schools owing to inefficiencies of cost. The out-of-state scholarship programs, such as Missouri's, were preferred by segregation states to creation of black colleges because they were cheaper.

Margold left the NAACP in 1933 to become the Solicitor of the US Department of the Interior, and in 1934 Charles Houston became the NAACP's special counsel. Margold gave his hearty endorsement for Houston to serve as his replacement.[52] Houston started as part-time while working at Howard University. He became full-time director of the NAACP's legal efforts in 1935. In 1945, Nathan R. Margold was appointed as federal district court judge for the District of Columbia.

When Charles Houston took over as the leader of the NAACP's legal defense, he maintained the basic structure of Margold's suggestions, but he also modified them and implemented a more practical strategy for litigation. Houston is frequently cited as 'the man who killed Jim Crow' and as the architect of the NAACP's legal strategy. William Hastie remembered Houston as "the architect and dominant force of the legal program" of the NAACP.[53] Historian Genna Rae McNeil writes that Houston "devised the legal strategy, charted the course, began a program of political education for the masses, and handled the civil rights cases. He called on former students to accept the challenge of civil rights law and brought into the campaign eager, alert and astute lawyers."[54] The Library of Congress electronic memorial to the civil rights struggle in the United States similarly refers to Houston as "the chief strategist of the NAACP's legal campaign that culminated in the *Brown* decision."[55]

Houston, the first African American director of the NAACP legal affairs, certainly deserves of this praise and was the most important force as the NAACP shifted from the planning stage to actually taking cases to court. This need not diminish the importance of Margold's basic strategy, but Houston had different targets in mind when he became the leader of the legal fight. It is certainly true that Margold did not address the question of graduate and professional education and paid very little attention even to undergraduate education, whereas graduate and professional education was a top priority for Charles Houston. As the dean of the Howard University Law School, Houston believed strongly in building a corps of black attorneys to not only fight the civil rights war, but to simply be the vanguard of a growing black middle class that would increase the overall economic power of blacks as a social class.

In the first of two essays published in late 1935 in the NAACP magazine, *The Crisis*, one in October and one in December, Houston wrote about the legal strategy he, William Hastie, Thurgood Marshall, and other attorneys working for the NAACP would pursue. In it, he outlined a strategy with a foundation built on the Margold plan, but aimed first at the highest levels of education, not at primary and secondary education.

As legal historian Mark Tushnet observes, there were many reasons for Houston's attention to graduate education early in the fight. For one, Houston simply had a personal desire to increase the number of black professionals. Second, there were more willing plaintiffs available at this level, even though far fewer people went to graduate school than to elementary school, because it was perceived that there was less personal risk at pursuing a case to go to law school than a case to attend the neighborhood white elementary school. In addition, Houston believed that the litigation would be more straightforward in cases of graduate education. As Tushnet observes, "Southern states did not have many graduate and professional programs for blacks, so the problems were not of 'separate but equal' but were rather problems of 'separate and nonexistent.'"[56]

In the introduction to Houston's October essay for *The Crisis*, his goals were similar to those Margold advocated in his report. Houston explained,

The National Association for the Advancement of Colored people is launching an active campaign against race discrimination in
public education. The campaign will reach all levels of public education from the nursery school through the university. The ultimate objective of the association is the abolition of all forms of
segregation in public education, whether in the admission or activities of students, the appointment or advancement of teachers, or
administrative control.

Houston continued, outlining a plan that was very similar to the Margold
prescription. "Where possible, it will attack segregation in schools. Where
segregation is so firmly entrenched by law that a frontal attack cannot be
made, the association will throw its immediate force toward bringing Negro
schools up to an absolute equality with white schools. If the white South insists upon its separate schools, it must not squeeze the Negro schools to pay
for them."[57] This was the strategy Margold recommended.

In his essay, Houston discussed the fact that pursuing educational equality
was but one part of a broader NAACP plan to attack segregation and discrimination in the United States, including campaigns against lynching, for the
economic and employment advancement of blacks, for the right to vote, the
right to serve on juries, the right to travel freely on public transportation, and
for the right to live wherever they wanted to live. NAACP Secretary Walter
White's priority for the NAACP and the organization's congressional lobbying emphasis had been passage of an anti-lynching bill. Houston wrote that
the education agenda

ties in with the anti-lynching fight because there is no use educat-
ing boys and girls if their function in life is to be the playthings of
murderous mobs. . . . The N.A.A.C.P. recognizes the fact that the
discriminations which the Negro suffers in education are merely
part of the general pattern of race prejudice in American life, and it
knows that no attack on discrimination in education can have any
far reaching effect unless it is bound to a general attack on discrimination and segregation in all phases of American life.[58]

Nearly all of these were topics addressed by Margold, who also recognized
the integrated nature of the many obstacles blacks had to overcome. As Margold observed in the introduction to his report,

Segregation coupled with inferior accommodations and instruction in public schools, segregation and inferior accommodations on common carriers, residential segregation, exclusion from jury service, disenfranchisement, peonage, and other impairments or deprivations of civil liberties are discussed in the appropriate memorandum as the primary evils in this country against which the campaign is to be directed.[59]

Houston's primary goal was to eliminate segregation and discrimination in education. Given the list of specific objectives that Houston identified in *The Crisis*, it is clear that he felt, as did Margold, that the attack on segregation would best be handled indirectly. He emphasized a plan to push first for *equality* of education rather than *desegregation* of education. The six educational objectives Houston gave were "(a) equality of school terms; (b) equality of pay for Negro teachers having the same qualifications and doing the same work as white teachers; (c) equality of transportation for Negro school children at public expense; (d) equality of buildings and equipment; (e) equality of *per capita* expenditure for education of Negroes; (f) equality in graduate and professional training."[60] The key difference in Houston's plan from Margold's report, as outlined in his October article for *The Crisis*, was the emphasis placed on graduate and professional education.

The highest levels of education were important to Houston because such programs were unavailable to blacks in the South. Houston wrote, "Although the southern states provide a measure of undergraduate instruction for Negroes on the college level, not one of them provides any graduate or professional training for Negroes." Some southern states, or states that might better be thought of as border states such as Missouri, Maryland, and West Virginia, had scholarship programs for black students to attend graduate or professional schools out of state, but this was unacceptable for many reasons, including the practical concern that such programs did not come close to fully paying expenses related to attending school out of state. Houston addressed this at greater length in a subsequent article for the December, 1935, issue of *The Crisis*.

On the one hand the number of Negroes in college is constantly increasing. Negro college enrolment jumped from 5, 231 in 1922 to 22,609 in 1932. This has brought a demand for graduate and professional education from below. On the other hand, requirements for teaching, higher standards in the trades and professions and keener occupational competition have brought on pressure for graduate and professional education from above.[61]

There were no integrated public universities in southern states with postgraduate programs that admitted African Americans, and only a handful of black universities with advanced programs.[62] Nevertheless, the demand for postgraduate education among African Americans was growing.[63]

The absence of postgraduate programs made litigation pertaining to equal opportunity easier. Houston wrote of the decision to go after segregation in postgraduate education first. Blacks in the South had opportunities for undergraduate education, although they were segregated. This was not the case with graduate education.

> The legal problem was simpler; and since much of its education program will involve pioneer work the association began with the simpler problem first. As regards primary, secondary and collegiate education in the South, there is a system, albeit inadequate, of separate primary and secondary schools and colleges for Negroes supported from public funds. A challenge to the inadequacies of these primary, secondary schools and colleges would raise the question whether the facilities offered by them are equal to the facilities offered in similar schools to whites. This would involve complex problems of comparative budget analyses, faculty qualifications, and other facts. But in the case of the graduate or professional training there are *no* facilities whatsoever provided for Negroes by the state, and the question narrows down to a simple proposition of law: whether the state can appropriate public money for graduate and professional education for white students exclusively.[64]

An assault on segregation could be more successful in the early stages in states when comparing postgraduate programs with white-only admissions and to nonexistent programs for blacks.[65] Once the precedent for equal opportunities was set, it could be used to press for integrated educational programs at other levels of the educational system. Moreover, Houston knew policies related to law schools well, he felt less comfortable with cases involving programs he knew less about. Houston was a perfectionist who wanted every detail correct. In a subsequent case involving graduate admission in journalism at Missouri, Houston felt he needed additional preparation. "In journalism I am in an entirely new field, and must be educated myself."[66] He asked for assistance from Roy Wilkins and other NAACP staff who worked more closely with the press. [67] A case involving law school admission would provide a stronger start to his overall legal strategy.

Houston also felt strongly about the need for black lawyers because he believed that only black lawyers would truly lead the kind of fight needed to win the struggle for equal rights. Houston once wrote, "Experience has proved that the average white lawyer, especially in the South, cannot be relied upon to wage an uncompromising fight for equal rights of Negroes."[68] While Houston was doing his best, through a revamped and newly accredited law school at Howard, to train black lawyers, it was obviously essential to expand the number of quality institutions black students could attend for legal training.

By 1935, when Houston's first essay on the education strategy of the NAACP appeared in *The Crisis*, the organization had already tried the *Hocutt* case in North Carolina and was involved in the cases of students wishing to attend graduate or professional school at the then-segregated institutions, the University of Maryland and the University of Virginia. The Virginia case involved a woman named Alice Jackson, who wished to pursue a Master of Arts degree in French at the University of Virginia. The case did not ultimately make it to court, but a history of Jackson's case, produced by the University of Virginia, attributes the creation of graduate education opportunities for blacks in Virginia to the threat which the case presented to the state of Virginia. Not only was a graduate school for blacks subsequently created at Virginia State University as a result of Alice Jackson's case, the state also established a scholarship fund for black students to pursue postgraduate education out of state. Although the out-of-state scholarship plan was an option Houston expressly opposed, Alice Jackson used the fund to get her master's degree in English, not French, from Columbia University.[69]

In his report, Nathan Margold specifically suggested against any legal action in Virginia, graduate school-related or otherwise. Unlike the other states on which he focused, Margold felt that Virginia's laws were more amenable to a suit filed as an original case in the US Supreme Court, taking advantage of the fact that the Court can be a court of original jurisdiction. However, Margold felt it would be a waste of limited resources to take that route because discrimination in Virginia was not as bad as it was in Alabama, Arkansas,

Florida, Georgia, Louisiana, Mississippi, or North Carolina. Ultimately, Margold's advice to focus on the states with the most severe forms of segregation was unheeded. It was in states with milder segregation, to the extent milder segregation exists, where the first important legal battles were waged and, to varying degrees, won, such as in Maryland and Missouri.

The Maryland case Houston discussed in the October essay in *The Crisis* was that of Donald Gaines Murray and, unlike Alice Jackson's case, it did go to court and was in the midst of litigation when Houston wrote his two essays.[70] Murray won his case at trial in June 1935 when Judge Eugene O'Dunne issued a writ of mandamus in his favor. Murray was admitted to the University of Maryland's law school even as the university and the state appealed the decision. The Maryland Court of Appeals resolved the *Murray* case in January 1936, also in Murray's favor, as Houston, Redmond and Espy initiated a lawsuit for Lloyd Gaines in Missouri.[71] Most accounts of the NAACP's legal strategy imply the Donald Murray litigation preceded the *Gaines* case. However, Gaines applied for admission to the University of Missouri, and the St. Louis NAACP legal office began background research, between the time of Murray's trial court and the state appeal.

In the December 1935 *Crisis* article, Houston addressed the Murray case extensively. Many of his remarks reflect a level of frustration with the fact that it was even necessary to file cases of this nature. For instance, Houston wrote,

> Nothing was said in Murray's petition about his being a Negro. From the standpoint of the N.A.A.C.P. the fact of Murray's color was immaterial since he was seeking admission to a state university under public control and supported in part by public tax money. The petition grounded itself flatly on the fact that Murray was qualified in all respects to enter the school of law, that he was a citizen of Maryland, and had been arbitrarily refused admission to the university. The university answered through the attorney general of the state and said it had excluded Murray because he was a Negro. It is interesting that both in the *Hocutt* case in North Carolina and the *Murray* case in Maryland, the attorneys general appeared to defend the policy of exclusion.

He added parenthetically an observation of the irony that he felt, "(Negro tax payers helping to pay the salaries of public officers who use their offices to deprive them of their rights)."[72] This was the basis on which the NAACP challenged the denial of admission of black students to graduate programs in segregated schools—that those students were tax-paying citizens and, as such, deserved the same opportunity to attend tax-supported public institutions as a white citizen.

Once *Murray* was resolved, after losses by the state of Maryland in its own courts and its decision not to appeal to the Supreme Court, the case represented a major, if localized, victory for civil rights. The case resulted in the desegregation of the University of Maryland, first, of the law school and, eventually, the entire university. The downside of the *Murray* case was that it was settled entirely in state court and presented no opportunity for a hearing in the federal Supreme Court, which could have set an important precedent for the nation. Despite this, however, the *Murray* case represented an enormous success by the NAACP's legal team in opening an institution previously closed to blacks.

The Maryland outcome not only established a model for cases going forward, it also served as evidence that blacks and whites could peacefully coexist at previously segregated institutions. Of Murray's experience when he was admitted to the University of Maryland, Houston wrote,

> At the University of Maryland Murray attends his law classes without a single unpleasant incident. White students sit on either side of him. He recites like any other student. He minds his business; they mind theirs. If the South will look at the question calmly it should see that there is no reason why the experience of the school of law of the University of Maryland with Murray could not be duplicated in every state university below the Mason-Dixon line. Negroes want better education so that they may lead fuller lives and become better citizens. They are not interested in settling old grudges but in building a new America of real democracy of opportunity for all.[73]

Houston's attentiveness to peaceful cooperation, however, was important and sincere. The historical past and public opinion regarding racial relations would continue to be a concern through and beyond the *Gaines* case.

Both Margold and Houston were interested in the question of how whites would respond to the NAACP's efforts. Margold dismissed concerns: "There remains for consideration only the danger of stirring up intense opposition, ill-will and strife as a result of any attack upon a custom so deeply entrenched in popular prejudice as is the segregation of races in public schools. A similar danger would be entailed by any sort of effective action which we can hope to take in our campaign."[74] Margold then asserted that this campaign was only necessary because of the injustice of *discrimination* and that existing legal precedents made it necessary for the legal goal not to be the dismantling of *segregation* but, rather, the elimination of *discrimination*, and that whatever inherent risks existed, the goal was worth it.

> In seeking to attack it, we are in effect seeking only to compel the states which desire segregation to provide for it in a form which will render equality imperative and provide Negro parents with effective, practicable means of forcing derelict educational officers to perform their duties properly. Approached from this point of view, and accompanied by extensive, carefully supervised publicity, I feel certain that the danger of inciting ill-will and alienating enlightened public opinion can be reduced far below the point where it is outweighed by the ultimate good to be accomplished.[75]

Facing *actual*, and not *hypothetical*, negative reaction in the Virginia and Maryland cases, Houston responded in a manner similar to Margold. Houston tied the situation of Alice Jackson in Virginia not only to the struggle for black rights, but also to the continuing fight for women's rights.

> The reactions of the white press of Virginia to this heretical attempt of a Negro girl to enter the graduate department of the University of Virginia are indicative of the opposition which the N.A.A.C.P. will face when its general educational program gets well under way. . . . White Virginians evidently cannot bring themselves to admit that the University of Virginia is a public institution, and not their own private property. It is a public institution, so the question put by the *Northern Virginia Daily* as to whether a Negro student "is wanted" at the university is beside the point. A Negro student can preserve her self-respect much more by standing up for her constitutional rights and facing the snubs and insults of the white students with calm and dignity than by supinely yielding up her constitutional rights. Unless the white students offer her actual physical violence, they cannot snub or insult her any worse than

the white men students snubbed and insulted the first white woman who dared enter the University of Virginia.[76]

Houston believed that the time had arrived to push things further and to
bring liberal whites to action, instead of just speaking in platitudes about justice. Houston's words are suggestive of what Martin Luther King, Jr., would
later write in "Letter from Birmingham Jail" about justice delayed being justice denied. Houston wrote, "Another point that the older white Virginians
make is that any attempt to force the university issue will disturb 'amicable
race relations' in Virginia. It seems strange that white people always use 'amicable race relations' as an excuse to discourage the Negro from insisting on
his rights."[77] In his December 1935 essay in *The Crisis*, Houston was even
more forceful, writing. "It is not necessary here to attempt to notice and re-
fute all the arguments which many white southerners are making against Negroes being admitted to state universities. Most of the arguments arise out
of hysteria and fear. They are not reasons but excuses under which in the last
analysis their proponents wish to continue the exploitation and suppression
of the Negro."[78]

For both Margold and Houston, the risks associated with this campaign
were outweighed by the possible gains, not only in terms of legal victories,
but also in changing the attitudes of whites. However, Houston was well
aware of the potential for violence and other negative response from whites,
and he expressed concern about violence surrounding Lloyd Gaines.[79] In addition, Houston worked behind the scenes trying to reduce the likelihood of
physical violence.

Like Margold, Houston held out hope for white Americans to see justice in
what the NAACP was pursuing. In the first essay, he observed that "the young
southern white students have not been heard from; but there are indications
that there is a growing sentiment among them for recognition of the Negro as
a real human being and citizen entitled to all the legal rights and public benefits as such."[80] In his second essay, Houston wrote, "The truth is that if Negroes attend state universities in the South, nothing ought to happen except
that the white South would throw off some of its fetters of prejudice and the
whole level of culture and civilization in the state would rise."[81]

The fight was, after all, about much more than gaining admission to
white-only schools. It was a fight for human rights and dignity, as Houston
summarized eloquently in his October essay in *The Crisis*:

The N.A.A.C.P. appreciates the magnitude of the task ahead of it, but it has its duty to its constituency and to the America of the future. It conceives that in equalizing educational opportunities for Negroes it raises the whole standard of American citizenship, and stimulates white Americans as well as black. Fundamentally, the N.A.A.C.P. is not a special pleader; it merely insists that the United States respect its own Constitution and its own laws.[82]

However, a case in federal courts had not yet been decided. In Missouri, Houston and Redmond saw the opportunity for adjudication in the nation's highest court.

3

Gaines and Losses

By early 1935, while litigating the *Murray* case in Maryland, Houston, Marshall, and their colleagues were looking for a case in Missouri. Missouri appeared an excellent venue for a test case on discrimination in postgraduate education admissions. The only state institution of higher education available to black Missourians, Lincoln University, offered a limited number of degrees compared to the state's flagship university and no graduate or professional degrees. Black Missourians, instead, could apply for out-of-state tuition scholarships, established by the General Assembly in 1921, for academic programs not offered at Lincoln. Other states had used Missouri's legislation as a model for maintaining white-only universities without creating the full range of alternatives for black colleges.[1] Houston's goal was to challenge graduate admission practices at the University of Missouri, in Columbia—and, by extension, challenge the practices of states that had copied Missouri's approach. Houston met with officials at the local NAACP office in St. Louis to plan and coordinate the litigation strategy. As Juan Williams observes, "Houston viewed the Missouri suit as key to the NAACP effort to desegregate schools nationwide. He was laying the groundwork for the argument that if no separate but equal schools existed for black students, there was no option but integration."[2]

Sidney R. Redmond was assigned the task of investigating the situation at the University of Missouri and providing the national NAACP legal counsel with a report.[3] Houston knew that Redmond and his partner, Espy, had recently argued the case for the integration of the Kiel Auditorium in St. Louis and that the city had reversed its position, which Houston considered an important local legal victory.[4] Houston trusted Redmond to handle the investigation, and the two men soon became co-counsel in what they referred to as the "University of Missouri case." Espy joined the legal team.

Redmond's charge was to obtain a substantial amount of information regarding the "Exclusion of Negroes from the University of Missouri and failure of the State to afford equal opportunities in lieu thereof." The agreement between Houston and Redmond outlined eleven points of information to be collected, including the constitutional and legal provisions for segregation, the rules of the University of Missouri, blank applications, financial data, financial and catalog comparisons between the university and Lincoln, a detailed record of the tuition scholarship program, and even photos of buildings at the University of Missouri.[5] Redmond set to work collecting background information for a case against the university.

The legal team needed a plaintiff. Charles Houston articulated the NAACP's judicial strategy of case sponsorship later, before the Missouri Supreme Court in 1939. The NAACP "did not seek cases but stood behind any Negro deprived of his rights who requested our aid."[6] The NAACP's legal agenda, noted Houston, depended on those willing to step up to the challenge. "This fight for equality of higher education essentially must be the fight of the young Negro college student and college graduate. The N.A.A.C.P. cannot go out and make students go into court. If the students themselves do not want graduate and professional education enough to make the fight the N.A.A.C.P. stands tied."[7] Although the NAACP attorneys could conduct background research, all depended on one or more persons to choose to file a case that the NAACP counsel could support.

The initial working agreement between the two attorneys became effective on July 18, 1935, a month after Lloyd Gaines initially contacted the University of Missouri for admissions information but before Gaines became a client. Houston, in the investigation memorandum, cautioned against proactively seeking a case. Even the acquisition of blank admission forms should be voluntary. "These must not be obtained under subterfuge, because we want our hands to be absolutely clean. Best way here is to let the prospective student or some of his friends obtain the blank in his or their own way." Houston wrote to Redmond: "Remember that it is not your job to find a client. I don't want you to be put in the position of fomenting litigation. I want the newspapers or interested laymen to find you your client. All I want you to do is to make the investigation and disclose the rotten conditions."[8] Redmond responded immediately that "I believe you will encounter some difficulty in getting a client" and warned against lengthy delay.[9] A month later, Redmond remained optimistic, but the attorneys officially had no client.[10]

Redmond soon suffered external pressure resulting from his inquiries. He felt "the Board of Curators of the University of Missouri, were out investigating me; they wanted to bring disbarment proceedings saying I was out chasing business."[11] Counsel for the university investigated Redmond and Espy in order to deter them from pursuing the case.[12] Word of pending legal action against the University of Missouri spread in the state's black community. Black teachers urged students to contact Redmond about applying for admission, but while Redmond encouraged students to request admission forms and to apply, he was careful to promise no additional personal support or legal action.[13] There were several applicants (actual and potential) who expressed interest in legal assistance for admission to graduate programs at the University of Missouri, but Redmond would later characterize most as "an unreliable group."[14] Houston responded, "The same thing has happened in every state we have entered. Frankly, the university program has slowed down to a walk for lack of suitable candidates both in the front line and in reserve." He continued, "What we must realize is that we are marking out new ground and that very few persons have the pioneer spirit. Consequently, do not be dismayed by the timidity and general unreliability of many of those with whom you come in contact."[15] One individual, however, seemed a strong and reliable candidate.

The black press was involved deeply in the Missouri case from the beginning, with the recruitment of potential litigants. Charles Houston encouraged editors of black newspapers to find potential students to apply for graduate admission at the University of Missouri. He gave Sidney Redmond instructions to allow others such as those in the newspaper business to help find a client for a test case.[16] Black attorneys and black newspapermen were close, particularly in St. Louis. They moved in the same social circles and shared office buildings;[17] they were politically active and were influential within organizations like the NAACP. In July of 1935, Houston wrote Joseph E. Mitchell, of the *Argus*, and Nathan B. Young Jr., of the *American* to publicize the legal program attacking educational discrimination in Missouri and to forward information about the successful Maryland case.[18] *St. Louis*

American owner and publisher Nathaniel A. Sweets had contributed funds to Gaines's undergraduate education, and, along with faculty at Lincoln, encouraged Gaines to apply for law school.[19] Sweets himself had applied for graduate admission to the University of Missouri School of Journalism, and he was one of the applicants deposed for the trial court.

In August, a potential client, Lloyd Lionel Gaines, visited the office of Sidney Redmond. Gaines, who had graduated first in his class at Vashon High School in St. Louis, earned a number of academic achievements, and graduated as an honors student from Lincoln University in Jefferson City in 1935, seemed a strong prospect for a test case.[20] Gaines described himself as "5'10", 160, medium brown, sober, courteous and conscientious."[21] The "wiry, chain-smoking"[22] Gaines and teacher Zaid Lenoir met with Redmond to discuss applying for admission to the University of Missouri Law School. Gaines and Lenoir met with Redmond on August 26, by which time Redmond was already referring to Gaines as "our client" suggesting earlier contact between Gaines and Redmond or Espy.[23] Later, Gaines testified that he was not yet a client.

The role of Lenoir in encouraging Gaines's involvement is unmentioned in later accounts. Nathaniel Sweets also relates a conversation he had with Gaines after instruction from Canadian-born, Harvard-educated English professor Cecil A. Blue. Sweets recalled that Gaines

> graduated and came back here and was sitting in my office one day and I said, "Lloyd, you know what you should do? You should go up to the University and make an application to go to the Law School there." He said, "Well, I'll believe I will. But I can't get in its needless for me to go over there." I said, "Well, you go ahead. And I'll go too, I'll make an application to enter," which is on the record over there, "the School of Journalism."

According to newspaperman Nathaniel Sweets, "the Gaines case had its conception right in our little office." He also alludes to the involvement of publisher and later Judge Nathan B. Young, Jr.[24]

Redmond responded in a manner similar to his interactions with other potential applicants. He described the encounter this way:

> [Gaines] came to my office and talked to me about going to the University of Missouri. I said, "A man with your qualifications and ability ought to be an asset to the school. And if you really want to

apply yourself and study, you should go. And all you need to do is to file an application." And he says, "Well, now, what kind of application should it be?" And I just reached in my desk there and got out a postal card, you know, one of these stamped cards, and told him to write the registrar and ask him to send you an application blank.[25]

Lloyd Gaines struck Redmond as a reasonable and suitable person for a test case. Gaines was smart and articulate, and he seemed to have a sincere interest in a legal career (an aspiration likely to appeal to judges). In addition, he was an academically sound student and a recent college graduate.

Unlike many other potential plaintiffs, Lloyd Gaines did request a form and followed with an application for admission. While Redmond seemed to think Gaines would make a strong plaintiff, he and Houston were prudent. Houston sensed potential problems. "Please keep after Gaines and above all, check his transcript yourself in order to see that he is an A-1 qualified student." Houston continued: "We do not want to back anybody as to whom there could be the slightest personal objection."[26] By late October, Redmond identified two other applicants and wrote "I beg to say that I am doing all I can to get additional persons to file their applications."

Lloyd Gaines received and completed the application for admission to the University of Missouri School of Law. Gaines originally asked for a catalog and admission information from the registrar on June 12, and a response was sent June 18. He requested an application for admission on August 19, and an application form was sent to him on August 26. The initial correspondence gave no indication that Gaines was a black applicant. The university registrar, Silas Woodson (Sy) Canada, asked Gaines to have his university forward transcripts for admission.[27] Gaines contacted Lincoln University's president, Charles W. Florence, and requested the transcripts be sent to the University of Missouri.

This process of sending transcripts was critical for more than mere certification of eligibility for graduate admission. Receipt of the transcript signaled to university officials whether the applicant was black. All students at Lincoln University were black; students at other state colleges in Missouri were white.[28] Thus, the registrar would know upon receipt of the transcripts that Lloyd Gaines was black, so they could potentially reject the application on any basis without overtly identifying a student's race. Attorney William Hogsett, lead counsel for the university, asked Gaines about this in his deposition later. Hogsett implied that Gaines tried to conceal his race by not identifying Lincoln University as the institution, asking if this was intentional or accidental. Gaines replied that it was incidental.[29]

Although it is difficult to establish in the written record, it appears that black university officials knew at least implicitly that they should not send transcripts to white-only schools. The *Hocutt* case in North Carolina could not go forward because President James Shepard of the North Carolina College for Negroes did not forward Hocutt's academic transcript to UNC. Since no complete application was received, his admission could be denied without a specific reference to race. It is important to note that Shepard, and other black college presidents, also had the incentive to expand their universities through cooperation with establishment authorities. If there was demand from applicants, new postgraduate programs, for instance, could be established at separate 'but equal' black colleges.[30]

Lincoln University President Charles W. Florence felt pressure to refuse to send transcripts. Gaines requested transcripts, and his legal counsel asked others to encourage compliance with his request. Redmond expressed concern to Houston that Florence seemed cooperative in a meeting with Espy, yet Florence did not meet with Redmond later as planned.[31] Raised in Pennsylvania, Florence received both bachelor's and master's degrees from the University of Pittsburgh. He taught at the Virginia Normal and Industrial Institute before moving to Missouri to head Lincoln University. During his tenure, he continued the tradition of his predecessor, Nathan B. Young, to improve the academic quality of Lincoln. He oversaw Lincoln's accreditation by the North Central College Association and created a sabbatical program to allow Lincoln faculty to earn advanced degrees in their fields.[32] Both he and members of the Lincoln faculty argued for greater educational opportunities, and Florence took the public position that Negro Colleges were not receiving their fair share of educational funding.[33] Ultimately, Florence demonstrated the courage to order that Gaines's undergraduate transcripts be forwarded to support his application for graduate study. On September 4, Lincoln Assistant Registrar Marguerite Hicks forwarded Gaines's transcripts, and they were received by the University of Missouri the next day. President Florence had difficulties with Lincoln's Board of Curators and was removed as president in 1937. It is not clear whether his cooperation with Gaines's counsel added to difficulties with the board members, half of whom were white.

The university realized that it received an application from a black student and initially procrastinated rather than making a decision regarding admission. The university's response was to refer Gaines's application back to administrators at Lincoln University.[34] Under Redmond's supervision, Lloyd Gaines wrote to and then wired President Florence of Lincoln, as well as writing to the University of Missouri president and Board of Curators member George Willson, requesting a decision on his admission application.[35] President Florence at Lincoln responded to Gaines through a telegram and a subsequent letter. Florence, under orders from his own board, referred Gaines to Section 9622 of the *Revised Statutes of Missouri*, the code that established tuition scholarships for study in adjacent states, and encouraged Gaines to contact the state superintendent of schools, Lloyd King.[36]

Lloyd Gaines continued to press for an admission decision, and Redmond and Houston decided that they had a responsible and reliable plaintiff. Redmond encouraged Gaines to request support from the national office. In a September 27, 1935, letter, Gaines made an official request for legal support from Charles Houston and the NAACP. Gaines described the segregated educational environment in Missouri and outlined his personal academic achievements. Gaines concludes

> I see no reason why I should be denied the opportunity of continuing my studies in a school of my choice, especially when that school—Missouri University—is a public institution of the state wherein I live and pay taxes. I am appealing to you in the name of social justice, to back my efforts to receive my rightful consideration. May I rely on your assistance at such an urgent time of need?[37]

The NAACP now had a plaintiff with standing to pursue a constitutional case on educational equality. Houston initially referred Gaines back to Sidney Redmond; however, the two became close. Houston would soon refer to Lloyd as "Brother Gaines" and Gaines to his mentor as "Brother Houston." They maintained a personal and mutual connection. Houston requested a biography and a photo from Gaines for publicity and an article in *The Crisis*.[38]

With Redmond, Houston expressed plans to make this case a significant one and outlined four important points. First, Houston's strategy included additional applications from qualified black students. "This gives you reserve material and puts you in the position to say to the court that it will do the state no good to try to dismiss the Gaines case on technicalities as there are other suits ready to be filed, and that it will save everyone's time, energy, and money to meet the case on its merits." Second, Houston insisted on detailed preparation on items such as the operation of the out-of-state scholarships: "I agree with you that there is no need for us to know facts if we cannot prove them." Third, he cautioned against hasty action with anything less than an "air-tight case." Houston cited the Alice Jackson case in Virginia as a success because of her refusal to accept a pyrrhic victory, forcing the state to confront its discriminatory practices. The University of Virginia refused to admit Alice Jackson because she was black as well as for other reasons. Jackson, through counsel, pressed for identification of any other reasons. This, in turn, forced acknowledgment that there were no other reasons. "The issues involved are so big that we cannot afford to omit any detail or preparation in a hasty attempt at grandstand play." Finally, Houston urged a search for inequality. "Missouri does make a gesture" at providing equal educational opportunity, so "we want to be prepared to show that uniformly Negroes fail to get justice."[39]

Named as the lead defendant in the litigation was the university registrar, Silas Woodson Canada. Sy Canada was a university man. Born and raised in northwestern Missouri, Canada came to Columbia for a college education and never left—the city or the university.[40] After graduation from the University of Missouri, Canada took a job in the registrar's office, and worked his way up to assistant registrar, and then to the top position. His draft card (for what would later be called World War I) describes Canada as medium height, "stout", with blue eyes and brown hair, and married. His wife, Evelyn Kehr, is never listed in the US Census as employed, but she was college educated. In fact, Mrs. S. Woodson Canada appears to have been the first married woman to attend and graduate from the University of Missouri.

Canada lived a comfortable life and held an important bureaucratic position as registrar at the university,[41] but he does not appear as a key decision-maker in the *Gaines* case. Correspondence indicates that S. W. Canada was thorough and knowledgeable, but he deferred major decisions, such as admission of minority student applicants, to his superiors, President F. A. Middlebush and, later, university counsel William Hogsett. He is named as defendant in litigation because Houston and Redmond sought an injunction compelling Canada to admit Gaines (and other black applicants) to the University of Missouri.

Frederick Arnold Middlebush became president of the University of Missouri on July 1, 1935. He was acting president in summer 1931 and again in 1934 during the illness of the incumbent, journalist Walter Williams. Middlebush replaced Williams shortly before his death. Middlebush had received his Ph.D. in political science from the University of Michigan, and, following appointments at several colleges, he became an associate professor at the University of Missouri in 1922. He co-authored a standard textbook on international relations.[42] Within three years, Middlebush was dean of the School of Business and Public Administration.[43] He continued to rise through university administration, and eventually became the longest serving president in the history of the University of Missouri, remaining until 1954.[44] His term as president was marked by expansion of the university, in terms of students, buildings and physical facilities, as well as the scope of educational programs and degrees.

When Gaines wrote to the Missouri university president directly, on September 24, he acknowledged his Lincoln roots but expressed a desire for a law school education with a "particular emphasis upon Missouri law." This emphasis was not available to any black student. "I am a student of limited means but commendable scholastic standing. May I depend upon you to see that I am admitted to Missouri University, where I am sure of getting what I want at a cost that is most reasonable? An immediate reply would be highly appreciated."[45] There is no record of a reply from Middlebush to Gaines.

Middlebush was a critical decision-maker in the *Gaines* case, although his personal views on educational equality and integration are unknown. Middlebush did not leave opinions on issues like this in writing. He was active in discussion of higher education policy nationwide, holding offices and serving on numerous committees relating to the discipline of political science, higher education curriculum, and national defense, and an elected member of the American Association for the Advancement of Science (AAAS). A native Michigander and a scholar devoted to teaching and learning, Middlebush had no background suggesting opposition to the admission of black students to the University of Missouri. However, his actions suggest that integration of education was not a priority for his administration. Satisfaction of state political decision-makers did seem a priority. Middlebush cooperated with the

Board of Curators generally, and his relations with the Board were "always . . . cordial and cooperative."[46] Canada referred the decision on admission of black applicants to Middlebush; he in turn referred these applications to the nine-member Board of Curators.

The Board of Curators governing the University of Missouri clearly opposed broadening admission standards to include African Americans. The president of the Board of Curators was Frank Mitchell McDavid, a lawyer and former state senator from Springfield.[47] F. M. McDavid took the lead on the political issue of educational equality and formally opposed Gaines's admission. In the meantime, McDavid professed he was noncommittal. Gaines wrote Senator McDavid on October 1, on November 4, and again on November 24; McDavid replied he had not spoken with President Middlebush nor with the board, which had a full agenda on "contracts for new buildings."[48]

The Missouri establishment resisted the efforts of the NAACP staff to contest any action by simply refusing to make a decision regarding Gaines's application. Both sides knew that litigation would center on the requirement for African American students in the state either to attend Lincoln University or to receive a scholarship for an out-of-state school. The statute regarding the University of Missouri was neutral on the issue of race. The law defined students admissible to the university to be "All youths, resident of the State of Missouri, over the age of sixteen" subject to "scholastic attainments and mental and moral qualifications" set by the Board of Curators.[49] Thus, Missouri University officials wanted to make no decision on applications from black students, but merely to forward them on to college administrators at Lincoln. Houston was undeterred, writing Redmond, "For our purposes, an unreasonable delay in acting on the request for review is just the same as a declination" and that "the continued procrastination is just as good as a refusal."[50]

Houston and Redmond expected the need to demonstrate inequalities based on race, so they began accumulating information regarding state higher education expenditures for black students compared to whites in Missouri. Redmond and his colleagues collected a massive amount of data on the discrepancies regarding educational opportunities, in preparation for a trial and a likely appeal. Houston was working tirelessly on cases in Missouri, Virginia, Tennessee, the *Murray* case in Maryland, and other states, while traveling, contacting the black press, and pressing individuals to help with the cause.

Meanwhile, attempts to encourage other applications from black Missourians persisted, in order to convince university officials that more was at stake than one prospective law student. Redmond wrote Houston that "Slowly but surely our efforts to secure competent applicants are bearing fruit,"[51] and the Board of Curators planned to make a decision on applications from the black students. Houston planned a visit to St. Louis and expected to file a suit in Columbia in late January 1936.[52] The *Murray* decision from the Maryland Court of Appeals officially was presented on January 15, bringing about integrated graduate education at the University of Maryland. Houston would use *Murray* as an important precedent for the case involving Lloyd Gaines.[53]

On January 24, 1936, the attorneys petitioned for a writ of mandamus to compel Registrar S. W. Canada to make a decision—either admit or deny Lloyd Gaines's application for admission to the University of Missouri School of Law. The two attorneys drove a borrowed car from St. Louis to Columbia through an intensifying snowstorm in order to meet with the circuit court judge.[54] Houston and Redmond expected the Boone County court to decide unfavorably and anticipated an appeal to the Missouri Supreme Court even before the preliminary case was filed.[55] Redmond wrote Houston that everything was completed "other than drafting our petition for the Supreme Court."[56] Circuit Court Judge Walter M. Dinwiddie initially resisted the notion of issuing a writ of mandamus requiring a decision regarding Gaines's admission and suggested filing the case in the state capital of Jefferson City—to avoid publicity and local resentment.[57] According to Houston's recollection, Dinwiddie said "there would probably be no trouble at U. of Mo. as long as only one or two Negro students were there . . . trouble would begin if 30 or 40 Negroes went there."[58]

When the case was filed in Boone County, one priority for Houston, White, and Wilkins was to ensure newspaper coverage of the legal action. Houston telegraphed Walter White: "Lloyd L Gaines against S W Canada Registrar No other defendants Filed Columbia today Papers in mail with report Suggest Schuyler try hand at special article for Negro press when [court] papers arrive Monday."[59] Author and journalist George Schuyler was renowned for articles about black progress, including articles for the *Pittsburgh Courier*.[60] Roy Wilkins soon telegraphed Schuyler "to do special feature story on University of Missouri case."[61] The NAACP followed press reports as well. From Toledo, Houston requested Redmond to "Please forward me to New York copies of the St. Louis papers for this week. I want to see what they did to our U. Mo. Story."[62] Within a week, Houston again wrote to editors at the *St. Louis Argus* and the *St. Louis American*, thanking them for covering the case and showing support for the NAACP and encouraging them to continue to follow the case "because we are in for a long, tough fight."[63] Houston through Espy sent press releases to sixteen black newspapers and Wilkins followed up with additional releases.

According to Houston, time was of the essence. "Release sent out under Espy's envelop so that it would not look like any encroachment on your territory as national officer. But we wanted to reach the papers this week with full story for the effect on country because next week would be stale especially after the Mo. papers had exhausted most of the details."[64] The NAACP knew its press constituency. Key black newspapers identified by Houston were *St. Louis Argus*, *St. Louis American*, *Kansas City Call*, Baltimore *Afro-American*, Norfolk *Journal & Guide*, *Washington Tribune*, *Black Dispatch* of Oklahoma City, *California Eagle* in Los Angeles, *Chicago Defender*, *Pittsburgh Courier*, *Amsterdam News* (NY), *New York Age*, *New York News*, *Philadelphia Tribune*, *Houston Informer*, and *Richmond Planet*.[65] The black press responded by regularly incorporating press releases written by Wilkins and others in coverage.

Local news coverage gave no suggestion the lawsuit had national implications. But as soon as Gaines asked the Boone County circuit court to issue a writ of mandamus to the University of Missouri's registrar ordering a decision on his application for admission, it drew interest from all over the country. For instance, the distant *Salt Lake Tribune* observed, "A negro student knocked at the door of the University of Missouri, but authoritative comment indicated tonight that his quest for admission would avail him little."[66] The black press gave notice, typically with detail provided by the NAACP press releases. The *St. Louis Argus* reported the legal activity matter-of-factly.[67] It was also argued that the current option for black Missourians to attend graduate school out of state with scholarships was unsatisfactory: "All the Negroes had was a pittance in out-of-state scholarships. These scholarships provided no railroad fare, no allowance for increased living expenses, and on the whole were an entirely unsatisfactory substitute for courses in the University of Missouri." The *Argus* also noted that Donald Murray had started attending law school at the University of Maryland and that Murray's "relations with the Faculty of Law and his classmates have been entirely satisfactory and there has not been a single unpleasant incident."[68]

One black newspaper offering extensive coverage of the legal action was the *Kansas City Call*. The *Call's* first story lauded Gaines's personality, character, and academic credentials.[69] Its initial coverage of the *Gaines* case was a front-page reprinting of the NAACP's motion for a writ of mandamus, including the charge against the registrar, S.W. Canada.[70] In addition, the story extensively quoted the charter of the University of Missouri about eligibility to attend, with nothing indicating that persons of color might be ineligible. This was a story clearly intended to build support for Gaines's legal claims. The *Call* also drew a parallel between the Missouri case and that of Donald Gaines Murray. In Maryland, the Baltimore *Afro-American* was highly critical of the University of Missouri and repeatedly argued that the Gaines case was identical to the Murray case on its merits. The article reiterated NAACP themes that blacks paid taxes to support educational institutions yet the institutions available to them were unequal and inadequate.[71]

Overall, the black press noted the potential scope of the *Gaines* case and its landmark potential. News reports cited it as "the first gun in the new battle for equal rights," a great legal attack against the educational color bar," and a "War against Missouri Jim Crow." As the *Call* had done, articles quoted the University of Missouri's charter, building a case for the desegregation of the university. The *Afro-American* brought back memories of the lynching of Jim Scott. The article's final paragraph read, "Some time ago a mob, led by university students, lynched a colored man accused of raping a white girl. Later, the man was proved innocent and the white girl's white lover was given ninety-nine years in the pen." The latter claim was unsubstantiated.[72]

Lloyd Gaines's initial action against the University of Missouri in January 1936 also attracted attention from the local white press. The *Columbia Missourian*, owned and operated by the University of Missouri's School of Journalism,[73] reported the facts in a straightforward manner, reflecting more positively on Gaines.[74] Likewise, the privately owned hometown newspaper, the *Columbia Daily Tribune*,[75] was objective on its front page, noting that Gaines was one of four African Americans applying to the university.[76]

Like the university administrators, Dinwiddie wanted to avoid making a decision. However, there was speculation that the case would ultimately be decided favorably for Gaines and the NAACP.[77] Redmond observed in early March:

> Matters are at a stand still, however, I was informed by [St. Louis attorney Joseph] McLemore that a member of the Board of Curators of the University of Missouri contacted our Supreme Court

and was informed that it would order the admission of Gaines to the University of Missouri. It seems that the Board of Curators of Lincoln and of the University of Missouri have appointed a commission to study several Negro schools. Perhaps the idea is to model Lincoln as a result of the survey.[78]

University officials decided not to leave the final resolution in the hands of the court. One of the university's local attorneys, Ruby Hulen (the county prosecutor at the time of the James Scott lynching), contacted Redmond and informed him that the Board of Curators would meet in March and make a decision regarding the application of Lloyd Gaines.[79]

The Board of Curators met to develop its legal strategy on February 8. McDavid advised the Board of Curators that "four negroes had applied for admission" to four graduate programs. All were graduates of Lincoln University and all met scholastic requirements for admission, but the University of Missouri had taken no action on the applications. In addition, McDavid explained that Gaines had petitioned in the Boone County Circuit Court for action on his application. The Board established a committee composed of its lawyer-members to investigate legal aspects of the Gaines case.[80] Although members engaged in "a lengthy discussion of the problem," the Board never seems to have considered seriously the option of allowing the admission of Gaines or the other black students.[81] The Board of Curators scheduled a meeting in March to make a final decision regarding Gaines and the other applicants.

In March 1936, the Board of Curators made its official determination to deny Lloyd Gaines admission to the University of Missouri. The lawyers presented their plan of action to "careful and thorough consideration of the entire problem."[82] The Board then adopted the resolution made and "properly seconded" that would serve as the foundation for the university's position:

> Whereas, Lloyd L. Gaines, Colored, has applied for admission to the School of Law of the University of Missouri, and
> Whereas, the people of Missouri, both in the Constitution and in the Statutes of the State, have provided for the separate education of white students and negro students, and have thereby in effect forbidden the attendance of a white student at Lincoln University, or a colored student at the University of Missouri, and

Whereas, the Legislature of the State of Missouri, in response to the demands of the citizens of Missouri, has established at Jefferson City, Missouri, for negroes, a modern and efficient school known as Lincoln University, and has invested the Board of Curators of that institution with full power and authority to establish such Departments as may be necessary to offer to students of that institution opportunities equal to those offered at the University, and have further provided, pending the development of Lincoln University, for the payment, out of the public treasury, of the tuition, at universities in adjacent states, of colored students desiring to take any course of study not being taught at Lincoln University, and

Whereas, it is the opinion of the Board of Curators that any change in the State system of separate institution which has been heretofore established, would reset to the detriment of both Lincoln University and the University of Missouri,

Therefore, be it resolved, that the application of said LLOYD L. GAINES be and it hereby is rejected and denied, and the Registrar and the Committee on Entrance be instructed accordingly.[83]

Although the motion was clearly intended as a general policy directive, the board made no direct mention of other black applicants. The Missouri Board of Curators specifically rejected the application from Gaines because he was a "colored student."

The Board of Curators sanctioned the separate but equal philosophy for higher education in the state, taking a position more definitive than either the legislature or the courts. The University of Missouri placed itself in the position of defending Lincoln University as a peer institution in terms of quality. That seems at odds with the fact that Lincoln did not have comparable programs. Moreover, although black students wanted to attend the flagship institution, white students were not petitioning for admission to Lincoln. McDavid, in particular, seems to have pushed for a defense of educational segregation and the motion to prohibit Gaines's admission. Leslie Cowan, the secretary to the Board of Curators, noted in a subsequent letter that McDavid appears to have violated the Board's administrative procedures by making the motion while serving as chairman of the meeting.[84]

Newspapers near and far covered the Board's actions. Suggesting that state leaders had already chosen their long-term response to Gaines's action, the

Post-Tribune noted, "It is understood that a course of law may be added to the curriculum of Lincoln University as a result of this suit."[85] The *Columbia Missourian's* report consisted almost entirely of reprinting the resolution issued by the Board of Curators and contained no sense of approval or disapproval of the action.[86] Again the local decision produced nationwide coverage, such as this wire service item in the *Circleville* (OH) *Herald*: "The board of curators of the University of Missouri today stood fast and unified in denying negroes the right to enter the university." The story was similarly reported in newspapers as far flung as the *Ogden* (UT) *Standard-Examiner* and the *Big Spring* (TX) *Daily Herald*.[87]

Meanwhile, broader problems within the NAACP legal effort emerged. Houston was overworked—in charge of not only NAACP litigation, but also publicity and other matters. Litigation in other states, such as Tennessee, was not producing desired results.[88] Other cases were distracting both the national office and the regional office in St. Louis.[89] In addition, money from the Garland Fund was running out.[90] In 1936, Houston hired Thurgood Marshall as assistant special counsel of the NAACP, an opportunity Marshall considered "the break of my lifetime."[91] Houston shared legal duties with his deputy.

The NAACP attorneys, Sidney Redmond and Henry Espy, continued working on the University of Missouri case pro bono.[92] Their expenses were reimbursed from the national NAACP office and amounted to no more than a few hundred dollars.[93] Publicity furnished by the NAACP may have encouraged activity from unpaid local lawyers, but the NAACP was obliged to provide full and accurate information about sponsored litigation on behalf of the volunteer lawyers. For instance, Thurgood Marshall and Bill Hastie identified errors and omissions in press releases to Roy Wilkins and George Murphy, who were in charge of publicity. Marshall chastised them for "inaccuracies in press releases tend to seriously handicap the spirit of the lawyers who are working with us without any fees at all. Since the bulk of their work is helping me in the legal department I, naturally, feel very bad when these mistakes occur and also when they are called to the attention of the lawyers and members of the Board of Directors."[94]

Houston, Marshall, and the national legal staff were paid a salary, but they were responsible for the full range of NAACP litigation. On the other hand, the university hired three law firms, in St. Louis, Kansas City, and Columbia, and each was paid $1,000 plus expenses to handle litigation in state courts.

The university's representation included the firms of Williams, Nelson, and English (St. Louis), Hogsett, Smith, Murray and Trippe (Kansas City), and Cave and Hulen (Columbia). Nelson was a member of the Board of Curators.[95] The intransigence of the board and of the university had begun to produce their intended effects; delay was costly and made legal challenges to segregation difficult.

However, others considered the resolution passed by the Board of Curators under McDavid a critical mistake. By identifying Gaines specifically and by acknowledging race as the reason for rejection of his application, the resolution gave the NAACP the ammunition it needed. Journalist Carl Rowan records Thurgood Marshall's reaction: "'Ho, ho, ho!' exclaimed Marshall when he read the resolution of the Missouri board of curators. . . . 'They gave us a legal gift that was bigger than anything we could expect. . . . '" Typically, state and local authorities refused to acknowledge the racial component of segregation, engaging in subterfuge about other issues, always suggesting any individual black was excluded "for practical reasons other than racial discrimination." "I couldn't believe it when the curators made it clear in their instructions to registrar Canada that Gaines was being rejected solely because of his race." Marshall continued, "the curators saved the NAACP about a hundred thousand dollars, which it didn't have, by that admission."[96]

On April 15, Houston, Redmond, and Espy filed a second petition in the 34th Circuit Court, Boone County, requesting an alternative writ of mandamus.[97] The petition claimed only that Gaines was a qualified Missouri taxpayer and met the qualifications for admission, so the registrar should be compelled to admit him to the university. Houston emphasized: "The issue is now squarely on the race question but in drafting the petition, do so without reference to color and make them plead color in the answer. This will give us the opportunity to challenge inequality and raise the whole question of equal provisions."[98]

Worth emphasizing is that the University of Missouri did not accept black applicants; however, Missouri state law did not prohibit the admission of black students. This was crucial from the perspective of Charles Houston. The Board of Curators directed the university's registrar, Silas Woodson Canada, not to accept Gaines, and other black applicants by implication. The refusal to admit Gaines and the bureaucratic discretion regarding tuition scholarships in other states meant that unelected state officials were making decisions about whether black applicants could successfully pursue postgraduate education. This was not implementation of state law, but a policy developed by the university's Board of Curators directing the actions of the registrar.

This led to the unusual name of the case: *Missouri ex relatione Gaines v. Canada*. Houston and Redmond claimed to act on behalf of the State of Missouri on the relation of Lloyd Gaines in order to require the university registrar to admit him according to requirements of state law. Thus, when counsel for the university claimed Gaines needed to turn to Lincoln or elsewhere on account of his race, they argued that the university's response was a violation of the equal protection clause. "When the board of curators was forced to consider Gaines' application and declare itself as opposed to his admission solely on account of color," Redmond stated in the NAACP press release, "the object of the first suit was won. Now we are down to the fundamental issue: whether the state of Missouri can exclude a qualified Negro citizen and resident of the state from the school of law of the University of Missouri, which is maintained by tax money which Negroes help to pay, solely on account of his color. We are resting the case squarely on the Fourteenth Amendment to the United States Constitution."[99]

The argument shifted to whether the rules "adopted and established by the board of curators" were constitutional.[100] The *Kansas City Call* summarized the new developments and justified the revised mandamus suit.[101] The *Call* noted that in addition to the denial of Gaines's application, the applications of two other African American men, Arnett Lindsey (law), and Nathaniel Sweets (journalism), were also denied. A brief United Negro Press story, published in newspapers such as the *Cleveland Call*, reported the story with an editorial flourish: "The Board of Curators of the University of Missouri thumbed its nose at Minerva, goddess of arts and the sciences, and turned a cold shoulder to Negroes applying for admission."[102]

The editors of the *Afro-American*, the out-of-state newspaper with the closest ties to the case, grew incredulous. A June 6, 1936 article quoted from a Houston-prepared press release,

> The University of Missouri, last week, in answering the NAACP's petition for a writ of mandamus requiring the school to admit Lloyd Gaines to its law course, denied that Lincoln University, the applicant's alma mater, is an accredited school. This is the first instance in the educational program of the NAACP where a state university

has attempted to defeat the action of a student seeking admission
by causing doubt on the standing of the State college for colored.[103]

Similar articles appeared in other black newspapers, such as the *Chicago Defender*, which quoted Charles Houston's release that the University of Missouri had "placed the state board of education in a very embarrassing position by denying that Lincoln University is an accredited and reputable institution."[104]

Setting a date for the trial in Boone County was difficult. In addition to Redmond, Espy, and Gaines, who would travel from St. Louis, Houston had to make time and travel from New York or wherever he would be at the time.[105] In addition, the university would be represented by a panel of six lawyers, geographically crossing the state from Kansas City to St. Louis, from Springfield to Columbia, and including a former state supreme court judge, a county prosecutor, and a state senator. Houston wanted Redmond to send a list of the university's counsel, not only to keep track of them but also for a press release as it "shows how important we are and how seriously they are taking this fight."[106] Press releases also emphasized the delay requested by counsel for "the lily-white University of Missouri" as "they could not complete their answer to Gaines suit" while the NAACP "is ready to proceed with the case at any time and is pressing for action." [107]

Kansas City attorney William Hogsett led the university defense team. Hogsett, in practice since 1906, had a prestigious legal career and was known as a "lawyer's lawyer."[108] He represented large corporations and other institutions and had represented clients before the Supreme Court. Hogsett was at the forefront of the political reform movement within Kansas City and, contemporaneous with *Gaines*, helped organize opposition to corruption and graft under the Pendergast machine. Hogsett graduated from law school at the University of Missouri and, while at the university, was the business manager of the school paper.[109] There is little documentation of Hogsett's personal beliefs regarding issues pertinent to the *Gaines* case. However, long after the case was concluded, Hogsett responded to an inquiry from S.W. Canada regarding the application of another black applicant to the University of Missouri and asked whether the applicant was "just another stooge for the N.A.A.C.P." The student's request, Hogsett thought "has the Houston touch, and I suspect it is the beginning of the old familiar N.A.A.C.P. routine."[110] Hogsett became Houston's legal nemesis throughout the litigation involving Lloyd Gaines.

The university investigated several options for its defense. Depositions were taken from Gaines and three other black applicants for postgraduate programs.[111] Counsel hoped to demonstrate that the applications of Gaines and the others were solicited by the NAACP or that they were controlled by Redmond, that they were not legitimate applications for admission to a professional program. Houston wrote: "The whole purport of the depositions was to establish collusion on the part of those applying, that the NAACP had fomented the applications, which were not supposed to be the voluntary acts of the four men desiring to exercise what they considered their constitutional rights. They attempted to show Redmond and I were the moving spirits. . . ." William Hogsett, who conducted the depositions for the university, attempted to show that the applicants were not seriously interested in attending the University of Missouri—either that they were pawns in an NAACP game or that out-of-state schools were a better and preferred option. Houston had predicted both legal tactics earlier. He wrote to Redmond regarding the depositions: "Two things you had better watch out for. The state may try to show that he is acting on suggestion rather than his own desire in trying to enter the Law School; and that he would rather have a scholarship."[112] Except for Gaines, the other applicants were years out of college, so Hogsett tried to link them to each other and to the NAACP. Houston concluded, "The four men took care of themselves well, so there is little to worry about now."[113]

The university tentatively took the position that no graduate of Lincoln University was sufficiently prepared for graduate and professional education. Houston found the point of view that no graduate of the state's only black college received a quality education to be scandalous. In a press release, Houston opined that "If the court should sustain this argument it would mean that the state of Missouri is more vulnerable than ever since it will stand convicted of not only failing to provide equal graduate and professional training, but regular college work as well." However, President Charles Florence's success in acquiring accreditation by the North Central College Association significantly weakened the university's perspective. If a Lincoln degree was substandard, then its graduates would not be suitable for graduate admission; however, this would also demonstrate that Missouri's segregated system of higher education discriminated against blacks. Conversely, if a Lincoln education was suitable for graduate education, then its graduates' applications for graduate study should reasonably be approved. The university ultimately took a different direction, defending Lincoln as well as strict segregation. Both sides of the lawsuit gathered information on books and instructional methods used at Missouri and comparable institutions in adjacent states. They collected a wealth of information related to in-state and out-of-state education: mileage and travel expenses and information on scholarship recipients.

Judge Walter M. Dinwiddie, a graduate of the University of Missouri Law School in 1909, wielded clout in local political circles. But Dinwiddie's circuit was busy around the intended time of the *Gaines* hearings, with even more sensational trials. Two prominent criminal trials coincided with the first and second petitions for a writ of mandamus on behalf of Lloyd Gaines and distracted the judge. [114] Dinwiddie also took time to attend the Democratic National Convention in Philadelphia in late June.

Redmond and Houston suspected that the University of Missouri lawyers wanted to hold the hearing on July 2, in conflict with the NAACP convention in Baltimore, making it difficult or impossible for the NAACP attorneys to attend or causing a delay until the fall term. Houston communicated his concern to the national office. [115] Walter White, the NAACP executive secretary, asked Houston "to look at its broadest aspects," demonstrating the tension between the national campaign for public opinion and the legal department's agenda. "The University of Missouri case is most important but it is, after all, but one link in the chain. Individual suits against universities are important, but equally important is the selling of the facts and the underlying philosophy in the whole education campaign to the public at large and particularly to Negroes." White reiterated the view that Houston and Redmond should attend the Baltimore convention. He added, "I have talked this over with Roy [Wilkins] and he is heartily in accord with me."[116]

Houston believed the court case was more important than the NAACP conference, and that his role in court was more important and that others could handle the public relations. [117] Nine months earlier, Sidney Redmond had complained to Charles Houston of an inconsistency between priorities in the national office and the realities of litigation.

> I think Walter White is using bad taste in talking about the cases to be filed. When you were here you mentioned the fact that a lawyer couldn't be placed in the position of soliciting business and his statements are certainly putting those who are cooperating with you in that position. I appreciate the fact that he wants to let people know

> the N.A.A.C.P. is doing something but I submit members are more
> interested in accomplished deeds than those to be undertaken.[118]

Redmond's comments were prescient; the university lawyers now were taking the position that the NAACP solicited the cases in the depositions and
in arguments.

The Circuit Court hearing was finally held on July 10, 1936.[119] Charles
Houston, Sidney Redmond, and Henry Espy drove from St. Louis to Columbia on the morning of the trial. Houston had hoped for a large turn-
out of friends from St. Louis, but only Robert Witherspoon joined, and four
St. Louis friends in an additional car journeyed with them. The lawyers and
Gaines left St. Louis at 6:00, but because of a detour, they did not arrive at the
courthouse until 9:15—fifteen minutes after the hearing was scheduled to begin.[120] The region suffered a severe drought, and, in Columbia "temperatures
had reached or exceed[ed] 100 every day since the 4th" of July, and on the 10th
the temperature reached 104°F.[121] The courtroom was stifling. One attendee
referred to the second floor courtroom as "the hottest place in the world," like
"sitting in a pool of melted varnish."[122] Judge Dinwiddie and the attorneys
agreed to conduct the hearing without jackets because of the heat, "so we had
a shirtsleeve trial." The university, that is, Canada and the Board of Curators,
were represented by William S. Hogsett, chief council, his partner Ralph E.
Murray (Kansas City), Nick T. Cave (Columbia), and Judge Fred L. Williams
(St. Louis).[123] Attending, in addition to Registrar Canada, were President Middlebush, and Board of Curators members McDavid and Willson.[124]

The NAACP attorneys were surprised that the crowded courtroom audience was not segregated. "Negroes and whites more or less sifted themselves
into separate groups, but folks sat where they could."[125] The courtroom was
full, particularly during part of the morning session, "packed with people all
down the aisles." Contemporary press reports indicate "The courtroom was
filled, with negroes constituting about a third of the spectators."[126] The *Kansas City Call* alluded to both the case and the region's prevailing drought and
high temperatures: "Fight for Admission of Young Man to Missouri University to Be Hot." The *Call* presented a David and Goliath tone to the proceedings noting "Opposed to an array of outstanding talent will be Attorneys S.R.
Redmond and Henry D. Espy of St. Louis, and Dean Charles Houston, New
York. . . ." The article concluded, "Both sides have indicated that they are
planning a fight to the finish."[127]

The trial in Judge Dinwiddie's courtroom was, among other things, a media event. Gaines and the NAACP staff arrived a few minutes late due to the long, detoured journey from St. Louis. As Charles Houston described the hearing: "There was a press table set up, which was crowded; but I did not have a chance to check or make contacts because we had to rush into the trial." Prominent Kansas City attorney William Hogsett represented the university, and, to Houston, "It was quite obvious that he was talking more to the press table than the court."[128] The NAACP, likewise, communicated with editors and reporters in the mainstream press behind the scenes.

A hundred or more students from the University of Missouri attended to see the proceedings. Farmers in overalls seeking drought relief aid through an office in the courthouse wandered upstairs to see the event. "Some of the farmers looked a little strange at us drinking out of the same fountain and using the same lavatories with them, but they did not say anything," Houston noted. The "St. Louisians" were timid and fearful of trouble because Columbia had a reputation for lynching, but the visit was otherwise uneventful. Indeed, "the crowd enjoyed the trial and on the whole was inclined to be generous in praising our presentation."[129]

Conditions within the courtroom were "quite cordial and informal." Redmond and Houston had no difficulties with Judge Dinwiddie in previous contacts or at the trial. Introductions were made among the lawyers who had not previously met. Houston noted, "The arrangements for counsel seemed odd to us."[130] All counsel sat at one table. "All during the trial we were looking down one another's throats. For private conference at the table we almost had to go into a football huddle."[131]

Redmond and Hogsett made opening statements. Houston thought Redmond "deliberate and not especially colorful" and his opening "a plain factual statement." Houston considered Hogsett "fiery and a showman,"[132] and his opening statement "very dramatic and driving." Hogsett's statement extolled the virtues of Lincoln University, arguing that it provided equality of education, and that the University of Missouri was thus intended to be for whites only.[133] Hogsett also defended the out-of-state tuition scholarships and the development of further programs at Lincoln. Houston disagreed completely, of course, but he noted that the attorney was respectful and "There was no Negro baiting in Hogsett's opening." Some observers characterized the general tone of the trial to be "the most polite disagreement over the most trivial of points" punctuated by a few childlike outbursts. Moreover, they found Houston to be "a man of a high type, with a rare patience and a long view in the battle he was waging for his race. . . ." Sidney Redmond told Charlie Houston later this "compliment paid you was well earned." [134]

Lloyd Gaines was the first witness called, and Redmond examined him. Houston wrote, "Gaines has courage and can't be bluffed, but he is not quick in his mental reactions. He likes to be meticulously exact, and being slow in thought sometimes under Hogsett's pounding on cross-examination he nearly gave us heart failure." Gaines worked hard before the trial, engaging in substantial background research, understanding the case, and studying the deposition and the pleadings. Houston believed that Gaines "takes the case very seriously and is in dead earnest about it." Houston and Gaines spent one morning in St. Louis discussing the case and its social background. "Consequently he was loaded when he went in Court and wanted to lay his position down unmistakably to the court. On direct he did fine. . . ." The key difficulty, from Houston's perspective, was the April deposition that Hogsett used to keep Gaines off-balance. Gaines "was a stickler for accuracy on immaterial items, while allowing Hogsett to apparently lead him into damaging admissions, but he came through." Houston's overall assessment was that Gaines "made a fair, but not a good witness."[135]

Next the attorneys called university officials to testify. Houston felt that Hogsett's "storming around at Gaines during cross-examination" needed an equal response, so when William Edward Masterson, dean of the law school, came to the stand, Houston "decided to demonstrate that two could thunder." Judge Dinwiddie then called Houston and Hogsett to the bench and requested they follow the local tradition of sitting while examining witnesses. For the most part, the two opponents moderated their behavior and cooperated.

University officials were not strong witnesses in defense of current admissions policy. "Dean Masterson, S. W. Canada, Registrar of the university, and [Tony David] Stanford, the Asst. Secretary of the U. Mo. had the most complete lapse of memory I have ever witnessed. None of them could tell us anything about the Law School." None could recall details about law school admissions, its budget, or its library or other infrastructure. Dean Houston's ire was directed at Masterson in particular. As the Missouri Law School was the only public institution in the state, Houston wanted to show its specialty in Missouri law, which Gaines claimed as a justification to reject alternative, out-of-state schools. "Masterson wiggled like an earthworm on this, and made just about the sorriest and most pitiable spectacle I have ever seen of a dean of an approved law school."[136] Masterson claimed that the Law School taught general law courses with no particular specialty for Missouri law, a claim which law students and observers in the gallery considered obviously false.[137] As dean, Masterson served as editor-in-chief of the *Missouri Law Review*, which made an annual report on the decisions of the state supreme court.

Registrar S. Woodson Canada admitted that students from many ethnic groups had been admitted—whites from Missouri and other states, foreign nationals, Chinese, Japanese, and Hindus—but no students of African descent. Although the lawsuit names Canada, his testimony at the trial was short and had limited impact on the case.[138] university President Middlebush was not called to the stand.

Many other witnesses were also called. Robert Witherspoon, the St. Louis attorney who accompanied Redmond, Houston, and Gaines, received his law degree from Howard University and was the current president of the Mound City Bar Association—the alternative regional organization for black lawyers. Witherspoon testified that there were only about 45 black attorneys in all of Missouri, and most had practiced law for many years. Only three or so black lawyers entered the profession in the entire state within the last five years. Witherspoon also testified that learning the subtleties in Missouri law was a handicap when educated out of state.[139] The latter point, a slight advantage for Missouri-educated attorneys taking the state bar exam, was also made by E. F. Elliott, the chief clerk of the Supreme Court, perhaps unintentionally.[140] Witherspoon was recalled to the stand to testify that Eden Theological Seminary in Webster Groves (near St. Louis) not only admitted white and black students but that they also shared a dormitory.[141]

Much was made of the 1921 act renaming Lincoln Institute and establishing the out-of-state tuition scholarship program. Although Houston does not mention it, the position of university counsel seems counterintuitive. Much evidence presented suggested that the University of Missouri was no better than, and arguably weaker than comparable institutions in Illinois, Iowa, Nebraska, and Kansas and that Lincoln University, in spite of the fact that it was limited to undergraduate programs, was likewise as good or better than the state's preeminent public university for whites. Lincoln Board of Curators President J.D. Elliff defended the academic quality of Lincoln University, although noting that there were no graduate or professional programs there. Houston questioned whether the institution was truly a university, despite such a description in the 1921 law. Elliff replied, "Lincoln is ready to go. As to the number of colleges it is not a— it is a university in the making. It is an embryo university."[142] The out of state scholarships were supposed to be supervised through Lincoln, but the program was underfunded and handled by the state superintendent of schools. Only one Missouri student received funds to attend law school in adjacent state (Kansas).[143] The defense argument that Lincoln was an institution of quality was a change from a trial balloon launched before the trial that graduates of Lincoln were inherently unqualified to attend postgraduate programs at Missouri University.

The defense took the position that the 1921 act institutionalized segregation in higher education. William Hogsett asked Missouri Board of Curator President F.M. McDavid what he thought of the admission of Negroes to the university. McDavid replied, "I think it would create a great amount of trouble."[144] Asked to elaborate, McDavid continued:

> I think that it would make discipline difficult. For this reason: everybody knows, every citizen knows, what the constitution of Missouri provides with respect to separate education of the races. Every citizen and every student is perfectly familiar with the general policies of the State of Missouri that have been recognized through the years. Every student and every citizen of this city where this school is located knows the traditions of this city and school, running through nearly a hundred years, respecting that matter. To admit a Negro into this school would, to my way of thinking, be subversive of discipline, which is so important on the campus, among the students and in the various departments of the university; and that was the thing that was considered, among other things, in ruling on this business.[145]

Acknowledging the seriousness of the issue, Houston asked McDavid whether hundred-year-old traditions should be allowed to hinder progress forever. McDavid responded, "I don't know what you mean by 'progress.'"[146] From this and similar testimony, observers characterized Frank McDavid as "a thoroughly crotchety old gentleman."[147]

Again appealing to the 1921 statute, McDavid offered, "They are building a University for Colored people and the place where they are to be educated, and the University here for the white people, and the Boards have the same power with respect to each." Houston responded, "They give Negroes . . . merely a piece of paper, just a legislative fiat, while the white citizens have an actual, existing School of Law?" McDavid retorted, "I would say that the Colored people would have no right to complain until they have made demand upon the body [the legislature] that had been given that power to create the thing which they wish." Houston tried to press the issue further, but Dinwiddie interrupted, saying "the Court is not interested in this testimony."[148]

During redirect, Houston questioned Dean William Masterson about comparable education at the Missouri Law School and what was essentially a proposed independent study of the law using the Supreme Court Library in Jefferson City. Former supreme court judge and member of defense counsel Fred Williams interjected that such a black student "is getting an education equal to or better than an education that he would get by coming to Missouri University." He continued, "It is wholly immaterial to the question of whether or not the law school that would be established at Lincoln University would give this man the same high grade of education he would get here, or even better because of the fact that is the only man who wants it."[149] Houston challenged that view and later referred to the exchange as "a little rumble between me and Judge Williams near the end of the trial."[150] Segregation of the races in education was presented as a cultural fact with legislative and state constitutional foundations.

Chief counsel for the university, William Hogsett, argued that Gaines had no claim against the university, rather that he should apply for a state tuition scholarship or for admission to Lincoln. Defense counsel claimed, somewhat paradoxically, the University of Missouri was not particularly special and praised the virtues of Lincoln and universities and legal training available in neighboring states. Houston, Redmond, and Espy marshalled evidence suggesting the superiority of the University of Missouri Law School for in-state residents. Gaines claimed that as a taxpayer and resident, he had a right to attend a professional program at a university in the state for which he was qualified.

The trial lasted until 4:00 in the afternoon, with only a recess at noon. Both sides waived oral arguments as Dinwiddie indicated he was concerned only about two items—"whether the act of 1921 . . . expressed the state

policy to exclude Negroes from U. Mo." and "whether . . . the state scholarships offered equal protection under the 14th Amendment." The defense already had a trial brief prepared, and attorneys for the plaintiff were given a
week to file. Houston notes that Dinwiddie "indicated he was against us but
was open to be convinced" and order Gaines's admission, however, he added,
"Well we belong to the class who don't believe he would do so."[151]

The NAACP issued a lengthy press release on the circuit court trial that
was picked up by black newspapers.[152] For instance, the *Afro-American* included a boxed section about the existing University of Missouri policy to
accept foreign students of various ethnicities, quoting liberally from the press
release drafted by Houston. Without attribution, much of the press release
was copied verbatim in the box and in the accompanying section, down to
the misspelling of "Hindoos" in reference to Canada's testimony.[153] The story
contained a detailed description of the trial, including an analysis of figures
discussed at the trial of what Missouri paid to send African American students out of state for their education. Sidney Redmond was quoted at length.
"We are determined to carry on this fight for equality of educational opportunity in Missouri until negroes get full university training, and complete
educational equality on all other levels, including equality of teachers' pay,
schoolterm quality, and equal outlay per school child. We realize we are in for
a long, desperate fight, but we are in it to the end."[154] Black newspapers, at
least those outside the state, could not pay to send reporters to cover the trial,
so there was dependence on information provided by the NAACP.

The *Kansas City Call* sent reporters to cover the trial firsthand. The paper
provided extensive and original coverage of the hearing in Judge Dinwiddie's
courtroom. However, *The Call* also noted with apparent skepticism that "the
university officials, including the dean of the law school, when questioned by
Gaines's attorneys, were unable to give fundamental facts concerning the operation of the school. They could not tell how much it cost to educate a law
student, the standards for an approved law school, the salaries of the various
law school teachers, or much about the fiscal administration of the university."[155] Active reporting by *The Call* provided an independent voice that broad-
ened appeal beyond the St. Louis area and emphasized the importance of the
case brought by Lloyd Gaines for the state as well as for the nation.

The two local, white Columbia newspapers initially covered the Gaines
litigation with neutrality. However, the tone of coverage began to differ by

the time of the hearing. Both papers misspelled Charles Houston's name as "Huston," otherwise there were few similarities. In a story about the week's schedule for Judge Walter Dinwiddie's courtroom, the *Missourian* offered no overt negativity directed toward Gaines, describing him as "a St. Louis Negro," attempting to "gain entrance into the University Law School."[156] The headline in the *Columbia Daily Tribune* offered a more blunt perspective, "Gaines Case Heard Today: St. Louis Negro, Trying to Force Way Into University, in Court." The story reiterated the perspective of Gaines as a man who did not belong.[157] Unlike the *Columbia Missourian*, the *Daily Tribune* had not yet adopted a convention of capitalizing "Negro." Instead, the paper alternated between capitalizing the word and not. In the Gaines story, it capitalized "Whites" in the same sentence with a lower case n for "negroes."

As the trial date drew near, other white newspapers, especially in Missouri, followed the event. The *Joplin* (MO) *Globe* reported on the university's brief, identifying two key arguments. Gaines "was neither qualified to enter the university law school or entitled under the state constitution to be a student." While the newspaper appeared unbiased, it detailed several points in the university's brief: Gaines was denied admission not because he was a negro, but because he did not meet the admission requirements; the state constitution provided for segregated education; there was no special advantage for the practice of law from studying at the University of Missouri; and Gaines was not a Missouri taxpayer.[158]

In the *Tribune*'s coverage of the hearing, Gaines's efforts to enroll at the University of Missouri were characterized not as an effort to pursue his constitutional rights, as they were in the black press but, rather, as a refusal to pursue the appropriate opportunities afforded him by state law: "He persisted in his efforts to enter the university here, instead of taking advantage of the statutory provisions for his education elsewhere, he said." In the black press, the testimony of Dean Masterson that there was no particular emphasis on Missouri law in the training provided at the state university was portrayed as uninformed or with skepticism. The *Tribune*'s interpretation was very different: "In his questioning of Dean Masterson, Huston sought to establish that the Missouri law school offered special opportunity for the study of Missouri law, and offered in evidence sections of the university catalogue and the university law review in support of his contention. Dean Masterson's evidence, however, brought small support for that line of argument."[159]

The front-page story of the *Tribune* on the following day prominently featured the testimony of University of Missouri Board of Curators president
Frank McDavid. He was characterized as ably defeating the arguments made
by Gaines's NAACP counsel, and Gaines's action was portrayed as unreasonable. According to the *Tribune*, McDavid "made a vigorous defense of the
board's action in denying Gaines's petition for admittance to the university . . . the board acted only after giving deep consideration to the problem,
raised for the first time in the nearly 100 years history of the university by
Gaines's attempt to enroll in the law school, and that his petition was denied
only because the board adhered to what it conceived to be the constitution,
the law and the public policy of Missouri in providing separate educational
facilities for the white and Negro races."[160] No testimony counter to this point
of view was given credence in the *Tribune*. The *Tribune* reviewed McDavid's
testimony about the options available, studying at Lincoln University or going to school out-of-state, and added, "It was this offer which Gaines ignored
when he sought to force his admittance to the university law school." An exchange between Houston and McDavid was reported in similarly unbalanced
language. The article concluded with a collection of statements about the inappropriateness of allowing "Negroes" to attend the University of Missouri:
"Canada testified that the university admits Japanese, Chinese, Hindu, and
Mexican students, but did not admit Negroes because, as he understood it, it
was against the law. [N.T.] Gentry and [C.B.] Rollins, both lifetime citizens
of Columbia, testified as to the university's traditions in which Negro students had no place . . . ."[161]

The tone of the *Columbia Missourian* was less hostile toward Gaines and
his attorneys. The general thrust of the *Missourian's* story was to demonstrate
that while Gaines might have a legitimate claim, he was making it against
the wrong defendants. The University of Missouri's lead counsel, William
Hogsett, was quoted, "'If equal educational opportunity were not provided, if the curators of Lincoln University failed in their duty, then the relator
would have cause to ask mandamus, but of Lincoln University, not of these
respondents.'"[162] While the tone was certainly more neutral than that of the
Daily Tribune, there remained a bias in favor of the university as nearly all
of the coverage on the front-page was devoted to the university's legal arguments and not until the bottom of the column did a subhead appear with,
"The Gaines Point of View."[163] Here, the *Missourian* offered several highlights

of Gaines's side and generally used positive language to describe the NAACP attorneys' efforts. For example, "Lawyers for the University entered many exceptions while attorneys for Gaines claiming 'we want the truth about everything' admitted all evidence with no objections." Testimony was frequently reported in ways that commented approvingly on the efforts of Gaines's attorneys. For instance, when Senator F. M. McDavid was on the stand, "Relator's lawyers ably pointed out in cross-examination that the Board was also called upon as a policy to carry out the Constitution of the United States and the 14th Amendment." Likewise, when E.R. Adams, the state director of teacher training was called to testify about the policy of paying out-of-state tuition for black students, the paper reported "plaintiff's counsel brought out that the state paid only the difference between the tuition at other schools and Missouri University."[164]

Other Missouri newspapers, such as the *Joplin Globe*, covered the trial through Associated Press reporting which focused primarily on McDavid's testimony. But the AP version was considerably more succinct than the *Tribune*. The *Globe* reported, "McDavid said the board acted on its interpretation of the constitution, law and public policy of the state, and added that he believed it would be 'most unfortunate' for the future of Lincoln university at Jefferson City, if a Negro were to be admitted to Missouri university."[165] Unlike the *Tribune* story, which reported that Gaines "ignored" the state's offer to supplement his tuition out of state, the *Globe* reported, "Gaines, denied admittance to the university, declined to ask state aid in entering a professional school in another state and filed suit against the university curators and Registrar S.W. Canada."[166] It was, like the *Missourian*, significantly different in tone from the coverage provided by the *Tribune*.

The *St. Louis Globe-Democrat*, the paper with the widest circulation in the state's largest city, covered the trial only briefly, apparently because it was seen as only the first engagement in a long war. Gaines's mandamus was "an issue that is apparently headed for the United States Supreme Court regardless of decisions in the Missouri State courts. . . . " This article gives few clues of the editors' opinion about the merits of the case, although rather than presenting Gaines as trying to "force" his way into the university he was "seeking the right to enter."[167]

Two weeks following the trial, Judge Dinwiddie ruled against Lloyd Gaines with a summary statement: "The finding of the Court is for the respondents

and against the relator and the writ of mandamus is quashed."[168] Redmond
and Houston were prepared for this outcome. Houston wrote immediately
after the trial, "It is beyond expectation that the Court will decide in our favor, so we had just as well get ready for the appeal."[169] Defense counsel also expected the judge's decision and planned for an appeal. Dinwiddie and defense
counsel cooperated in expediting the process,[170] so Redmond and Houston
made an appeal directly to the Missouri Supreme Court. They hoped the case
would eventually reach the US Supreme Court.

State black newspapers followed the ongoing litigation closely. St. Louis
newspapers reported on the activities of those involved in the case. The *Kansas City Call* offered original content regarding the lawsuit and emphasized
its importance in the fight against segregation. When Lloyd Gaines and the
NAACP lost the case in Boone County in July 1936, the *Kansas City Call*
summarized the case effectively.[171] The support from the *Call* was more than
merely editorial. On a driving trip to the West, Charles Houston took time
to visit the editor. "I stopped in Kansas City and called on Mr. [Chester A.]
Franklin of The Call. He promised unlimited support of the case and said the
Call was going to raise some money for us. He had me address the entire Call
staff. I told them the differentials in teachers' salaries, and Mr. Franklin said
the Call was going to give us a teachers' salary case."[172] Houston's efforts were
gaining traction beyond the St. Louis region.

The local press, of course, followed the case closely. The *Columbia Daily
Tribune* renewed its opposition to the admission of Gaines and other black
students. The *Tribune* continued to assert that refusal to admit Gaines was
a matter of law which the Board of Curators was simply enforcing.[173] The
Columbia Missourian made no suggestion that Dinwiddie's decision meant
continued segregation at the university. The *Missourian* provided an extensive
review of the case, including the legal arguments of both sides and discussion
of similar actions taken by the NAACP in other states, focusing on the *Murray* case in Maryland. It provided much background material and implied
that not all was lost for the supporters of desegregation.[174]

The request for a writ of mandamus in a remote central Missouri courthouse had national importance, and the mainstream press corps recognized
this immediately. Roy Wilkins observed that the *Gaines* case in Missouri attracted much more press interest than the *Murray* case in Maryland: "people all over the country are watching Missouri."[175] *Time* magazine contacted

Wilkins for information on the circuit court case, and Wilkins sent a telegram to Houston and Redmond for "the latest dope" on the case, July 11, 1936. Houston sent his undated, three-page "Memorandum for Time," prepared shortly after the Columbia trial, as well as a subsequent revision. *Time* staff appeared to have reviewed the memo, although the publication included other information as well.[176]

The acerbic item in *Time* reported how the "NAACP and Negro Lloyd Gaines marched into Circuit Court at Columbia, Mo. to see whether the University of Missouri, lily-white since its opening" could be "forced across the color line." The editors at *Time* downplayed the university attorney's "rehearsed" arguments. On the other hand, "NAACP attorneys demanded to know how the state of Missouri could blow hot by claiming that its black and white colleges were equal, blow cold by allowing its University to reject Lincoln credits." Judge Walter Dinwiddie presided over "an acrid hearing" and later "flatly refused to issue an order compelling the University of Missouri to admit Blackamoor Gaines."[177] According to Roy Wilkins, the journalists at *Time* were interested in why Dinwiddie made his decision, but the judge issued a summary judgment and NAACP attorneys had no information on the rationale behind his decision.[178]

Houston, White, Marshall, and Wilkins recognized the impact the white press coverage could have on the legal agenda. Thurgood Marshall remembered, "I felt great . . . when Time magazine, the New York Times, the New York Herald Tribune, began to write about how we were stirring up a 'revolution' in higher education. Charlie Houston was contagiously excited when he told me that Time was going to do a piece explaining the Missouri challenge, and tell the nation that this was only the beginning." Journalist Carl Rowan noted that the NAACP leadership "courted the press as assiduously as they did the judges."[179]

Reports in the black press acknowledged that the Missouri case was to be a long legal fight. The *St. Louis Argus* set expectations for the next steps: "Both parties [in the lawsuit] have indicated that they will not be content with the state supreme court's ruling in the case and that eventually it will be carried to the United States Supreme Court."[180] As the case awaited its hearing before the Missouri Supreme Court, the *Cleveland Call and Post* reported that the NAACP legal team "expected to lose in the lower court in Missouri and they may lose in the state supreme court. They are confident, however, of victory in the United States supreme court."[181] Similarly, the *Chicago Defender* reported, "It is understood that if the appeal is lost in the state supreme court, the case will go to the United States supreme court."[182] The latter quotes directly from the NAACP press release on the upcoming oral arguments before the Missouri Supreme Court.[183] Black newspapers had limited staff and resources, so NAACP releases were an important source of information for articles. When original information was available, it supplemented NAACP releases. For instance, the Baltimore *Afro-American* again observed that the Gaines case was "almost identical" to the *Murray* case in Maryland.[184]

Shortly before Gaines's appeal was made to the Supreme Court, Houston again contacted Chester Franklin along with Charlie Calloway about staging public protests for a favorable decision. Houston reminded Franklin that "last summer you stated that you would give us support on the University of Missouri fight." Attorney Charles H. Calloway was the president of the Kansas City Branch of the NAACP.[185] Houston informed Franklin and Calloway that the state supreme court appeal of the University of Missouri case was scheduled for May 18. "We have never carried this case home to the people of Missouri and I am wondering whether it would be possible to arrange a mass meeting for Wednesday, May 19, in Kansas City, at which we could present the University of Missouri case and the story of the fight to pass the Gavagan Anti-lynching bill in the House of Representatives, together with the next steps in each."[186] Houston hoped for "a united front consisting of the Kansas City Branch of the N.A.A.C.P., newspapers, fraternities and sororities, churches, businesses, labor unions, political clubs, etc. We want the entire population of Missouri to know the significance of this fight for equal education."[187]

The next stage in the case was the appeal to the state supreme court. Houston wanted to be prepared on all fronts.

4

Substantially Equal If Separate

Although both sides in the litigation had issues they hoped to resolve on appeal, the legal process moved at a glacial pace. All the participants knew that the circuit court proceedings were only a "scrimmage." The real contest would be played before the US Supreme Court.[1] The NAACP was eager to move forward, and university counsel and court staff appeared cooperative.[2] Sydney Redmond explained this to Roy Wilkins: "Ordinarily it does take two years to try a case in the Supreme Court of Missouri after it is appealed. However, in this case both sides have agreed to file jointly a motion requesting the court to advance the Gaines case on the docket, and in view of that it should be heard about November, 1936. The appeal has already been taken and has been lodged in the Supreme Court."[3] Redmond expressed the view that the Supreme Court could order Gaines's admission to the Missouri Law School for the next year. That prediction would prove overly optimistic.

In the meantime, the question became what to do with Lloyd Gaines. Donald Murray, in Maryland, was admitted to law school quickly. William Redmond, in Tennessee, seemed to have personal funds and the wherewithal to wait on a decision regarding his application to pharmacy school. Gaines, however, received limited financial support from his family and had only intermittent employment. His employment history provided no experience for future legal studies.[4] Gaines felt the urge for postgraduate education and decided, while awaiting the appeal, to seek a master's degree in economics at an institution such as the University of Illinois or the University of Michigan. Houston and Redmond agreed with Gaines on this course of action. It would be a year before the case would likely be resolved, and they felt additional education would improve his prospects of success at the University of Missouri Law School.[5]

The problem was that Gaines could not afford the cost of a master's program. Gaines received considerable financial support from his brother George, a Pullman worker, and seemed willing to support himself by working. But, Gaines wrote to Houston via Redmond, to attend a graduate program "and at the same time continue an active fight in interest of the University of Missouri suit, would be to exceed my limited resources. Subsequently, any suggestion of possible relief in the matter would be welcomed and appreciated."[6] The NAACP, however, was created to represent and to lobby for the rights of blacks, not to provide educational scholarships. Houston hoped friends would offer a contribution for the fall semester and added that "if he survives the first semester," the Alpha Phi Alpha fraternity would contribute later.[7]

Doubts began to arise about whether Gaines would continue to act as a plaintiff throughout the appeal without some financial support. A committee was formed to decide whether to use money from the Garland Fund to advance scholarships to Gaines and William Redmond, the litigant in the Tennessee case. Houston wrote to Walter White and NAACP legal committee head Arthur Spingarn in New York, "Both students need help and have requested me to try to arrange some assistance for them. It is imperative in Gaines' case."[8] The Missouri case was stronger and more likely to receive timely consideration before the US Supreme Court, so Houston wanted to push for Gaines in particular.[9] Gaines considered requesting a tuition scholarship through Lincoln University for study in an adjacent state for a master's degree, and he discussed it with his counsel in St. Louis. Espy strongly opposed this option as damaging to the lawsuit, and Redmond encouraged Gaines to correspond with Houston first.[10] Houston concurred with the St. Louis attorneys. If Gaines applied for a state tuition scholarship, it "would be a very bad move." Houston pleaded with Sydney Redmond, "For Heavens' (all the heavens) sake don't let him ask for state aid."[11]

Gaines had decided to attend the University of Michigan, and he wrote Walter White asking that the NAACP cover his tuition payments of seventy-five dollars per semester.[12] but the NAACP leadership felt conflicted about making a direct payment to a client in litigation the association sponsored. Yet Gaines's counsel and the NAACP felt the pressure to request supplemental educational funding on his behalf in order to preserve the case. Although never mentioned explicitly in the correspondence, it may have been that Houston and Redmond preferred Michigan to Illinois because it was not adjacent to Missouri. As Houston continued to White and Spingarn,

> Gaines is from the State of Missouri, which provides scholarships. He asked me about accepting a state scholarship to study economics. Of course I told him he could not do this and continue on with the suit because his position would be too inconsistent—even making allowances for the fact that law is more localized than economics, and the law studied at the University of Missouri will be somewhat different in emphasis and content from law studied outside the state. But basically I do not think he could consistently accept a scholarship for economics, and refuse one for law.

Houston suggested that reimbursement of full tuition was appropriate.[13]

The recommendation for reimbursement following a receipt for tuition in lieu of advanced payment suggests some suspicion of Gaines's motives. In his memorandum, Houston suggested that William Redmond be given a grant of fifty dollars up front, with a certification of enrollment provided afterward. In both cases, however, Houston also recommended that the actual source of the money be hidden from each recipient. Houston recommended that he write each client indicating that he had "located a friend" to loan the money under the condition that it be repaid within five years.[14] White corresponded directly with Gaines. Reemphasizing that "as Mr. Houston has explained to you, the Association is not financially able nor is it within its purpose to give scholarship aid," White wrote, "I am happy to be able to report to you that a friend has agreed to advance the necessary sum of seventy-five dollars for each of the two semesters." White outlined the conditions: it was an interest-free loan, was to be repaid within three years after degree completion, and would be a reimbursement following a receipt of enrollment. He concluded, "I am glad that we were able to locate this friend who is able to help."[15] Gaines accepted the conditions and expressed his gratitude, asking that his thanks be conveyed to the anonymous friend.[16] White responded that he shared the message and warmly added, "He and we will be best repaid by the fine work we are sure you will do."[17] Gaines, however, did not wait for reimbursement. Instead, he told the registrar at the University of Michigan that the NAACP would pay for his tuition directly.[18] To White, Houston repeated his expectation that the Alpha Phi Alpha fraternity would pay for the second semester.[19] However, the NAACP was billed for Gaines's second semester in the M.A. program as well.[20]

During his second semester at Michigan, Gaines asked for more money. He asked White for an additional loan of seventy-five dollars, to be repaid in September, and he told Redmond twenty-five dollars would be needed immediately. Gaines hoped to finish the degree requirements in the summer, but financial difficulties troubled him. The alternative, he confided to both men, would be the need to work for summer, so Gaines also asked for employment references.[21] On receipt of White's letter, Houston reminded Gaines that "you told us you could make it yourself if we could find someone to advance your tuition charges. It is very difficult to go back to the friend who advanced your tuition charges and ask him to increase the loan. I am quite sure you appreciate the difficulty." He encouraged Gaines to use his own employment contacts. Within days, Gaines somehow got his finances in order. In a handwritten note, Gaines asked Houston to disregard the previous request for a job contact. "During the interim, everything has worked out satisfactorily and good possibilities for the summer are assured."[22]

Houston chided Gaines about his academic performance. When he first learned of Gaines's admission to Michigan, Houston was congratulatory to his "Dear Brother Gaines" but he added a warning to "study your head off at Michigan because you are a marked man now and folks will be watching every move you make. You simply cannot afford to go there and make anything but an excellent record. You carry the banner for all of us." Houston knew that academic preparation at colleges like Lincoln might be "insufficient preliminary preparation" for a strong graduate program and urged him to consider transferring to undergraduate studies.[23] Before leaving for Michigan, Gaines assured Houston that "you need not worry about the scholastic angle—not that I make light of your word of warning, but to assure you that it is well taken and though confident I am equal to the occasion, I will proceed with added caution."[24]

Later, in consultation with his economics department advisor and instructor, he reduced his course load, which also meant he needed to extend his time at Michigan.[25] Gaines received further advice from his mentor, Charlie Houston: "May I as an older brother . . . offer a little suggestion: in your studies this year make clarity and simplicity a goal. Anytime you see yourself about to use two adjectives, stop and search to find one which will do the work of both, and strive for simplicity of language. Simplicity of language leads to the directness of thought, and as a public speaker that is what you will need."[26] Gaines boasted to Walter White about his successful first semester, but Houston considered his academic performance lackluster. Houston confided, "I hope you can improve and make a B-plus or A for the second semester."[27]

In the meantime, Sidney Redmond felt the pressure of the Missouri Supreme Court appeal. He was concerned about when the case would reach the docket, as it could be within a month after a request to hear the appeal.[28] Houston's crucial input was difficult to obtain because he was out of state. Houston's main concern was the anticipated appeal to the federal court, but first they had to pass the state, or as he put it, "I do not want the Supreme Court to throw us out on any ground of lack of form." Houston expressed confidence in Redmond: "In the matter of procedure please note that the entire responsibility is yours. I do not know Missouri procedure and will not interfere. I am demanding on you to make up the record in perfect shape. . . . Do not leave any stone or expense unturned which may be necessary to perfect the case." He scolded Redmond for delays as he and university attorney Hogsett made corrections to the transcript, while reassuring his colleague of his trust: "If it were anybody but you I would also caution against letting the case drag and depend on perfecting the record in the last few days. But I know your record for punctuality and promptness, and therefore only say I'm glad it is in your hands because I know that you will have the whole thing perfected and file way ahead of time." Houston relied on Redmond but wanted to control the case as well. "I won't be able to do much work on the brief out here, and will depend on your office for the bulk of the research. But I should like for you to arrange so that we will not have to file the brief before December 1. That will give me a chance to spend about ten days with you in November polishing it up. But once again the decision is yours."[29]

Within a week, Houston had begun to voice doubts about the strength of the case and sought new information. Houston told Redmond that he had forwarded his files to Thurgood Marshall, "asking him to make his own independent research." Again Houston assured Redmond, "This is not to supplant what you and I are doing but to supplement it. I believe that from the standpoint of time the Missouri case will be the first to reach the United States

Supreme Court; and therefore I want all our strength concentrated on it."[30] Still focused on a federal appeal, Houston reminded Redmond that when he next traveled east, either he or his father would need to move Redmond's appeal to the US Supreme Court. Meanwhile, Houston gave Redmond more work: "Don't slacken your own work in the slightest. As a matter of fact I have a special research job for you. I want all the bills, statutes, debates, etc. on Negro education rechecked. I think it ought to be done in Jefferson City. I know you did the job once, but I think they ought to be combed again for the appeal."[31] Houston also suggested speaking again with Charles Florence and Irvin C. Tull as well as Walthall Moore or, "if he won't talk," Joseph Mitchell of the *Argus*. Concerning the publicly funded tuition scholarships, Houston wanted to know all the rules, the attitudes, and the arguments of Missouri decision-makers.[32] Houston knew this was a tall order and offered to send in Thurgood Marshall to assist. "In short, while I do not want you to neglect your regular practice I do hope you will live, sleep and breathe this case. To my mind both the Maryland and Tennessee cases are walkovers compared to the problems raised in this Missouri case."[33]

Sidney Redmond was concerned about coordination and guidance and hoped for more direct input from Houston. "My experience leads us to believe that divided responsibility is no responsibility at all."[34] Redmond traveled to Columbia and to the state capital, as Houston requested, but he uncovered no records of consequence and no new information. He drolly observed, "Jefferson City is a place where nobody knows anything and everybody takes a month to move."[35] Neither Marshall nor Houston seemed to contribute much as they waited for the appeal hearing. Redmond recognized the distractions from other demands but remarked, "It seems to me that it is better to work a little all along than it is to put a rush act on at the last moment."[36] Redmond pursued the appeal and waited for Houston's brief. On February 11, Redmond wrote, "Time is becoming of the essence and in spite of the pressure of other matters this one must be given consideration." Houston responded on March 1, "We are so darn rushed here that it is hard to get detached long enough to do any consecutive thinking." A few days later, Houston responded to another complaint by humorously addressing the letter to "Dear Aunt Sidney" and suggesting, "Go chase yourself."[37] Redmond's response indicated no amusement and inquired, "What about the brief in the Gaines case?" and concluded, "I realize that you have many types of duties, as well as enough work for three men, but I dare say none of the other matters are more important than this one."

Arguments before the Supreme Court of Missouri were scheduled for May 18, and briefs had to be submitted thirty days in advance. Moreover, counsel for Gaines had promised to provide drafts to university counsel even earlier, and printers would typically take ten days for such a job.[38] Houston wanted to prepare the arguments for the case, but the deadlines to file were encroaching, and Redmond thought *Gaines* could be dismissed on procedure.[39] Houston promised to get to St. Louis as soon as possible, but, after additional delay, Redmond boarded a train to Washington. The visit motivated Houston. Despite other obligations, with only a few days remaining to finish, Houston concentrated on the brief. After Redmond returned home, he worked with Andy Ransom on the brief, sending incomplete versions to university counsel in Kansas City.[40] On April 14, Redmond threatened in a telegram, "If brief does not arrive tomorrow case will be dismissed."[41]

Charlie Houston was overworked. Later, he would comment, "I wound up nearer exhaustion on this case than on any job I can remember."[42] He was traveling across the country on behalf of the NAACP. The Tennessee case was moving forward—arguments were made in Memphis in mid-March. An anti-lynching bill, which was Walter White's priority legislative issue, seemed to be making headway in Congress, requiring Houston's presence on Capitol Hill in late March and early April. Another case about racial discrimination in the selection of jury trials, *Hale v. Kentucky*, was reaching the US Supreme Court.[43] The stress was taking its toll on Houston's health, his family life, and on the overall NAACP legal agenda. His workload during *Gaines* litigation did permanent damage; his "marriage never failed so much as it slipped away."[44] Houston was "litigating himself to death—simply destroying his health by rushing from Missouri to Maryland, Texas to Tennessee. The man never lay awake at night worrying about one crucial case; there were always four, or nine, each of almost the same level of importance as the Gaines case."[45]

Houston would turn to trusted colleagues such as Andy Ransom, William Hastie, and Thurgood Marshall for assistance. Marshall had proven himself invaluable on the University of Maryland case, the Baltimore County schools case, and in other ways, and the time had come to make him a permanent member of the NAACP legal team. In October 1936, Sidney Redmond offered Marshall his "congratulations upon your appointment to the staff of the N. A. A. C. P. You have a wonderful opportunity and I am sure the race will benefit from your efforts."[46] Marshall was "deeply appreciative" of the opportunity and the confidence in his legal skills.[47]

Houston finished the brief and sent it by train. It arrived on April 15. Redmond made several corrections and took the brief to the printers. To Houston, he responded, "It takes only a little calculation on your part to see that I was not trying to scare you when I stated it was absolutely necessary for the brief to arrive today, Thursday."[48] Redmond thought the brief was generally strong, although more so at the beginning than at the end. His concern was that the argument allowed two interpretations. Houston insisted that Gaines was entitled to admission to the existing state law school, but Redmond thought the stronger claim was that Gaines was entitled to his rights under the law. The latter could be satisfied if the state established and admitted Gaines to a segregated law school. Of course, there was no state law school for blacks, so Redmond saw no immediate concern.[49] He added, "As a whole the brief is unanswerable. I await the maneuvering of the univ."[50] Houston later responded that he wanted the legal argument to follow a single track ending with admission to the University of Missouri, so the brief did not mention the possibility of creating a black-only law school. Gaines did not apply to Lincoln for creation of a law school, and to raise the issue of an independent black law school would obscure the focus of the case.[51] Houston did not seriously consider that the state would respond by promoting a non-existing program at Lincoln University because of the unnecessary financial cost it would entail.

The Missouri Supreme Court heard the case on May 18. The court had seven members, chosen through a partisan election for a ten-year term. The court had two divisions: one heard criminal cases; both one and two were assigned civil cases. Under certain circumstances, the court would hear a case en banc, composed of all seven judges from both divisions.[52] Because of its constitutional character, the appeal in *Gaines* was heard en banc. Three of the sitting judges had attended the University of Missouri Law School (though one for only a year), and two others had law degrees from private schools within the state.[53]

The challenges faced by Houston and Redmond in segregationist Missouri were not only legal ones. Houston asked for assistance from Lincoln

University President Charles Florence because he had no place to stay over-night in Jefferson City. Houston hoped to visit the Supreme Court Library before the hearing to refresh his memory on Missouri law before presenting oral arguments. Moreover, Redmond and a group of about ten supporters drove in on the day of the hearing but knew of no place in town where they could eat.[54] White attorneys for the university faced no such restrictions on accommodations or dining.

On the eve of oral arguments before the Missouri Supreme Court, the *Columbia Missourian* reported on the case. It referred to *Gaines* as a case "which attracted wide attention when he sought admission into the University of Missouri," a significant departure from the language asserting Gaines was forcing his way into the university that appeared in other newspapers. The *Missourian* reported succinctly the positions of both sides, but highlighted aspects seem to reflect subtle support for Gaines. First presented was a quote from the NAACP's brief: "Missouri is an island of prejudice in education ex-cept her southern border. The real question is whether Missouri will remain fettered by the past, or whether it will calmly face the future of greater civic participation by her Negro citizenry." Following this passage was a statement from the brief outlining the university's position supporting tuition scholar-ships.[55] In the direct quote from the NAACP brief, readers get the sense of forward thinking, of advances in education. In the summary of the univer-sity's case, readers get a sense of an institution of higher learning afraid of change, despite the change occurring all around it.

The appeal before the Missouri Supreme Court reemphasized the key points from the circuit court. University counsel took the position that ed-ucation segregation was legally required and that the state's sole college for blacks, Lincoln University, was substantially equal in quality to the state's flagship university. In addition, they defended the out-of-state scholarship program for Negro students when Lincoln did not offer necessary courses.[56] Gaines's attorneys pointed out that the state had no law school for black Missourians and attacked the equality of tuition scholarships.[57] They argued that students at the state university had the advantage in overall costs as well as the emphasis on Missouri law (as Gaines aspired to practice in St. Louis after graduation). In addition, they pointed out that expanding Lincoln for a law school was not feasible. Houston argued that "not a cent had been ap-propriated since [public authorization in] 1921 to make it possible to expand

Lincoln university, and that all the money had been appropriated for college work and that Lincoln university is a university in name only" limited to "undergraduate collegiate instruction." A key argument was that the University of Missouri admitted other minority citizens as well as international students while it "excluded active Missourians who helped to support the university through their taxes, and called on the state to be just to its own citizens before attempting to be so generous to strangers."[58]

William Hogsett, lead counsel for the university, asserted that the case was "merely part of a national campaign on the part of the National Association for the Advancement of Colored Persons." In particular, Hogsett claimed that the NAACP pushed an agenda of social equality irrelevant to the case and not acceptable to the general public. Houston agreed that the *Gaines* case was part of "a nation-wide campaign to educate Negroes to their citizenship rights, and up to the limits of their resources [NAACP lawyers] were going to accept every worthy case of discrimination." Then he took university counsel to task on the subject of social equality: ". . . Negroes were not fooled or disturbed about the cry of social equality . . . because they knew it was the last desperate effort to deprive Negroes of equal rights, and that the sooner white people relegated the bugaboo of social equality to the limbo of the past the better off they and the country would be."[59]

Reporting in the *St. Louis Argus* praised the arguments made by Redmond and Houston. "Last Tuesday was an epoch making event in the history of Negro education in the state of Missouri. . . . At the opening of the case, the court was crowded with interested spectators. . . . The judges gave a great deal of attention to the arguments produced by Houston and Redmond and the spectators at times had difficulty in restraining their emotions." The *Argus* continued, "Attorney Sidney R. Redmond opened the case for the plaintiff, and for forty-five minutes the spectators and the Court was charmed by his eloquence, as he cited case after case, law after law, custom after custom, in support of his contention that Gaines was only seeking the opportunity to pursue the study of law in his own state as any other citizen." Quoting Redmond at length, the article presented the crux of the NAACP argument: "'The question has been raised by the defense that the plaintiff is seeking social equality. We deny this. This young man is only seeking equal educational opportunities as provided by the state of which he is a citizen. Any successful attempt to force him to further his education in another state does him an irreparable wrong, a wrong the extent of which cannot be estimated.'"

Dismissively, the paper reported, "Attorneys for the defense made the usual plea that Gaines was seeking social equality and that he had not availed himself of the opportunity to study law in some other state, saying that the constitution of the state of Missouri provides separate schools for white and colored children."[60]

Mainstream papers tended to carry wire stories about the hearing, but some added their own interpretations of the case. News in the *Joplin Globe*, for instance, consisted almost entirely of the case presented by the University of Missouri. It was capped by the headline, "Attorneys Oppose Negro Entering M.U.: Supreme Court Told Efforts of St. Louis Black Is Contrary to 'Unvarying' Policy of State." The headline was noteworthy for its use of a term that was unusual in coverage by the white press at the time. Gaines was described not only as colored or a "Negro," but also as a "St. Louis Black." This was an early, unusual use of the cultural term "black" in the press. Its sister Joplin newspaper, the *News Herald*, also referred to Gaines as a "St. Louis Black."[61]

In the *Globe*, Hoggsett was quoted arguing that the policy of separate education "runs throughout the whole warp and woof of the state's educational laws" without change since the Civil War. The *Globe* reported that Judge Ernest M. Tipton interrupted Houston to ask him "if it would be 'satisfactory' to have a professor from the University of Missouri law school conduct classes at Lincoln. 'I would say—you're asking me as an individual—that would be satisfactory,' the Negro attorney replied." In this exchange, the reading public received an unrepresentative statement of the NAACP's case—that segregation might be acceptable—to "the Negro attorney."[62]

Despite initial optimism after the appeal, Redmond and Houston expected the Supreme Court of Missouri to affirm the establishment's case and looked forward to a federal appeal. The Missouri high court did not include the *Gaines* decision in the first release of decisions in early August. Houston made a lengthy trip west. Redmond wrote to Houston, "I have an idea that it will be September before the method of our being trimmed is known."[63] Charlie Houston traveled to Reno, Nevada, for several reasons, including a divorce from his first wife, Mag, the former Margaret Gladys Moran. Within a few months, he had married the legal secretary in his law firm, Henrietta Williams.[64]

During the Supreme Court's delay, state leaders took action. Charles Florence was dismissed by the Lincoln Board of Curators. Although the motivations for his ouster were not fully clear, it is possible that cooperation with the NAACP and its allies was a factor.[65] Redmond commented, "The ouster of Florence can do Lincoln no good and I fear will do much harm. The politicians want the pie."[66] Even J. D. Elliff, president of the Lincoln board, who had testified that Lincoln was a university in the making, felt Florence's dismissal was politically motivated. He submitted his resignation to the governor, expressing concern that educational quality of the institution was endangered.[67] Lincoln was not the only university experiencing alleged politically driven machinations. Months later, William E. Masterson, the Missouri law school dean so reviled by Houston on the witness stand in the circuit court trial, resigned from his position. In a written statement, Masterson blamed "certain intolerable, petty conditions that have existed within the school for some years and . . . a constant attempt at meddling in the affairs of the school by a small and noisy group of 'politically-minded lawyers.'"[68]

In Maryland, the initial legal success was slipping. An out-of-state tuition scholarship program similar to Missouri's was expanded, and it looked like other black students would be excluded from the University of Maryland. Houston wrote to leaders of Greek letter societies and NAACP youth groups, "After the victory in the University of Maryland case, two Negro students were admitted but recently the State of Maryland has increased the out-of-state scholarships provisions and moved to bar Negroes from the University of Maryland. If no new qualified Negro students present themselves to challenge such exclusion, the doors of the University of Maryland may be closed again."[69] Failure to achieve quick success in *Gaines* seemed to be damaging the broader effort for equality in education. Sixteen states imposed some form of racial segregation in education, and the state where the NAACP had previously scored its greatest success seemed in retrenchment from equality of opportunity.

The Missouri Supreme Court, on December 9, affirmed the circuit court ruling. The unanimous opinion, written by Judge William F. Frank, took the view that "the established public policy of this state has been and now is to segregate the white and negro races for the purpose of education in the common schools and high schools of the state."[70] Though there was no constitutional mandate for segregation in higher education, "the Legislature has the authority to enact laws providing for such separation."[71] The court noted a lengthy legislative history of statutes regarding Lincoln University as an institution for African Americans in order to "show a clear intention on the part of the Legislature to separate the white and negro races for the purpose of higher education. The provisions of the 1921 Lincoln University Act, if it stood alone, would leave no doubt on that subject."[72] This history demonstrates a "clear intention" to provide "equal opportunity for higher education, but in separate schools."[73] More, the tuition scholarships for blacks to attend a college confirm the intention for segregation.[74] The act that allowed "all youths" to attend the University of Missouri was effectively redefined by the statutes regarding Lincoln.

The Missouri Supreme Court had previously held that racially segregated education did not violate the Fourteenth Amendment to the Constitution, even when a school district had no schools for blacks.[75] Opportunities, the court repeated several times, need only be "substantially equal." "However, equality and not identity of school advantages is what the law guarantees to every citizen, white or black."[76] Frank noted that Gaines had not applied to Lincoln in order for the board of curators to act, and that would have been the appropriate action. Statutes show "it is the mandatory duty of the board of curators to establish a law school in Lincoln University whenever necessary or practical." The opinion accepted the views of university counsel regarding the equivalence of instructional style, travel distance, living expenses, and so forth, to sanction the out-of-state scholarships for black students. The court explicitly rejected comparisons to the *Murray* case, arguing that Missouri was "so radically different" from Maryland because of the Lincoln University Act.[77] Should Lloyd Gaines be allowed to matriculate at the University of Missouri? The court responded, "The answer is obvious. It is clear that the legislature intended to bring the Lincoln University up to the standard of the University of Missouri, and give to the whites and negroes an equal opportunity for higher education—the whites at the University of Missouri, and the negroes at Lincoln University."[78]

The court did not accept the state's case on all points. The opinion did declare a portion of the 1935 appropriations act unconstitutional. Although the 1921 wording was vague on the extent of out-of-state tuition covered for black Missourians, the 1935 appropriations act specifically gave the Lincoln Board of Curators the discretion to pay the difference between in- and out-state tuition. The 1921 Act (section 9622 of state statutes), however, granted authority to the board to pay "reasonable tuition fees." The state supreme court ruled this provision unconstitutional and null because an appropriations bill could not legislate on another matter.[79] The Lincoln board could cover full tuition scholarships for out-of-state students. This part of the decision, however, had no bearing on the complaint in *Gaines*.

The decision accepted the arguments provided by university counsel and, to the NAACP attorneys, ignored the basis of their appeal. Redmond believed "opinion really overlooks facts in our favor."[80] After drafting a motion to re-hear, he added, "The opinion seems somewhat fair to one unfamiliar with the facts but just about all of our evidence has been overlooked, and I fear intentionally. Those two exhibits about the [*Missouri Law*] REVIEW and costs of education were completed ignored in spite of their importance."[81] Houston summarized the ruling in a letter to fraternity and NAACP youth leaders:

> The Court held it was equal protection under the 14th Amendment for Missouri to create a paper university out of Lincoln Institute, renamed Lincoln University (Mo.) whose Board of Curators should have authority to establish a law school when the Curators felt the demand justified the same, and until such law course should be established to pay the tuition of Negro students in law to attend a university in an adjacent state.[82]

The NAACP counsel registered disappointment but no surprise with the decision. Redmond wrote Houston, "There is nothing left for us to do but appeal. The judges should want to jump in the river."[83]

Black newspaper reports agreed with Redmond's assessment. *The Call* juxtaposed results in the Missouri case with the NAACP's efforts in Maryland. Donald Murray, who entered the University of Maryland Law School, "has been attending Maryland U for two years and his relations with the faculty and his classmates have been entirely satisfactory."[84] The *St. Louis Argus* noted how the opinion by Judge William F. Frank explicitly rejected a comparison to the Murray case.[85] Newspapers such as the *Afro-American* reported that the NAACP attorneys had expected a state supreme court victory but were planning an appeal to the US Supreme Court.[86] The *Chicago Defender* offered this criticism of the University of Missouri and Missouri state law: "'No blacks may enter here' might well serve as an appropriate sign to hang from the portals of the University of Missouri. This would proclaim that the State supreme court, on December 9, denied Race students the right to enter the institution."[87]

Coverage of the state supreme court in the *St. Louis Argus* emphasized the prevailing opinion among black observers that the decision was made *in spite of* the Missouri constitution. The newspaper with its connections to black lawyers in St. Louis offered a perceptive legal analysis of the state court decision: "In denying Lloyd Gaines admission to the University of Missouri Law School, the State Supreme Court held that there was no constitutional law in Missouri which prohibits white and Negro students attending schools together for higher education and neither was there any constitutional provision which required the separation of the races for higher education."[88] Instead, support for segregation was inferred from laws passed by the state legislature over the course of several decades. "Therefore the court held that in the absence of such constitutional provision, the Legislature would control in this case," and the *Argus* reported the lengthy list of statutes cited in the decision. It was undoubtedly galling to the *Argus* staff and the paper's readers that the lower-court decision was allowed to stand in spite of the fact that the state's foundational legal document, its constitution, did not insist on racial segregation. Allowing segregation was not the same as mandating it. The next challenge would necessarily require interpretation of the federal constitution.

When the Missouri Supreme Court declared that Lloyd Gaines should not be admitted to the University of Missouri, state newspapers' positions on the case were predictable. In the *Joplin Globe*, for instance, a section, appearing midstory, labeled "Intention Clear," showed where the *Globe* stood. The subhead was a line restructured from the court's opinion that the state legislature "showed a clear intention" to segregate education in Missouri when it passed the Lincoln University Act in 1921.[89] The story concluded with a further quote from the opinion that expressed a similar sentiment: "The fact that the two races are separated for purposes of receiving instruction deprives neither of any right. As said in the case just cited [which the *Globe* neglected to name] 'equality, not identity of privileges and rights, is what is guaranteed the citizen.'"[90]

Noting the strange diminution of the quality of Missouri's law school, the paper repeated the Court's finding that four neighboring states' public law schools were at least as good and all admitted black students. One unusual aspect of the Missouri case was that in its fight to keep out black students, the University of Missouri Board of Curators, its legal counsel, and here the local press, consistently argued that there was nothing special about the University of Missouri—except that it was for whites only. The *St. Louis Globe-Democrat* was more sympathetic to Gaines, and it issued the headline "Negro Loses Fight to Enter State U.: Members of Race Denied Right to Go to Missouri Institution." Readers were sent a message that this was a loss for an entire group of people, not for an individual student, and this theme continued in the opening line, "The State Supreme Court today denied Negro students the right to enter the University of Missouri."[91] Both the *Globe* and the *Globe-Democrat* referred extensively to the state supreme court opinion, but the former emphasized its defense of the separate but equal doctrine; the latter focused on the rights lost to an ethnic group.

The *St. Louis Post-Dispatch* offered more details about the legal action. The story reported, "The public policy in Missouri has been to segregate the white and Negro races for purposes of education in the public schools, and there is no constitutional prohibition against such separation for purposes of higher education, the Missouri Supreme Court en banc ruled late yesterday in a test case . . . ."[92] In a section similar to the *Joplin Globe*'s declaration "Intention Clear," the *Post-Dispatch* offered a subheading using quotation marks to meaningful effect, "'Adequate Provision' for Negroes." In this section, it was reported that "Judge William F. Frank . . . overruled several constitutional points raised by counsel for Gaines, and held the Legislature had made adequate provision for higher educational opportunities for Negroes, equivalent to those furnished at the University of Missouri."[93] The *Post-Dispatch* also used quotes from the opinion not included in other stories. Bias for the state is implied in the penultimate paragraph, which suggests questionable behavior on Gaines's part. "Gaines, a graduate of Lincoln University, admitted in the Circuit Court hearing that he had not applied to the Board of Curators of Lincoln University for payment of his tuition in any of the law schools of State universities of the adjoining States of Illinois, Iowa, Nebraska and Kansas, which admit Negroes."[94] The wording suggests someone made an error. The story emphasized the court's extension of out-of-state tuition, but, like other coverage, did not mention the lack compensation for the travel required or that appropriations did not fund all applications.

Redmond forwarded a copy of the *Post-Dispatch* item to Houston. In this correspondence Redmond wrote to his colleague, "Read this editorial from the POST DISPATCH. There is nothing left for us to do but appeal. The judges should want to jump in the river."[95] The NAACP distributed clippings of the *Post-Dispatch* coverage of the hearing before the Missouri Supreme

Court. Frances Harriet Williams, of the National Board of the YWCA, responded to Houston, "I like very much the quotation from the brief which begins, 'On the East, North, and West, Missouri, surrounded by states which admit Negroes to the state university without social disorder, etc.' This shows that your good mind is at work. The article by Mr. Carroll seems to show also that you are moving with a certain degree of equilibrium and poise. So, I congratulate you."[96]

The *Columbia Daily Tribune* was positive about the decision.[97] The first line of the *Tribune's* story emphasized the victory: "The refusal of University of Missouri authorities to admit a Negro student had the approval of the state supreme court today."[98] It repeated the incorrect assertion that Gaines could have attended law schools in four neighboring states with full tuition paid.[99] The story ended with this quotation from the 1890 state decision of *Lehew v. Brummell* cited in the court's opinion: "There are differences in races, and between individuals of the same race, not created by human laws. . . . If we cast aside chimerical theories and look to the practical results, it seems to us it must be conceded that separate schools for colored children is a regulation to their great advantage."[100] Presented without comment on the part of the *Tribune*, this final passage stands firmly as an endorsement of both the decision and the separation of whites and blacks in education.

The *Columbia Missourian,* based on United Press reporting, was largely supportive of the decision and the state's case. It dealt with the out-of-state travel and tuition issues in a tone favorable to the state and Judge Frank's opinion on the matters.[101] On the question of tuition, it was reported, "Attorneys for Gaines contended equal opportunity was denied if he did choose an outstate law school since the state would only pay the difference between charges of the University of Missouri and the other school. Frank held that provision of the 1935 appropriation act as unconstitutional. The full tuition would have to be paid, he said."[102] There was no suggestion of motivations for Gaines.

Capital coverage of the Missouri Supreme Court's decision in the *Jefferson City Post-Tribune* was similar to that of the *Columbia Daily Tribune*. The newspaper emphasized aspects of the unanimous opinion, written by Judge William Frank, reflecting Missouri's constitution. Within the section, "Lincoln U. for Them," it reported, "Frank pointed out that while the constitution fails to require separation of whites and negroes, it also contains no section forbidding education of the races in separate schools."[103] There was little analysis, as in other articles about the decision, provided about the arguments of Gaines's legal team. Of course, Redmond and Houston's complaint was that the state supreme court opinion likewise ignored their arguments. Coverage was nearly identical in the *Post-Tribune*'s sister publication in Jefferson City,[104] but the *Daily Capital News* did include a short sidebar about the *Gaines* team's next move. It reported, "Counsel for Lloyd Gaines said tonight the defense is hopeful of carrying the case to the United States Supreme Court. 'I can not state definitely our best move until I have read a copy of the state supreme court opinion,' explained S.R. Redmond.... 'But if the opinion is so phrased, giving us permission, we will appeal to the supreme court of the United States.'"[105] This was considerably more attention for the Gaines side than other white newspapers gave.

Like every aspect of the *Gaines* case, the court's decision garnered attention far outside of the state. For instance, a brief Associated Press story in the *Billings* (MT) *Gazette*, "Court Bans Negroes," observed, "The state supreme court Thursday denied Negro students the right to enter the University of Missouri."[106] That was certainly correct and with the decision of the Missouri Supreme Court, Gaines and his team had exhausted nearly every legal path available within the state.

Redmond and Houston filed a motion for a rehearing before the Supreme Court of Missouri, but it was denied. Houston had difficulty returning to St. Louis in time to work on the motion. He was occupied with progress with the Anti-Lynching Bill on Capitol Hill and with the teachers' salary case in Baltimore.[107] On February 25, the Missouri Supreme Court overruled the motion for a rehearing without comment.[108] Immediately following the Missouri Supreme Court's announcement, Houston wrote Redmond asking him to request the Court grant a petition for a writ of certiorari from the United States Supreme Court.[109] Redmond handled the legal procedures within Missouri, and Houston worked on arrangements in Washington, DC.[110] They requested an additional extension of time for the petition for certiorari in order to perfect the case. Sardonically, Houston wrote Redmond, "I suppose that that would be satisfactory with [Hogsett], because they want to delay the case as much as possible in any way."[111] Houston wanted to ensure that no procedural elements blocked the appeal to the US Supreme Court. The goal was a federal decision on the merits of the case and on the constitutionality of educational equality. This would overturn the separate but equal doctrine from the Court's decision in *Plessy*. Taking the *Gaines* litigation to the US Supreme Court had been the goal all along. The petition for certiorari asked the federal court to resolve inconsistencies between the highest courts in the states of Maryland and Missouri on whether equal protection was violated if a state provided differential educational opportunities for its citizens solely on the basis of race or color. Houston's vision was a national application of the equal protection clause of the Fourteenth Amendment that would apply to all states and communities.

Houston and Redmond filed the appeal on May 24, 1938. As Houston was filing, the NAACP provided leaders of the black press background information on the case. Houston directed Redmond to give copies of the appeal to Mitchell at the *St. Louis Argus* and Young at the *St. Louis American* encouraging them to write editorials in support of the NAACP.[112] Houston asked several editors to encourage potential students denied out-of-state scholarships to contact him.[113] Many black newspapers, such as the *Kansas City Call* and the *St. Louis Argus* emphasized the organization's view concerning the Fourteenth Amendment's equal protection clause.

> The test of equality under no circumstances can be whether a Negro student outside the state has to pay as much for his education as a white student inside the state, but whether the state itself does more for its white students than it does for its Negro students. The force of this is realized when it is considered that state scholarships for Negroes in Missouri total only $7,500 per year against an appropriation of more than $500,000 for the University of Missouri.[114]

It was the US Supreme Court's discretion to grant a writ of certiorari to review the *Gaines* case. However, unrelated to the legal rationale, two severe problems plagued the NAACP attorneys just as the case was reaching the highest court. The first was the status of their plaintiff, Lloyd Gaines, and the second involved funding to pursue the case further. Both issues were critical and could have ended the appeal before it could be heard by the Supreme Court.

While Lloyd Gaines studied at the University of Michigan, his attorneys lost track of their plaintiff. During the summer, the university registrar,

Boyd C. Stephens, forwarded a note to his "business agent" Charles Houston asking for Gaines's current address.[115] Houston forwarded the registrar's address form to Sidney Redmond noting, "I have been called many things in my life, but to be denominated as a business agent is new."[116] Redmond responded by giving Gaines's previous Ann Arbor address, adding "since he is in the city I assumed that he did not want to communicate with [university officials]. I was informed that he has a job cooking."[117] A month later, the news about Gaines sounded more sinister.

Lloyd's family sounded the alarm. As Redmond wrote Houston in July, "Gaines' family has not heard from him in over a month. His brother was in my office a few days ago and seems to think he has been kidnapped. They are having an investigation made. If I get any more information on the subject, I will advise."[118] Houston had no additional information.[119] The two colleagues did not exchange further correspondence about Gaines's location that remains, but Gaines was in Lansing, Michigan, where he remained through the end of 1938. After a year in the master's program in economics, Gaines took a job as a WPA clerk in the state Civil Service Department.[120] He had not contacted his family from his new location.

The other major problem involved funding necessary to pursue the appeal. The appropriation from the Garland Fund, the American Fund for Public Service, had been exhausted. No money remained for the *Gaines* appeal to the US Supreme Court, or for other legal projects. As Executive Director Walter White confided to Sidney Redmond just after the Supreme Court petition was filed, "We have been able to finance the educational fight in Missouri, Maryland, Tennessee and other states through a grant from the American Fund for Public Service. But we have received the tragic news that the resources of the American Fund are exhausted and we will not receive a renewal."[121] The funding crisis dogged Houston as he prepared the brief for the federal appeal. He wrote Redmond in April, "We haven't been able to get any money out of the Garland Fund for briefs and expenses. I have been tailing onto Roger Baldwin but have not been able to get him to commit himself."[122] Baldwin was the secretary of the American Fund for Public Service.[123] The difficulty was that the poor economic environment of the Great Depression and the many demands on the Garland Fund had depleted its resources.

Walter White, the dapper African American who wore tweed suits and could pass for white,[124] preferred appealing to wealthy, white benefactors for major funding for the national NAACP campaign. While *Gaines* worked its way up through the courts, White wanted an informative but research-laden brochure on the education agenda that would appeal to rich entrepreneurs.[125] White wrote Sidney Redmond that *Gaines* cost the NAACP national office $1,900 through early 1938 and the filing of the petition for a writ of certiorari. If the writ was granted and the Supreme Court heard the appeal, White estimated the cost "will amount to approximately $2,000" of additional funding, money the national organization did not have.[126] White admitted to Redmond that his own legislative priority for a congressional anti-lynching bill produced a "heavy drain on our budget from the unexpected duration of the anti-lynching fight." Funds otherwise available for the *Gaines* case were not only unavailable, there was a deficit of $2,000. White appealed to Redmond to ask the St. Louis Branch for contributions to help pay for *Gaines* litigation. The letter concluded, "We *must* not lose the benefit of the long fight which has already been made, because of lack of funds to complete the task."[127] White asked Houston to draft a letter to Redmond for his signature, using the model of a letter to Arthur Packard to solicit a contribution from John D. Rockefeller.[128]

Although the national office of the NAACP was in dire straits, the St. Louis branch had plenty of money. A recent fund drive had elicited over $1,900 and was expected to pass the $2,000 goal.[129] To Houston, Redmond expressed concern that "we have so much money in our [Branch] treasury that I fear there will be raids and believe we should make a gift to the national office. At first my inclination was to give toward the Gaines case but in view of your letter our gift should be an outright donation." Redmond asked for the letter from White and hoped for further requests from him in order to sustain a second drive for the *Gaines* case in particular, rather than an appeal for general operating funds.[130] In the meantime, the St. Louis Branch contributed $350 to the national office with the assumption that it would help finance legal efforts and the *Gaines* appeal.[131] Although Houston wrote a letter of thanks to the St. Louis branch, the absence of any acknowledgment by Walter White would irritate Redmond for months.[132] Whether from animosity or financial exigency, White preferred that Redmond receive no fee for the Supreme Court appeal.[133]

In July, Houston left the New York office for Washington. He was closer to judicial decision-making there, as well as to his law practice with his father.

He stayed on as special counsel for the NAACP but, as he told attorney Osmond Fraenkel, "off-salary."[134] The Board of Directors of the American Fund for Public Service considered a provisional extension of a $700 grant for the *Gaines* appeal. Two conditions were attached. First, the NAACP would need to provide matching funds, thus, the need for the St. Louis branch to donate to the national office rather than make a direct contribution for expense reimbursement. Second, a statement from reputable counsel outside the organization should confirm "that there is a fair chance of winning the case." Houston called Morris Ernst, a prominent New York attorney and cofounder of the American Civil Liberties Union, for assistance. Ernst agreed, but suggested that Houston contact someone else—none other than Nathan Margold, who had prepared the original report on the NAACP legal strategy under the auspices of the Garland Fund. Margold was now a solicitor for the Department of the Interior.[135] Margold, however, was on an extended trip to the West and did not see Houston's letter until almost a month later.[136]

In the meantime, Houston contacted Osmond K. Fraenkel, co-counsel of the New York Civil Liberties Committee and one of the attorneys for the Scottsboro boys in the US Supreme Court case of *Norris v. Alabama* (1935), an important precedent for Houston, Hastie, and Marshall in *Hale v. Kentucky* (1938).[137] Houston went a bit further than the Garland Fund directors intended, asking Fraenkel for an amicus curiae brief to strengthen the petition for a writ of certiorari.[138] Fraenkel could not understand the purpose of writing Roger Baldwin, secretary of the Garland Fund, as a condition for the fund's support. "Am I to assume the role of prophet? Because surely if the Supreme Court grants certiorari the fund should support the appeal. On the other hand, if the Supreme Court denies certiorari I do not see why the fund should have to pay out money on my guess." Unfortunately, Fraenkel thought the Supreme Court would deny certiorari, both because Gaines did not apply to Lincoln University and because of doubt that the Hughes Court would rule that equality was denied if payment was offered to another, out-of-state school. Houston admitted that "the chances of the court granting the writ are not as bright as we might wish." He responded to Fraenkel with a clear assessment of his expectations:

> a court disposed to dodge the question could rest on the omission
> to make formal application to Lincoln University. A court not dis-
> posed to dodge the question would find from President Florence's

letter and the testimony in the case that applying to Lincoln University would have been a mere idle gesture. The tuition scholarship situation is analogous. A tuition scholarship is not equal protection, but as you say the court may find the subject too hot to handle. What I really hope for out of the case is a pronouncement on the question of the scholarship equivalent. This would affect the entire South and 9,000,000 Negroes.[139]

On October 10, 1938, the United States Supreme Court granted certiorari. Houston telegraphed White immediately: "Missouri Certiorari Granted. Argument about November 7. Notify American Fund."[140] White wrote to Roger Baldwin and the board of directors of the Garland Fund: "We trust that this accomplishment meets the conditions laid down in your letter of May 28, 1938" for the financial contribution.[141] Houston was pleased when the American Civil Liberties Union agreed to file an amicus curiae brief on behalf of the NAACP's position.[142] University counsel, however, refused to provide consent for the ACLU brief, and, under Supreme Court rules, it could not be included as part of the petition.[143] In any case, the *Gaines* appeal would be heard by the United States Supreme Court.

Roy Wilkins sent telegrams and letters to ten black newspapers on the day the Court agreed to hear the appeal.[144] A broader press release was also issued, boasting but setting high expectations. "The case marks the eleventh appeal of a case by the N.A.A.C.P. to the highest court in the land. The association has won all but one of the ten previous appeals before the high court."[145] The *Afro-American* noted the historic nature of *Gaines:* "This is the first time the issue has gone to the Federal Supreme Court."[146] Black newspapers anticipated the outcome and how the justices would respond. Washington Rhodes, the editor of the *Philadelphia Tribune*, wrote back to Wilkins: "We hope that the Association will win this case for the benefit of colored Americans. It will be interesting to observe the position Justice K. K. K. Black will take."[147]

The Supreme Court under Chief Justice Charles Evans Hughes seemed receptive to application of the equal protection clause of the Fourteenth Amendment but reluctant to make major changes in constitutional law. Southerners on the Court included James McReynolds of Kentucky and new appointees Hugo Black of Alabama and Stanley Reed of Kentucky. McReynolds led the "Four Horsemen," an influential bloc of four conservative justices on the Court that opposed the New Deal and the expansion of the federal government. However, two members of this bloc, Willis Van Devanter and George Sutherland, retired and were replaced by Black and Reed. Pierce Butler of Minnesota remained a conservative ally of McReynolds. African Americans protested Black's confirmation to the Supreme Court because he was a member of the Ku Klux Klan in Alabama. Associate Justice Benjamin Cardozo died in July and his seat remained vacant. Charles Houston faced a Court that was more moderate than it was recently, and he sensed the opportunity for a ruling that would expand equality of opportunity.

Oral arguments were made on the afternoon of November 9. Houston had requested an extension of time for oral arguments to ninety minutes rather than the traditional hour, though it is unclear whether his motion was granted. He argued: "The case presents many questions which have never been before the United States Supreme Court. The decision is likely to chart the course of state development of professional and graduate education for Negroes in the South for the immediate future. It is in the public interest that ample time for argument be allowed."[148] Houston and Redmond represented Gaines, while Hogsett and Williams represented the state university.[149] According to contemporary accounts, the Court responded to the two sides differently. "Houston and Redmond were permitted to speak almost without interruption but their opponents were subjected to searching interrogation in which Chief Justice Hughes took the lead, and in which most of the Associate Justices found occasion to intervene."[150]

During oral arguments Williams and Hogsett claimed that Missouri was a pioneer among states, establishing Lincoln University as an institution of higher learning exclusively for blacks that was equal in quality to the University of Missouri was for whites. Moreover, the state, Williams claimed, was willing to organize a program of legal education for $10,000 if requested, and it would pay $150 annually in out-of-state tuition scholarships until the program was organized. The Missouri Supreme Court, Williams continued, made this mandatory, though Justice Owen Roberts questioned whether this could be mandatory given the existence of the out-of-state scholarships.[151] Hughes followed by asking why, if the program was mandatory, the Missouri Supreme Court had not already ordered Lincoln to establish a law school. He inquired whether Lincoln University was in a financial position to accomplish this task. Williams, the former Missouri Supreme Court judge, insisted Lincoln did have the capability, though he acknowledged that Lincoln regularly operated at a budget deficit, and it could utilize the resources of the Supreme Court Library in Jefferson City, "one of the best in the country, comparable even to that of the United States Supreme Court." Hughes wondered aloud about the difficulty for a university to incur dramatic, new costs once a budget was already prepared.[152]

The position of university counsel was that racial segregation was a nondebatable issue. Justice Harlan Stone interposed, "This is the law in some states. But there is also a national point of view, which is opposed to racial discrimination." Chief Justice Hughes added, "How can you say that Negroes have equal educational opportunities in Missouri, when they are compelled to leave their own state to find such equality of professional training in other states?" University counsel responded that the tuition differential of $150 was an advantage over white students. Justice Hugo Black interrupted with the question, "Do you mean to suggest that a pecuniary payment would be adequate compensation for loss of civil rights?"[153]

William Hogsett declared "that in the history of the University of Missouri, Gaines was the first Negro to apply for entrance to its law school" and that, on advice of counsel, he refused to say whether he would attend legal courses at Lincoln. Justice Louis Brandeis raised the question of whether state law prohibited blacks from enrolling at the University of Missouri. Counsel responded that there was no such statute, but "the rejection of Negro students has been held by the State Supreme Court to be a question of public policy." Justice Pierce Butler asked about the number of black lawyers within the state.[154]

Justice James McReynolds said little during oral arguments, but claims of his inappropriate behavior during oral arguments have become legendary, a symbol of resistance to racial equality. When Charles Houston addressed the Court, McReynolds is alleged to have turned and kept his back to Houston during oral arguments, refusing to acknowledge the black attorney.[155] Robert L. Carter offered a personal recollection of the oral arguments for *Gaines*. "The case had a personal resonance for me. I was a law student at Howard at the time, and it was the first Supreme Court argument I had heard. At the hearing, when Houston rose to begin his argument Justice James McReynolds turned in his chair and kept his back to Houston throughout his presentation." Carter remembers no negative reaction to this discourtesy, "Nor do I myself recall feeling any outrage at the time."[156] The problem with accounts such as Carter's is that they are otherwise unsupported. No reports published at the time in either the black or white press mention this behavior. Still, McReynolds's behavior during oral arguments was described as a bit unusual. As the NAACP press release described it, "The full bench of eight Justices sat during the argument, except that Mr. Justice McReynolds left the bench after N.A.A.C.P. counsel had finished their argument, and when counsel for the university were half through."[157] The lone biography of James McReynolds portrays him as cantankerous and an ardent segregationist, but an individual who was personally respectful to African Americans.[158]

Charles Houston pressed the point that the University of Missouri was the only public law school in the state and Gaines was a citizen and a taxpayer; thus the rejection of Lloyd Gaines's application was a denial of his fundamental rights. "Houston's argument, dignified and restrained, but with an undercurrent of emotion, was heard by the bench with closest attention, and virtually without interruption." As guaranteed by the Fourteenth Amendment, Gaines was entitled to equal protection under the law. Houston told the Court, "The records show that Missouri University has admitted Filipinos, Chinese, Hindus, Mexicans—in fact, every race save its own Negro citizens. My client applied for admission under a triple handicap—he belonged to the wrong race, the wrong class, the wrong section."[159]

Coverage of oral arguments was ubiquitous in the black press, as opposed to the white press, where the hearing itself received spotty attention. When oral arguments were heard in November, the Associated Negro Press noted the entry of an important ally of the NAACP into the case, reporting, "Charging that equal protection of laws guaranteed by the 14th Amendment to the U.S. Constitution had been denied, the American Civil Liberties Union will file a brief amicus curiae in behalf of Lloyd Gaines."[160] The *St. Louis Argus,* in a brief front-page story accompanied by a photo of Gaines, proudly reported that "Attorneys Charles H. Houston of Washington and Sidney R. Redmond of St. Louis represented Gaines and were permitted to speak almost without interruption by Chief Justice Hughes and the seven associates."[161]

In front-page coverage, the *Afro-American* focused exclusively on the brief delivered by Charles Houston, pointing out in bold print that, "Mr. Houston emphasized the public importance of the case. He pointed out that it was the first to reach the Supreme Court involving the question of graduate and professional education for colored people." The newspaper reported Houston's argument that international students were admitted to the University of Missouri but not persons of African descent. Houston "also ridiculed the question of social equality raised in the brief filed in behalf of the University of Missouri." Adding a detail, the paper reported that Houston "may have shocked the eight justices, though they showed no traces of shock, when he told them that evidence of social equality was written into the features and complexions of colored people." The *Afro-American*'s analysis of the justices was saved for the final two paragraphs, "Sitting on the bench at the time were three Southerners, Justices James C. McReynolds, Hugo L. Black, and Stanley F. Reed, and a Westerner, Justice Pierce Butler, who has been none too liberal in his opinions involving the rights of colored persons. Justice Harlan F. Stone, who was dean of Columbia Law School, followed the argument of Mr. Houston intently."[162] It is noteworthy that none of the black newspapers reported the story which would later spread—apparently facetiously—that McReynolds turned his back on the black attorneys as they addressed the court.

Wire service reportage of the hearing published in newspapers such as the *Cleveland Call* and the *Chicago Defender* was scornful of the University of Missouri's case.

> The University of Missouri "belongs to white people" and any insistence on the contrary connotes a desire on the part of Race members for social equality with whites. These were the views expressed with a straight face by counsel for the University of Missouri. . . . They were expressed only after severe questioning on the part of the justices forced the defense counsel to admit that this was the reason for the university's exclusion of Gaines from its law school in September, 1935, on the ground that "he is a Negro."

The Court was, in the opinion expressed by the *Defender*, supportive of the NAACP's arguments.[163]

Regional white paper coverage of oral arguments before the Court on November 9, 1938, varied substantially. In the *Jefferson City Post-Tribune,* for instance, the coverage was limited to a one-sentence statement, "The supreme court took under advisement yesterday the appeal of Lloyd L. Gaines, St. Louis Negro, from a Missouri supreme court decision upholding the right of the University of Missouri law school to exclude him from its classes."[164] The *Daily Capital News* added that Gaines "contended he was denied the equal protection of the laws by his exclusion from law classes."[165] Both papers credited the Associated Press, but the *Post-Tribune* mentioned only the university's "rights," as opposed to the *Daily Capital News* that also mentioned those of Gaines and other African Americans.

If the *Missourian's* coverage of the Missouri Supreme Court decision could be read as supportive of the state's side of the issue, when *Gaines* was argued before the US Supreme Court, the *Columbia Missourian* reported the proceedings in a tone that suggested the clear superiority of the NAACP's case. This difference in tone may have much to do with the fact that the *Missourian* did not offer its own reporting. The story about the US Supreme Court decision in the *Missourian* was built from the report of the Washington correspondent of the *St. Louis-Dispatch*, who provided the best and most complete coverage of the oral arguments before the high court.[166] The *Post-Dispatch* was less antagonistic toward Gaines and the NAACP than many Missouri newspapers covering the story. In contrast to the *Missourian's* positive—for Gaines—coverage of the hearing, the *Columbia Daily Tribune* appeared hardly to have noticed the event. Following the US Supreme Court hearing, the *Columbia Daily Tribune* ran only a brief notice at the bottom of the frontpage. The item is noteworthy for its continued emphasis on the correctness of the state's perspective, noting the Missouri Supreme Court upheld the university's right to deny Gaines's admission.[167]

The Court took little time to reach its decision. The Supreme Court released it on December 12, just over a month after oral arguments. In a 6–2 decision, the US Supreme Court ruled in favor of Lloyd Gaines. The Court decided that Missouri had to provide equal educational opportunities for black graduate and professional students within the state that were equal to those offered for whites, overruling the practice of discretionary tuition scholarships for study in an adjacent state. In the majority opinion authored by Chief Justice Charles Evans Hughes, the Court found that out-of-state tuition scholarships for blacks were an unconstitutional violation of the equal protection clause of the Fourteenth Amendment.[168]

The majority opinion declared that "the fact remains that instruction in law for negroes is not now afforded by the State, either at Lincoln University or elsewhere in the state, and that the State excludes negroes from the advantages of the law school it has established at the University of Missouri. It is manifest that this discrimination . . . would constitute a denial of equal protection."[169] The Supreme Court thus struck down racially based out-of-state tuition scholarships as a violation of the Fourteenth Amendment. The Court, however, did not go on to compel the University of Missouri to admit Gaines to its law school. Instead, the majority opinion noted that the 1921 Missouri statute establishing Lincoln as a public university gives discretion to its curators on whether to establish a black law school or to provide an out-of-state tuition scholarship. The discretion of public officials cannot guarantee an individual's equal protection. The Court cited both the *Murray* case in Maryland and *Yick Wo v. Hopkins* as precedents.

Chief Justice Hughes dismissed issues of casebooks, legal specialties, travel distances, and so forth as irrelevant. The key issue is "what opportunities Missouri itself furnishes to white students and denies to negroes solely upon the ground of color."[170] Hughes continued,

> By the operation of the laws of Missouri, a privilege has been created for white law students which is denied to negroes by reason of their race. The white resident is afforded legal education within the State; the negro resident having the same qualifications is refused it there, and must go outside the State to obtain it. That is a denial of the equality of legal right to the enjoyment of the privilege which the State has set up, and the provision for the payment of tuition fees in another State does not remove the discrimination.[171]

In the Court's view, states were constitutionally required to provide equal protection of law within their own borders, not rely on another state to provide constitutional protection. Hughes wrote that "the protection of equal laws can be performed only where its laws operate, that is, within its own jurisdiction. It is there that the equality of legal right must be maintained."[172] The Court rejected any argument that the number of individuals involved was a relevant factor for constitutional safeguards.[173] Gaines's right "was a personal one. It was as an individual that he was entitled to the equal protection of the laws, and the State was bound to furnish him within its borders facilities for legal education substantially equal to those which the State there afforded for persons of the white race, whether or not other negroes sought the same opportunity."[174] The majority opinion also rejected the notion that a temporary violation of rights (out-of-state scholarship during the period that a professional program is created) passed constitutional muster.[175]

The Court's opinion reversed the Missouri Supreme Court's interpretation of federal rights and concluded, "We are of the opinion that the ruling was in error, and that the petitioner was entitled to be admitted to the law school of the State University in the absence of other and proper provision for his legal training within the State."[176] However, elsewhere in the opinion, the Court reasserted the legality of separate but equal education, suggesting that an all-black law school in Missouri could be an acceptable solution. Rather than compelling the university to admit Gaines, the Court remanded the case to the Missouri Supreme Court for further proceedings. The opinion left open the issue of whether the establishment of a black law school could be an acceptable way to resolve the case. No such alternative then existed within the state. The Court was a long distance from its future reasoning in *Brown v. Board of Education* and that separation is inherently unequal. Nevertheless, the Court solidly rejected out-of-state scholarships on the basis of equal protection of the laws.

Justices James McReynolds, joined by Justice Pierce Butler, wrote a dissenting opinion which supported the Missouri Supreme Court ruling and maintained the validity of the separate but equal doctrine. McReynolds predicted that Missouri would either "abandon her law school, and thereby disadvantage her white citizens without improving [Gaines's] opportunities for legal instruction" or integrate schools and thereby "damnify both races."[177] Out-of-state scholarships, for McReynolds, satisfied "reasonable demand for specialized training." He was influenced by the fact that "never before has a negro applied for admission to the Law School, and none has ever asked that Lincoln University provide legal instruction." In McReynolds's view, Missouri "should not be unduly hampered through theorization inadequately restrained by experience."[178] McReynolds's position was cited by defenders of segregation, who were not yet willing to give up the status quo.

Legal counsel and college administrators for the University of Missouri had difficulty accepting the majority opinion of the US Supreme Court. On December 31, counsel for the university asked the Court to reconsider its decision in the *Gaines* case. The decision, Williams and colleagues argued, "is a new interpretation of the equal protection clause, and one which (so far as our research discloses) has never before been applied by this Honorable Court."[179] According to the state's representatives, who cited numerous cases, the Fourteenth Amendment's equal protection need not be guaranteed within a state's own jurisdiction. Moreover, they protested, "no authority is cited for the construction now adopted. We believe no authority exists."[180] They repeated that Gaines had refused to apply to Lincoln, the black-only institution, which could create new courses in law on his behalf.[181] Moreover, according to university counsel, the "principle of race separation in educational facilities is firmly established" and a "deeply rooted tradition;" racial segregation is "a condition, not a theory." The protestations of counsel for the university indicated how sharply the US Supreme Court turned in the application of the equal protection clause.

The *Gaines* decision meant that Missouri and six other states "will be compelled either to admit negroes to sit with white boys and girls in state universities, or to build separate negro universities within their borders to take care of any demand for higher education for negroes which might arise."[182] Since these seven states would not abandon segregation, counsel for the state complained of the unnecessary cost involved for this new definition of equal protection.[183] They repeated words from McReynolds's dissent and objected that the problem "is intensely practical, and must be solved with due regard for the actual needs of the two races, rather than upon the basis of purely theoretical considerations."[184] "Obviously the whole basis of the petition," said Sidney Redmond in a NAACP press release, "is a determination on the part of the State of Missouri to segregate Negro citizens and then make them pay for the segregation. The petition illustrates the state's dual standard of morality, and the utter inability of the officials of the state of Missouri to conceive of Negroes as an integral part of the state."[185] The Court quickly rejected the petition.

The implications of the Supreme Court ruling "sent shock waves through the South, affecting sixteen states."[186] The *Gaines* decision "caused immediate consternation in the states having separate systems of education. The reaction to the decision varied in different states."[187] None of the states with some form of racial segregation in education was ready to abandon it, but each realized the broader implications of what was likely to come.

Houston touted the magnitude of the *Gaines* case. A press release issued after the US Supreme Court's decision announced the future of NAACP litigation: "The sweeping opinion . . . ordering the State of Missouri to provide Negro students with the same facilities for studying law as are provided for white students will be the wedge in a campaign all down the line to the smallest rural school. . . ."[188] But Houston and the NAACP also knew the limits of the decision. Hughes wrote in the *Gaines* decision that "The admissibility of law separating the races in the enjoyment of privileges afforded by the state rests wholly upon the equality of the privileges which the laws give to the separated groups within the state."[189] Although the Hughes Court emphasized the need for racial equality of opportunity, the NAACP attorneys also recognized its overt permission for the 'separate' component in a newer judicial doctrine of 'must be equal if separate.' The NAACP press release continued to presage *Brown*:

> N.A.A.C.P. officials and their legal staff point to [this] sentence in the broad opinion of the supreme court as one of the most significant in the whole opinion and one upon which a further campaign for equality of elementary and secondary education will be based. . . . the N.A.A.C.P. proposes to redouble its efforts to improve education for Negroes in the rural and city elementary schools in the South, in the high schools; in bus transportation for Negro rural pupils; and in the allocation and administration of the millions of dollars of federal funds given to the states each year for educational purposes.[190]

Following the Court's ruling, Houston issued a statement: "This decision affects all types of education in every state having separate schools."[191] The Court ruling influenced graduate and professional education in all states, but *Gaines* had broader implication; issues of funding and educational equality followed naturally. Houston noted that *Gaines* "establishes that constitutional rights are personal rights not dependent on the volume of demand." He foresaw that the *Gaines* decision signaled the end of legally sanctioned segregation and the expansion of federal constitutional protections. *Gaines* v. *Canada* established the precedent that would lead to a series of cases regarding segregation in education.

The *Gaines* doctrine established the Supreme Court's expectation that educational facilities, at least, if separate, must be shown to be equal.[192] Although World War II, an intransigent court, and other factors would slow progress, the Supreme Court's decision was the beginning of the end of segregation in education. Houston would not live to see the final victory—this was a battle Marshall and other protégées would finish. But in Houston's words, the

Gaines decision "gives America a chance to practice the same race tolerance that is now preaching on all sides to Nazi Germany."[193] This point of view would be shared in the black press as well as in postwar political culture.

Walter White also promoted the significance of the *Gaines* decision. Contacted by the national newsmagazine, *Time*, White "declared the decision more sweeping than he had hoped. To Negroes it means far more than a chance to go to professional school." He commented on the vast inequity between spending for educations of whites and blacks, and he believed the court's ruling meant there should be parity in school spending from the graduate level down to primary education (what would eventually be the stage for the ruling in *Brown*). *Time* also quotes "Realist White" saying, "We still have a struggle ahead to get the States to obey the court's mandate."[194] Nevertheless, in his press statement, NAACP secretary White announced, "It may well be that the decision won yesterday may advance the cause of Negro education more than any other pronouncement the court has ever made."[195]

In addition to the legal strategy of the NAACP, Houston concurrently pushed a public relations agenda. Congratulatory notices came to the NAACP from all across the nation, and contributions eased the pressures from insufficient funding. Lucile Bluford of the *Kansas City Call* wrote to Roy Wilkins that she considered the legal decision "the most significant victory Negroes have won in recent years."[196] To no one's surprise, the black press praised the outcome of the 1938 *Gaines* case. Some mainstream publications did as well, although evaluations of the decision were mixed. Generally, the press and the informed public knew that major social and political change was in the wind. Journalist Oswald Garrison Villard, an early contributor to the NAACP, wrote that *Gaines* "is an epoch-making decision, a milestone in the Negro's fight for his rights as a citizen, and it will cause consternation throughout the fifteen states which now deny to Negroes the advantages accorded to whites."[197] The case of Lloyd Gaines, however, was not yet over.

5

Gaines in the Press

The US Supreme Court's decision in *Missouri ex rel. Gaines v. Canada* was news across the country. The NAACP legal strategy was part of a coordinated effort to overturn de jure segregation in the states that involved black newspapers and decision-makers. The defenders of racial segregation were less monolithic, in part because racial segregation was practiced actively in only part of the country. The mainstream or white press was less coordinated.

The black press responded to the *Gaines* decision in a variety of ways. To be sure, black newspapers hailed the decision as groundbreaking. Some news outlets enthusiastically predicted the end of segregation in education; a few went further and suggested the decision would alter race relations in other areas. Other news organizations voiced caution and concern about implementation of the decision. Following the announcement, the black press in general relied less on NAACP releases, and local papers provided more distinctive news coverage and original assessments of the political and legal environment.

As the largest hometown black newspaper, the *St. Louis Argus* was enthusiastic, declaring in an enormous headline, "Gaines Wins In Supreme Court: Decision Has Far-Reaching Effect in So." The story used front-page photos of Charles Houston, Sidney Redmond, and Lloyd Gaines. The *Argus* summarized the news media's coverage: "The decision handed down by the United States Supreme Court in the case of Lloyd Gaines versus the University of Missouri, et al, was hailed by the press, and particularly by the Negro press, as a great victory for colored people seeking equal educational facilities in the several southern states."[1]

The *Pittsburgh Courier* joined in the celebration with a large, front-page headline, "Supreme Court Smashes Color Line in Southern Universities: Rules Missouri University Must Admit L. Gaines."[2] A week later, on Christmas Eve, the *Courier* reiterated this version, printing a photograph of Gaines with the headline, "Kills Dixie Color Line."[3] The *Courier* reported the words of former representative in the US House and radio news correspondent George Hamilton Combs Jr.: "'Your reporter has only to say . . . that as an alumnus of the University of Missouri and of that law school, this is one decision of the Supreme Court which he heartily applauds . . . it is democracy at work!'"[4] The *Amsterdam News* proclaimed "Court Hits Dixie Death Blow" in large all-capital letters. The story asserted, "Encouraged by the sweeping decision of the United States Supreme Court this week that the University of Missouri must let down its color bar against the Negro and admit Lloyd L. Gaines, 28-year-old student to the law school, Negro leaders all over the country are girding themselves for a smashing attack upon the citadels of prejudice and discrimination in the Southern States. . . ."[5]

An editorial published in the *News* the same day opined, "there are few victories ever been won by the race that equal the one over the University of Missouri which, in effect, is a victory over educational discrimination in this country because of race or color." It concluded,

> The Amsterdam News believes that the fight waged in the Gaines case that must be waged by the Negro group as well as all other minority groups for equal protection of the law and for equal opportunity. It is the democratic way. It pits brain against brain; mettle against mettle; men against men. And if those who are entrusted with the tremendous task of interpreting the constitution fairly for all of the people, regardless of race, color or religion, do so, they cannot but help render such decisions as did the Supreme Court in the already famous Gaines case.[6]

The passionate coverage of the *Gaines* decision by Baltimore's *Afro-American* illustrates the truth of an old adage that says news coverage of events is not history, it is merely the first draft of history. "The U.S. Supreme Court ruled, Monday, that the University of Missouri must admit Lloyd L. Gaines of St. Louis, as a student in the law school, pointing out that a State must give 'equality' in educational privileges to colored and white law students alike."

The article quoted from Chief Justice Hughes's majority opinion and inferred that "Gaines will be the first colored student to enter the University of Missouri in its ninety-eight years of existence."[7] The newspaper underestimated the stamina of the segregationists. In a separate item discussing the implications of the decision, the *Afro-American* went further. Repeating the assessment that Gaines would be admitted, the paper extended: "Decision in Missouri U. case means equal opportunity in Pullman Cars and National Guards, too."[8] Implying that *Gaines* overturned *Plessy*, the *Afro-American* concluded, "So sweeping is the Court's decision that it is immediately evident that it goes beyond law schools and railway cars to include State-supported colleges, medical, art, and music schools, to National guards, to Civil Service or any other 'opportunity' offered citizens by any state." Citing the importance of the Maryland case as a precedent, the *Afro-American* referred to an editorial in the *Baltimore Evening Sun* urging southern schools not to fear desegregation and declared, "So, with one swift dash of the Supreme Court pen, Uncle Sam makes it plain that opportunities—whether they be State universities or Pullman cars—provided for one citizen must be provided for all citizens black or white."[9]

Coverage of the decision in the *Kansas City Call* was jubilant but tempered. The *Call* acknowledged a second possibility: "The supreme court ruling will do one of two things: 1.—Wipe out the color line in state universities, or 2.—Build great negro universities, calling for a great outlay of money for buildings, libraries, equipment and high-salaried teachers." A sidebar acknowledged the work of the NAACP in the legal fight for equality. "The winning of the Gaines case is a new feather in the cap of the National Association for the Advancement of Colored People. It was the N.A.A.C.P. legal staff which sponsored the Gaines case from the start and which pushed it up from the trial court to the highest tribunal in the country."[10] Sidney Redmond and Henry Espy received special front-page recognition (including a photo of Redmond), along with Charles Houston, for their contributions to the effort.[11]

The *Chicago Defender* was also laudatory, thought its coverage was sober and reserved. A *Defender* editorial observed, "The association and its attorneys deserve great credit for a well-earned and merited victory. It would do well however to consider the meaning and implications of the *Gaines* decision. The Supreme Court merely decided that the University of Missouri must admit Gaines to its law school until it had provided for another law school for Race students at Lincoln University." The editorial concluded, "The net effect of the Gaines decision is to gain for the Race people of Missouri some sort of law school for the students at Lincoln University. The decision of the Supreme Court in this case is of limited character and effect."[12] Likewise, the *Cleveland Call* hedged, reporting that the Court's decision meant Missouri would need to provide equality, but not that desegregation of the University of Missouri was coming soon.

Some papers offered editorial comment on the dissent written by Justice McReynolds. The *Cleveland Call* noted, "The intolerant voice of southern ancestors spoke through the mouth of Justice James Clark McReynolds of Elkton, Ky., who wrote a vigorous dissenting opinion in which 'Hoosier' Justice Pierce Butler of Waterford, Minn., concurred."[13] A *Los Angeles Sentinel* editorial declared, "The supreme court decision was almost unanimous with only Justice McReynolds of Tennessee and Justice Butler of Minnesota, both diehard reactionaries, dissenting," and the *Sentinel* took a cautious approach to the decision: "It is hard to predict what Missouri will do in the light of the decision: Maryland faced with a similar dilemma simply admitted the Negro student and, despite all predictions to the contrary, he has had no trouble in keeping pace with his fellows. Missouri, being a border state where race feeling is not too intense, may do likewise."[14]

Meanwhile, a column by Floyd J. Calvin in the *Cleveland Call and Post* referred to the *Gaines* case as "a welcome Christmas present to the group in the field of civil rights," and argued that, "In the hardbitten, prejudiced Missouri, it had been ruled by the State Supreme Court that the Law School was a 'white man's school'. The U.S. Supreme Court, however, saves the day." Notably, Calvin added something in his column that was conspicuously absent from much coverage in the black press; he praised Lloyd Gaines, the man, writing, "We wish to commend young Gaines for his courage to fight the case, and his brilliant attorney, Sidney R. Redmond, who saw him through."[15]

At home, the assessment of *Gaines* was positive and buoyant. An editorial published in the same issue as its coverage of the decision, the *St. Louis Argus* proposed the following rosy outlook:

> Based upon this mandate from the highest legal tribunal of the nation we take it for granted that Gaines will, at the beginning of the next school year in September, enter the law school at the

University of Missouri, located at Columbia, Missouri. We make
this statement because it is hardly possible for the state to build and
equip a law school at Lincoln University in Jefferson City comparable with that which is provided for white students at Columbia.
Nor do we presume that there will be any opposition on the part
of the state in obeying the mandate of the Supreme Court in this
matter . . . it is a reasonable assumption that the denial of Negroes
to the schools of medicine, pharmacy, agriculture, journalism, etc,
at the University of Missouri is as violative of their rights as that
in the case of law, because none of these courses is provided by the
state at any other place. It is probable, therefore, that other Negroes
will be knocking for admission at the doors of these schools. . . .
We believe that this decision will also hold good in the case of all
public conveyances and places of public accommodations, such as
hotels, inns, etc. Thus, we hail this decision as an indication of the
liberalism of the United States Supreme Court.[16]

The optimism of the *Argus* and other papers would prove unfounded. Forces
for segregation in education would not give up so easily.

For its 1938 Christmas Eve issue, the Baltimore *Afro-American* compiled
editorials from newspapers and statements from university presidents that
supported the Supreme Court's decision in *Gaines*. One article, with a cre-
ative interpretation, reported, "The decision of the U.S. Supreme Court in
the Gaines vs. Canada case, directing the University of Missouri to open its
law school to Lloyd Gaines, won unanimous approval of Southern college
heads as 'rational and just.'" Of course, it was neither accurate to say that the
Court ordered desegregation of the University of Missouri, nor that the leaders of Southern colleges were unanimous in their support of the decision. The
'rational and just' line came from the statement of the president of Atlanta
University, Rufus Clement, "Rational and just decision imposes upon leaders of both races [a] test of rational planning so as to avoid either establishing
of inferior separate schools for colored people or increased racial friction."[17]
Atlanta University was, however, a black-only university, so it is not surprising that its president interpreted the impact of the *Gaines* case in this way.
University leaders quoted by the *Afro-American* were all presidents of black
colleges with the exception of John Hugh Reynolds, president of Little Rock's
Hendrix College. Reynolds gave something less than a ringing endorsement

of the decision, and his school, a private college, was not directly affected by *Gaines*. He said, "If colored students were admitted to the South's State-supported 'white' colleges and universities, there probably would be trouble at first—some hot-headed Southern boy might bash a colored student's nose—but in a year or two we would get used to it."[18]

The *Defender* reported the objections of Dr. John Brown Watson, college president of Arkansas A.M. and N.[19] His reaction, like President James Shepard's in the *Hocutt* case, serves as a reminder that black colleges had much to lose by educational integration. With the headline, "Watson an 'Uncle Tom' Says N.A.A.C.P. Head," the article reported,

> Dr. Watson said there is not a Race student in Arkansas who wants to attend the University of Arkansas. He said a recent check had shown that there are 27 Arkansas Race students studying medicine and seven studying law in universities all over the country. "I am not excited over this Supreme Court decision," Dr. Watson said. "Colored people in Arkansas get along much better than in any state in the South. They don't have as much money as Negroes in other states but there is a better friendship and a more healthful relationship between the Negroes and whites in Arkansas than in any southern state."[20]

The *Defender* critiqued Watson's position in subsequent editorials: "It is strange, indeed, that while we are fighting for economic, political and cultural advantages; fighting for those rights which are guaranteed us under the constitution that we should have to face enemies within our own ranks. Arkansas with its lynchings, peonage farms and general disregard of the rights of its black citizens is held up by Dr. Watson as an ideal state. . . ."[21] In another, it argued,

> The attitude of some Southern Race educators on the Supreme Court decision in the Lloyd Gaines case, has brought despair to the thinking members of the Race. Many people, who heretofore had held some degree of respect for the administrators of our southern colleges, are unable to explain their mentality. They are beginning to question, and rightly so, the usefulness of that type of leadership that forfeits hard-won rights in order that it might remain in the good graces of some white benefactors.[22]

In a similar vein, the *Chicago Defender* attacked pessimistic comments made by Rufus Clement, the president of Atlanta University, whose remarks earlier had been extolled by the *Afro-American*. Clement suggested several ways for states to respond to the *Gaines* decision and mentioned "that the admission of 'Negroes' to graduate schools in Southern state universities 'probably will not happen during our life-time.'" The *Defender*'s editors charged, "Any attempt on the part of any of our educational leaders to formulate a policy in deference to Southern sectional racial bias and discrimination is a distinct betrayal of the legitimate rights of black America as well as a flagrant prostitution of the American theme of 'equality of opportunity.'"[23]

While the *Afro-American*'s coverage continued to be celebratory as the end of 1938 approached, there had been a change in the paper's characterization of the Supreme Court decision. A December 24 article commented that the ruling could be interpreted to allow equal and separate universities for blacks and whites.[24] The same article mentioned one black college administrator's plan for a regional university for black graduate and professional students. The *Afro-American* also pointed out that two of the most important civil rights decisions involved Missouri and that the "Supreme Court ruled with the State on Dred Scott," but that the Court changed the previous week and ruled against Missouri in *Gaines*.[25] Two weeks later, the *Afro-American* reported a more accurate and nuanced interpretation of the opinion.[26] This interpretation of the Supreme Court's decision in *Gaines* persisted. For instance, in a 1947 article about segregation in medical schools, the *Afro-American* summarized the *Gaines* decision this way: "The Court laid down the plain rule that if a State chooses to provide within its borders specialized educational facilities for citizens of one race, it must make similar provisions, also within its borders, for citizens of other races."[27]

A common theme in black newspapers, as the Nazi control of Germany and its treatment of Jews and other ethnic groups became bigger news, was to point out the hypocrisy of Americans who criticized the Nazis in Europe while blacks were afforded such poor treatment at home. One provocative example was a *Los Angeles Sentinel* editorial entitled "Home Grown Hitlers."[28] Similarly, the *Afro-American* asserted, in a front-page story, "This country, it is believed, cannot continue in the anomalous position of insisting that the German Government abate its campaign against Jews while condoning discrimination against colored people within its territory." It concluded, "The United States must first purge itself of racial discrimination before breaking with Germany over the Reich's anti-Jewish decrees."[29] Indeed, for Houston and another generation of black soldiers, the inconsistency of foreign and domestic policies shook the foundations of segregation.

In a sharply worded editorial, the *Afro-American* took aim at a proposed meeting of the leaders of several southern white public colleges and universities. The plan, according to the paper, was to create regional graduate schools at several historically black colleges in return for financial support from the black schools. The editorial referred to the biblical story of Jacob and Esau in which Esau gives his inheritance to his brother, Jacob, in return for a bowl of stew. "There was a man who sold his birthright for a mess of pottage, and we would not be surprised if some of our leaders do the same thing in the jim crow educational appeasement matter."[30] Walter White complimented Carl Murphy, the editor of the *Afro-American*, for the "swell editorial."[31]

As the NAACP anticipated further litigation before realizing actual gains from the *Gaines* decision, it made public appeals for financial assistance, which were publicized by the black press. For instance, the *Cleveland Call* reported, "An appeal . . . to give financial support so as to press forward the drive against inequalities in public education was made here today by Walter White, N.A.A.C.P. secretary." White was quoted, "If we are to receive the full benefit of the broad decision of the U.S. supreme court, there must be funds to press other test cases, to make surveys, to draft legislation and mobilize public opinion in support of it. The amount of good the race receives from this University of Missouri case will depend largely on the amount of financial support it is willing to give to the organization." White expanded on the importance of *Gaines* and the priorities of the NAACP,

> This decision is sweeping in its language and opens up vast possibilities for the improvement of Negro education all down the line to the smallest rural school. The N.A.A.C.P. does not intend to confine itself to college cases, but we expect to use this victory to help us secure better elementary schools, more and better high schools, and improved bus transportation for little colored children in rural areas. This fight for better education is not as spectacular or emotional as an anti-lynch fight, but as the years go by, it may prove to be more important even than anti-lynching work.[32]

In a summary of the most important stories of 1938, published on the same day as the NAACP appeal for money, the *Call* added emphasis to White's words, referring to *Gaines* decision as the "most significant event" of the year.[33]

In January 1939, the University of Missouri asked the Supreme Court to reconsider its decision. The black press reported this development with scorn, as in, for instance, this a *Los Angeles Sentinel* headline: "State Seeks New Trial School Case: Missouri Whines That Supreme Court Overlooked Law."[34] The *Amsterdam News* characterized Missouri as "Unwilling to admit the justice of the recent sweeping Supreme Court decision which ordered the University of Missouri to admit Lloyd Gaines."[35] The *Chicago Defender* reported, "The petition, which upholds the minority opinion expressed in the dissents of Justices Butler and McReynolds, contends that the decision does not take into account the fact that the problem of the races in the South is practical, which must be solved on the basis of actual needs rather than upon purely theoretical considerations."[36]

The *Kansas City Call* gave extensive coverage to the state's request, reporting that university officials doubted Gaines's seriousness in wanting to attend law school. The thrust of Missouri's case, according to the *Call*, was that state officials felt that the Supreme Court's majority simply did not understand what they were asking Missouri to do. The *Call* explained the petition: "Segregation is a condition, not a theory" meant "southern states will never accept interracial education. They would either abolish state universities if obliged to open to Negroes or revert to private institutions, say petitioners." The *Call* also noted the university's opposition to creating a law school at Lincoln: "Further the opposers say that to establish a university at Lincoln equal to Missouri's would mean a useless expenditure of money, idle teachers, empty class rooms."[37] The Kansas City *Call* reported extensively on the Supreme Court's rejection of Missouri's petition, including the "new way of justifying exclusion of Negro students" that the *Pittsburgh Courier* had earlier predicted that Missouri officials would create. The *Call* reported that "attorneys for the university are still seeking legal methods to bar Negroes from the campus." Their chief method was to file yet another appeal with Missouri's highest court, this time alleging that Gaines's request for a writ of mandamus was inappropriate on the grounds that it was "inimical to the public good."[38]

The court denied Missouri's petition for rehearing. A story by the Associated Negro Press noted "the prompt, decisive action of the court came as a distinct surprise to all concerned."[39] The *Pittsburgh Courier* offered this short observation: "University of Missouri officials must think up a new way of justifying exclusion of Negro students. Last week the United States Supreme Court refused to re-consider their plea for a re-hearing of the Lloyd Gaines case. There's a lot of head-scratching going on in Missouri now. In other States, too."[40] The *St. Louis Argus* interpreted the Supreme Court's rejection of Missouri's appeal as definitive, "a state must give equal educational advantages to all persons."[41]

Following the Court's refusal to rehear the case, *Atlanta Daily World* columnist Cliff Mackay wrote, "Missouri's Board of Curators last week found themselves at rope's end after your Supreme Court stood firm on its original position that the University of Missouri must admit Lloyd Gaines to the law school." Mackay suggested that Missouri had just three options in responding to the Supreme Court's decision, "leaving those in charge of higher education in Missouri in the dilemma of either admitting a blackface in the classrooms of a school which during its entire 92-years' history has been maintained 'for white only;' or establishing graduate courses at Lincoln University, or abolishing all graduate work at the University of Missouri."[42] Mackay's forecast was quite accurate. Over the next several years, the State of Missouri tried all three.

Response to the decision was muted in white newspapers. Few papers devoted more than a paragraph or two to the news, and some large newspapers did not carry any coverage. A typical approach was that of the *Chicago Tribune,* which ran a two-paragraph story on page seventeen, published the day after the decision was issued. The story was set off from the many short items around it with a boxed headline, but it was still buried deep in the paper. The story reported, "The United States Supreme court ruled today that the University of Missouri law school must admit Lloyd L. Gaines, a St. Louis Negro, as a student."[43]

Most newspapers reporting the decision used Associated Press coverage, although the editing of the AP material varied dramatically and, of course, the headlines differed in emphasis. The lead story in many newspapers on December 13, 1938, was one that tells us that little has changed about the press: celebrity news leads. The story garnering the biggest headlines and front-page coverage in most white newspapers across America on December 13 was that comedian George Burns pled guilty to smuggling into the United States several thousand dollars' worth of jewelry which was intended to be a gift for his wife, comedienne Gracie Allen. While the *Gaines* story made the front-page of the *Washington Post*, for instance, it was below a story, complete with a picture of Burns, about the comedian's legal troubles. The AP version of the *Gaines* decision rated front-page coverage in the *Louisville Courier-Journal*, appearing in the upper-left corner of the paper. Kentucky, like Missouri, was a border state targeted by the NAACP. But even in Kentucky, the Burns story was immediately to the right of the Gaines story and accompanied by a photo. It even warranted, in the editor's estimation, a much larger headline. The Burns story reported, "Assistant United States Attorney Joseph V. Delaney asked consideration for the comedian because he had co-operated with the Government in a broad investigation of smuggling which began with a raid late in October on the Park Ave. apartment of Mrs. Edgar Lauer, wife of a State Supreme Court Justice, by Treasury agents in search of smuggled Parisian knick-knacks and finery."[44]

In addition to the competition from the Burns story, news of the *Gaines* decision was easy to miss because coverage was shared with another decision announced concurrently. The Supreme Court declined to hear an appeal by the National Labor Relations Board on behalf of a group of unionized sailors who were fired after a strike. In the *Washington Post*, the NLRB story was mixed, in alternating paragraphs, with the story of the *Gaines* case, and its headline gave no mention of a landmark decision regarding civil rights: "Labor Board Loses Plea for 'Mutiny' Crew." The *Gaines* decision was treated as the less important: "The high court also ruled that the University of Missouri should admit Lloyd Gaines, colored, to its school of law." The story did provide some idea of the potential scope of the decision with an extended paraphrasing of Houston's words, "the decision probably would increase higher education facilities for colored people in 16 States which now bar them from State professional schools." It went on to provide information on the decision's effect in border and southern states. Another feature of the story, common to coverage of the decision in many newspapers, was this detail (in the case of the *Washington Post*, appended to the end of the story in parentheses): "In Lansing, Mich., where he is employed on a WPA-sponsored survey, Gaines declined to say whether he would enter the school, which previously had refused to admit him."[45] There is no indication of what readers were to draw from that, but it seems to suggest that if Gaines did not decide to attend the University of Missouri, he had wasted everyone's time.

News coverage in border states, the region that had elements of both north-ern and southern cultures, commented on the likely impact the decision would have locally. Another DC newspaper, the *Washington Star,* carried a brief story about the decision that was indirect and dismissive. Appearing at the bottom of page two, the story featured this headline: "Virginia Seen Forced to Aid Colored Students." The story makes the newspaper's position clear, denigrat-ing the optimistic interpretation of the decision common in the black press and suggesting negative consequences for Virginia. The story read, in part,

> Non-legalistic interpretation of the Supreme Court's decision that the University of Missouri Law School should admit Lloyd Gaines, colored, made it seem likely that Virginia must either provide post-graduate and professional study facilities for Negroes at the state college at Petersburg, or admit them to corresponding courses in such state institutions as the University. Virginia now has a provi-sion for caring for Negroes seeking postgraduate study similar to that of Missouri.[46]

Like the black newspapers, but without the optimistic tone, the *Louisville Courier-Journal* implied the decision was a game-changer. The newspaper was particularly focused on the broader implications of the Court's decision, and a quotation from Charles Houston drove the point home: "Charles Hous-ton, counsel for Gaines, said the decision 'affects the entire scope of gradu-ate professional training' for Negroes in sixteen southern states which do not provide such training within their borders." There was, however, one aspect of the story reported by the newspaper that was not emphasized in the op-timistic coverage of the black press. It attributed an alternative solution to Charles Houston, "He expressed the opinion Missouri could avoid admitting Gaines to the State Law School by establishing an adequate School of Law at Lincoln University prior to the next regular admission date at the University of Missouri."[47]

As the *Courier-Journal* story continued inside on page six, it shifted focus to the implications for the state of Kentucky. "I don't believe the question [of educational segregation] has ever been brought to an issue in this State,' [Assistant Attorney General J.K. Lewis] said, adding that if it were to be, he could see no reason why the same decision would not apply to Kentucky." The story concluded, "The Missouri Negro's petition named Kentucky as one of sixteen States excluding Negroes from State universities, and one of six States providing aid for Negroes studying in universities outside the State. There are no publicly supported law schools in Kentucky and no Negro students in any of the three law schools of the State."[48] News coverage in many border and southern states often made similar, local connections.

Southern newspapers' coverage of the *Gaines* decision tended to be negative. In Georgia, the *Atlanta Constitution* buried the story, again combined with news of the NLRB case, on page nine. Like much of the black press's coverage, the *Constitution* suggested that the decision meant the desegregation of the University of Missouri. Most papers provided quotes from Chief Justice Hughes's majority opinion, and most also provided a quote from the dissent written by Justice McReynolds. The *Atlanta Constitution* and other southern newspapers, including the *Courier-Journal*, gave the longer coverage to McReynolds's dissent, quoting him at length, with special attention to his assertion that integrating education in Missouri would "damnify both races."[49]

The *Dallas Morning News* allowed McReynolds the final word. "Dissenting Justice McReynolds said the Missouri Supreme Court had arrived at a tenable conclusion and its judgment should be affirmed. 'That court well understood the grave difficulties of the situation,' he said, 'and rightly refused to upset the settled legislative policy of the state.'"[50] In the *Arkansas Gazette*, coverage of the decision was within a larger story about Supreme Court decisions of the session. As with the coverage in other southern newspapers, it concluded with McReynolds. In the *Gazette* story, there were seven paragraphs of quotes from McReynolds's dissent, essentially the entire opinion.[51]

Negative news coverage of the Supreme Court's decision dominated the South, but there were exceptions. *The State*, a newspaper in Columbia, South Carolina, published a thoughtful discussion of the *Gaines* decision. It compared local circumstances to those addressed by the Court decision.

> Last spring or summer a Negro made formal application for admission as a student to the University of South Carolina's school of law. Now that Negro has what is apparently an unequivocal decision of the Supreme Court of the United States to support his application. The highest court says he must be admitted, or afforded equal facilities in a state Negro institution for the study of law. The case decided by the Supreme Court was not brought by the South

Carolina Negro. It went up from Missouri, but the fundamental facts are almost identical.

The article discusses the *Gaines* decision and its implications and asks, "What can South Carolina do about this?"[52]

The *State* listed several options. First, establish a law school at the State College for Negroes in Orangeburg. It identifies this as the simplest short-term response but notes that many other professional schools would need to be established later, suggesting a significant long-term cost. Second, admit students to white schools. "South Carolina will not do that willingly unless and until public opinion changes radically." Third, abolish courses offered only for whites, an undesirable outcome. Fourth, do nothing, though the "Ultimate effects of a policy of ignoring the decision can only be guessed at." Finally, the *State* identifies the "Worst Possible Course." "Physical violence would solve nothing. On the contrary it would create problems more acute and more threatening to the South than any it now faces. No, there should be no violence. In its place, the South must manifest calmness, wisdom, justice and tolerance. The South can gain nothing by arousing the hot ill will of the public outside of the South."[53] NAACP secretary Walter White was taken with this article and asked for a copy to be included within NAACP press packets distributed to influence public opinion.[54]

The typical, smaller southern newspaper, such as the Burlington (NC) *Daily Times-News* offered the standard AP coverage. Like Kentucky, North Carolina was facing litigation, and the headline reflected the impact the decision might have on the state: "Court Upholds Negro: Right of Negroes to Attend Law Schools In Any State Upheld by Supreme Court Ruling Favoring Negro in Missouri Court Test." Noteworthy in the wording of this headline and the story is the lack of an assertion, prominent in many newspapers, that the decision meant Lloyd Gaines would be allowed to attend the University of Missouri as a result.[55] Rather, the story emphasized the fact that the Court found Missouri's plan of paying out-of-state tuition to be unconstitutional.

If a smaller southern city saw the Supreme Court's decision in this way, a small northern city newspaper, such as the *Middletown* (NY) *Times Herald*, used a headline to baldly state its view: "School Must Admit Negro." Newspapers that disapproved of the decision mentioned how Gaines had spurned an offer to have the state pay his out-of-state tuition, as if his actions were unreasonable. On the other hand, this newspaper and others supporting the Court's decision relied on the same wire service information, rephrasing it slightly, "Gaines, however, refused to accept the offer on the grounds that since he wished to practice law in Missouri, he wanted to study within the State."[56] The University of Iowa was integrated, and the *Iowa City Press-Citizen's* coverage of *Gaines* was distinctly favorable. It ran an AP story beneath the headline, "Missouri U. Loses Action: Supreme Court Rules Negro Law Student Must Be Admitted." The story gave no mention of the dissenting opinion of McReynolds and Butler.[57] The evolving legal positions of the parties to the lawsuit were reflected in the newspaper reaction to the Court decision.

Although newspapers around the country used text from wire services, usually the Associated Press, their headlines told readers how to interpret the story. In general, headlines in southern newspapers emphasized that Missouri was forced to do something: "Supreme Court Decrees Negroes Must Be Admitted To Missouri Law School: Holds Provision to Pay Tuition Outside State Inadequate; Texas Listed Among States Denying Negroes' Admission" (Denton, TX),[58] "'Equality' For Negro Ordered By High Court: Supreme Court Rules Missouri Must Allow Negro to Attend College" (Kingsport, TN),[59] and "U.S. Supreme Court Rules Missouri Must Admit Negro Student" (Miami, OK).[60] In northern and western newspapers, headlines emphasized individual rights: "Court Upholds Negro's Right" (Lima, OH),[61] "State Must Give Negro Equality in Education Court Rules" (Reno, NV),[62] "Court Orders Negroes Given Equal Educational Rights" (Wisconsin Rapids, WI).[63]

Newspaper perspectives were reflected not just in the headlines but also in editorial selection and modification of content from AP or UP reports. For instance, the space devoted to the dissenting opinion of Justice McReynolds serves as one indicator of newspaper ideology. Editorial decisions, such as whether to add quotation marks around the term *equality* has an impact on how readers perceive the Court's action and its implications for the future, even when the rest of the story is presented in a straightforward, nonjudgmental manner. These subtle influences can only be determined in a comparative study of news reports.

It was not simply a difference in tone, although, as was mentioned above, southern papers tended to be more negative and northern papers more positive. Southern papers emphasized the loss of state's rights (the "rights" of a public university) and northern papers, the constitutional protections of groups' or an individual's rights. Coverage in border regions tended to be more practical and focused on what the Supreme Court decision meant for educational policy within the state. Coverage in the mainstream press supporting segregation reinforced the view that Lloyd Gaines had not taken opportunities available to him as a black man in a segregated society. Initially, such news suggested that he should apply for and accept the out-of-state tuition scholarship. When the Court eliminated that possibility as unconstitutional, the point of view articulated in the mainstream press transformed into pressure for alternatives such as creation of a black-only law school. For many papers, south and north, racial integration of higher education, even in graduate and professional schools, seemed an impossible expectation.

One border state newspaper, the *Baltimore Sun,* covered the decision more extensively than did the average mainstream newspaper. Like the *Afro-American*, the editors of the *Sun* commented on similarity to the *Murray* case against the University of Maryland. Though it relegated the story to page two, the *Sun* featured a headline on the *Gaines* case ("Negro's Right to Attend Law School Upheld"), while the National Labor Relations Board case was demoted to a subsection ("Gave the National Labor Relations Board its second setback in as many weeks").

The *Sun*, sympathetic to Donald Murray and his lawsuit, also adopted a positive perspective on *Gaines*. "Every Southern State that maintains a law school must admit Negroes to that school if no other State law institution is provided for them. It is not enough that such a State may pay or offer to pay the tuition of Negro law students in schools outside that State. Nor is it enough that a State may declare its intention, even by an act of the Legislature, to provide a school of law for Negroes. . . ." Observing that sixteen southern and border states practiced educational segregation, the *Sun* called the decision "an open invitation to Negroes in any section to apply for and demand their full educational rights."[64]

The *Sun* erred in its claim that "The Missouri case is not the first involving this issue to reach the Supreme Court. A few years ago a similar issue was raised in Maryland and a similar decision was rendered by the same court." The *Murray* case never left Maryland state courts.[65] The *Sun's* comparison of the two cases shows a disposition in favor of integration of higher education: "The Missourians, however sought to differentiate their case from that of Maryland by setting up the claim that Missouri actually had initiated plans for a Negro law school at Lincoln University, which is supported in part by the Legislature. But the court found that plan had never been consummated and Missouri was just as guilty, in fact, of racial discrimination as Maryland was found to be." The article in the *Sun* contained details emphasizing the importance of the *Murray* case as an influence on the Supreme Court. The story quoted extensively from the majority opinion's discussion of the *Murray* case. Maryland was cited in reference to Missouri's program of out-of-state scholarships for black graduate students, and the *Sun* quelled opinion supporting out-of-state scholarships within Maryland.[66]

Nationally oriented papers saw the Supreme Court's decision as an advance. The *Christian Science Monitor* declared, "Race Tolerance Begins at Home." Its editorial argued that if the United States wanted to distinguish itself from the ever dimmer human rights record of Nazi-led Germany, something needed to change: "If today's headlines about Germany's plan to link forced emigration of its Jews to exports stress anew the need for racial tolerance, then readers doubtless also will see today's headlines about the Supreme Court ruling in a case involving a Missouri Negro carry that emphasis even farther." Without demanding Gaines's admission to the University of Missouri, it makes this argument:

> In fact, many who read the majority opinion . . . will rightly regard
> it as carrying the humanitarian view of the race question to its logi-
> cal conclusion. . . . It is now believed the state will take steps to pro-
> vide equal opportunity "within its borders" by adding an adequate
> law department to Lincoln university, which the state maintains
> for Negroes. This willing compliance and the ruling that evokes it
> breathe the spirit of tolerance and equality before the law, the best
> safeguards of democracy.[67]

The *Monitor*'s editorial was reprinted in other newspapers; the *Helena* (MT) *Daily Independent*, for example, included it as the "Best Editorial of the Day."[68]

In the West, the *Los Angeles Times* offered a different tone compared to southern newspapers. Its story, "Negroes Upheld in College Case: Right to Attend Missouri University Affirmed by Court," stood separate from the NLRB action. The *Times* offered no coverage of McReynolds's dissenting opinion; instead, it concluded with the quote from Charles Houston about the broad scope of the decision.[69] While the San *Francisco Chronicle* covered the story by following the common path of subsuming the *Gaines* case under a headline about the NLRB, it tracked the *Los Angeles Times* by offering no coverage of McReynolds's dissent, other than to note, "Justices McReynolds and Butler dissented."[70]

The *New York Times* front-page headline summarized the case accurately: "Court Backs Negro On Full Education: Orders Missouri to Admit Him to State Law School or Provide Equal Training." An original news report outlined major points from the majority opinion and concluded with a discussion of the dissenting opinion authored by McReynolds.[71] A supplemental AP story included Charles Houston's comments about the meaning of the decision for increased educational opportunities for blacks. It implied that Gaines might decide law school at the University of Missouri was not for him. "Mr. Gaines . . . will consult counsel as to seeking his legal training in Missouri."[72] While the initial *Times* coverage of the *Gaines* decision was balanced and more accurate than many newspapers', the *Times* would soon publish reports less favorable for equal rights in education.

In smaller cities around Missouri, the decision was also front-page news. Most newspapers carried wire service coverage, offering headlines that emphasized the state's university would be *forced* to admit Gaines. In the *Joplin News Herald,* the headline read, "Court Holds M.U. Must Admit Negro."[73] The brief, edited version of the AP story focused on the decision and reported nothing about the dissenting opinion. The paper also published a sidebar, also by the AP, "Would Be First Negro to Attend University," mentioning that Gaines had no comment about the case.[74] The next morning, the front-page headline of its sister publication, the *Joplin Globe*, was long, identifying an escape route for the University of Missouri: "State University May Open Doors to Negro Student: Supreme Court Holds That Board of Curators Cannot Legally Bar Lloyd L. Gaines; One Way to Enforce Exclusion Order: State Can Keep Black Out by Establishing Lincoln U. Law School—Plan under Consideration."[75]

In Moberly, the *Monitor Index*'s headline was also long, "Must Give Equality to Negro: Negro Has Right to Enter M.U. Law School, the Supreme Court Rule." Another section led, "Affects Several States; McReynolds and Butler Give Dissenting View."[76] On an inside page, the *Monitor-Index and Democrat* ran the story about Gaines being the first black to attend the University of Missouri: "No Comment Made by Lloyd Gaines: University Also Silent on Admitting Negro Student to Law School; Case Is First of Kind in State."[77] In Sikeston, the *Herald* offered a one-sentence summary of the case, "If Lloyd

Gaines avails himself of the opportunity presented by the ruling of the high court, he will be the first Negro to attend the University of Missouri in its 98 years of existence."[78]

The *Kansas City Star*'s coverage used a large headline for its lone, brief AP.[79] The George Burns story had front-page coverage in the *Kansas City Star*, but the Gaines story received higher billing in the form of a larger, boldface headline. Unique in the *Star*'s coverage was a brief addition, "Dr. Fredrick [*sic*] A. Middlebush, president of the University of Missouri, said today he had 'no comment' to make on the Supreme court ruling that Lloyd Gaines, St. Louis Negro, should be admitted to the school of law. J. Coy Bour, acting dean of the law school, also declined to comment."[80] In its weekly edition two days later, the *Star* offered a different interpretation. With the same AP content as its daily edition, the story makes clear that equality did not necessarily mean admission to the University of Missouri, only that Gaines had a chance to attend law school in-state.[81] The weekly *Star* also contained a story noting that the State of Missouri's likely response to the Court's decision would be to create a black law school at Lincoln University, reflecting developments in Jefferson City in the immediate aftermath of the decision. The *Star* predicted,

> The establishment of a law school at Lincoln University for Negroes at Jefferson City was indicated by the reaction to the ruling . . . from several sources came indications that a law course would be added to the Lincoln university curriculum as an alternate to the admittance of a Negro student to the state university at Columbia. Members of the board of curators of the University of Missouri and members of the governing board of the Negro university appeared to be in agreement on the best way to settle the question.[82]

The *St. Louis Post-Dispatch* coverage, featuring a large headline and placement in the upper right-hand corner of the front-page, was more accurate and complete than most newspapers'. The *Post-Dispatch* had a reporter in Washington and was able to provide non-wire service coverage of the decision.[83] The coverage was straightforward, offering lengthy quotes from the majority opinion and several quotes from Justice McReynolds's dissenting opinion. Buried deep in the story was a brief summary of the major legal arguments made by both sides. The *Post-Dispatch* provided information and left room for supporters of the decision and those who objected to it to find something to get worked up about.

Another story in the *Post-Dispatch* offered details about Gaines: noting he was from St. Louis, listing his mother's home address, and reporting his current location in Lansing. It also reported reaction to the decision at the University of Missouri, indicating a preference for creating a law school at Lincoln, quoting cost estimates from the university's legal brief. Within a few days, a *St. Louis Post-Dispatch* editorial rejected the wisdom of the Court's decision while accepting the futility of further legal appeals. It concluded: "The United States Supreme Court brushed aside the more realistic approach of the Missouri Supreme Court, deciding the issue on a basis of pure logic, and since the court of last resort has spoken, there is nothing for the State to do but open the University of Missouri to Negroes who apply for law degrees or to provide a law school at Lincoln University."[84] The editorial was reprinted elsewhere, for instance, in the *Joplin Globe*.[85]

The *Globe Democrat*, a competing, morning St. Louis paper, combined news of the Court decision with an AP story about the reaction of Lincoln University officials. Its headline, with an expansive interpretation of the decision, "Missouri U. Opened to Negro: Supreme Court of U.S. Rules Lloyd L. Gaines Must Be Admitted," was limited by the story's first line, "Unless the Missouri Legislature acts quickly to add a law course to the curriculum of Lincoln University, a precedent of 99 years' standing is likely to be broken by admission of a Negro student to the University of Missouri." The *Globe-Democrat* quoted the new president of the Lincoln Board of Curators, Joseph L. McLemore, who said the *Gaines* decision was "a step toward democracy for a minority group." McLemore expressed doubt that Lincoln University could quickly create a law school on par with the University of Missouri's school: "It took 300 years to make Harvard University Law School what it is today. I don't see how we could be expected to accomplish much in a short time at Lincoln University. Of course, it seems to me if we should attempt to establish a law school at Lincoln next fall, our efforts will be pitiful," adding that Gaines's attendance at the University of Missouri would result, "'in steps being taken rapidly toward making Lincoln a real school and toward setting up a law department.'"[86] This, of course, is distant from the position that the admission of Gaines would lead to permanent desegregation of the University of Missouri. The *Post-Dispatch* ran the same story. The impression left by the story is that the decision was a chance to improve and establish new programs at Lincoln University rather than a path toward permanent desegregation of the University of Missouri.[87]

In the *Globe-Democrat*'s coverage of the decision, attorney Sidney Redmond added weight to the notion that Gaines would attend the University
of Missouri: "S. R. Redmond, St. Louis, chief attorney for Gaines, also expressed pleasure at the verdict and said Gaines probably will enter Missouri next September."[88] The *Globe-Democrat* addressed long-term implications
and concerns some white readers might have had about the *Gaines* decision.
For instance, the *Globe Democrat* reported: "Emmet T. Carter, attorney for
the Board of Education, said last night, in his opinion, the question of whether Negro students could attend the white public schools in St. Louis could
not arise as a result of the Supreme Court decision in the case of Missouri
University. 'We furnish the Negro students with all of the facilities of education the white students have,' Carter said, 'and as I see it, this question could
not arise in reference to the public schools.'"[89]

The potential impact of *Gaines* on developments at Lincoln University was
front-page news for the *Jefferson City Daily Capital News*. The headline read,
"Class in Law May Be Added at Lincoln U." and "Follows Ruling M.U. Must
Enroll Negro." The reporting identified urgency and a need for immediate
action. The first line read, "Unless Missouri acts quickly to add a law course
to the curriculum of Lincoln University, a precedent of 99 years standing is
likely to be broken by admission of a Negro student to the University of Missouri." The article offered no other options than the creation of a law school at
Lincoln. Lincoln University officials and Gaines's attorney Henry Espy were
quoted, but none suggested that Gaines might actually attend the University of Missouri. Instead, the article offered the familiar quote of Joseph Mc-
Lemore's referring to the decision as "a step toward democracy for a minority
group," and his comment about "steps being taken rapidly toward making
Lincoln a real school and toward setting up a law department."[90]

The hometown *Columbia Daily Tribune* took a rather negative view of the
Gaines decision, with two front-page stories. The first, in the upper right
corner, reported the Supreme Court's decision, with a section prominently
noting "Two Justices Dissent" and with the word *equality* consistently placed
within quotation marks.[91] The second article, in the center of the page, reported the university's response to the decision. Though university officials
refused to comment, the *Columbia Daily Tribune* explored the possibilities
suggested by Justice McReynolds: "The high court's decision, however, apparently left two ways open for the state to avoid offering legal education to
white and Negro students in the same class rooms. One, rather obviously,

would be abandonment of the law school altogether. Where would be equality of opportunity for whites and Negroes if there were no opportunity at all? The other alternative would be for the state to immediately establish a school of law at Lincoln University at Jefferson City." The newspaper was dismissive of this option, asserting in negative tones that African Americans would not be content with such a solution:

> Establishment of a law school in Lincoln University, however, would probably serve only as a stop-gap in the campaign of Negroes for admission to the university here. At the same time Gaines was applying for admission to the law school to start the present litigation, another Negro sought to enter the school of journalism, another field in which professional education is not offered in Lincoln university. Presumably negro organizations which have backed Gaines' suit will shift their attacks to other professional divisions of the university until Negroes are admitted to all of them.[92]

The *Columbia Daily Tribune* also addressed the assumed distress of white students troubled by the prospect of an integrated M.U. The story contained this speculation about the student body and what it might be facing: "For the proportion of it that has a southern background, the announcement that Negroes might be admitted here was no small shock. On the other hand, since the state schools of all the surrounding states except Oklahoma and Arkansas already admit Negroes, *there would be no place for the Missouri student to turn*, unless they should choose to enter a private school which does not permit Negroes to enroll."[93]

A follow-up story published in the *Tribune* the next day reported that the Lincoln Board of Curators was already at work on a plan to create a law school at Lincoln University. The story noted, "Prospects of obtaining such a school were materially enhanced, Negro educational leaders believe, by yesterday's United States supreme court ruling that Negroes must be provided 'equal' educational opportunities within the state of Missouri."[94] Yet another high-profile celebrity scandal also made front-page headlines, even in the town potentially most affected by the *Gaines* decision. The headline opposite the Lincoln University story read, "Ruth Etting Tells Jury How Ex-Husband Shot Pianist in Musician's Hollywood Home." Again entertainment news struggled with equal protection for the news spotlight, "Torch Singer Ruth Etting, calling herself 'Nutsy' in a telegram to Pianist Myrl Alderman, faced cross-examination today on her accusation Martin (the Gimp) Snyder shot Alderman at the musician's Hollywood home last October."[95]

America's sweetheart of song, Ruth Etting, and Lincoln University continued to share the front-page of the *Columbia Daily Tribune* throughout the week. On December 17, the *Tribune* reported that Lincoln curators had "discussed informally today the decision of the United States supreme court in the Lloyd L. Gaines case but agreed to take no action until further study of the matter." The story also contained this observation: "Comment following the decision indicated widespread agreement that the situation should be met by establishment of a law school at Lincoln University, the state's institution of higher education for Negroes here, rather than through altering Missouri's policy of separation of the white and Negro races in schools."[96] Use of the term *situation,* as well as the general perspective of the *Tribune's* coverage, suggests a temporary problem to be resolved and forgotten, rather than what the black press saw as a decision of sweeping importance that would forever alter the landscape of racial politics. Featured two columns to the right was a story about Martin (The Gimp) Snyder, ex-husband of Ruth Etting on the witness stand.[97]

The *Columbia Missourian* reported the Supreme Court's decision in a more positive light, with a headline that was a relatively unique combination of optimism and realism: "U.S. Supreme Court Rules M.U. Must Admit Negro Till Lincoln U. Gets Law School." The main story in the *Missourian* consisted largely of quotes from Chief Justice Hughes's majority opinion, with a sidebar devoted to major points from the dissenting opinion of Justices McReynolds and Butler.[98] A third item, "Gaines Refused Admission in 1936," reiterated Gaines's legal claims and portrayed him as a reasonable man denied at every turn.[99]

In a fourth article, the *Missourian* reported that legislators at the General Assembly in Jefferson City were preparing to create a black law school at Lincoln University.

> Observers here were unanimous in forecasting that the next Legislature would provide law courses at Lincoln University, state supported school for Negroes here. . . . A school of law or law courses will be instituted at Lincoln probably before the next semester opens at Columbia, a responsible official said. He pointed out that since Missouri became a state, separate schools have been provided for whites and Negroes and that there was little chance for deviation from that course which is more than 100 years old.

The story also offered several statements suggesting that Gaines would be uncomfortable attending the University of Missouri. For instance, Albert Heckel, the University of Missouri dean of men, was quoted, "I don't think he would be very happy here, but I am certain the faculty would show no resentment," and it was reported, "Members of both legal fraternities, Phi Delta Phi and Delta Theta Phi also expressed the view that Gaines would be 'unhappy' at Missouri. Law students once threatened a walkout if Gaines were admitted." The remainder of the news item reiterated the state supreme court's decision in *Gaines,* with a particular emphasis on the elements supporting separate education for blacks and whites. [100]

As has already been noted, mainstream (white) news coverage on *Gaines* was driven by wire service content. Few news organizations (the *St. Louis Post-Dispatch, New York Times,* and local papers at early stages of the case being exceptions) produced original content. Originally, the Court's decision was framed as a victory for the NAACP and for black Americans. Earlier stories interpreted the decision to mean that Gaines would be admitted to the University of Missouri. Within days of the announcement of the decision, particularly within Missouri and the South, alternative frames were constructed in the white press. The revised interpretation was that Gaines should not be admitted to MU, and alternative proposals, such as the construction of a new law school at Lincoln University, would be a preferred outcome. Of course, many mainstream papers provided no news coverage of the decision at all. Although Gaines lived in southern Michigan for over a year, newspapers in Detroit, Ann Arbor, and Lansing, gave no report of the *Gaines* decision.[101]

Black press coverage of the *Gaines* decision was initially jubilant but became more tempered as time passed. Original coverage dominated papers in St. Louis and *The Call* in Kansas City. For most newspapers, coverage depended on NAACP press releases as well as American Negro Press content. Black reporters and editors put more original analysis into the impact of the US Supreme Court decision, leading to increasingly divergent interpretations of its long-term impact. The political and social culture of segregation was resistant to change. Optimism gave way to legislative and bureaucratic intransigence.

6

Public Reaction and
Legislative Response

Newspaper reporting provides critical insight into elite opinion about the NAACP legal strategy for ending segregation in higher education and the Supreme Court's decision in *Missouri ex rel. Gaines v. Canada*. The black press generally supported the NAACP's legal agenda. The white, or mainstream, press divided along regional and ideological lines in reporting on the significance of the *Gaines* litigation and the Court's decision. What a newspaper covers serves as one important indication of the general predisposition of its readership,[1] but there is little direct evidence from the 1930s of public perceptions about educational equality in general and the *Gaines* case in particular. There is some information about local reaction to the case among individuals potentially affected by the *Gaines* decision. As indicated by news coverage within a week of the decision, college administrators and legislators began to take action immediately after the Supreme Court's decision. The *Gaines* case was remanded to the Missouri Supreme Court for additional action, and the NAACP attorneys had to return there. The state court, however, took an unusually long time to reconsider the case.[2] The work of Charles Houston, Sidney Redmond, and Lloyd Gaines was far from finished.

Student reaction can be gauged by coverage in campus publications. In fact, an editorial that was itself widely covered in both the mainstream and the black press was from the *Missouri Student*, the weekly student-run newspaper of the University of Missouri. This publication is distinct from the *Columbia Missourian*, the newspaper published by the University of Missouri School of Journalism, which was operated by journalism students for training purposes but supervised by faculty. The *Missouri Student* was prepared for students by students with limited oversight by university officials.[3] Except for the editorial and the opinion pieces it produced, the student newspaper offered little news coverage of *Gaines,* largely due to timing. Many of the developments in the case took place during summers, when the *Student* was not published.[4] The editorial, however, served as a catalyst for public opinion formation after the Supreme Court announced its decision. The editorial sparked innumerable discussions about educational segregation among students and faculty on campus. In addition, the item was reprinted in newspapers across the country, producing additional commentary on segregation.

An exception to the student paper's relative dearth of news coverage came on October 26, 1938, roughly two weeks after the Supreme Court granted Gaines certiorari. A front-page story reported briefly on the status of the case, noting, "Within the next few months the U.S. Supreme Court will hand down a decision in the case of Lloyd Gaines, Negro, vs. S.W. Canada which will determine whether Negroes may be denied admission to the University of Missouri." With no passage in this story indicating how the editorial staff felt about the potential of breaking the color barrier at the university, it briefly presented both sides of the case.[5] The mere appearance of the article may have signaled the views of the new student editor, William Edward (Bill) Macklin, on the case.[6] In the middle of the three-paragraph story appeared the line, "The appeal was granted under the 'equal provisions' clause of the fourteenth amendment," and the final paragraph restated the university's position: "The University lawyers maintain that Lincoln University in Jefferson City provides most courses. They add that a school fund which pays tuition fees at other colleges for students to study courses not included in Lincoln's curriculum does grant equal privileges to Negroes in Missouri."[7]

The *Missouri Student* contained no further coverage of *Gaines* until the US Supreme Court reached its decision. Then the newspaper drew national attention, particularly in the black press, for an item by Macklin, printed on page two of the December 14 edition. The editorial, with its provocative title, appears in its entirety here.

The Inevitable Mr. Gaines

The Supreme Court's decision on Monday may prove to be a pebble dropped into a calm pool. The pool measures nearly a score of states. At least, the total effect of the decision will be realized only as instances come up in the next few years.

A report from the state capitol indicates the legislature may provide a law school for Negroes at Lincoln University. But what about Journalism? What about Engineering? Our University has the best in Journalism. To what extent can the legislature provide equal opportunity in Journalism for the Negro? To what extent can it provide equal protection in education in any of the studies outside of those taught at Lincoln University?

Here, then, we meet the question: Can Missouri provide for the Negro a University of the completeness of the state University? It is apparent the state will employ every trick in its hand to maintain its traditional policy of separation of whites and Negros in schools. At the same time it is fighting an uphill battle that measures as high as all the states who allow the Negro to mix with the white in educational institutions, American tradition of racial equality, and topping it all, the written constitution. The hill is steep, and rugged, and the fight looms as a losing battle.

Of immediate importance to students is the possibility of Gaines occupying a seat in a Missouri University classroom. The law students were convinced Monday that Gaines would be "treated like a dog"—if he entered. Outspoken students said they would not sit by a Negro in class. Stronger voices announced they would leave school, if Gaines were admitted. The logic of the latter statement is ridiculous. Where would they go? The Supreme Court decision holds for the nation: consequently, all southern schools will be forced to allow whites and Negroes to study in the same institution.

In the trigger discussion, one caught the scent of Nazi anti-semitism, saw a race magnified in its role of an underdog. Lincoln University for the Negro. The Ghetto for the Jew. For, wherein is there a basic difference?

The south has come to reconcile with the Yankee; the war that tore them apart gave the Negro equality. The question was settled 75 years ago; the consequences have been long in arriving. While the string is sharp, it will wear off. The Supreme Court decision was inevitable. The University knew when it went beyond the state's boarders to uphold its tradition of racial segregation in education that it had a slim 50 to 1 chance of winning. And now we have the decision.

We who are students will have no say as to what will be done about the Negro attending school, but it is we who will go to school with him. Few will have the money to come, and those who do will come for advanced education and, for the most part, will be a superior Negro.

Our actions in accepting him will define our status as Americans. Our pilgrim, continental, Gettysburg tradition is freedom and racial equality for all. It is our cue to pioneer the nation out of this last frontier of racial prejudice and superstition.[8]

The editorial, a brave statement in support of social progress, spurred many responses from whites both inside and outside the university. A student commentator referred to the editorial as the "first narrative spark to kindle the idle pens of students" and, as a result, "persons throughout the nation have sent letters to the editor."[9] Walter White called it "a fine editorial" and made plans to distribute it along with similar items to editors and opinion leaders.[10] Macklin's editorial was republished or discussed in a number of articles about *Gaines,* particularly by editors in the black press in their own newspapers, including the *Afro-American* and the *New York Amsterdam News.*[11]

Charles Houston likewise praised the editorial in the *Missouri Student,* calling it important. He quoted from the editorial in later arguments before the Missouri Supreme Court, arguments in which he also drew attention to a protest started by Missouri students when the university refused to participate in a track meet in which a black athlete would be competing. Reporting on the case's second hearing before the Missouri Supreme Court, the *Kansas City Call* noted that Houston "read the editorial appearing in the 'Missouri Student' last December in which students expressed their willingness to accept Gaines as a fellow-student. He cited the incident of this spring which Missouri U. students protested against the action of the university officials in refusing to play Wisconsin unless that university's star athlete, a Negro, were left at home." The *Call* noted university counsel's attack on the editorial as irrelevant and came to Macklin's defense. "Mr. Hogsett, the first attorney to speak for the state . . . charged that the editorial in the 'Missouri Student' was written by a non-Missourian." The *Call* suggested the feebleness of such an argument. Macklin had been born in Iowa and raised in Minnesota, but he was, after all, a student at the University of Missouri.[12]

An initial undergraduate response to the editorial appeared in the *Missouri Student* a month later, after students returned from winter break and the newspaper resumed publication. It presented a far less tolerant view. It is reproduced below in its entirety.

Try No Half-way Solution to Gaines Case, Says M.U. Student

To the editor:

After reading your editorial before Christmas, I feel that the other side of the Gaines question should be presented. A number of the native Missourians enrolled here feel that you have missed some of the main objectives to the entrance of a Negro into the University.

A college education is more than the mere sitting in a class room and listening to some professor lecture. It does include, I believe, all of our outside activities which at times loom larger and more important than our class assignments.

It is in this part of our school life that we present our most forceful objection to Negro. Justice Hughes in his opinion concerning the case said that the Negro should have "complete equality in education." Now just what does this phrase mean?

To the native Missourian it means that we must:

1. Associate with the Negro students in school and out.
2. Pledge them to our sororities and fraternities and admit them to our Independent organizations.
3. Number them among our friends for the all night "bull-sessions" and "beer busts."
4. Room with them; lend them our money and clothes; and talk over our vital problems with them.
5. Permit them to cut in on our dates at the SGA dances.[13]
6. Compete with them on equal basis socially and economically as well as scholastically.
8. And finally we are supposed to like it.

My personal opinion is that the Board of Curators should try no half-way solution of this problem. Either it should disband the School of Law and keep him out or welcome him to the University with a big brass band and force the students to treat him in every respect as an equal.

If the latter course is followed and the people of the state of Missouri by the ballot feel that they want to support a State University

under such conditions, then those of us who do not care enough
for an education to abide by the rules had better get out of the University of Missouri."

—Glenn Van Horne[14]

The first letter chosen to represent opposition to Macklin's position is
not particularly well written. It emphasizes social interactions and equality
and dismisses the importance of educational attainment for both blacks and
whites. So objectionable was racial integration to this "native Missourian"
that dropping out of school was preferable to sharing the campus, closing
schools and programs for whites preferable to educational equality for blacks.
Additional letters published over the next several weeks supported both sides
of the controversy, but the student editorial staff maintained independence
and refused to retreat from the position established by Macklin. The editor
affirmed the newspaper's commitment when introducing another angry letter: "The Student stands firm in the previous statement that Negroes should
be admitted to the University. However, we gladly print this letter in opposition to our views."[15]

As early as 1935, Walter White encouraged students such as Oklahoman
and journalism major Charles M. Spencer to mobilize public opinion in favor
of the NAACP. Spencer attended a summer service group course on "national, racial and other problems" in New York. White saw Spencer as a representative of younger Americans "who, in my opinion, give great hope of a
just solution of many of our racial problems."[16] Charles Houston contacted
Spencer for "authentic" information on campus attitudes regarding the admission of Negroes.[17] Spencer, active in student government, responded in
early 1936, "Almost everyone now is informed of the case and has an opinion
concerning the move by Mr. Gaines. Quite a number are sympathetic, but
more are openly hostile. Among the faculty are those who view unbiasedly
the situation of inter-racial education, but they are reluctant to take a position
in the open in support of Mr. Gaines." This was before the curators had voted
to reject Gaines's application, so Spencer may have been a bit melodramatic.[18]

Student opinion regarding the admission of Gaines remained salient and
bitterly divided. Campus discussion about admission of African Americans to
the University of Missouri occurred from the early stages of the litigation on-
ward. After the Supreme Court decision, George Frank Cech, student president of the University of Missouri YMCA, described how "Race prejudice

has come face to face with the unbiased minds in a verbal "free-for-all" on the campus to determine the educational status of the Negro in our state." Legal decisions occurred beyond the university, but Gaines remained on the collective mind of the student body. Cech observed that

> student opinion is still unharnessed and works its way into almost every "bull session" or "jelly" date on campus. There is a noisy group that would use the full power of its vocabulary to keep the Negro out of school; there is a calm group that occasionally mentions its willingness to help make the Negro's stay here a pleasure—if possible; and there is also the middle-of-the-road group that remains indifferent. To say that any group is in the majority or in the minority would be merely expression of personal opinion because no one definitely knows.[19]

Cech perceived that student religious groups were more likely to welcome Gaines to campus.[20] Similarly, Walter White extolled a letter of support from Wendell McKinsey, the chairman of a special committee of the MU Students' Religious Council.[21]

Moreover, according to Cech, students understood the broader consequences of the case. He writes presciently that

> One of the issues being discussed is the far-reaching implications of decision. Will Negroes be able to attend the high schools and grade schools of the white students for courses not offered in their own schools? If the answer is in the affirmative, a rapid summary of the opinion on this tangent of the decision can be clearly stated: either the state establishes a complete duplication of educational facilities for Negroes throughout the state, or it must admit Negroes to the schools hitherto open only to white students. This is elementary reasoning, yet it is essential to understanding of the problem as a whole.

The letters to the editor in the *Missouri Student* likewise seemed to understand this and reflected the broad scope of the debate occurring at universities across the nation.[22]

In the black press, the only positive reports about the university or the State of Missouri were accolades for the author of the *Missouri Student* editorial, which urged Gaines's admission. An article in the *New York Amsterdam News* praised William Macklin, who "courageously tackled two dangerous bogies when he exclaimed, 'In the trigger discussions, one caught the scent of Nazi anti-Semitism, saw a race magnified in its role of an underdog. Lincoln University for the Negro; the Ghetto for the Jew. Wherein lies the basic difference?'"[23] The *Afro-American* also printed a message from the editorial, set off in a separate section from its news coverage of the case.[24] The *Pittsburgh Courier* went further in its praise, reprinting his editorial in its entirety.[25]

It is worth wondering, in today's oversaturated media environment, about the importance of a student editorial in a college newspaper intended for campus readership, but the words of William Macklin[26] expressed a view that was salient to many whites. The time to admit African Americans to the University of Missouri had come. The black press understandably saw this point of view from a young, white opinion leader as a significant and newsworthy event.

On January 9, 1939, Lloyd Gaines spoke to the St. Louis branch of the NAACP about the US Supreme Court's decision made a month earlier. Gaines had returned home from Michigan at the end of 1938, and he was treated as a local hero within the black community. His remarks to the NAACP were interpreted rather differently in the black and the mainstream presses. The white press accounts indicated that Gaines was uncertain about attending the University of Missouri. In the black press, his words were conveyed to reaffirm his full intention to attend the University of Missouri. A few days earlier, the *Kansas City Call* had reported that Gaines "told a *Call* staff member that he intends to remain here until September when he expects to enter the law school of the University of Missouri. Until that time, he hopes to work [in St. Louis]. Gaines expressed his appreciation to the press for the news space given him and his cause."[27] Similarly, the *Argus* featured a front-page photo of Gaines being congratulated by editor Mitchell along with the story about Gaines returning to St. Louis and going immediately to meet with Sidney Redmond, reporting that Gaines "consulted with him regarding his entrance to the University of Missouri next September." The article went on to note that Gaines was excited about attending law school at Missouri: "He was highly pleased with the court's decision, and is happy over the thought that he can attend the law school in his own state. It is understood that Mr. Gaines expects to get work in St. Louis where 'I will be on the ground when the time comes for me to enter the university.'"[28] The story also publicized Gaines's up-coming speech at a meeting of the St. Louis branch of the NAACP.

Because most black newspapers were published weekly, reporters covering Gaines's speech had the opportunity to comment on not only what Gaines had to say, but also on how the white press covered the story. Some articles in the black press were critical of the mainstream press's coverage of Gaines's comments. The controversy involved direct accusations by the black press of misreporting. It was suggested in white newspapers that Gaines had said he favored the opening of a black-only law school over desegregation of the University of Missouri. The response in the black press was insistent that he had said nothing of the sort.

One such story in the white press was published by the *St. Louis Globe-Democrat*. After the speech, the newspaper reported, "Unless a law school is established at Lincoln University, Lloyd Gaines 27-year-old St. Louis Negro, of 3932 West Belle place, announced yesterday he has decided to enter the law school of Missouri University in the fall." The crucial phrase, in the view of critics in the black press, was the "unless" clause. The black press reported no ambivalence on Gaines's part; the *Globe-Democrat* expressed the idea that Gaines would be as satisfied with an alternative, "He said he would be 'hap-py' to enter a law school at Lincoln University, for Negroes, provided one is established there by the State Legislature."[29]

The *Globe-Democrat* went further, quoting what it reported was his re-sponse to the William Macklin editorial in the campus newspaper the *Missou-ri Student:* "Commenting on an editorial in Missouri Student, campus weekly at the university, urging a 'decent reception' for Gaines should he decide to enter the university, the prospective law student declared: 'I can understand their point of view, but I think it would be better if a law school were estab-lished at Lincoln University.'"[30] In comparison to the coverage in many white newspapers, the reporting in the *Globe-Democrat* was generally favorable to-ward Gaines, but even in a newspaper considered forward-thinking, the story was quite different from anything run by the black press.

An Associated Press story, published in newspapers such as the *Joplin News Herald*, reported that Gaines said both what the black press and what the lo-cal white press emphasized. The AP reported, "Lloyd Gaines, St. Louis Ne-gro who carried his fight to enter Missouri university to the United States supreme court and won, said today he is planning to enroll there next fall. At the same time, however, Gaines explained he would prefer to attend Lincoln university, the state-supported Negro school at Jefferson City, if a law school is established there." The AP repeated Gaines's satisfaction with other options as had the *Globe-Democrat*.[31]

The *Pittsburgh Courier* wrote of the controversy with sarcasm evident in the headline, "Gaines Didn't Say It!" The *Courier* went on the offensive, "Oddly enough, neither Gaines nor any of the group present heard such a statement with the exception of the representatives of the white daily press. 'I intend to enter the University of Missouri in the fall,' Gaines asserts, 'I don't see how they could say what I know that I didn't say and which, of my own will and upon the advice of my counsel, I have refrained from saying.'"[32] Without addressing comments in the white newspapers, the *Argus* reported a similar version of his speech. It observed, "At the regular monthly meeting of the local branch of the National Association for Colored People at the Pine Street Y.M.C.A. last Monday Night, Lloyd L. Gaines spoke before a crowded house. He warned his hearers that if they wished to enjoy their full rights as citizens, the fight has just begun. He said that he expected to enter the University of Missouri next September and was now laying plans to that end."[33] This coverage contained no mention of his not attending the University of Missouri.

The speech by Gaines also made news in the *Missouri Student*. Consistent with other mainstream news outlets, the *Student* reported, "Gaines said Monday he would prefer to attend a Law School at Lincoln, if one is established, but would enter the University here in the fall as a second course." However, the same story in the *Missouri Student* is noteworthy for its clear depiction of concern about public relations. Despite the fact that university officials had fought to keep Gaines out, they apparently worried about how the university was perceived from the outside. Passages from the *Missouri Student* make that point clear: "Officials feared that, if Gaines comes, the lead in demonstrations against him would be taken by Columbia residents, 'drug store cowboys,' but would reflect upon University students regardless. Prejudice among Columbians is more outspoken and unanimous than among students."[34] Reflecting a town/gown divide, one concern was that local residents might react more negatively than university students. However, the university officials also clearly worried about the *actual* sentiment of Missouri students, because the main thrust of the *Missouri Student* article was about the suppression of a story in the *College Farmer*, a monthly, student-run publication from the School of Agriculture.

Agriculture students working for the *College Farmer* had conducted a public opinion poll of university students about attitudes toward the admission of Lloyd Gaines and possible desegregation. Dean Merritt Finlay Miller asked that staff postpone publication of the poll results in part because the *Farmer* was "primarily an agricultural magazine." The *Missouri Student* reported,

> Coincident with a public statement by Lloyd C. Gaines in St. Louis Monday came word of suppression, by University authorities, of the College Farmer's Gaines poll. The Gaines poll, conducted mainly by Harry Barger, Farmer associate editor, was "postponed" by requests of Dean F. M. Miller of the College of Agriculture and, it was reported, by President F. A. Middlebush. Dean Miller said he thought it wise not to publish results of the poll which Barger said totaled 3,950 student votes, because they might "aggravate the present situation." . . . The College Farmer's poll, it was learned, showed a rather overwhelming student opposition to his entrance into the University.[35]

Reporting in the *Missouri Student* and the *College Farmer* demonstrates the thin line university officials were trying to walk with regard to *Gaines* and integration. They did not want to admit Gaines (nor other black students), and they feared the turmoil having Gaines on campus would bring, but they also cared what the rest of the world thought of the University of Missouri. The poll results were never published in the *College Farmer*. Associate editor Harry Barger received financial offers for a story on poll results from other state papers, but administrators apparently quashed the attempt to publish elsewhere.[36] One final mention of the findings of the poll in the *College Farmer* itself was this short statement at the end of the January 1939 issue. The column "With the Editor . . . " read, "We were sorry to disappoint readers by not publishing student opinion on the negro question. College Farmer representatives do, however, owe an apology to University authorities for conducting the poll without permission."[37] In a companion essay, the *College Farmer* noted Dean Miller and President Middlebush had given permission to publish the poll results "with no coloring of editorial matter such as the 'Student' reporters used in a story with the hues of a rainbow." The original plan had been for a feature article on the "negro situation," but concerns about influencing legislative activity or public opinion caused them to pull the results. "We feel the controversy should receive no aggravation whatever from our publication or our findings."[38] The two student publications, however, were exceptions to the mainstream press, including the university-published *Columbia Missourian*, which made no attempt to gauge or engage public opinion on the issue.[39] University administration quelled efforts for open discussion on issues pertaining to educational segregation.

African Americans living in Columbia had strong interests and opinions regarding the *Gaines* litigation and pending desegregation of the University of Missouri. As early as the initial trial in Columbia, Houston remarked on public discussion about the case. He claimed, "Several spectators in the court room were heard to comment on the unfairness of using tax money, which Negroes help to pay, to run the University of Missouri, and then take more tax money to pay lawyers to keep Negroes out of the University which they help to support." [40] In 1938, after the state court decisions but before final disposition by the US Supreme Court, sociology graduate student Audrey Kittel conducted master's thesis research on the black community in the city. When interviewing black Columbians regarding racial attitudes, Kittel noted that the case of Lloyd Gaines "was frequently brought into the conversation as a means of getting an expression of opinion on race relations."[41] Black residents of Columbia had strong opinions, and few were unfamiliar with the case.[42]

Black professionals fervently favored Gaines's admission to the University of Missouri. Kittel offers two representative comments. "Of course there is no reason to exclude him except prejudice. They talk a lot about the dangers, but I don't think there would be any trouble at all if handled properly." "I used to live in Chicago where Negroes have their rights—at least more than they do here. The argument that Lincoln University offers the same opportunities as the State University is absurd. Actually, it is inferior in every way. But any segregated school is bound to be inferior because they will always discriminate in funds." The opinions of black workers were divided, and Kittel shared three. "Well, if they give him money to go somewhere else, that's O.K. He don't havta go here." "I don't think he should try it. It's too dangerous. I know he probably would get along all right, but I wouldn't want my son to take a chance like that." "Lloyd Gaines should never have tried to get in here. They may get in in Maryland, and they may get in in Tennessee, but he'll never get in in Missouri." Among black Columbians overall, Kittel found "attitudes of resentment or mere submissiveness." With some, she noted, "it was impossible even to discuss race relations. They simply accepted segregation as part of the scheme of things and never thought of anything different."[43] Kittel found this passive acceptance limited to older Columbians and sensed that younger generations were no longer satisfied with the status quo. While some rejected "stirring up trouble," professional and younger African Americans were optimistic that race relations would improve.[44]

The tolerance of segregation as an acceptable state of affairs was not limited to those directly affected. The *New York Times* heralded the Supreme Court's opinion in *Gaines* when first announced. In continuing coverage of the decision a week later, the *Times* featured a story about how southern states prepared to deal with the decision. "Southern college and university presidents and state officials are holding hurried conferences with a view to appraising the situation. There is virtual unanimity among them, and a good many Negro leaders agree, that maintenance of separate institutions for Negroes should be the general policy, rather than admission of Negroes to graduate and professional schools heretofore attended exclusively by whites." The author was Virginius Dabney, editor of Virginia's *Richmond Times-Dispatch*.[45] Dabney, a distinguished writer as well as a segregationist, won the Pulitzer Prize in 1948 for editorial writing during the previous year.[46] In an Associated Press story published in many newspapers, including the *Baltimore Sun* (where it ran beside, and in contrast to, the paper's positive take on the *Gaines* decision), Dabney was described as "an authority on interracial matters," who "said today the Supreme Court would make it necessary for Virginia either to develop professional and post-graduate courses at the State College for Negroes in Petersburg, at considerable cost, or admit Negroes to white State schools. Dabney said he believed the latter course would injure racial relations."[47]

One implication of Dabney's piece in the *New York Times* was that black leaders were on board with alternative policies that would not integrate the University of Missouri. While some in Missouri and elsewhere agreed, the implication of general approval for such a policy by black leadership is misleading; it was not, for example, even remotely acceptable to the NAACP, which led the legal struggle. Dabney claimed that black leaders were "anxious to avoid stirring up the inter-racial friction" from future admission applications by black students. Instead, Dabney claimed, leaders would allow "white officials, Legislatures and educators an opportunity to provide adequate facilities before forcing a showdown. Few, if any, States can by next September make the necessary adjustments required to provide separate but 'equal' instruction for Negroes."[48] A second story, published on the same page, reported the expected Missouri reaction in benign terms. While subsequent reporting in black newspapers would report the cost to the state for maintaining separate educational facilities as extreme and unnecessary, the tone of the *Times* story is one which implies the cost of black-only law school is comparatively modest.[49] The story concluded with a report of Gaines's future plans that was similar to that in many other newspapers but different from the *Times'* initial reporting: "Gaines, now employed outside the state, says he is uncertain whether he will take a law course now that it is offered to him."[50]

The responses of the University of Missouri and the state legislature were uncertain as well. As soon as the US Supreme Court refused to rehear arguments for its decision, establishment leaders considered the options available to them. The University of Missouri Board of Curators met to decide "whether they will throw the doors of the university open to Negroes in those divisions of the institutions which are not duplicated for Negroes at Lincoln University at Jefferson City, or whether they will urge the legislature to expand the educational facilities of the Jefferson City institution."[51] Newspapers across the state recognized this "serious dilemma upon states practicing race separation."[52] The Lincoln Board of Curators also met, and a brief Associated Press item published in newspapers such as the *Joplin Globe* and the *Moberly Monitor-Index and Democrat* reported the curators would take no action. President Joseph McLemore, according to the report, "said no recommendation would be made to the legislature which convenes in January until Gov. Lloyd C. Stark's advice had been sought and until the board has 'had an opportunity to see the many implications that are involved in the decision.'"[53]

The legislature, and presumably the governor, would not wait. Before the legislative session opened in January 1939, efforts were underway to create an alternative to desegregation of the law school. Representative John D. Taylor, Democrat from Keytesville and chairman of the House Appropriations Committee,[54] announced that he would sponsor a bill to grant Lincoln University the authority to set up graduate and professional programs. House Bill 195, more commonly known as the Taylor Bill, would do just that. The state General Assembly seemed ready to act with uncharacteristic swiftness.

The US Supreme Court remanded the *Gaines* case back to the state, and the NAACP attorneys were concerned about the delay before the Missouri Supreme Court would reconsider it. Houston wrote to Redmond asking about state procedure for the rehearing. "What is the Supreme Court going to do? I understand that it is going to write a new opinion. Will we have the chance to argue the case again or will the opinion just be cooked up and sent down?" Redmond responded that the case was set on the state Supreme Court's May docket. This seemed an unusually lengthy delay. Redmond related,

> I talked with a lawyer here who has had considerable experience along this line and he stated that none of his cases had ever been held up this long and suggested it would be advisable to go up and talk to the chief justice about it. There are two explanations to this action one is that they want to keep Negroes out of the summer school at the University of Missouri as Lincoln University will not have begun about that time and the other is that they want the opinion to consider laws that will be enacted in the present session of the legislature.

The concern was that the Taylor Bill, or similar legislation, would be enacted to thwart the federal court's ruling on equal protection. Redmond suggested another tactic, "What about filing a suit in the federal court on behalf of some other student?"[55]

The press recognized the pending *Gaines* litigation as the motivation for the proposed legislation. The purpose of the Taylor Bill was to avoid desegregation of the flagship university, and all parties knew this. An AP story on educational equality for Negroes acknowledged in the first line that the bill offered "an alternate to admitting Negroes to the Columbia school."[56] The US Supreme Court had "dealt what appeared to be a death blow" to segregation, and the bill was intended to resurrect it.[57] The *Kansas City Star*, for instance, linked developments in the *Gaines* case to legislative action. The focus of the article was the introduction of HB 195, the Taylor Bill, complete with an emergency clause to make it effective immediately on gubernatorial approval. Representative Taylor expressed belief that "his bill would meet all the objections in the United States supreme court opinion as it permits the Negro school to meet University of Missouri standards in all departments." The *Star* also noted that the university registrar "refused admission to a Kansas City Negro girl who applied for admission to the school of journalism."[58]

University officials justified the rejection "on the grounds formal notification of the Gaines decision had not reached them."[59] An item by the United Press went further, indicating that since a decision would need to be written after the May term, "it will probably be another year before the new opinion comes down that may open the University to Negroes."[60]

The bill provided no appropriations for any new programs at Lincoln. The initial *Gaines* decision before the Missouri Supreme Court, in a section not overruled in the US Supreme Court's decision, declared that legislative creation and appropriations had to be in separate bills under the state Constitution. In section 9622, the Taylor bill also specifically allowed for out-of-state tuition scholarships for programs not offered by Lincoln, although the US Supreme Court clearly declared this as a violation of equal protection. In addition, the bill did not require Lincoln University to create the law school or other postgraduate programs in Jefferson City. The assumption had always been that programs would be situated at or near the Lincoln campus in the capital, but the bill allowed schools to be established anywhere within the state.

The Taylor Bill advanced through the General Assembly quickly. In the House of Representatives, Democrats, who held the majority, lined up to support the bill as Republicans generally opposed it. During preliminary debate on the bill, in a process known as perfection, Representative O. B. Whitaker, a Republican from Hickory County, spoke against the bill. His inflammatory remarks on the floor, according to the *Columbia Daily Tribune*, were "'I am opposed to denying to colored people the right to attend the state university when we admit Japs who may some day come back to slaughter our American boys!'"[61] The black press correctly interpreted Whitaker's comments as supportive of desegregation and equality.[62] Not all Republicans agreed with Whitaker. Representative Murray was quoted as saying, "I believe Negroes should have instructors of their own race: if they want equality, let them get it at Lincoln U." The *Tribune* emphasized the reaction to Whitaker's statement from Democrats, and it emphasized shock at support for African American rights. For instance, Democratic Representative Claude Arnold said, "It makes my blood boil to see a political issue made of a problem of this kind by these demagogic remarks." Representative Guy Abbey, another Democrat, spoke with incredulity about Whitaker's advocacy, "I never expected to hear any member of this house support the doctrine of racial equality."[63]

Taylor defended his bill with questionable claims. "Not one-half of one per cent of the native-born Missouri Negroes want to go to the state university,"

Taylor claimed. "They want to raise the standards of Lincoln U. to make it a really fine institution, and that is what my bill seeks to do." Of Gaines and the NAACP, Taylor's words were factually inaccurate but echoed those of the university's attorneys in court: "The Negroes who are trying to get into Missouri University have been sent here from outside of the state by an organization which wants social equality."[64] While the *Columbia Tribune* offered an overwhelmingly positive endorsement of the bill, the *St. Louis Post-Dispatch* characterized debate on the bill "as designed to circumvent the United States Supreme Court decision in the Lloyd L. Gaines case." Though the bill would direct "the Board of Curators of Lincoln University to establish any new department necessary to provide Negroes with the opportunity for training up to the standards of the State University," the *Post-Dispatch* reported, "there is no pretense among the sponsors of the bill of an intention to provide at Lincoln the full facilities had by students at the State University in Columbia, they believe that it will meet the decision of the Supreme Court." Taylor's objectives with his legislation were revealed, as far as the paper was concerned. "Though not directly making the assertion, Taylor intimated he was of the opinion that the efforts to obtain admission for Negro students at the State university were in furtherance of a plan to force recognition of race equality, rather than merely to obtain educational advantages. 'Negro agitators have been transported into Missouri to arouse this issue,' Taylor said." His bill, the story suggested, was Taylor's way of defeating the agitators.[65]

The Taylor Bill passed the House of Representatives 102–19 before opposing interests could organize. Joseph McLemore, the recent president of Lincoln's board, black St. Louis lawyer, and notable Democrat, wrote an impassioned letter to Senator Michael Kinney urging that the senate quash the bill.

> There cannot be the slightest doubt as to the intention of this bill. It proposes to prevent Missouri Negroes from entering Missouri University by setting up at Lincoln some fashion of graduate work. By what stretch of the imagination can this bill be expected to measure up to the mandate of the Supreme Court? Does the author of this bill think for one moment that there can be established at Lincoln a school of law by next fall when Gaines will be ready to begin his law course?

McLemore points out the absurdity of the alleged equality of institutions, that "with six months time and two hundred thousand dollars, there can be

produced at Lincoln University what it took seventy five years to produce at
Missouri University. What manner of SUPER PEOPLE does he think Missouri Negroes are?"[66] McLemore outlined a host of problems with the bill.
The cost, and resulting tax burden, would be enormous; costs would grow,
particularly as new graduate programs such as medicine and engineering were
added each time one black application was received; it continued the unconstitutional provision of out-of-state tuition scholarships for nonexisting programs; equivalence to existing MU programs would be impossible to achieve,
particularly for prestigious programs like the school of journalism; it was undemocratic; and, comparing the state government's reaction to Hitler's treatment of the Jews in Europe, it was racist.[67]

To McLemore, the Taylor Bill was an "insult to the two hundred thousand
Negroes who make up a substantial part of Missouri's citizenry. And it is an
insult because persons of all creeds, races and even foreign lands are made
welcome at the University of Missouri."[68] McLemore was, himself, a trailblazer in racial equality, a graduate of Howard University Law School and winner
of the Democratic primary for Congress in 1928, making him what *Time* described as "the first negro in a border state or southern state to be nominated
for Congress by the Democratic Party," so it is difficult to know for certain
how he really felt about what would, or should, happen next.[69] Kinney was a
veteran legislator who had represented St. Louis in the Missouri General Assembly since 1912, and he would go on to become the longest-serving legislator in American state legislative history.[70] He was an influential and cagey
politician who knew how to represent his district and how to succeed in the
legislative process. McLemore complimented Kinney on continuing support
for blacks in St. Louis, particularly, echoing Missouri's evasion of harsher
forms of segregation from *Plessy*, for the "the bill many years ago to have separate railroad coaches in Missouri, which . . . you did so much to defeat."[71]

Walter White saw McLemore's letter to Kinney and thought it was "su-
perb." He found the letter "so uncompromising and so unequivocal that I am
taking the liberty of asking [NAACP correspondent] George Murphy [Jr.] to
send a story out on it in our press releases this week."[72] The press release denounced the "determined effort on the part of the Missouri state legislature to
get around the recent U.S. Supreme Court decision which opened the doors
of the University of Missouri to Negroes," and a number of black newspapers
picked up the story.[73] Thurgood Marshall drafted and White signed a letter to

Senator George Whitlow, chair of the Senate University and School of Mines Committee, protesting the Taylor Bill.[74] Large delegations from both Kansas City and St. Louis arrived in Jefferson City to oppose the Taylor Bill during the committee deliberations.[75] The primary arguments presented were that the bill was a restatement of the current law that had failed to bring Lincoln up to parity with the University of Missouri since 1921 and had been decreed inadequate by the US Supreme Court.[76] In a related hearing before the state House Appropriations Committee, *St. Louis American* journalist Nathaniel A. Sweets testified, "'We don't need new courses at Lincoln now that the U.S. Supreme Court has ordered the University of Missouri to admit Negroes. Give us good undergraduate work and we can take our special courses at Columbia (U of Mo).'"[77]

The unity in opposition to the Taylor Bill covered cracks in the single-minded purpose of the NAACP strategy. Redmond, Houston, and the Howard University cohort in St. Louis wanted to pursue the *Gaines* case further, but they needed additional support. Roy Wilkins and the Kansas City branch wished to pursue a different agenda. As noted earlier, Wilkins had ties to the region and to Kansas City's *Call.* Kansas City resident Lucile Bluford had worked for the *Call* as well as the *Atlanta Daily World.* Bluford had earned an undergraduate degree in journalism from the University of Kansas, and she applied for the graduate program in journalism at the University of Missouri in January 1939, shortly after the US Supreme Court's decision. Inspired by *Gaines,* she sent her application and requested her transcripts.[78] University registrar S. W. Canada accepted her application, but he asked her to pick up an enrollment permission form because of the brief time before the beginning of the semester.[79]

When Bluford arrived on January 30 to pick up her form, she was escorted out of line and taken to Canada's office. He read a prepared statement from the University of Missouri Board of Curators: since the Gaines case was "still pending in the Supreme Court of Missouri for further consideration," she could not be admitted.[80] It was her application, rejected by S. W. Canada, to which newspaper journalists and politicians referred while the final stages of the *Gaines* decision languished.

Even as Houston, Redmond, and Espy neared the end of the litigation on behalf of Lloyd Gaines, the focus within the state began to shift westward. D. A. Holmes, longtime pastor of Kansas City's Paseo Baptist Church, met with Columbia residents at the city's black high school for a "vigorous and frank discussion" of events surrounding desegregation efforts. Holmes called *Gaines* "a human problem and not a race problem." He also took regional responsibility for political mobilization efforts. "We in Kansas City, sent Lucille [*sic*] Bluford down to enter the graduate school of the School of Journalism, only to see her denied admittance. We are going to send thirty or forty more down, and we will ask St. Louis to do the same until we gain recognition of rights, and Negroes are allowed to enter graduate and undergraduate schools."[81]

Similarly, Wilkins claimed that the Kansas City Branch "is carrying on a real fight against the bill . . . which would make a mockery of the Gaines decision." Moreover, Wilkins complained to Walter White that "Kansas City would like you to write Sidney Redmond, who they say has been doing little except speaking at banquets and accepting bouquets on the Gaines case," and rally the St. Louis black community. He added that Kansas City members "claim St. Louis did nothing on the House protest while Kansas City sent twenty witnesses (with good arguments) to appear before the committee."[82] White did as Wilkins asked. He wrote Redmond, Houston, and Senator Whitlow, and he spoke with US Senator Bennett Clark in order to influence Governor Lloyd Stark.[83]

On April 9, Marian Anderson sang for a crowd of 75,000 or so spectators outside the Lincoln Memorial after she was denied permission to sing at Constitution Hall in Washington, DC, on account of her race.[84] On April 10, the committee ignored black opposition and approved the Taylor Bill directing Lincoln University to establish separate graduate programs with the intent to deny blacks admission into the University of Missouri on account of race. Kansas City and St. Louis witnesses testified at the committee hearing, and a large number attended,[85] but to no avail. They observed that other states were watching Missouri in order to see how they should respond to the US Supreme Court's decision in *Gaines*.[86] Senator Whitlow acknowledged White's letter and wrote that it was reviewed by the full committee, but HB195 was approved and reported to the floor.[87]

On April 19, the senate passed the Taylor Bill with ease, 25–6. There were no changes to the house bill, so it passed the General Assembly. A United Press report noted "There was little senate opposition to the measure, which had no trouble passing the house." Naming the six senators voting against the bill, the article reported, "In the short senate debate there was only a hint of the Negro demand to be permitted to attend the University of Missouri until such a time as Lincoln University professional schools are established on demand, as called for by the bill." The article noted the case of Lucile Bluford, without mentioning her by name.[88] The *Jefferson City Post-Tribune* described it as "an alternative to the admission of negroes at the Columbia institution." In support of the bill, Senator W. B. Whitlow characterized it as "an attempt to iron out the situation created by last December's United States Supreme Court ruling in the Gaines case in keeping with Missouri's traditional policy of separate education for Negroes."[89] The opposition focused on financial considerations, and none used the fiery words along the lines of the debate in the House of Representatives. Senator W. E. Freeland could not "see where this bill will be a solution of the situation."[90] The *Post-Tribune* quoted Senator Michael Kinney at greater length: "'It is impossible to establish complete equality between Lincoln University and the University of Missouri without a staggering financial burden.' He also pointed out that Negroes had already indicated they intend to press their rights to enter the state university under the Gaines decision and 'it will inevitably be some time before the equality which this bill proposes could possibly be achieved.'"[91]

The Taylor Bill was sent to the desk of Missouri Governor Lloyd C. Stark for final disposition. Walter White sent first a telegram to Governor Stark, followed by a longer letter, asking him to veto the Taylor Bill, which he called "a deliberate attempt to evade the United States Constitution as interpreted by the United States Supreme Court in the case against the University of Missouri." White urged Stark to take the correct action. The bill was "not only unconstitutional but a disgrace to the State of Missouri."[92] The Missouri General Assembly acted with "total disregard of the Fourteenth Amendment to the United States Constitution." He implored Stark to do his duty by "refusing to sign an unconstitutional as well as an unjust law." White outlined the basic dilemma, effectively providing a summary statement of Houston's general legal strategy. "Either the attempt will be a mere sham without furnishing equality, or it will prove to be too expensive for the State of Missouri to maintain."[93] White outlined the basic problems with the bill—appropriations and infrastructure for Lincoln would not be enough, the out-of-state scholarships were unconstitutional, and the intent was discriminatory toward African Americans, though they were state residents, voters, and taxpayers.[94] White concluded with a veiled threat that the NAACP would pursue legal action against the state in federal courts if Stark signed the bill.[95] White also wrote to Senator Bennett Clark asking for assistance.[96]

The NAACP also mobilized supporters within the state and across the country. The organization sent out a provocative press release that was picked up by black newspapers, declaring "The decision in the Gaines case threw Missouri into an uproar," adding the legislature's response was unacceptable. "Citizens feel that the Missouri legislature in the Taylor bill has thumbed its nose at the United States supreme court and has told the Negro citizens of the state that they are not to have equality in public education regardless of what the highest court in the land says."[97] The Taylor Bill, "'double crosses' Negro citizens of this state," and the governor was urged to veto it.[98] Mobilization efforts extended further. White telegraphed branch leaders in St. Louis, Kansas City, Springfield, and Macon.[99] Thurgood Marshall wrote a "Memorandum to Branch Officers in Missouri Branches" which included additional information on NAACP objections to the bill. The memo requested leaders to wire to Stark as well as requesting all executive committee leaders to do so. In addition, leaders were pressed to contact "churches, fraternal organizations, labor unions, YMCA, YWCA, social clubs, etc." and ask leaders to send telegrams as individuals and on behalf of their organizations. Marshall pleaded, "You are facing one of the most crucial periods in the history of Negroes' rights in Missouri. We do not want an inferior separate school for Negroes. The only proper thing is to admit them to graduate schools of the University of Missouri. IMMEDIATE ACTION IS IMPERATIVE."[100] Roy Wilkins led a mass meeting at a Kansas City church and declared that if Governor Stark signed the Taylor Bill, the NAACP would sponsor additional litigation.[101]

Governor Stark signed the Taylor Bill on May 3.[102] Henry Espy forwarded Walter White a tiny clipping from the *St. Louis Globe-Democrat*. The short AP item reported that Stark "signed the Taylor bill designed to bring Lincoln University for Negroes [in Jefferson City] up to a par with the University of Missouri and remove the necessity for admitting Negroes to the Columbia institution under the United States Supreme Court Gaines decision."[103] Espy added in his note to White, "I suppose that is about all that we could have expected but nevertheless we protested to the limit of our ability."[104]

The St. Louis branch of the NAACP passed a resolution expressing dissatisfaction with Stark on May 15. The *St. Louis Argus* reprinted the resolution adopted by the St. Louis NAACP chapter in full. Under the headline

"Oppose Gov. Stark's Federal Appointment," the resolution exerted pressure on the Roosevelt administration to not name Stark, a Naval Academy graduate and a former naval officer, as the new Secretary of the Navy.[105] White congratulated Redmond on the St. Louis resolution and suggested further publicity. Redmond responded that releases were sent to the "colored press" and several radio stations made announcements.[106] To Espy, White noted that Stark should lose any support from African Americans if he aspired to future elective office.[107]

Although they probably were unnecessary, White offered encouraging words to Espy, "Don't think, however, that your protests are unavailing. Many times it seems as though standing uncompromisingly for a principle has been a futile business. But always—and I speak from twenty-one years of experience—in the long run it turns out right if one has really stood uncompromisingly for a principle."[108] On the other hand, Espy had also informed White that Sidney Redmond was in Jackson, Mississippi, for a meeting (though he did not tell White) recognizing the contributions of African Americans, in particular, his father, Sidney D. Redmond. White added in his letter to Espy, "I note your statement that Sidney is attending a "Seventy-five Years of Progress" in Mississippi. *What* progress?"[109]

Dissatisfaction was not limited to Governor Stark and the legislature. Even after an appropriation of $200,000 to establish the new law school at Lincoln, some black newspapers criticized the "paper law school" and those who supported it. They included the new curators and Lincoln University's president, Sherman Scruggs. The *Afro-American*, for instance, expressed "some surprise" that "Lincoln University officials did not await further action on the part of the association before accepting the proposal" to set up the program in law. The NAACP planned additional pressure on Lincoln officials, the paper continued. "Advised that President Sherman D. Scruggs and the board of regents had begun preparations for opening a law department in September, Mr. Marshall said the answer must be applications to other departments of the University of Missouri."[110] With understated sarcasm, *Atlanta Daily World* columnist Charles Howard wrote, "To make the Taylor Bill effective, a $200,000 appropriation was provided so that Lincoln University (Negro) might become the equal of University of Missouri (white). Most interesting, however, was that the same legislature appropriated $3,000,000 to the University of Missouri for maintenance and improvements."[111]

Enactment of the Taylor Bill into law pushed the NAACP into further action. During its May 1939 board meeting, the NAACP voted to expand its litigation efforts in Missouri.

> In view of passage by the Missouri Legislature of the Taylor Bill to set up graduate study for Negroes in the state's Negro college, Lincoln University, and thus circumvent the United States Supreme Court decision in the University of Missouri Case, it was the consensus of opinion that the N.A.A.C.P. should handle the case of any qualified colored student who applies and is refused admission by the University of Missouri.[112]

Certainly the NAACP, as well as Houston and Redmond, had encouraged other qualified black Missourians to apply for graduate and professional schools at the State University, but the pressure before had been to encourage a conciliatory resolution of the case concerning Lloyd Gaines.

With passage of the Taylor Bill, it was clear, as it would be in the future decisions of *Brown v. Board of Education*, the legal victory of constitutional principles would be insufficient without a second case ensuring enforcement of that previous decision. Missouri had simply refused to acknowledge the US Supreme Court's decision. As noted in an April NAACP press release, "the mandate of the supreme court containing its official opinion delivered December 12, 1938, has never been acted upon by the Missouri supreme court. The University of Missouri, therefore, has not been officially informed of any change in the situation which existed before the case was brought."[113] The university, as it did in the case of Lucile Bluford, could continue to act as if nothing had changed. Houston and Redmond still were working on this problem.

The hearing before the Missouri Supreme Court was scheduled for May 22, 1939. Before leaving for Jackson, Redmond updated Houston regarding the status of the second appeal to the state Supreme Court: "Espy and I went to Jefferson City Monday and talked with the acting chief justice and the clerk of the Court. It seems that it is the practice to put cases like ours on the docket for argument and there seems to be nothing for us to do except be there." Redmond spoke with one judge he did not identify, who seemed to admit problems with the original decision. Redmond felt those matters were already resolved. To Houston, he confided, "The whole plan is to try to benefit because of the dissenting opinion of the two justices." Redmond advised that no brief needed to be filed.[114]

Charles Houston, however, had no intention of going to court silently or unprepared. He asked Walter White to provide financial support for the trip to St. Louis and a week in Jefferson City.[115] He asked Thurgood Marshall to bring "all legal material" on *Gaines* along with "statistical studies with special reference to the administration of scholarships in Missouri."[116] Houston, no longer paid a salary by the NAACP, seemed weary of distractions from his legal work. He wrote to Marshall of "a telegram from Roy which I did not like the tone of." Wilkins had asked Houston to speak at the Kansas City branch of the NAACP on May 28. Though the source of his dissatisfaction was not entirely clear, Houston complained, "I do not intend to put out my money on any misunderstanding. I am carrying my own expenses, and the expenses of my household and the office, and I do not have any reserve sufficient to wait a long time for misunderstandings to be ironed out." He wrote Wilkins and, as he related to Marshall, "if he thinks I am going to wait around a week losing money to speak to the Kansas City Branch May 28 he has another thought coming."[117] Houston also asked Marshall for any additional editorial comments from the clipping service and reminded him, "don't forget the legal and statistical material."[118]

On May 22, counsel for Lloyd Gaines and the University of Missouri met for a second hearing before the state supreme court in Jefferson City. Redmond wrote to White, "Our appearance in the Supreme Court Monday was treated with more sympathy than we had anticipated." Houston described, "I went in court fully convinced that we were simply to go thru the motions, that the court's mind had already been made up and it was just a question of the formalities of a hearing to make things look regular. During the course of the argument my opinion changed sufficiently to believe now we have an open chance to get the court to order the writ issued." Houston and Redmond were modestly surprised. They had a positive reception from the judges.[119]

Thurgood Marshall, Donald Gaines Murray, and Charles Houston, during litigation against the University of Maryland. From the Library of Congress Prints and Photographs Division.

Lloyd Gaines as a student. From the University of Missouri School of Law Digital Collection.

Walter White, NAACP executive secretary (left), and Charles Houston, NAACP special counsel (right). From the Library of Congress Prints and Photographs Division.

Sidney Redmond (right) with Elmer Mosee and Daisy Lampkin, supporting the NAACP anti-lynching campaign. From the Library of Congress Prints and Photographs Division.

(Left) Silas Woodson Canada, registrar of the University of Missouri, after his retirement in 1946. From *Missouri Alumnus*, June 1967, courtesy of University Archives, University of Missouri.

(Below) Charles Hamilton Houston, NAACP special counsel and lead counsel for Lloyd Gaines, in 1939. From the Library of Congress Prints and Photographs Division.

William Sloan Hogsett, lead counsel for the University of Missouri. From *Dick Fowler, Leaders in Our Town.*

Attorneys Sidney R. Redmond *(center, standing)*, Henry D. Espy *(right center)*, and David Grant *(center, sitting)*, and Colored Clerks Circle organizer Frank Jones *(center left, sitting)*. From the Bennie G. Rodgers Photograph Collection, State Historical Society of Missouri.

Chief Justice Charles Evans Hughes follows US Supreme Court Clerk Charles Crop-ley into House Chambers during celebration of Congressional Sesquicentennial. Dissenting Justice James McReynolds, trailed by Pierce Butler, walks aside Hughes. In the background, Hugo Black looks into the camera. From the Library of Congress Prints and Photographs Division.

Students outside the Lincoln University School of Law in St. Louis. From the Lincoln University Picture Collection, Inman E. Page Library, Jefferson City.

Future NAACP Board Chair Margaret Bush [Wilson] as a student at Lincoln University School of Law. From the Lincoln University Picture Collection, Inman E. Page Library, Jefferson City.

Portrait of Lloyd Gaines by Judge Nathan B. Young, Jr. Son of a Lincoln University President, Ben Young was a Yale-educated lawyer and co-founder of the *St. Louis American* who knew Lloyd Gaines. From the Nathan B. Young Painting Collection, St. Louis University Archives.

7

The Case Returns to Missouri

The US Supreme Court gave Missouri a choice—either admit Gaines to the University of Missouri School of Law or create a separate and substantially equal alternative. Originally, Charles Houston considered the establishment of new black professional schools unlikely. In 1933, he wrote, "No southern state today could, or would, erect a separate law school or medical school for its Negro citizens. The cost is entirely out of reach."[1] The Missouri General Assembly, through the Taylor Bill, gave Lincoln University curators the authority, or more correctly, the mandate, to create a school of law for blacks only. The Taylor Bill was law by the time attorneys returned to argue *Gaines* before the state supreme court, but no appropriations bill had yet passed.

At first, the university's lawyers announced no plans to alter their position, essentially expecting to argue the same points from the first. The expectation, articulated by the attorneys and in the press, was that the hearing was merely "a technical step necessary before the circuit court at Columbia and the University of Missouri receive official notification" of the US Supreme Court decision.[2] Gaines's attorneys filed no brief because they had won the decision in the appeal before the Court. Oral arguments were to commence on a Monday. On the Wednesday before, university counsel suddenly filed a new brief. Houston, Redmond, and Espy had no time to prepare a response, though Houston began working on a brief immediately, and the attorneys received a leave to file a response within ten days of the hearing.[3] Oral arguments were heard by the Missouri Supreme Court sitting en banc on May 22, 1939.

University counsel now made two new claims. First, enactment of House Bill 195, the Taylor Bill, mandated that the Lincoln University Board of

Curators open law courses, and, in fact, open any graduate and profession-al courses upon the demand of a black applicant and that this new mandate fulfilled equal protection of the law. Gaines, according to university counsel, should be required to proceed against Lincoln, not the University of Missou-ri, for law school admission. The US Supreme Court had noted that Lincoln had no law school, but now the "objection can no longer be made." Before, Lincoln could either supply a law school or tuition scholarships, now the re-vised statutes compelled Lincoln to create a law school. University counsel quoted the Hughes opinion that Gaines should be admitted to the universi-ty "in the absence of other proper provision for his legal training within the State," but now such training would be organized. Second, counsel argued that the writ of mandamus was discretionary. Out-of-state tuition scholar-ships were at the option of the (Negro) applicant, not that of public officials. Mandamus could be withheld if its issuance would create confusion or public disorder.[4] Acceptance of either position required the state supreme court to rule against Gaines.

Houston responded to the university counsel's position on both counts. First, he claimed that the US Supreme Court decision applied to existing fa-cilities, not to hypothetical degree programs. In his letter summarizing the proceedings to Walter White, Houston noted that the court raised this ar-gument in questions, before he could. "One of the judges picked up on this point on his own even before I could state it (Judge [Ernest] Gantt), and asked me whether that wasn't the essence of the case." Houston responded af-firmatively and added "it was impossible for the state to establish a law school at Lincoln U. equal to the U. Mo. within two years" because equality, in the state court's first decision, was comparability to public law schools in adja-cent states. All were members of the American Association of Law Schools, and potential membership for Lincoln could not be considered for two years, until December 1941.[5] The *Kansas City Call* reported a similar exchange.[6] Sidney Redmond argued that the Taylor Bill, which required Lincoln to be made the equal of the University of Missouri, was nothing more than a "pa-per change" that had no real impact. The *Cleveland Call* quoted Redmond before the state supreme court as saying: "No problem is settled until settled right. We urge your honors to decide this matter purely on a legal basis, and not on extraneous matters injected by opposing counsel. Negroes have fought this case four years and if necessary will continue on the same legal front four more years and four times four to the end that justice prevails."[7]

Second, on the discretionary nature of mandamus, the judges noted that jurisdiction of mandamus was already taken by the court and it recognized mandamus as a proper remedy. Houston also pointed out that the university's brief "stated (and urged) that Gaines did have a right to mandamus Lincoln U., but argued that he did not have a right to mandamus against U. Mo. I attacked their dual moral standards in urging mandamus against the Negro school, and denying it against the white school." According to reporters at the hearing, Gantt again interrupted to point out the inconsistency of the state's case.[8] Houston also gave another Fourteenth Amendment justification. Although state judicial procedures are generally not reviewed by the US Supreme Court, failing to grant appropriate remedy to Gaines would simply be to deny his constitutional rights of due process.[9]

In oral arguments, according to Houston, the university counsel "were driven to the point of admitting that if no law school is started and ready at Lincoln U. by September that Gaines is entitled to be matriculated at the U. Mo."[10] This was after much protest by former judge Fred Williams, who argued that the court should be required to wait to determine how Lincoln's law school developed. Houston, of course, responded that the court could not wait indefinitely to make a ruling. Moreover, it "would have to remand the case anyway to the lower court even if Lincoln U. did start a law school" unless it wished to conduct its own fact-finding mission, and "no appellate court would go that far on judicial notice." The General Assembly had not yet passed an appropriations bill to fund any courses or programs at Lincoln. Williams assured the court that an appropriations act would be passed within ten days, but judges "asked him whether [they] could speculate on the future. He said no but that by the time the court would write its opinion such a law school would be there."[11]

At this point in his explanation to Walter White, Houston articulated the fundamental point in the case for Lloyd Gaines following the US Supreme Court ruling. He explained this to the several visitors from Kansas City and St. Louis after the hearing but told them that White "would have the last say."[12] Houston noted that "every one here thinks the appropriation will be made because there is a group...which is determined to keep Negroes out of the Univ. at all costs. So," Houston explained, "we are faced with a condition not a theory." He continued by stating that the NAACP was "opposed to segregation, but that if segregation were forced on us we wanted to make it to serve our purposes as far as possible and to make it ultimately defeat

itself." Houston encouraged black applications to all professional and specialized programs at the University of Missouri in order to "demonstrate that
the $200,000 [appropriation] is merely a pittance toward establishing a real
university at Lincoln." He encouraged Missourians to demonstrate that this
comparatively small amount of money should be spent in other ways, such as
improving undergraduate programs. If white leaders demanded separate educational institutions, he said, make them pay for equal ones. The economic
incentives would ultimately bring down segregation. Nevertheless, Houston
asked White, "Now if I did wrong, write out immediately."[13]

Walter White wrote back a gracious letter, acknowledging that "you and
Sidney did a swell job before the Missouri Supreme Court." However, White
also took an unyielding position.

> Now as to the suggested course of action you discussed with the
> Missouri folks. I can understand your desire to see that the greatest
> amount of benefit be secured by the people of Missouri. But it does
> not seem to me that the N.A.A.C.P. should do anything but stick
> without compromise to the principles we are organized to advance.
> In the Missouri situation the issue is clear. The United States Su-
> preme Court has said that Missouri must provide absolutely equal
> facilities for the two races or admit Gaines to the University of
> Missouri until such time as equal facilities are established.

The legal decision, of course, required "substantially equal" facilities, but
White the idealist wanted a complete victory.

> We greatly fear that advice from an Association representative
> such as you gave may result in splitting of our forces and confu-
> sion. To advise the Missouri people to influence the spending of
> the $200,000, if and when it is appropriated, on undergraduate
> study so that no money will be left to set up a law school may be
> good strategy but we fear that it will result in the dissipation of
> energies instead of keeping their fight aimed at the only goal we
> should aim toward. As you pointed out to the Court, it is impos-
> sible for Missouri to establish an absolutely equal law school with-
> in two years. Our fight, therefore, must be squarely behind and
> solely towards getting Gaines into the University of Missouri in
> September.[14]

The difficulty was that the NAACP was not in a position for an absolutist stance. Funding for legal defense was again threatened, so simultaneously, White asked Marshall if the St. Louis branch would cover half of Houston's expenses.[15]

The editorial staff of the *Kansas City Call* were among the courtroom visitors and characterized the work of Houston and Redmond as a "brilliant plea before state court."[16] Houston had also noted that the university attorneys attacked the NAACP as

> outsiders stiring [*sic*] up trouble, that Gaines was merely a figure-
> head in the Association's campaign for social equality, that Gaines
> was not acting in good faith because he had concealed his race in
> his correspondence with the Univ. for two months in the hope of
> "ambushing" the Univ . . . that Gaines refused to contact Lincoln
> U. when instructed by the U. Mo. to do so, that the Asso. lawyers
> were trying to build a case.

Redmond addressed some of the points in the hearing, in particular, explaining how the NAACP was local. Houston handled others, including that the organization sponsored but did not initiate lawsuits, that the legal team "took great pride" in telling Gaines not to contact Lincoln as the US Supreme Court confirmed they were right, and that "if the U. Mo. was ambushed it [was] because it was wrong, . . . the only ambush Gaines laid was his refusal to compromise his constitutional rights."[17]

The editors of the *Kansas City Call*, who had pronounced Houston and Redmond "brilliant," used no superlatives to describe the oral arguments of the university's attorneys. For example, when asked to address Houston's argument that the Lincoln law school would require accreditation to be considered the equal of the university's law school, the *Call* reported, "Mr. Hogsett faltered a moment, then answered, 'It doesn't make any difference whether a student can wear a badge saying "I'm from an accredited school." What counts is what is in his head.'" Many of Hogsett's comments dealt with the argument that allowing blacks to attend the University of Missouri would cause social unrest. As reported in the *Call*, Hogsett argued, "'The history of race separation runs through 100 years in Missouri. . . . This man [Gaines] is a mere figure head for an institution [NAACP] which is trying to force the mingling of the races and trying to destroy the state's laws and policies.' He accused the NAACP of inciting litigation in a frontal attack on Missouri's policies."[18]

Likewise, Fred Williams argued that the NAACP was "trying to outwit the state of Missouri. 'They are more interested in social equality,' he thundered as he pounded his fist on the speakers' stand, 'than they are in education.'" Charles Houston responded with eloquence, as reported in *The Call*:

> "Any time a Negro stands on his feet as a man, he is accused of ambushing somebody," he said, "We have been accused of pumping Gaines in this case. If aiding a young Negro get his constitutional rights, then we are pumping him." Houston said that it was social equality when he and his associates, Redmond and Espy, sat across the counsel table with the attorneys for the state. "Why is it any more social equality for a Negro boy to sit in the classroom with a white boy while learning to be lawyers than it is to sit at counsel tables together later? We are fighting," Mr. Houston said, "for a single standard of honor and morality before the law."[19]

Indirectly, Charles Houston also reminded the judges of their place in history. He referred to both the Macklin editorial in the *Missouri Student* on "The Inevitable Mr. Gaines" and the December 13 *Baltimore Sun* editorial on Maryland's experience with the admission of Donald Murray to its law school.[20] In his handwritten draft of the conclusion to the brief, Houston wrote:

> Some day, perhaps when present respondents are deceased, their descendants will be ashamed that the respondents raised the excuse of "social equality" as justification for depriving appellant of his constitutional rights. At all events, appellant is neither to be persuaded nor intimidated for exercising his constitutional rights because of such arguments. What appellant seeks is a legal education, as good and as valuable in all respects as the legal education furnished by the state to white students Missourians in the School of Law of the University of Missouri. He is not willing to accept an inferior substitute because he is a Negro. He respectfully asks the full and complete protections of his constitutional rights by this Court.[21]

The Missouri Supreme Court did not issue its opinion until August 1. In the meantime, legislative and bureaucratic activity proceeded briskly. House

Bill 584 passed the General Assembly; Section 3 appropriated $200,000 for Lincoln University for "employing additional teachers and instructors and the purchases of necessary equipment for the purpose of opening new departments" to comply with the Taylor Bill and the newly revised Section 9618 of the Statutes of Missouri. In addition, a resolution of the Lincoln University Board of Curators on June 26 required President Sherman Scruggs "to proceed immediately to set up a Law School to be opened by September 1, 1939."[22] By the time the state supreme court issued its opinion, the state had all the statutory structure of a black-only law school, though the school would not open until September.

The black press expressed skepticism about the ability of the state to create an equivalent black-only law school. For instance, the *Pittsburgh Courier* published a series of items on the Missouri case. The *Courier* alleged that the supreme court was a "Missouri Mule," intent on rewriting its decision, which had been overturned by the US Supreme Court, with the goal of delaying a decision long enough to prevent blacks from applying to the University of Missouri for the fall term. "Some observers are pondering whether or not the State Supreme Court should be cited as being in contempt of the federal court through its failure to carry out the mandates in the *Gaines* case. It looms that further legal action may be needed to speed up the admission of Negroes to the University of Missouri." The same article also suggested that a high level of vigilance should be directed to black leaders in Missouri who might sell out to the state on a deal to create graduate programs at Lincoln University. "Already rumors of 'sell-out' are floating around and certain so-called leaders are being closely watched because most of the Negro citizens of Missouri are anxious that they be given all entitled to under the court's ruling."[23]

Another *Courier* article detailed black opposition to legislation increasing funding for Lincoln University: "Whites continue to attempt to 'duck' High Court ruling."[24] An editorial a week later declared, "The various Southern educational systems are getting JITTERY. . . . They have become almost PANICKY because of the recent decision of the U.S. Supreme Court in the case of Lloyd Gaines versus the University of Missouri demanding equal educational facilities for students of BOTH races in State-supported colleges."[25] Another *Pittsburgh Courier* editorial, entitled "Ducking the Issue," decried the Taylor Bill and attempts to create a black law school at Lincoln University, arguing,

It is amazing to what lengths some of our white people will go to violate the letter and spirit of the law where we are concerned. . . . It takes more than buildings to make graduate schools. The Missouri legislators know this but they hope that this inadequate provision will close Negroes' mouths and enable the state to continue to flout the Federal tribunal. The enlightened Negroes of Missouri and elsewhere will not be satisfied with this makeshift. Missouri Negroes help to maintain the University of Missouri and they have a right to its facilities in acquiring the education they seek.[26]

As the parties awaited a decision from the Missouri Supreme Court, the black press kept up the pressure. In an editorial based on the work of Charles Thompson, professor at Howard University and founder and editor of the *Journal of Negro Education*,[27] the *Chicago Defender* argued,

These opponents of liberty would make the granting of equal educational facilities depend upon the number (arbitrarily fixed, say at ten) of Negro students who might apply for such opportunities; and would arbitrarily fix other conditions, equally invalid under the decision of the Supreme Court. Group rule opens the door to group rule. The individual must demand, as his Creator wishes him to demand, that he be respected for what he is.[28]

The Missouri Supreme Court declared its unanimous decision on August 1.[29] The opinion, written by Judge C. A. Leedy Jr., reversed the court's earlier decision and noted the developments in the state legislature and the board of curators. Leedy also quoted from Houston's brief on behalf of Gaines that the state supreme court was not the appropriate body to consider the equivalence of Lincoln and the University of Missouri law schools; the trial court was. On this point of law, Leedy noted, the court agreed completely with Houston, "In this we think the appellant correct."[30] Repeating the words of Chief Justice Hughes in the Supreme Court's opinion, Leedy added, "it cannot be said that a mere declaration of purpose, still unfulfilled, is enough."[31] The court remanded *Gaines* back to the circuit court in Boone County. "If the facilities at Lincoln University, to be available at the commencement of the next school term, which is in September, are in fact substantially equivalent to those afforded at Missouri University, the writ should be denied; otherwise it must issue, as a denial under those circumstances would amount to an arbitrary exercise of discretion."[32] Attorneys for Lloyd Gaines had won again. The Missouri Supreme Court fully accepted the legal reasoning of Charles Houston.

In press reports, many black newspapers emphasized the opportunity in the Missouri high court's decision for the eventual desegregation of the University of Missouri. While the mainstream press also reported this possibility, the emphasis was different. To readers of newspapers in Kansas City and Baltimore, there was still reason to expect African American students might soon be attending classes at the University of Missouri. The Baltimore *Afro-American* concluded, "The State's highest court, by its opinion, does not order the university to admit Gaines to its law school, but does not shut the university to him."[33] The *Kansas City Call* included lengthy passages from the Missouri high court's decision and suggested the case was not fully resolved and, more important, that Gaines would still end up at the University of Missouri.[34]

The reaction of the white press generally supported the establishment of a separate black law school. The Associated Press story, carried by many mainstream newspapers, described the legal development in these terms: "In a unanimous opinion reflecting a recent ruling of the United States supreme court that Gaines must be allowed to enter the Columbia school unless 'equal' educational opportunities were available elsewhere within the state, the Missouri supreme court directed the Boone county tribunal to decide whether Gaines would be provided such advantages at Lincoln (Negro) University."[35] The *Globe-Democrat* added a sentence to the AP report, making it one of the few mainstream papers to acknowledge that Gaines's lawyers were victorious: "The court's ruling reversed its previous decision denying Gaines admittance to the University of Missouri law school and remanded the Negro's mandamus action to the Boone County Circuit court for re-trial."[36] The United Press story, like that sent out by AP, focused on the black law school to be opened at Lincoln: "The question now rests on whether the new law, dubbed the Taylor Bill . . . brings Lincoln University up to the standards of the University of Missouri at Columbia.[37]

Throughout the state supreme court's reconsideration of the case, the Lincoln University Board of Curators had been active. Curators' meetings were sometimes raucous. Joseph McLemore, the St. Louis attorney and Democratic politico who had written the fiery letter to the governor, had been appointed to the board by Governor Stark. McLemore became president of the board following the annual nomination process in 1937. J. D. Elliff, board president for many years, had testified in the original *Gaines* hearing. Elliff's renewal was simply assumed. But in 1937, McLemore was nominated as an alternative candidate. The vote split along racial lines: the three black curators voted for McLemore; the two white curators, for Elliff. As presiding officer, Elliff could not vote; however, he ruled that "three members of the Board did not constitute a majority." The ruling was appealed, and Elliff admitted defeat, announcing, "By your ballot you have elected Mr. McLemore as President of the Board."[38] But Elliff would not go quietly.

Joseph McLemore became the first black president of the Lincoln University Board of Curators. He immediately had to confront a number of urgent issues, including allegations of staff selling state property for personal profit, suggestions of an inappropriate relationship between the dean of men and the dean of women, and decisions to be made in connection with the university's purchase and improvements of Dalton Vocational School, a trade and technical school for blacks within John D. Taylor's House District.[39] A decision was made to remove Charles Florence as university president, giving him a one-year leave of absence followed by termination.[40] Within a few months, the board had selected Sherman D. Scruggs as Lincoln University president.[41] Scruggs, the former supervisor of elementary schools of the Kansas City, Kansas, school district, would exert strong leadership in the tradition of Nathan B. Young.[42] He would also divide the black community over his efforts to expand Lincoln University at the cost of cooperation with establishment forces to maintain educational desegregation within the state.

Within a week of McLemore's election as board president, Elliff fired off a letter of resignation to Governor Lloyd Stark, complaining of politics, factions, and "illegal organization" within Lincoln University.[43] Stark refused to accept his resignation.[44] Elliff, who had worked with Florence to secure Lincoln's accreditation through the North Central Association of Colleges and Secondary Schools, now contacted colleagues within the organization to initiate an investigation of the university.[45] Again he tried to resign, and again Stark refused to accept it.[46] Elliff, previously a fervent supporter of the academic development of Lincoln, stopped attending curators' meetings. When McLemore reached out to him for help regarding compliance with the North Central Investigating Committee, Elliff responded, "Frankly, Mr. McLemore, I can see no reason for such a conference as you suggest," adding that any problems were for "only the Governor and the Board to solve."[47] Elliff later wrote the curators to "approach this problem from just one point of view, namely, the best interests of the University and the Negro race. Personal prejudices, social and professional pride, political affiliations, and self-betterment must be left out of your considerations." Elliff's solution: the curators should write the governor and resign.[48] However, accreditation and stability were necessary to the state's defense of the quality of this segregated educational institution.

Immediately following the US Supreme Court decision in *Gaines*, the Lincoln Board of Curators considered the implications for the university. Under McLemore's guidance, "delegations from various groups and organizations of the state were present and desired to express to the Board their opinions and points of view with reference to the recent Supreme Court Decision in the Lloyd Gaines Case." Herman Dreer represented a group from St. Louis that "urged the establishment of a state supported university in St. Louis, Missouri, in case Negroes were not admitted to the State University at Columbia."[49] Chester A. Franklin, editor of *The Call* in Kansas City, appearing with Lucile Bluford, presented "the statewide views of the Negroes in respect to the Gaines Decision. He expressed the view that Negroes should take full advantage of the rights and privileges accorded them by the Supreme Court Decision." Presumably, this meant continued pressure for integration of graduate and professional programs at the University of Missouri.

Officers of the General Lincoln University Alumni Association "presented the opinion of the Lincoln University alumni on the Gaines Decision and asked that the Board study the case and listen to opinions before taking steps."[50] Likewise, the president of the Kappa Sigma chapter of Phi Beta Sigma fraternity wrote a letter requesting that "the Board take no action relative to arrangements until such time as all phases in the matter have been carefully weighed." Another letter from fourteen members of the St. Louis Negro Welfare Association (including teacher Zaid D. Lenoir, who had initially encouraged Lloyd Gaines to apply and litigate) argued "unequivocally against a hastily formulated expanding program, not based on scientific inquiry and not having due regard for the future welfare of the Negroes." According to the letter, "It was the unanimous opinion of our body that the most judicious procedure now is to await the further developments and in the meanwhile, to make an effort to arrive at some definite educational policies for Negroes in

Missouri."[51] McLemore and the curators would have no opportunity to act in an official capacity as they would soon be replaced.

Along with passing the Taylor Bill and the supplemental appropriations for Lincoln, the legislature reorganized the Lincoln University Board of Curators. The governor signed House Bill 364, which changed the composition of the board.[52] Under the new statute, the board went from six members appointed concurrently to nine members appointed to staggered terms. Previously, whites and blacks had equal representation; the revised statute created a board with five whites and four blacks, eliminating the ability of black curators like McLemore to take over the board through a strictly racial vote. McLemore remained as president through February 1939, but new appointees were sworn in and replaced the old membership at the board meeting on March 17.[53] At least one new member, Kansas City physician John Edward Perry, had learned of his nomination through a written announcement received a week earlier, and, he said, it was "the first received by the author that such designation was under consideration."[54] The expansion to nine members became effective at the next meeting, where its controversial agenda on the state's defense of segregation was a central issue.[55]

The new nine-member board met on June 26 to consider the "virtual mandate" to create a law school at Lincoln University.[56] The first curators' meeting was "a rather stormy session."[57] A motion was made to "authorize the setting up at Lincoln University of a Law School by September 1, 1939" and to direct President Sherman Scruggs to employ acting Dean William E. Taylor of Howard University Law School, "or a man of equal educational qualifications, and one other instructor."

Several of the black members of the board went on record as protesting the plan. Among their criticisms was concern that such a proposal could violate past or pending court decisions (the Missouri Supreme Court had not officially released a decision in its reconsideration of *Gaines*) and that establishment of a law school should not take preference over creation of other professional programs such as one for journalism. In these two cases, the curators would need more time to evaluate alternatives. J. Edward Perry, a physician and board member from Kansas City, was blunt. He "characterized the setting up of a Law School at Lincoln University at this time as a subterfuge, stating that an effective Law School could not be established and operated at Lincoln University under such a plan." A substitute motion satisfied some complaints, such as removal of the specific identification of the person to be selected as dean. A majority approved the motion to "authorize and direct President Scruggs to proceed immediately to set up a Law School to be opened by September 1, 1939 employing necessary and qualified teachers or instructors and that the setting up of the School be in accordance with the co-operation, suggestions and advices of the representatives of the North Central Association of Colleges and Secondary Schools."[58]

Jefferson City's *Post-Tribune* called the decision "a first step in a legislature-authorized program to bring the institution to an equal educational level with the University of Missouri."[59] The wire services offered similar reports. An Associated Press story, for instance, characterized the decision to open a law school at Lincoln in this way: "Establishment of the law school—first step in a program to bring the Negro university to an educational parity with the University of Missouri at Columbia—was authorized at a meeting of the school's new board of curators."[60] The AP item described the role of the new school in the state's overall strategy against integration: "Attorneys for the university used that legislation as the bed work of their plans against admission of Negroes at the Columbia school. They argued that the act met requirements of the Gaines' decision."[61] NAACP legal counsel disagreed.

When Charles Houston left Howard University to become special counsel for the NAACP, William E. Taylor succeeded him, becoming acting dean of the law school in 1934. Taylor had joined Howard in 1929 and was recognized as a strong supporter of the university. He had encouraged many black lawyers to begin a career there.

Taylor now visited Lincoln University in Jefferson City and met with President Scruggs and some of the curators. A special committee of the board of curators discussed a range of items relevant to the creation of a new law school. Members also visited the University of Missouri School of Law in Columbia for ideas.[62]

William Taylor accepted the deanship and the opportunity to create the nation's first black public law school. His motivation is not clear. Perhaps he wanted to leave the East Coast and return to his midwestern roots. He was educated at the University of Iowa and had practiced law in Iowa and Illinois. Taylor had attended Lincoln University before transferring to Iowa, although he had to retake courses as Lincoln was not then accredited.[63] William Hastie replaced Taylor at Howard on July 1, and this may have encouraged the acting dean to move on. "Perhaps," as noted by Howard legal historian J. Clay Smith Jr., "he saw a greater challenge in becoming the first dean at the newly formed black Lincoln University Law School."[64]

Charles Houston did not have a positive view of William Taylor. He referred to the environment Taylor had created during his deanship at Howard as an "atmosphere of terror and spying," and Houston believed that he then transferred that to the new law school.[65] Taylor did refuse to release the names of students registered at Lincoln's law school, and Gaines's attorneys improvised a method to gather information from students themselves on who attended classes.[66] Houston warned Redmond to be prepared to utilize any Missouri court procedures in order to compel Taylor's actions "because you may be certain that Taylor is neither going to appear himself nor produce any documents voluntarily" at a deposition.[67] Later, during a visit to Taylor's office for the deposition, Houston noticed the paintings in the exterior office. One painting was of George H. Woodson, first president of the National Bar Association, the organization founded to support black lawyers. Houston recognized it as one which "I had got and given to Howard University School of Law. Fortunately, it had my handwriting on it, so I challenged Taylor in front of Scruggs, the lawyers and all, telling him he had my picture and calling attention to my writing. He said he did not know, it must be some mistake, that the picture had hung over his desk for the last four years and he had probably got it mixed up with his things."[68] In his deposition, Houston wrote to Thurgood Marshall, Taylor "Lied as usual."[69]

Others, including Margaret Bush Wilson, remembered William Taylor fondly. She recalled introducing herself to Taylor in his office at the "controversial law school" at the former Poro College and saying "I'll consider going to your law school, if you will provide me with a scholarship to pay for my tuition and fees, and a part-time job to pay for my books and spending money." Wilson continued, "He hardly paused, and said, 'Young lady, if you're bold enough to ask me for it, I'm bold enough to give it to you.'"[70] Wilson become only the second black woman to practice law in Missouri, headed a major law firm in St. Louis, and became president of the national NAACP Board of Directors. Opinions of William Taylor and the legitimacy of the Lincoln University School of Law produced division within the black community in St. Louis as well as in the greater community across the nation. Some, like Wilson, perceived advantages from greater educational opportunity and appreciated his leadership role. Others, and they made up the larger group, saw Taylor as a self-interested promoter whose efforts to advance his personal ambitions impeded achievement of the greater public good—educational parity for blacks and whites.

Funding immediately became an issue for the black law school. The initial appropriation of $200,000 did not appear to be enough to create a brand new law school in such a short time. Lincoln requested an additional appropriation from the General Assembly, but it was denied.[71] Moreover, the governor would not release additional funds. When the Lincoln University Board of Curators met on August 9, one week after the Missouri Supreme Court issued its second opinion, options were few. There were insufficient funds for construction of a new facility, no available space in Jefferson City, and a month remaining before the semester was to begin. Lincoln's curators were divided on whether and how to accomplish the tasks assigned to them by the Missouri legislature. Despite these differences of opinion, they cooperated to establish the new, segregated postgraduate programs.[72] It was difficult to create a new law school with so few resources and in so little time. Curators had considered one remaining alternative, but it went unmentioned in official releases. The board unanimously approved a motion to give the university president discretionary authority to establish the new law school in St. Louis.[73]

St. Louis seemed a reasonable urban location, particularly because of its large African American population and its proximity to two private, white-only law schools with faculty and other resources, those at Washington University and St. Louis University.[74] These justifications were repeated by the American Negro Press and its newspapers, such as the *Atlanta Daily World*. "Dr. Scruggs said there was not enough space at Lincoln university in Jefferson City, and St. Louis offered advantages for students in contact with practicing lawyers and proximity to two white university law schools whose faculty members might be available as part-time lecturers." The story also contained a strong suggestion that it would be difficult for the school to equal the law school at the University of Missouri. The report continued,

> Although Dr. Scruggs said he considered $200,000 ample to begin the law school in a rented building, many other Negro leaders consider the sum inadequate. . . . The institution must have a library of 10,000 volumes, a librarian, four professors and a clerical staff in addition to suitable quarters to be accredited by the American

Association of Law Schools. Failure to win this rating may mean Gaines could force admission to the state university law school.[75]

As evident from the minutes of the Lincoln University Board of Curators meetings, the real reason for relocating to St. Louis was that there was neither sufficient time nor money to establish a law school in Jefferson City, given the legal demands of *Gaines*.[76] There were also questions about the legislative authorization for new construction, but it was a moot point. Buildings could not be raised by September.[77] Given these substantial constraints, President Scruggs, Dean Taylor, and others did a remarkable job of creating a law school from scratch within a matter of months.

The new law school took over space from Poro Beauty College in St. Louis. Poro College, established in 1918, was the center of a hair and beauty products empire owned by Annie Turnbo Malone. She had detected an untapped and potentially lucrative market among African American women. Malone had success selling her special hair treatment door-to-door, and after her products received a positive reaction at the 1904 World's Fair in St. Louis, she established a network of trained assistants who would market her beauty products worldwide. Poro manufactured beauty products for black women, but the company also provided more. Poro offered black women a sense of self-respect and a feeling that their lives could be improved. By the end of World War I, Malone was a multimillionaire, the first African American woman to achieve this status. She was arguably the richest person in Missouri. Poro College served as a cosmetology school and training center for her assistants and as the hub of her activities. The five-story complex contained dormitories, classrooms, a gymnasium, an auditorium, dining rooms, a movie theater, and facilities for manufacturing and sales. Poro colleges were established in other cities as well, but St. Louis was the center of Poro universe. Annie Malone was also a philanthropist, supporting institutions in St. Louis and African Americans throughout the United States. On Herman Dreer's list from the 1950s of the most influential Negro leaders in St. Louis, Annie Malone rated fourth.[78]

A bitter divorce and ongoing legal issues caused Malone to move her business to Chicago in 1930. She hoped that Poro College in St. Louis would remain a cultural center for the black community.[79] However, in 1937, she was forced to sell her St. Louis property, and the Poro College buildings became available for other uses. Annie's former husband, Aaron Malone, had served as a curator on and vice president of the Lincoln board in the late 1920s.[80] Through political and business connections in St. Louis, Scruggs was able to secure Poro College as a location for the new Lincoln University Law School.[81]

The mainstream press characterized the location in St. Louis as necessary to give the school both adequate resources and an adequate student base. According to a United Press story, "Members of the Lincoln board of curators decided to establish the law school in St. Louis because there were at least 30 Negro lawyers here from whom lecturers could be drawn. In addition, they felt that they could obtain the cooperation of the Washington and St. Louis University law schools. About half of Lincoln's students are from St. Louis, another factor in establishing the school here." The story referred to the physical location of the new law school as "a remodeled hair tonic factory." It also reported that Gaines intended to attend the new law school: "Gaines, who until his Supreme Court victory was a civil service employee of Michigan, said he expected to attend the new law school this fall. He returned to St. Louis and members of the National Association for the Advancement of Colored People have raised funds to finance his education." These claims were not quite correct, and there was neither a direct quote from Gaines nor any indication of when he was supposed to have made such a statement. The article ended by repeating some previous reportage on the Supreme Court ruling in *Gaines*.[82]

The general reaction from the black press was that the state's creation of a Lincoln law school, and its insistence on speed, which forced Lincoln's administration to set up in St. Louis, had no purpose other than to circumvent the US Supreme Court's decision in *Gaines v. Canada*. Reporters and editors for black newspapers made the connection clear. Articles described the work necessary to create a new, quality law school from scratch.[83] A *Pittsburgh Courier* editorial offered a pessimistic perspective of the state's actions.

> This is just another stall, an example of how so-called courts of justice work to perpetuate the status quo against which Negroes are in revolt . . . the Missouri supreme court must wait until the obvious is proved before it acts to compel the University of Missouri to admit a taxpayer (who helps support the university) to its law school. Of course this will take a long time to prove because the Lincoln University law school has not even been established and the state

is not hurrying to do so. So we have an elaborate stall: a legal de-
vice which will give the University of Missouri another breathing
spell in which to devise methods to avoid admitting Negro graduate students.[84]

The Lincoln University School of Law opened at the old beauty college
and began its first session on September 20, 1939. Offices and classrooms
took over two floors, and the third floor served as a dormitory.[85] Dean William E. Taylor led a serious effort to establish a legitimate program of legal
studies, and the law school's legitimacy would soon be recognized by national associations.[86] Taylor voiced expectations for a first-year class comprising
about sixty students.[87] When the semester began in September 1939, thirty
students enrolled.[88] State funding, staff, and resources for Lincoln's School of
Law, however, were far lower than that available for the white-only law school
in Columbia.

Public reaction to the establishment of the Lincoln University Law School
was mixed. Certainly it offered educational opportunities otherwise unavailable to black Missourians, and many black students began successful legal ca-
reers there. However, many in the black community considered Lincoln to be
a symbol of segregation and continuing inequity for African Americans. The
Colored Clerks' Circle, a group organized in the early 1930s to picket Wool-
worth's and other businesses until black clerks were hired, protested creation of
the segregated black law school in St. Louis.[89] The St. Louis American initiated
a campaign that used the slogan, "don't spend your money where you can't
work," supporting jobs for blacks as retail clerks, motion-picture operators, at
pharmacy counters, and in other similar positions. The Colored Clerks' Circle
organized protests against the "Jim Crow Law School." Picketing outside Poro
began on the day the law school opened. Protesters picketed daily outside the
building and tried to prevent students from registering. The Cleveland Call,
in a front-page story on the new law school, claimed, "Some applicants last
Wednesday were persuaded not to enroll by the pickets."[90] Police officers were
sent to break up the demonstration. The protests led to the arrests of many, including attorney David Grant and newspaperman Nathaniel Sweets.[91]

How the NAACP should respond to the demonstrations was unclear. Redmond assured the national office that in St. Louis black public opinion about
the new law school was almost universally negative.[92] Roy Wilkins, visiting St.
Louis, urged radical action. Wilkins believed "the great majority opinion [in

St. Louis] is for a militant fight and absolutely against the new law school."
He wrote to Walter White, "The question of the law school has the town
split wide open. To picket or not to picket? Are the young folks right? They
have been trying to get me to make a statement ever since I arrived Wednesday night. The straight story seems to be that Gov. Stark has sent word that
the pickets must be removed at once. They were still there yesterday when I
went by Poro."[93] Wilkins forwarded White an editorial from the *St. Louis Call*
demanding statements regarding the picketers and the law school from the
NAACP and the Mound City Bar Association, as well as immediate action.
"If the pickets are on the wrong track, it is because they follow in the wake
of leaders who stopped fighting in the heat of battle. These young people say
they don't think Negroes should stop fighting just because a desire has been
sidetracked."[94]

A subsequent strident editorial in the *St. Louis Call* equated "the 'Poro' law
school" with the vestiges of slavery. The editorial lashed out at the traditional supporters of segregation, as well as others who received benefits from the
black law school. This list included Governor Stark and state politicians who
had organized the new law school, the Lincoln University Board of Curators
(St. Louis NAACP branch member Frank L. Williams in particular),[95] those
who accepted jobs at the new law school, and the traditional black press. Although praising Lucile Bluford's attempt to register at the state university, the
St. Louis paper condemned the *Kansas City Call* for accepting money to publicize Lincoln University.[96]

Wilkins cautioned White,

> Of course Sidney Redmond's attitude of not fighting has aroused
> these young people and I think the editorial is directed mainly at
> local NAACP heads and others who are regarded as conservatives.
> But the point is that we might do well to study the situation and
> issue a statement of policy which will not sacrifice all the prestige
> we have won in this Gaines fight. Most important, I think, is the
> attitude which Charlie will take when he comes out here in the
> next few days. May I suggest that you get in touch with him and
> have some understanding of what he is going to say and do when
> he arrives? If he should happen to say the wrong thing, we stand
> to lose face. We must come to some understanding with the local
> NAACP people on philosophy and procedure.

Wilkins perceived a lack of consensus within the organizational and the legal ranks, in particular, a division between older and younger attorneys.[97]

Earlier, Houston had written Redmond that the legal case should not be influenced by claims made in the press. "The fact that a lot of newspaper talk is being spread about the separate law school which is being set up does not prove anything. We still do not know, and the public at large does not know, that the reports are true. They do not know the official basis on which the school is run, its program or what not."[98] The NAACP's Committee on Administration unanimously approved a statement on the University of Missouri case emphasizing the need to hold the course on its legal agenda. Thurgood Marshall distributed the policy to state representatives:

> The position of the N.A.A.C.P. is that it is necessary for the trial court to decide whether the law school at Lincoln University satisfies the decision of the United States Supreme Court and the Supreme Court of Missouri. In order to do this, application has been made for the regular hearing of this case upon the mandate as sent down from the Supreme Court of Missouri. This is the usual procedure in court cases which have been appealed.[99]

The publicity department created a longer press release on the NAACP policy statement for national dissemination.[100]

Throughout the semester, the protests organized by the Colored Clerks' Circle continued outside the Poro Building. Coverage in the black press included information from press releases from Lincoln University and from the NAACP and, often, photos of the picketers.[101] The *Cleveland Call* described the Colored Clerks' Circle as "a militant organization that has won several job fights."[102] These protests, designed to put pressure not only on the State of Missouri, but also on students who might consider attending the new law school, continued in St. Louis long after the new law school opened for business.

On January 5, 1940, the Society of American Civil Liberties joined a protest with the Colored Clerks' Circle. As the *Afro-American* reported, "They appeared, according to Frank M. Jones, president and organizer of the Clerks' Circle, 'in protest to the undemocratic procedure and waste of public funds' in establishing a separate law school rather than drop the color bar at the State University."[103] The Society of American Civil Liberties was led by the

Reverend Harold Wilke. A United Church of Christ Minister, Wilke was, for a time, the minister at The Chapel in Columbia. A white, armless man, Wilke remained a civil rights advocate throughout his life, later turning his efforts to the rights of the disabled.[104] Of this protest, Wilke said that students from Lincoln, Washington University, and the University of Missouri participated, repeating the words from Jones, "in protest of the undemocratic procedure and waste of public funds represented by the present law school."[105] The *Atlanta Daily World* also reported that a large number of whites participated in the protest, including students. Frank Jones added

> The Lincoln university law school is a farce . . . and is inferior in every respect to that of the University of Missouri school of law and in no wise does it meet with the decision of the supreme court for equal educational facilities. The results obtained by the school are not enough to pay for the principles relinquished. The Colored Clerks circle will continue its fight that Negroes as American citizens shall receive their rights of equal educational facilities.[106]

An editorial in the *Pittsburgh Courier* lambasted the Lincoln law school and any blacks who might support it. It declared,

> When the United States Supreme Court handed down its decision in the University of Missouri versus Lloyd Gaines case, it struck such a deadening blow at educational discrimination based on color and "race" that the apostles of segregation throughout the South were appalled at the prospect which unfolded. . . . Then some genius who for discreet reasons will perhaps always go unsung and unhonored, at least in public, thought up the jim crow or toy university. . . . Educational Uncle Toms were called in and given their orders which, as usual, they obeyed with alacrity. Suddenly a Law School, trumpeted as equal to the long-established University of Missouri Law School, was set up in an abandoned hair-straightening emporium in St. Louis as an adjunct to Negro state "university," and Negroes were found to solemnly hail it as "de same ting."[107]

As the NAACP university cases proceeded through the courts, the black press noted the changing makeup of the US Supreme Court and suggested it would have a positive influence on the desegregation effort. In late November 1939, for example, the *Afro-American* reported the death of Justice Pierce Butler, one of two dissenters in *Gaines*, describing him as a "consistent voter against colored people where a question of their constitutional rights was concerned."[108] The subtext of the article was that with Butler off the Court, his anti-desegregation vote could be replaced with one more favorable to the advancement of civil rights.

In an editorial published two months later, William N. Jones expressed hope that more changes were coming to the Court during the Roosevelt administration. Former US attorney general Frank Murphy was confirmed to take Butler's seat on the Court. Using language that was at times critical of the Roosevelt administration, Jones still felt that the situation was, on balance, positive for blacks. "While many of the New Deal fiscal and social security policies—especially the lending-spending programs—have not only been ineffective but harmful, the Supreme Court outcome may well be regarded by colored citizens as one of their distinct gains."[109] Describing the changes, Jones wrote, "Ten years ago it would have been questionable whether it would have been worthwhile to take the University of Missouri or a Maryland salary equalization suit into a Federal court. But the composition of the Supreme Court for many years now—thanks to the acts of God and Roosevelt—will be the kind of body to which the average citizen may look as a bulwark against arbitrary and reactionary disregard of his civil rights."[110] With hopeful words to describe a societal shift that would require many more years to reach fruition, Jones concluded, "It will not matter much what the local courts do to thwart justice so long as we have a liberal court of last appeal and the will of a people to fight it out through that body."[111]

Attorneys for Gaines continued to press for a favorable judicial conclusion consistent with the US and Missouri Supreme Court decisions. The key issue at the circuit court hearing would be whether the newly created Lincoln University School of Law was substantially equal to what was offered to white law students at the University of Missouri. Charles Houston preferred waiting to pursue the case on behalf of Gaines until after the segregated law school opened, "Then we can show as a fact, and not a theory, all the detailed inequalities."[112] If the circuit court judge could not find equivalency, the only reasonable legal solution would be to issue a writ of mandamus to compel the University of Missouri to admit Lloyd Gaines. Charles Houston, along with Gaines's other attorneys, Sidney Redmond and Henry Espy, needed evidence, statements on the record from Lincoln law school faculty. Depositions were taken from all four members of the faculty at the new law school in the old Poro building. Charles Houston examined the faculty members. William Hogsett led university counsel, which also included Judge Fred Williams and Ralph E. Murray. Nearly all of the questions at the hearing were directed at Dean William E. Taylor.[113]

Howard University was well represented on the faculty at the opening of the Lincoln Law School, and Houston knew them all. Taylor had been on the faculty at Howard for ten years, and had served as interim dean for the last four years. He hired three Howard Law graduates to fill out the Lincoln faculty: Scovel Richardson, James Claiborne Bush, and Virgil H. Lucas. Even the librarian, Constance Mapp Barbour, was recruited from the Howard Law Library.[114] Lucas and Bush had both been assistants under Taylor. Bush and Richardson were ranked first and second, respectively, in their 1937 graduating class at Howard. Lucas received his degree in 1934, ranked second, and practiced law in St. Louis for five years. Richardson briefly had a law firm in Chicago.[115] With the exception of Taylor, none had teaching experience.[116]

Houston endeavored to show the weaknesses and lack of preparation involved in the arrangement of the Lincoln School of Law. Under intense questioning, Taylor admitted that, although the "total number of persons who made steps toward matriculation was thirty," the correct number of students was "[a]bout nineteen now at the present time." All were first-year students in class during the day; eight of the students were employed in some fashion at the law school.[117] Houston also had Taylor testify on the record that the St. Louis facilities were small, leased, and available for a time "subject to the will of the legislature."[118] Taylor noted that the library contained "upwards of thirteen thousand volumes now."[119] Houston tried to show that the faculty were chosen on the basis of convenience and personal ties rather than proven experience, particularly in the classroom. His efforts to get Taylor to compare qualifications of faculty at the University of Missouri Law School to his own faculty found limited success.[120] Taylor read catalog excerpts, but he testified to a lapse of memory regarding his own school's salaries, courses, and other factors necessary to make comparisons.

Taylor, with Hogsett's prompting on redirect, compared his own experience in organizing Lincoln Law School to Houston's tenure as dean at

Howard University. Taylor pointed out that two members of the Howard faculty, William Hastie and Bernard Jefferson, had been selected before completing degrees at Harvard University School of Law.[121] Thus, Lincoln faculty members were no less experienced than those at Howard. Moreover, under questioning from Hogsett, Taylor took for himself half the credit for improving Howard Law, saying of himself and Houston, "Yes, sir, we were the two men who were selected to qualify the school, to accredit the school." Taylor replied affirmatively when Hogsett asked, "Then, what you and he did for Howard University, in building it up as a law school you are now undertaking to do for Lincoln University?" Hogsett followed by asking, "And you have been through that work once in establishing the Howard School?" Yes, sir," Taylor assured him.[122] Moreover, Houston's argument that Lincoln was inferior was made more difficult because Will Shafroth, representing the American Bar Association, had inspected the Lincoln School of Law on September 28 and found it "now worthy of admission to probationary status among the approved schools of the association."[123]

Overall, Houston thought the hearing went well, writing to Thurgood Marshall that Taylor, taking his deposition in front of faculty and students, "will probably have a few more explanations to make tomorrow."[124] Of his own performance, Houston regretted missing "a marvelous opportunity to hit on the question of whether [Lincoln] was a Negro school, but in the rush I slipped it."[125] Taylor, however, said, "This is a colored school, so in my opinion we ought to have a colored faculty."[126] Counsel for Gaines would need to show for the record in circuit court that the law school at Lincoln was not equivalent to that at the University of Missouri, and this was because of the policy of racial division. University counsel felt Houston was rough on Taylor. Fred Williams objected "to counsel arguing and quarreling with the witness." Houston replied, "I think the witness had been arguing all afternoon." When Williams protested that Taylor "should be treated with the respect he deserves," Houston retorted, "He has been given that respect."[127]

Coverage in the local black press was not always favorable toward the NAACP. The *St. Louis Argus*, an early and strong supporter of the organization's legal agenda, reported: "Dean William E. Taylor occupied the witness stand for more than two hours on Tuesday and amply defended the school. . . . Dean Taylor never faltered any of his answers which were to clarify the procedure of the new law school and to qualify the professors."[128] The front-page story reported that Taylor did a more than adequate job in

defending the new law school and described the rancorous interaction between Taylor and Charles Houston:

> At several times during the direct testimony, Dean Taylor an-
> swered questions of Mr. Houston to similar tactics he, Houston,
> had employed while raising the rating of the Howard University
> Law School. At two or three times Dean Taylor refused to answer
> questions and asked Mr. Houston what he was attempting to ar-
> rive at, and stated that he would give only those answers which he
> thought were relevant. At the end of Dean Taylor's examination,
> Judge Williams entered his objection to the manner in which the
> questioning had been conducted by the plaintiffs to which Attor-
> ney Houston replied that he did not believe the questioning was
> objectionable.[129]

The *Argus* concluded, "Dean Taylor displayed excellent knowledge of law
schools, their requirements and sources of necessary material."[130] It was,
overall, a positive review of Taylor's performance. That is perhaps surprising in a newspaper that had long advocated the integration of the University of Missouri, given that Taylor was dean of a school created to circumvent
desegregation.

Houston, nevertheless, was confident that the final stage of the lawsuit was
progressing properly. However, in his description of the proceedings at Lincoln Law School, Houston acknowledged a potential problem to Marshall.
Although they had not requested his appearance, their plaintiff, Lloyd Gaines,
had not attended the hearing held in his hometown. After the depositions of
Lincoln Law faculty members were taken, Houston wrote to Marshall, "counsel for the University hit us in our tender spot: they asked to take Gaines' deposition, which brought out the fact we do not know where Gaines is."[131]

8

The Mystery of Lloyd Gaines

In August 1939, as he prepared for the circuit court trial, Charles Houston expressed concern about the difficulty in locating Lloyd Gaines. The NAACP attorneys had lost track of him.[1] When Gaines returned to St. Louis after the US Supreme Court decision in December 1938, he was treated like a celebrity. When he spoke at local NAACP events in St. Louis and Kansas City, large crowds gathered to hear him. But before long Gaines drifted out of the limelight and maintained only occasional communication with his attorneys and his family. Outwardly, Houston appeared unconcerned about Gaines's absence, but he encouraged Redmond to find him.[2] The appeals to the US Supreme Court and Missouri Supreme Court did not require Gaines's appearance. Even if he could not reach Gaines immediately, Houston thought that the case could be continued. "We do not have to carry Gaines to Columbia to have him apply. Really we do not have to have Gaines in court at all. It seems to me that all we need is a motion for the writ [of mandamus] to issue."[3]

By September 11, Houston had acknowledged that it seemed Gaines could not be found; nevertheless, he continued to press the case remanded to the circuit court in Boone County. He suggested to Sidney Redmond that he should "telephone the clerk at Columbia to the effect that he has not heard from Gaines whether Gaines can be present by September 15 or 18," and, if the case was delayed further, Houston would postpone his trip. The litigation on behalf of Lucile Bluford and her admission to the University of Missouri School of Journalism was at its early stages. Houston asked that Bluford, with Redmond accompanying her, attempt to register again on September

209

15, and, knowing her efforts would be thwarted, he instructed Redmond to file a case in the circuit court the same afternoon. Then, "Redmond can also straighten out the matter of calendaring the Gaines case while he is in Columbia." Houston would remain in Washington in order to save funds for expenses to be incurred later.[4] Funds to cover legal expenses remained a central concern of the NAACP. Walter White wrote to Redmond, as representative of the St. Louis branch, and Prentis J. Hoffman, the acting president of the Kansas City branch, that money from the Garland Fund was exhausted and more was necessary to pursue the legal agenda in Missouri.[5]

Houston continued to express optimism on the following day, writing in a longer memo on the *Bluford* case,

> We have yet to find Gaines, but whether we find him now or in the middle of the year we will press his case to test out the issues of equality raised by the "new law school". To this end time is not fatal. The more of a record the "new law school" makes for or against itself, the more we reduce the field of speculation and get down to concrete demonstration of inequality and discrimination. We are in for a long fight. Delays are not fatal if we make them serve our ends.[6]

Houston decided against filing a case on behalf of Bluford in September, concerned that speed would replace accuracy. Houston was unwilling to sacrifice his, and the NAACP's, unblemished record on the university cases. He asked Redmond to "use Thursday at Columbia to lay the groundwork for another perfect case."[7] As he organized the depositions to be taken in St. Louis for the Gaines case, Redmond was not as optimistic. "An intensive drive has been made to locate Gaines but to no avail. All our leads have proven groundless."[8]

Depositions in the *Gaines* case were taken at the new Lincoln University School of Law in St. Louis on October 10, and three days later, a new lawsuit against the University of Missouri was filed for Lucile Bluford. She was refused admission for graduate study in journalism in February 1938 and again in September. The *Bluford* litigation filed in October progressed simultaneously with *Gaines*, which allowed Houston, as well as the other lawyers, to travel only once for both cases. Representing Bluford were attorneys Houston, Redmond, Espy, and John A. Davis. The NAACP press release announcing the *Bluford* lawsuit also reminded readers of the organization's legal achievement for Gaines at the US Supreme Court and assured them, "Action in obtaining rehearing of the case is planned by the N.A.A.C.P. in the near future."[9]

Immediately following depositions of the Lincoln Law School faculty, University of Missouri counsel asked Houston, Redmond, and Espy about their last contact with Lloyd Gaines. Houston explains:

> A long discussion developed about when Gaines had last been in touch with us. The last communication from Gaines was received in April (so he said) by Frank Wethers [*sic*], an assistant in the library at Lincoln U. Law School. Wethers could not remember where Gaines was at the time; said Gaines had written him about his frat pin, and he in turn had written to a fellow at Lincoln who has now graduated. The St. Louis Post-Dispatch and Globe-Democrat are starting to look for Gaines. If we do not find him soon we will have to advise the court, because counsel suavely suggested that if we had no client the cause was moot. Counsel told Taylor and Wethers to help us locate Gaines because they want him too. Better send out word in press release this week that no contact with Gaines since spring, that we have been trying to locate him, that his family does not know where he is, and any one knowing his whereabouts will please contact the N.A.A.C.P. No secret.[10]

When the Missouri Supreme Court released its ruling, finding for the university, in December 1937, Gaines was living in Michigan, pursuing a master's degree in economics at the Horace H. Rackham School of Graduate Studies. He had kept in contact with Houston and Redmond during his first two semesters in Ann Arbor, but, by the summer, they no longer maintained an active correspondence. Gaines maintained an irregular correspondence with his older brother George and his mother. By late November 1937, Lloyd complained to George that he "getting kind of tired of Ann Arbor and feel like leaving any minute."[11]

Although Lucile Bluford and others who knew Gaines believed he earned a master's degree in economics at Michigan, he did not.[12] Gaines completed only two semesters of graduate study at the University of Michigan and did not return to his studies.[13] Another student, Heman Sweatt, attended classes at Michigan and lived around the corner from Gaines in Ann Arbor. Sweatt would be a plaintiff in a subsequent, important NAACP test case on educational equality in Texas.[14] Sweatt remembers Gaines at Michigan as a minor celebrity, knowledgeable about and committed to civil rights. Sweatt, however, also found Gaines arrogant and said they were not that close.[15]

In addition to his studies, Gaines held several jobs. In Ann Arbor, he took a number of part-time jobs, including teaching for the local black school in the city and waiting tables.[16] However, he could not cover his expenses, even with tuition paid by the NAACP. Lloyd frequently asked his older brother George, a Pullman porter, for loans that he had difficulty repaying.[17] Gaines seemed sensitive to claims that he spent money attending parties and shows. Lloyd assured his brother that studies and work took almost all his time.[18] He asked Houston and Redmond for financial assistance during the summer of 1937.[19] Gaines seemed to value his graduate education, but he disliked Ann Arbor.[20] Gaines found a job in Lansing, Michigan, working as a WPA clerk on a survey for the state Civil Service Department.[21] It was around this time that Gaines stopped regularly communicating with his family, friends, and the attorneys litigating his case. Because they had not heard from him, his family mistakenly believed, for a while, that Lloyd had been kidnapped.[22] However, Gaines was working in Michigan through the end of 1938, and in 1939, he returned to St. Louis, where he gave the speech before the local NAACP branch.

Some of the information in the press about Gaines's activities was jumbled. He was, according to an incorrect report in the *Kansas City Call*, studying law.[23] By the time of the US Supreme Court's decision in December of 1938, however, the *Call* reported that Gaines had left the University of Michigan. "Gaines was in Michigan when the news of his victory in a three-year fight reached him. He went there to study law at the University of Michigan but now is employed as clerk in the Michigan State Civil Service department at Lansing, Mich."[24] The latter was correct, but, of course, if Gaines had been studying law there would be little justification for continuing the lawsuit against the University of Missouri. In January 1939, the *Afro-American* reported that the NAACP voted to provide Gaines with financial support when he entered the University of Missouri's law school the following fall. Gaines, meanwhile, was reported by the *Afro-American* to be studying at the University of Michigan, working on a master's degree and preparing for law school.[25]

Lloyd Gaines's movements in 1939 are the subject of conflicting reports. In early 1939, Gaines was living and working in St. Louis. His speech in St.

Louis on January 9, 1939 attracted much press attention and adulation. The *Pittsburgh Courier* reported that Gaines returned to live in St. Louis and was given a job at the Careful Cab Company by Benjamin Austin, the owner of the cab company and the leader of the St. Louis Negro Business League. The *Courier* continued,

> Gaines, who had been working in Detroit pending the outcome of the Supreme Court decision, returned to his home town with the expressed desire of being a real Missourian and showing the world that he could make it in Missouri. However, the congratulations didn't keep the old pot boiling nor did it stack up the shekels needed for study. Some few persons had offered to assist him. For that, Gaines was quite grateful but above all, he wanted to work and help himself. . . . And Gaines is out to make good on the job and then make good in law school in his state.[26]

Gaines worked at a gas station in St. Louis. However, he felt overworked and underappreciated during his employment with Benjamin Austin. Gaines found his employer, Austin, disreputable, his business model poor, and his activities corrupt. Gaines found the job "distasteful from the first." He quit this job near the end of February.[27]

Lloyd Gaines left St. Louis and traveled to Kansas City to give a speech at the Centennial Methodist Church to a crowd of over a thousand, an audience rivaling that drawn by Roy Wilkins and Charles Houston.[28] The following day, Gaines spoke to an assembly at Sumner High School in Kansas City, Kansas. He again searched for a job, but he found no employment opportunities in Kansas City and decided to travel to Chicago.[29] Lucile Bluford found his visit inspirational. She remembers that she "accompanied him to the Union Station the night he left for Kansas City and saw him board the train for Chicago." She recalls his plans to spend a few days in Chicago before returning home, although Gaines "never returned to St. Louis as far as his family and his lawyers know."[30]

Gaines left Kansas City on February 27 during a heavy snowstorm and arrived in Chicago on February 28. After visiting a former girlfriend from St. Louis, Eddie Mae Page, and her mother, Nancy Page, he rented a room at the Wabash Street YMCA through March 7. He then moved temporarily to the Alpha Phi Alpha fraternity house, where fraternity brothers loaned him some money. Gaines obtained a temporary job in the South Center Department

Store in Chicago. Gaines arranged to take the Pages out for dinner on March 19, but he did not follow up on the date. A few days later, Eddie Mae Page checked the Alpha House for him, but she was told by the housekeeper that he had been gone for about ten days. The housekeeper told her that one night Gaines left to buy some stamps, but he never returned. He left only a small bag of personal items at the fraternity house.[31] Gaines did not return for the Supreme Court arguments in Jefferson City in May, but there was no need for him to appear.[32]

However, by October 1939, as Houston and Redmond were taking depositions about the quality of the new black law school established in St. Louis, it became clear that something unexpected had happened. Gaines had not been seen by anyone in the NAACP or his family since sometime in the spring of 1939. In its coverage of depositions taken in St. Louis, the *St. Louis Argus* reported,

> Along toward the end of the session the attorneys for the University called for Gaines' deposition and were informed by Attorneys Houston and Redmond that they had received no message from Gaines since March, and that they, along with Gaines' mother, were exhausting every possible means of locating his whereabouts. This situation finds the N.A.A.C.P. attorneys in a very embarrassing situation, for they are presenting a case and cannot produce the client. The opposing attorneys however, offered every means at their disposal in helping to locate the client.[33]

The story in the *Argus* was joined on the front-page by a photo of Gaines, two columns to the right, in the middle of the right-most column, with the headline, "Where Is He?" The caption read: "Principal in the famous Gaines Case who failed to answer when his name was called for taking of depositions at the Lincoln U. Law School Tuesday. The N.A.A.C.P. has been conducting a search for him since last may but without success."[34] The official depositions, however, do not indicate that university attorneys called Gaines or any other witnesses.[35] It is clear, however, that university counsel asked about his status.[36] Houston and Redmond asked that reporters in the black press also inquire about his status.[37]

Newspapers in the black press responded. On October 20, 1939, the *Call* in Kansas City offered extensive coverage of the lawsuit just filed by its own editor, Lucile Bluford, against the University of Missouri for refusing to admit her to graduate school in journalism. In the same issue, the *Kansas City Call* printed a photo of Gaines with a headline spanning the full range of the top of the front-page: "Where is Lloyd Gaines—Have You Seen Him?" The accompanying story reported that Gaines was believed to be in Michigan or Illinois, but that no one who was known to be close to him, including his mother, had seen him in months.[38] On October 21, 1939, the *Afro-American* carried a front-page story headlined "Lloyd Gaines Said to Have Vanished," with the first line, "Lloyd L. Gaines has disappeared!" It reported that his mother, Callie Gaines, had not heard from him since spring and "is said to be frantic with anxiety." Clues as to his whereabouts were few and the *Afro-American* reported, "Somebody at the law school received a post card from Gaines this summer sent from Ypsilanti or Ann Arbor, Mich., but the card has been misplaced and the return address lost. It is believed that Gaines is somewhere in Michigan or Illinois. Mr. Houston has requested the nation's press to help locate Gaines, who started the educational 'rumpus' in Missouri."[39] Likewise, the *New York Amsterdam News* reported, "Lloyd Gaines has disappeared! Neither his attorneys nor his family know the whereabouts of Lloyd Gaines. . . . Gaines' presence is desired at a hearing to be held in the Boone county circuit court to determine whether the new law school in the Poro building is the equal of the law school at the University of Missouri."[40]

Of immediate concern to the NAACP was the fact that his absence made it impossible for him to give a deposition or to appear at the circuit court in Boone County. The *Afro-American* and other black newspapers published a plea, on behalf of Sidney Redmond and the NAACP: "Any person knowing the whereabouts of Gaines or anyone who has any indication of where he might be, is asked to asked to contact Sidney R. Redmond. People's Finance Building. 11 N. Jefferson Street, St. Louis, Mo."[41] *Afro-American* columnist Louis Lautier wrote that unless Gaines was found quickly, the lawsuit would be dismissed. He asserted that Houston, whom he referred to as "Cholly," had long been aware that Gaines was missing. Lautier wrote, "Gaines' disappearance has been known to NAACP officials for months, but they were keeping it secret. But when Cholly was taking depositions of witnesses in St. Louis the other day, lawyers for the State asked him to produce Gaines so they may take his deposition."[42] The *Chicago Defender* reported, "The sudden disappearance of Gaines has led to a variety of rumors here in St. Louis where public interest in the fight is at its highest. At almost every gathering place, one runs into persons with 'inside information.' They'll tell you confidentially, that Gaines has either been threatened with bodily harm if he returns to St. Louis, or that he has been paid to drop out of sight." The article further suggested, "That, it is said, has been done to weaken the case of the N.A.A.C.P. . . . They'll get a paper and point out to you that Former State Supreme Court Justice Fred L. Williams, who is representing the University of Missouri in the court fight, has said that the case will certainly be dismissed if Gaines cannot be produced."[43]

Indeed, Judge Williams contacted Sidney Redmond to inquire into Gaines's whereabouts. If Gaines lived in Michigan, Illinois, or another state, then he might no longer be a Missouri state resident subject to the parameters of the US Supreme Court decision. Moreover, given various statements, it was uncertain, at least to the state's counsel, whether Gaines still intended to go to law school in Missouri. In either condition, the case would be moot and should not be continued. Redmond wrote to Houston on October 20,

> Judge Williams just called and asked for a setting in the Gaines case. He wanted to know if we would dismiss the case if Gaines is a non-resident of the state or if Gaines says he does not wish to enter the University of Missouri. I told him that Gaines' suit was based on the contention that he is a resident of the state and when that condition ceases the duty of Missouri to him will end. As to the other matter I told him that I couldn't appreciate Gaines foregoing his determination to become a lawyer. So far I have not heard one word from him. If nothing is learned by the 25th, I think we might as well give up, for the papers have certainly flooded the country with his disappearance.[44]

Williams's query is curious because, publicly, the university attorneys had no more knowledge about whether Gaines was within the state and intending to enroll than did his own counsel. Houston was not ready to surrender the case and responded, ". . . I suggest that you set the Gaines case for the first day in the January, 1940, term if you can persuade Hogsett and Williams to wait that long. If not, set the day as far in advance as possible. Let Hogsett and Williams know that we will not go forward unless we have him."[45]

University counsel agreed to the additional delay, and Redmond got a circuit court hearing scheduled for January in Columbia. Efforts to locate

Gaines remained fruitless. Redmond wrote again to Houston on December 19, "Judge Williams just called to know if we are going to dismiss the Gaines case in the event Gaines cannot be located. You have told me that you would not go to trial without him so please give me a definite answer in that matter."[46] William Hogsett, the lead attorney for the university, also wrote to Redmond, "In accordance with the recent telephone conversation which you had with Judge Williams last Tuesday, we beg to advise that the above case will be called in the Circuit Court of Boone County, at Columbia, on January 2d, 1940. Unless we hear from you to the contrary, we assume that at that time you will dismiss the case."[47]

News stories in the black press initially were supportive of Gaines and sought information on his whereabouts. The aim was to help the NAACP and its lawyers move forward with the case. However, the litigant did not always receive the same amount of praise as others involved in the case. For instance, when the *Afro-American* announced its 1938 "Honor Roll," following the victory in *Gaines v. Canada*, it lauded the achievements of Charles Houston and Thurgood Marshall, but not Lloyd Gaines, noting the attorneys' role in the university cases in Missouri, Maryland, and elsewhere.[48] In its coverage of the US Supreme Court decision in *Gaines,* the *Chicago Defender* lauded not the plaintiff but his alma mater, Lincoln University, "[a]n institution that has come into the limelight by virtue of its involvement in the recent U.S. Supreme Court decision calling for equal educational opportunities within the state for the Race, is one, strangely enough, that few people know much about. . . . Lincoln University, standing midway between St. Louis and Kansas City, has for the past 72 years been doing quite a job of providing Race youth with advanced training."[49] The article mentioned Gaines only once, to note that he had graduated from the school in 1935 with "high honors."

As the disappearance of Lloyd Gaines became a crisis, negative views of Gaines began to find their way into print. Allegations of irresponsible behavior began to leak and be reported in the black press. For instance, a short column in the *New York Amsterdam News* scolded him, calling his "strange disappearance" and the anticipated dismissal of his case a

> a most unfortunate setback to the National Association for the Advancement of Colored People and others who are fighting for justice and democracy in education and other matters in the United States. Fortunately, however, the failure of Gaines to show up

at the recent trial in St. Louis . . . will not do more than delay
the fight against the southern state universities for discriminating
against Negroes, since the Supreme Court has already ruled that
those states which bar Negroes from their universities must provide
equal educational facilities or admit them to state schools.[50]

The *Amsterdam News* reported the lesson, "which Gaines' disappearance
into thin air has again emphasized," that decision-makers in the NAACP had
also learned:

> Any individual who takes upon himself the noble task of acting in
> any capacity to help his race or nation should stick with that task
> until the bitter end. For after all anybody who assumes the role
> Gaines enjoyed in his fight against the U. of Mo. took on himself a
> public duty which he could not under any circumstances let go to
> pot. It is hoped that Gaines is well, secure and in all other ways all
> right. It is also hoped that if he hasn't been killed or isn't being held
> in bondage that he will come out of hiding so that the fight to seat
> him in a classroom at the U. of Mo., Law School can be renewed if
> such is desired by his lawyers.[51]

The NAACP legal defense team's dependence on a litigant was a lesson that
they would remember. In a subsequent case, Thurgood Marshall wrote to
Heman Marion Sweatt, Gaines's fellow student at the University of Michigan and the plaintiff in a later equal protection suit against the University of
Texas, about an attorney's need for dependability of the litigant. "None of us
knew Lloyd Gaines in the Missouri Case very well and we took a chance."
Marshall continued that the *Gaines* case cost over $25,000 but Gaines disap-
peared when they needed him.[52]

Commentary in the black press about the impossibility of locating Gaines
evolved into several news frames. First, Lloyd Gaines was a victim of foul play,
typically at the presumed hand of supporters of segregation. Second, he simply lost interest in the ongoing litigation and withdrew from visibility. Third,
Gaines took a bribe in exchange for abandoning his court case. Little or no
evidence was provided for any of these theories.

Some articles in the black press portrayed Gaines as a victim. For example, an October 1939 *Pittsburgh Courier* editorial suggested sinister
motives behind his disappearance. However, while the article suggested

the possibility that something bad had happened to Gaines, it also entertained the notion that he had accepted money to leave and then withdrawn voluntarily. Using uppercase words for emphasis, the editorial offered salacious speculation:

> Why is it impossible for the lawyers handling Lloyd Gaines'
> case against the University of Missouri to find ANY TRACE of
> the young man? Why is it that even the young man's MOTH-
> ER has received no word of him? . . . . If Lloyd Gaines is alive
> and free, it is VERY STRANGE that he should DISAPPEAR
> without a word to ANYBODY. . . . The N.A.A.C.P. lawyers
> are eager to find Lloyd Gaines but the lawyers for the state of
> Missouri obviously do NOT want him found. Has this de-
> sire of Missouri ANYTHING to do with the disappearance of
> Lloyd Gaines? If he is VOLUNTARILY in hiding, is it possi-
> ble that someone is making his disappearance FINANCIALLY
> WORTHWHILE? If he is held somewhere against his will,
> WHO IS RESPONSIBLE for that? The surmise will not [die]
> down that there is something very MYSTERIOUS and EVEN
> SINISTER about the disappearance of Lloyd Gaines. We MAY
> be wrong, and we HOPE we are. Lloyd Gaines MAY turn up
> any day with a PLAUSIBLE explanation of his long absence.
> But there is SO MUCH involved in this case, that we are frank-
> ly NOT optimistic about Mr. Gaines' return until AFTER the
> separate law school is well established.[53]

The belief of black leadership was that Gaines had expressed dissatisfaction with his plight and walked away from the lawsuit. The *Afro-American* reported, "NAACP officials are reported as saying that Gaines instantly walked out on them when they declined to make him certain monetary advances for his personal support. The association, in refusing, said it was not marrying him, but defending him in the courts. With Gaines gone, however, it might have proved cheaper for the NAACP to 'marry' him."[54] Louis Lautier, columnist for the *Afro-American*, suggested Gaines could have been bribed or killed. He began with these questions: "Why did

Lloyd Gaines disappear? Was he bribed by unknown influential persons, or is he a victim of foul play?"[55] By suggesting the possibility of bribery, the *Afro-American* began a storyline adopted by other black newspapers: that Gaines was missing because of less than honorable behavior.

For his part, Charles Houston did not accuse Gaines of taking the money and running, but he did accuse Gaines of running. The *Afro-American* quoted Houston, "I do not know why Gaines disappeared and even where he is at the present. The idea of anyone thinking bribery or foul play had anything to do with the boy's disappearance is most absurd." As Houston continued, his frustration with the plaintiff in his case was apparent: "Gaines was not indispensable and any other student could pick up his application at Missouri University and take up where he left off. But Gaines must be found to be present at the decisions, the hearing of which are now delayed when they should not be." In the same story, it was again suggested that Gaines was disgruntled over monetary issues and concluded with another plea for anyone knowing his whereabouts to contact the NAACP.[56]

The frequent claims that Gaines demanded additional money from the NAACP is unsupported by NAACP correspondence. Although Gaines requested funds to attend the University of Michigan and for support in summer 1938, NAACP records do not include written requests for support in 1939. Perhaps he verbally requested additional financial resources in St. Louis or Kansas City, but no first-person accounts of these requests remains.

The mainstream press offered no theories on Gaines's disappearance. In Columbia, the city most directly affected by the *Gaines* case if the plaintiff succeeded in gaining admission to the University of Missouri, the *Missourian* matter-of-factly reported the news of Gaines's disappearance on its front-page on October 11, 1939. The story reported that his court case "may come to an unexpected end in the Boone County Circuit Court. For it was disclosed yesterday that Gaines has been missing for more than four months, and efforts to locate him have so far been futile." The story further reported that the NAACP lawyers asked Judge Walter Dinwiddie to postpone the case. "No word from Gaines has been received at his mother's home in St. Louis for several months," the story noted. "His mother, Mrs. Callie Gaines, is said to be frantic, and St. Louis police have been asked to contact Michigan authorities in an effort to locate the missing Negro."[57]

In Gaines's hometown, the *Globe-Democrat* reported his disappearance under the headline, "Law School Case Figure Missing: Lloyd L. Gaines, Negro

Who Won Appeal, Can't Be Found." The story noted "The whereabouts of Lloyd L. Gaines…is a mystery, it was disclosed yesterday." The brief story further reported that Sidney Redmond and Charles Houston "revealed their dilemma at a deposition hearing at the Lincoln University School of Law, 4300 St. Ferdinand Street, which was established to conform with the Supreme Court's decision that equal instruction be provided for Negroes in the state." The article went on to describe the purpose of the hearing.[58] In the *Post-Dispatch*, Gaines's disappearance was presented more as legal wrangling between the two sides than as a missing person case.

> Counsel in the suit of Lloyd C. [*sic*] Gaines, St. Louis Negro, to compel the University of Missouri to admit him to its law school, are seeking to find Gaines for a deposition preparatory to final disposition of the case. . . . Counsel for the two sides hold opposite views as to whether the case can be carried to a conclusion if Gaines does not appear. Gaines' lawyers assert that his presence is not essential but express the opinion he will appear if he learns his presence is desired. Attorneys for the university propose to move for dismissal of the suit, on the ground of apparent abandonment.[59]

The *Columbia Daily Tribune* modified an AP report and presented the same options available to counsel.[60]

When Sidney Redmond and Charles Houston officially announced that they did not know where Lloyd Gaines was, the story was covered by both the black and the white press. The tone of the coverage sometimes varied dramatically, even within the same newspaper. For example, the *Jefferson City Daily Capital News* published an Associated Press story which reported that "Attorneys for Lloyd L. Gaines…disclosed today they have not heard from their client for several months." The story also mentioned that his mother was "frantic" and that authorities were asked to search for him.[61] A one-paragraph item two days later in the same newspaper offered opinion with the news, including a disturbingly hopeful conclusion about Gaines's disappearance:

> It seems that Lloyd Gaines, the St. Louis negro who has been trying to get himself enrolled in the Missouri University law school is missing, and his case is liable to be thrown out of court if he does not show up pretty soon. It is said that nothing has been heard of Gaines for four months and his whereabouts are unknown. It

would be a much desired end of a very vexing and troublesome problem should he not be found.[62]

The first report was factual, but the second concluded that Gaines's disappearance was a resolution to an undesirable situation.

As the NAACP attorneys attempted to keep the case alive in state courts, the *Columbia Missourian* reported this legal activity without reference to Gaines's status. The *Missourian* summarized the last stage of the suit. "In his reply Gaines denies that the School of Law established in St. Louis by Lincoln University is equal to the School of Law at the University of Missouri; he also states that such action denies him rights assured under the state constitution and under the Fourteenth Amendment of the federal constitution."[63] Nowhere was an indication that Gaines was missing or that this could impact the lawsuit.

The deadline for the circuit court hearing was fast approaching, but Redmond, Espy, and Houston could not locate their client. In addition to the case for Lloyd Gaines, the attorneys were also pursuing two cases on behalf of Lucile Bluford against the University of Missouri: one in the circuit court requesting a writ of mandamus to compel her admission to graduate study in journalism, and another in federal district court seeking damages from Registrar S.W. Canada for a denial of Bluford's civil rights. The attorneys had hoped for a quick resolution for Gaines, but Sidney Redmond had spoken with Fred Williams and subsequently received a letter from William Hogsett. They expected Gaines to appear in court. If he could not establish his current Missouri residence, for instance, the case would be moot. The inability to reach Lloyd Gaines threatened legal enforcement of the US Supreme Court decision. Thurgood Marshall advised Houston against going forward: "As to the Gaines case, I do not see how you possibly can try the case without Gaines being present."[64]

Although he did not want it publicized, Houston had decided how to handle Gaines's case in the circuit court. By December 28, 1939, Houston had already prepared an affidavit for the case.[65] Houston wrote to Redmond, "Since we cannot find Gaines we cannot go on. But I think we should leave on record an exact statement of our position so that in the future people may know exactly why we did not proceed. To that end I have prepared and herewith hand you my own affidavit to be filed in the cause. You can file a companion affidavit if you and Espy want." Houston assured Redmond that he could tell

attorneys Fred Williams and Nick Cave that they would not resist a motion
to dismiss the case. "I consider the statement that we will not resist a motion
to dismiss a full performance of my agreement with Judge Williams that we
will not attempt to proceed without Gaines." Houston encouraged Redmond
to wait until the affidavit was filed, then to release copies to the Associated
Press and the United Press.[66]

Redmond filed the affidavit and, at the beginning of the new year, Judge
Dinwiddie dismissed the case of Lloyd Gaines. Redmond reported to Roy
Wilkins that the affidavit said "we had made a diligent search for Lloyd
Gaines, but had been unable to find him, and for that reason will not plead
further. The court on its o[w]n motion, or on motion by the respondents,
dismissed the case."[67]

All was not over. A few days later, the Gaines legal team filed a motion requesting that Judge Dinwiddie reverse an order made on dismissal of the case
on January 1. The *Columbia Daily Tribune* reported the development in this
way: "Lloyd Gaines...today filed a motion in the circuit court for a modification of the order...which assessed the costs of the trial of the cases against him
and he asked the court to change the order and assess the damages against the
respondent, the university authorities." The reasoning of the NAACP attorney was "Gaines, who now, in view of the opinion of the United States court
decision, claims that he won the case and states that he had won relief by the
decision and he prays the court for this relief in his motion filed today. He sets
out plainly that he won the case and asks the court to assess the costs against
the University."[68] Redmond observed that he had received a bill for court
costs, but he "filed a motion to modify the order and assess same against the
respondents for the reason that we did not lose the case."[69]

When Judge Dinwiddie dismissed the case in the circuit court on January
1, 1940, the *Gaines* case again made national news. The front-page of Reno's *Nevada State Journal*, for instance, ran an Associated Press story with the
headline "Court Dismisses Student's Suit." "Gaines' counsel Saturday filed an
affidavit saying they had no knowledge of Gaines' whereabouts. They were
unable to confirm the allegation of respondents S.W. Canada and Missouri
University that Gaines no longer was a Missouri citizen. He last was heard
from on March 6, in Chicago."[70] The news story presents an abrupt end to a
civil rights case that had gone on for the better part of a half decade. Moreover, it is one of the few examples of a white newspaper referring to Gaines

simply as a "Student." The same story ran in the *Wisconsin State Journal*, with the headline, "Negro Student's Suit Dismissed." This version of the story also included a different, and important, final sentence: "The case was filed 48 months ago and resulted in creation of equal scholastic opportunities in a Negro state school."[71] It was accurate in that it did not claim Gaines won admittance to the University of Missouri, yet it lends weight to the accomplishments of Gaines and his attorneys.

Closer to home, the *St. Louis Globe-Democrat* also reported the story with the help of the Associated Press, under the headline, "Negro's Suit to Study at Missouri U. Fails." The brief story explained that "The dismissal followed receipt of an affidavit from Gaines' attorneys in which they said they would not plead the case further. They have not heard from Gaines since March, 1939, they said."[72] The story concluded with a strange factual error: "The University of Missouri since has established a branch law school for Negroes in St. Louis."[73] It is difficult to imagine how this high-profile detail was reported incorrectly in a St. Louis newspaper.

In Columbia, the dismissal of Gaines's case was front-page news. The *Columbia Missourian* suggested the finality of the judge's decision in its first sentence, "Forty-five months after Lloyd L. Gaines, St. Louis Negro, first sought court aid in his attempt to enter the School of Law in the University of Missouri, Judge W. M. Dinwiddie today dismissed the case in Boone County Circuit Court." When the NAACP lawyers filed their affidavit that they had no knowledge of Gaines's whereabouts, they were effectively dropping the case. As the *Missourian* concluded, "Gaines' lawyers, however, contended that the educational standards of the newly created [the Lincoln University School of Law] for Negroes did not compare favorably with those in the University of Missouri."[74] Without a litigant, however, they were unable to put that assertion to the test in court.

The *Columbia Daily Tribune* gave the most detailed account of the affidavit filed by Charles Houston and his colleagues. The paper reported,

> Houston, in his affidavit, informs the court that he and his associates are unable to contact their Client, Gaines, and that they have no information or knowledge as to where he is. They set out that they have caused to be printed in the colored press of the country a notice seeking to obtain knowledge of the whereabouts of Gaines. The petition says that he is no longer a citizen of Missouri

and that when they last learned of him he was in Chicago trying to get work.

Given the relative hostility of the *Tribune* to Gaines, it is no surprise to see such attention given to the details of the NAACP's surrender; however, the paper reported, "The petition concludes with the statement that counsel for Gaines does not imply that in their opinion the state of Missouri has satisfied its constitutional obligations to satisfy Negro citizens of Missouri who wish to study law at the University of Missouri but that the affidavit is filed solely because the council is unable to make contact with its client, Gaines." The article contained an interesting out-of-context detail about Houston: "Houston is chief attorney for the Association for the Advancement of Colored People. Negroes of the United States have asked President Roosevelt to name him for the vacancy in the United States supreme court."[75] Roosevelt instead nominated Frank Murphy.

An editorial from the *East Tennessee News*, a black newspaper in Knoxville, reprinted in the *Atlanta Daily World*, chimed in. The consensus view by January 1940 was that Gaines's disappearance was a matter of his own choice. The editorial claimed that the sudden disappearance of Lloyd Gaines "offers another very evident need for Negroes employing some means of correcting grave problems within their own racial group. Just where young Gaines is, or what his motive is for staging a disappearing act just at the most crucial period of the law suit is extremely difficult to fathom, but thoughtful observers have their opinions, one of which is a downright certainty that his disappearance is not based on fear of bodily harm."[76] The editorial concluded with this admonition:

> One of the contentions waged by opponents of establishment of professional schools for Negroes is that the racial group is not ready for such elaborate set-ups. Judging from the outcome in Missouri and North Carolina, it does appear that an educational program from within the racial group, with a view of preparing eligible Negroes for the opportunities demanded will go far toward relieving the race of embarrassment as well as avoiding needless expenditures of taxpayers' funds.[77]

For some in the black press, the name "Gaines" became a word for absconding and failing to fulfill responsibilities. In a column about communism,

Daily World columnist Gamewell Valentine referred to the Scottsboro Nine case and the fact that the young men in that case were defended by an attorney with communist party ties. Valentine added, "The humor in the case was reached when one of the 'victims,' Ruby Bates, after testifying that all nine boys attacked her, did the 'Lloyd Gaines', only to pop-up after a short interval in New York City, where she publicly declared that the boys had never touched her and that her testimony was part of a grand frame-up."[78] It is remarkable that Gaines, central to a landmark victory in the Supreme Court, became so quickly dismissed and accused.

Editorial opinion seemed to reflect the perceptions of NAACP officials that Gaines disappeared of his own volition and, in so doing, did great harm to the legal case against the University of Missouri. However, the *Afro-American* published a letter to the editor from Pauli Murray, a civil rights and women's rights pioneer who met with Thurgood Marshall about suing the University of North Carolina for admission to its law school. In her letter, she defended Gaines—to a degree—and urged the NAACP to press forward without him, if necessary. She wrote,

> The disappearance of Lloyd Gaines, the temporary set-back to the fight for equal educational opportunity, has raised some editorial criticism of Gaines's motives. I do not feel, however, that Gaines is entirely to blame. I am convinced that if he had rested upon the continuous organized support of the masses, he could have been neither intimidated nor bought off. What actually happened after the decision was handed down? Gaines saw his own leaders thrown into confusion and wide disagreement over the implications of the decision. If Lloyd Gaines has failed, his failure rests squarely upon the shoulders of the colored people. It is our failure, lack of idealism, our disorganization, and our proneness to do little more than mouth our grievances beyond 'the big gate.' Find Lloyd Gaines if he can be found, if not, finish the job he left uncompleted.[79]

While Murray's words of support for Gaines were qualified, they were more than many black leaders and journalists were willing to offer on his behalf. However, as time wore on and Gaines remained missing, opinions about his whereabouts, and about Gaines himself, moderated.

Murray's opinion was seconded, somewhat, by a story in the *New York Amsterdam News*, which summarized *Gaines* and previewed Lucile Bluford's case, "The case is scheduled to travel the same road as its predecessor—county court to state court to Supreme Court. And if the Supreme Court decides as it did previously, and there is no reason to believe it will not, the State of Missouri will find itself in a more embarrassing position than after the Gaines decision." This article was less critical of Gaines than had been the paper's earlier coverage. Instead, it portrayed a hostile atmosphere at the University of Missouri:

> The attitude on the campus of the University of Missouri illus-
> trates the manner in which a racial struggle affects an institution of
> higher learning, presumably dedicated to the more lofty pursuits
> in life. A spokesman for the legal fraternities loudly proclaimed,
> "If he's admitted he'll be treated like a dog: there aren't any of us
> who'd like to sit by a Negro." Another legal fraternity warned he
> wouldn't stay long because "he'd be busted out." Genteel Missouri-
> ans, who can be more Southern than the Southerners, hinted dark-
> ly that they would know how to "welcome" Gaines if ever entered
> the University.

In this article, all that was reported of his disappearance was that he "could not be found when the time came for him to appear in court."[80]

After the case was dismissed, the views of the NAACP leadership became apparent. Gaines had simply withdrawn from participation in the case. He expected the organization to provide support it could not, so he disappeared. Although the last confirmed sighting of Gaines was in March in Chicago, Frank Weathers, the Lincoln law student and assistant librarian, claimed to have received a postcard from him in April. Charles Houston was told Gaines had been seen in Chicago several months after that. "When I was in Chica-go, Tuesday, October 17, I talked to William H. Patterson, Vice President of the I.L.D. He told me he had talked to Gaines in Chicago about a month ago, that the whole burden of Gaines' complaint was the N. A. A. C. P. had not done anything for him, and that he did not trust Gaines because he felt Gaines was trying to saddle himself onto the N. A. A. C. P. indefinitely."[81]

Many believed that Gaines, who always seemed to need money, accepted a payment to disappear. Nathanial Sweets, publisher of the *St. Louis Ameri-can*, one of the many papers searching for information on the absent litigant, believed the story of bribery. "Gaines was, in my opinion, from all the inves-tigation that I can make, Gaines was paid to leave Missouri after the United

States Supreme Court had rendered its decision. . . . "[82] Walter White also expressed the belief that Gaines accepted a bribe. White received word from none other than Lucile Bluford. He wrote to Sidney Redmond, "Lucille [*sic*] Bluford writes me that she has heard that one of the students or somebody at the Poro Law School has received a card from Lloyd Gaines, post marked in Mexico, stating that he was having 'a jolly time on the Two Thousand Dollars he had been given to leave the country.' Will you check this and let me hear from you as quickly as possible?"[83] The national NAACP leadership seemed to accept this explanation, that Gaines accepted a substantial payment to withdraw from the case.

Sidney Redmond recalled receiving several reports about Lloyd Gaines and checking on their accuracy. None were confirmed.

> I heard that he was in Kansas City and got some information I thought was true. And his mother and brother lived on West Belle in St. Louis. I got in touch with [his brother], and he went to the hospital in Kansas City and said that it was not Gaines. They were really anxious to find their brother and son. But I have heard reports, I don't know what's to them, someone said that a certain editor in Missouri gave him some money to go to Mexico. You see, we wanted Gaines to go on and use him to try to get him admitted to the law school here. And somebody, or Gaines himself just disappeared.[84]

Despite an absence of evidence, some newspapers in the black press began to publish stories that Gaines betrayed the cause.

As the *Bluford* trial was heard in Boone County, the search for Gaines continued, with many rumors making the press. One asserted, on the basis of the report to the national NAACP office, Gaines "had been seen in Mexico City, Mexico, enjoying life, with plenty of money to spend." This same article repeated an earlier accusation, that "Gaines had complained previously, according to published reports, that he should be getting money for his role," and concluded, "This was refused." [85] A common narrative formed about Gaines as a manipulator, not a victim, but with no explanation of why he might have fled as far away as Mexico.

Regardless of the reasons for his disappearance, the NAACP attorneys were forced to admit the case could not proceed. University counsel requested that

Judge Dinwiddie dismiss the case, which he did on January 1, 1940. Din-widdie was more than happy to grant this request. After all, it allowed him to avoid having to make a decision in the case. As the *Cleveland Call* reported in a wire service story printed in many black newspapers, "Finis was written to the efforts of Lloyd Gaines to enter the University of Missouri as a law student when the case was dismissed last Monday in Boone County Circuit court by Judge W.M. Dinwiddie." The NAACP attorneys gave Dinwiddie an out: "Gaines has been missing for ten months and his attorneys, unable to plead a case for a client they can't find, requested dismissal of the suit."[86]

In March of 1940, the NAACP raised the issue of his location and expressed frustration, drawing coverage from the black press. In a press release picked up by many black newspapers, Charles Houston said, "The N.A.A.C.P. has exhausted all means of locating him." Houston acknowledged he was unable to contact him and urged anyone with information to contact the national office in New York.[87] Gaines remained missing, of course, and periodically the black press would run brief stories reminding readers of the search. The *Philadelphia Tribune* in September asked, "Was he a victim of foul play or did he sell his birthright for a mess of pottage? Did he become tired of it all and attempt to escape publicity? There are some of the questions being asked by everyone." It further reported, "The known trail of Gaines leads to Chicago and there it ends. He left his home in St. Louis in May, 1939, to attend an NAACP mass meeting and disappeared a few weeks after the meeting. In past years Gaines has remember[d] to send his mother gifts and greeting cards. . . . But he has not sent any word or contacted members of his family during the past year."[88] Thus were the doubts about Gaines's motives and the mystery surrounding his whereabouts starkly presented.

In June 1941, a year and a half after the case's dismissal, Roy Wilkins dis-cussed the Gaines situation again. Reported in an Associated Negro Press sto-ry printed in publications such as the *Afro-American* and the *Defender*, "If the question, 'Where is Lloyd Gaines' has been on one pair of lips, it has been on a thousand pairs, and the question goes unanswered." Wilkins told the ANP that "in order to win compliance by the state with the decision either Gaines would have to be produced or another suit would have to be instituted. And yet, if Gaines reappeared tomorrow it was not clear just what effect it would have upon his original case, that is, whether a statute of limitation would be-come operative and militate against him."[89] The *New York Amsterdam News* reported, "Still a mystery after several years, the disappearance and where-abouts of Lloyd Gaines, Lincoln University student and central figure in a case against the University of Missouri for equal educational opportunities for Negroes, is the biggest hitch to continuance of the case...."[90] "The NAACP," declared Wilkins in a press release, "is still seeking to locate Gaines and will welcome any information leading to his whereabouts."[91]

As the years passed, there were occasional references to him in the black press. These indicated his disappearance was still within the collective mem-ory. One mention, for instance, was a non sequitur at the end of a column about the 1944 Supreme Court decision in *Smith v. Allwright*, the Texas white primary case,[92] by *New York Amsterdam Press* columnist S. W. Garlington. "By the way, wonder what happened to Lloyd Gaines? Do you think he 'sold out' to the reactionary opposition?"[93] Another instance, a 1950 article in Balti-more's *Afro-American*, reminded readers of important civil rights litigation such as *Murray* and *Gaines*, and added, "Interestingly enough, the plaintiff in the latter case, a man named Lloyd Gaines, disappeared soon after the deci-sion and is still a 'missing person.'"[94]

In 1948, two *Pittsburgh Courier* reporters, Gene Hudson and Harry B. Webber, conducted an investigation about Gaines, noting he had been miss-ing for ten years. The story featured interviews with his mother and siblings, as well as quotes from Gaines's last letter to his mother. His siblings, Dorothy and George, seemed to believe that Gaines was still alive, living anonymous-ly somewhere. George Gaines said, "Yes, Lloyd is still missing. One reason could be the promise he gave the NAACP to repay his tuition. He always hat-ed debts he could not pay," while his sister Dorothy said that he hated pub-licity and objected when the reporters wanted to take pictures of his family. A quote the reporters pulled from Gaines's last letter to his mother also leaves the impression that Gaines disappeared on his own: "Don't worry. I'm a man and can take care of myself." Gaines's mother, Callie, seemed torn between hope and doubt. She said, "I'm the only one who believes Lloyd is dead. . . . If he were not dead, I feel he would have come home by now. However, I re-member he often said he did not like St. Louis and did not really want to live here." The article concluded with a bit of sensationalism: "Mrs. Gaines un-consciously threw a bombshell when she said she believed him dead. 'Were he not dead, he would have left whatever world he moved to and come home.'"[95] On balance, however, the story leaves the impression that Gaines disappeared of his own volition.

The most exhaustive analysis of Gaines's whereabouts was in a story published in *Ebony* magazine in 1951. Author and editor Edward T. Clayton,
who wrote about the murder of St. Louis attorney Homer Phillips, leaves
readers with the strong perception that Gaines chose to disappear, rather than
fell victim to foul play. At the outset, the story suggests three possible explanations for Gaines's disappearance: "Had he met with foul play at the hands
of hired hoodlums? Had he run out under threats from Ku Kluxers? Or had
he weakened under promise of a lucrative bribe and accepted a pay-off to disappear into some foreign land?" By the end of the story, readers are presented
with another possible explanation—that Gaines chose to disappear because
he was simply tired of the notoriety of being "the first Negro to bring court
action against a state school."[96] Of course, Gaines was not, but his was the
first case to make it to the US Supreme Court.

The story in *Ebony* is not unsympathetic to Gaines, referring to him as "a
legal guinea pig for the St. Louis branch NAACP," but the preponderance
of the evidence presented paints a picture of a debt-ridden, angry man who
chose to start a new life elsewhere.[97] Sidney Redmond is quoted extensively,
expressing his frustration with Gaines's disappearance. Nowhere in his account does Redmond suggest Gaines could have met with foul play:

> I haven't the slightest idea where he could have gone or why. He
> had cooperated with us fully on the case, and at that time it was al-
> most impossible to get anyone who would be willing to take part in
> that kind of law suit. Even some of the lawyers we first asked were
> a little reluctant to be associated with it. It was that kind of thing.
> Of course, it wasn't necessary for Gaines to be present at all hear-
> ings after we filed his petition, but we were reasonably certain that
> he was going all the way with the suit. We had checked him pretty
> closely as a student and knew his attitude about such matters. You
> can't imagine how we felt when he failed to show up even after the
> case was won.[98]

Like the reporters from the *Courier*, Clayton interviewed several members
of Gaines's family, including his aging mother, Callie. When asked about
Lloyd's whereabouts, Callie Gaines said she had no idea where he was but also
said that the family had never filed a missing persons report with the police.
She did mention receiving both a letter and a card from Lloyd. When Clayton asked her about the contents of the card, she said, "'It wasn't more than

a half-dozen words. He said, 'Goodbye. If you don't hear from me anymore, you know I'll be all right.' We haven't heard from him since. Of course, we heard a lot of reports about where he was, but none of them mean anything. We heard once that he was in Mexico; another time somebody said he was in New York. But nobody knows any more than we do.'"[99]

Clayton then asked Callie Gaines about the case, saying, "Do you think his disappearance had anything to do with the suit against the school?" She responded,

> I don't know. But I do know he never intended going there. He said he wasn't. We never talked much about the case, but I remember once I asked him if he was going to that school, and he said "No." I told him then that I thought it would be too dangerous, but he didn't say anything else, except that he wasn't going and I knew he wasn't. Lloyd was like that. Whenever he wanted to do something, he did it, and if he didn't want to do something he was the same way. He wouldn't do it.[100]

In this revelation from his mother, readers are given the impression that not only did he probably disappear of his own volition, but also that he never intended to attend the university whose doors his legal team fought so hard to open.

Clayton also contacted Gaines's oldest brother, George, who painted an unflattering picture of Lloyd Gaines as a man who struggled with persistent financial difficulties and who was upset that he was not receiving proper support from the NAACP. George Gaines said, "'He was always writing here asking for money and I tried to send it to him whenever I had it. We had an understanding that he was going to pay it back later, but I haven't received a penny and haven't heard from him in all this time. That organization—the N-A-A-P-C or whatever it was—had him going around here making speeches, but when he got ready to go to Kansas City I had to let him have $10 so he could get himself a white shirt.'"[101] Lloyd Gaines's requests for money were a persistent theme from the beginning of the case.

Clayton got access to the last letter from Lloyd Gaines to his mother and quoted extensively from it. The passages quoted signal a sense of extreme frustration on Gaines's part: "Dear Mother, I have come to Chicago hoping to find it possible to make my own way. I hope that by this letter I shall make very clear the reasons for such a step."[102] He explained that his conscience prevented him from continuing to work in St. Louis, but he had difficulty finding another job. Gaines wrote of his role in the landmark court decision.

> As for my publicity relative to the university case, I have found that my race still likes to applaud, shake hands, pat me on the back and say how great and noble is the idea; how historical and socially important the case[.] But—and there it ends. Off and out of the confines of the publicity columns I am just a man—not one who has fought and sacrificed to make the case possible; one who is still fighting and sacrificing—almost the "supreme sacrifice" to see that it is a complete and lasting success for thirteen million Negroes— no!—just another man. Sometimes I wish I were just a plain, ordinary man whose name no one recognized.[103]

Gaines signed off, saying, "Should I forget to write for a time don't worry about it; I can look after myself ok. as ever, Lloyd."[104]

Clayton devoted a lengthy passage in his story to his interviews with Nancy and Eddie Mae Page, whom he described as two of the last people to see Gaines before he disappeared in Chicago. In the interview, both women reported that Gaines was "moody and disturbed" when visiting with them, building on the impression gained from his letter that Gaines was fed up with being part of a momentous Supreme Court case.[105] Clayton described the NAACP as officially "left holding the bag" and quoted Walter White, the NAACP's executive secretary, suggesting strongly that Gaines was alive and well somewhere:

> We were very disappointed at his disappearance. Naturally there was much conjecture at the time as to where he could possibly be, but we didn't really know what to think. We had a lead that he was in Mexico, and although we did not have ample money to make an intensive investigation, we did make a check through friends there. Still, there was no trace of him. Our report was that he had been seen there and had an ample supply of money. I'm reasonably certain that it might have been Gaines as the person who reported it seemed to be very confident that it was.[106]

Had anyone at the NAACP thought Gaines met with a violent end, White surely would have found an adjective other than "disappointed" to describe his emotions.

Clayton concluded by quoting one of Gaines's sisters, though he does not say which one: "We think Lloyd is still alive. We really don't know, of course, but if he is, he is probably somewhere where he doesn't want to be bothered. And if Lloyd doesn't want to be bothered, I don't see why we should interfere." But regardless of her optimism, the Lloyd Gaines case remains one of the strangest mysteries in the history of American race relations.[107] Eddie Mae Page expressed confidence that Lloyd Gaines was dead "but prefers not to disclose her reasons." However, she also shared a recollection that she looked out a window and saw Gaines—or someone who looked like him—pacing outside her house recently.[108] Amid all the speculation, the only thing that can be said with certainty is that Gaines disappeared from the public spotlight in 1939 and it is impossible to know if anyone who knew him ever saw him again. The preponderance of coverage in the black press reflected the view that Gaines's departure was voluntary. The press took its cues from the NAACP, and the organizational leadership had no other explanation as to how or why he vanished. His attorney, Sidney Redmond, could only conclude, "Lloyd Gaines is a mysterious person."[109]

The circumstances of Gaines's disappearance and the decision of the Supreme Court have been revisited occasionally over the years. The NAACP sought the assistance of the Selective Service System to locate Gaines, but this was "to no avail."[110] Journalist Juan Williams wrote, "In 1995 Gaines's remaining relatives said they still had not heard from him; the Social Security Administration said that year there was no record of Gaines's death."[111] In 2007, the *Riverfront Times*, an alternative newspaper published in St. Louis, ran a lengthy story on the disappearance of Gaines.[112] Reporter Chad Garrison interviewed three of Gaines's family members: his nephew George Gaines, and his great nieces, Paulette Smith-Mosby and Tracy Berry. The story followed from a request filed by the NAACP for an FBI investigation of Gaines's disappearance. It was one of many such requests made by the organization. While the relatives suggest that Gaines must have met with a violent end, the article presents evidence that, on balance, tilts the scales toward Gaines having disappeared of his own volition. The article relies heavily on the earlier investigative work and conclusions drawn by Edward Clayton for *Ebony*.

The *Riverfront Times* also reports the story of an encounter with Gaines by one of his former professors at Lincoln University, historian Lorenzo Greene. He died in 1988, so Greene's story was told secondhand by librarian Sid Reedy and confirmed by his son Lorenzo Thomas Greene. The elder Greene

related that while traveling to Mexico City in the late 1940s, he had a telephone call with Lloyd Gaines. According to Reedy, Greene "recognized it was
the voice of Lloyd Gaines." Over the phone, "They talked for awhile. Gaines
said he had grown tired of the fight, and wanted to start over. He had some
business in Mexico City and apparently did well financially." Greene's son
claimed that telling the authorities was not a realistic option as it could result in an FBI investigation. "There wasn't a lot of trust there. FBI agents had
already been to our house to question my mother about my father's involvement in civil rights matters." The younger Greene continued, "Even if my father went to them with that information, I really don't think they would have
cared." According to the story, Lorenzo Greene and Lloyd Gaines planned
to meet at a restaurant in Mexico City, but Gaines did not arrive. Garrison
reports that the FBI twice denied requests to conduct an investigation into
Gaines's disappearance, once in 1940 and again in 1970. Of a modern FBI
investigation, Garrison quotes Berry, an assistant U.S. attorney in St. Louis,
saying, "It would be good to finally end the speculating.... Then I think it's a
positive thing—no matter what they find."[113] Reporter David Stout and the
New York Times revisited the disappearance of Lloyd Gaines in 2009. Stout
notes that living relatives George Gaines and Tracy Berry suggest that Gaines
must have disappeared as a result of foul play, but also comments that "while
his case was winding through the courts, [Gaines] had behaved erratically
before."[114]

Contemporary, undocumented stories abound that Lloyd Gaines was a
victim of foul play. Most of the stories suggest Gaines was captured by the
Ku Klux Klan or another white supremacist group, possibly brought back
to Missouri, killed, and buried. However, no evidence has been offered to
support this sequence of events. Although some have called for a criminal
investigation, there is no firm evidence of a committed crime. No active
missing-person report was filed for Lloyd Gaines, and no FBI investigation
conducted. The Department of Justice inquiries into unsolved civil rights
cases were limited to victims who were killed. Since there is no evidence that
Lloyd Gaines suffered a suspicious death, his fate is not among the cold cases.[115] What happened to Lloyd Gaines remains unknown; his disappearance
is "the mystery of the century."[116]

Lloyd Gaines himself was mysterious and hard to pin down. He was an
intelligent young man willing to take his place in the vanguard of opposition
to racial injustice. Yet he was also solitary by inclination, devoted to friends

and family but with a fiercely independent streak. He worked hard in his studies at Michigan, but was unable to stay the course and left before completing a degree. He was a conscientious worker but seemed unable to find and maintain long-term employment. He was constantly in need himself yet under pressure from others, who expected much of him. He made a personal sacrifice that few others would and found himself drawn, unwillingly, into a limelight others might have sought. And when it was time to step again into the light for the final test, Lloyd Gaines was nowhere to be found.

9

The *Gaines* Legacy

The direct impact of the litigation involving Lloyd Gaines continued after his final appeal was dismissed. Houston, Redmond, and Espy picked up a similar case in Missouri. Like other segregationist states, Missouri held firm and resisted integration of education. The national NAACP pursued reliable plaintiffs in other states and initiated new lawsuits with similar circumstances, expanding from the organization's success in *Missouri ex rel. Gaines v. Canada*. Ultimate triumph over segregation in education remained elusive in Missouri and elsewhere.

Lucile Bluford's attempt to enter the University of Missouri School of Journalism was inextricably linked to the *Gaines* case.[1] Houston and Redmond handled her lawsuit as *Gaines* was remanded from the US Supreme Court to state courts. Despite the *Gaines* decision, university officials refused to accept Bluford's graduate application and directed her to apply to the state's only university for African Americans. Lincoln University administration, in the midst of creating a new law school in St. Louis, had neither funding nor time to establish a new graduate program in journalism in Jefferson City. While organizing depositions for the *Gaines* case, Redmond wrote Houston on September 30, "Professor Frank L. Williams called me this morning and stated that the Board of Curators met on the 28th and decided that they were not in a position to do anything toward establishing a School of Journalism."[2] On October 12, 1939, Bluford filed suit against the University of Missouri, seeking a writ of mandamus ordering her admission.

The trial was held in Judge Walter Morris Dinwiddie's circuit court in Boone County, the same location as the original trial for Lloyd Gaines, on

February 10–11, 1940. Central to Houston's argument were the US Supreme Court decision in *Gaines v. Canada* and the second Missouri Supreme Court decision requiring admission or substantially equal facilities. The implication was that Bluford must be admitted to the University of Missouri since there was no other graduate program in journalism within the state. William Hogsett, representing the university, argued that Bluford's suit should be against Lincoln University, that Canada was not the responsible person for denying her admission, and that Bluford was "merely acting for the National Association for the Advancement of Colored People in order to gain publicity for that organization."[3]

At the end of May, Judge Dinwiddie refused to issue the requested writ of mandamus. Dinwiddie decided that Bluford had no real intention to pursue graduate education, that she merely was part of an effort by Houston and the NAACP for publicity.[4] In part, Dinwiddie's rationale involved the failure of Gaines to pursue his case to its culmination at the second hearing in his circuit court.[5] Segregation, according to the judge, was "for the good of both races."[6] Houston and Redmond appealed the circuit court decision to the Missouri Supreme Court in April 1941.[7] Oral arguments were made in May, and the hearing provided some initial reasons for optimism that the Missouri Supreme Court would favor Bluford.[8] However, the court, in a unanimous opinion by Judge Albert Clark, ruled, "It is the duty of this court to maintain Missouri's policy of segregation so long as it does not come in conflict with the Federal Constitution." The court also ruled that Bluford had not made "proper demand" to allow authorities to create new courses of study.[9]

Meanwhile, Bluford filed a civil case in federal district court against Registrar S. W. Canada for violating her civil rights, seeking $20,000 in damages.[10] Marshall and Houston expressed confidence, believing the case for Bluford was stronger than those for other litigants, including Gaines. Hogsett again argued that the lawsuit was primarily for publicity and for dismantling a legally sanctioned system of segregation, rather than from a true interest in graduate study on Bluford's part. According to Hogsett, Bluford "wanted a rejection as a basis for a law suit to get better publicity and keep the public stirred up about the issue. They want to break down the policy of racial separation not only in college but in grade and high schools of Missouri."[11] Bluford later recalled, "Well, that was true, but we couldn't admit it. . . . We were trying to break down that barrier of discrimination. That's exactly what we were trying to do."[12]

However, the federal suit did not go well.[13] District court judge John Caskie Collet[14] agreed that the court had to follow *Gaines,* but he interpreted the Missouri Supreme Court's decision to allow "the authorities at Lincoln University until the next term to furnish the facilities."[15] Moreover, citing *Plessy v. Ferguson*, the federal court explicitly upheld the state's right to impose racial segregation in education: "The State has the constitutional right to furnish equal facilities in separate schools if it so desires."[16] The federal court scoffed at the notion that a black citizen had a constitutional right to demand admission for higher education already offered to a white Missourian. [17] Collet said Bluford could not claim Canada "has deprived her of her constitutional rights until she has applied to the proper authorities for these rights," that is, to Lincoln University, "and has been unlawfully refused. She may not anticipate such refusal."[18] Bluford's attorneys opted for other damage suits against the University of Missouri and its administrators. That litigation fared no better.[19]

President Sherman Scruggs and Lincoln University were unable to open a journalism school until February 1, 1942.[20] When Lincoln failed to meet an earlier announced deadline to open a journalism school by January 1941, the University of Missouri shut down its own graduate program in journalism. The justification offered was a decrease in demand, but most understood the actual reason for the closure was to prevent admission of Bluford or other black students.[21] The *Pittsburgh Courier* lambasted the state for its "Organized Negrophobia."[22] Bluford refused to enroll at Lincoln, and, in May, she reapplied to an allegedly closed University of Missouri Journalism School.[23] It had come to Charles Houston's attention that the school was, in fact, teaching graduate students in courses labeled as undergraduate. He was prepared to continue the appeal in court when Walter White, the NAACP secretary, decided the organization did not have the resources to continue pursuing the case.[24] All the *Bluford* cases were lost, and none were appealed outside the state. Lucile Bluford applied for graduate admission to the University of Missouri eleven times, but her application was refused each time.[25]

Missouri's loss in the *Gaines* case did not lead immediately to integration in education. On the contrary, the delays to integration led some politicians to press more strongly for racial segregation. It was an established practice to provide separate primary and secondary education institutions for blacks and whites within school districts in the state.[26] Within a decade of Lloyd Gaines's original application for admission to the University of Missouri, the state held a new constitutional convention and replaced its state constitution. The 1945 constitution had added language mandating educational segregation in state schools. Section 1 of Article IX required that "Separate schools shall be provided for white and colored children, except in cases otherwise provided for by law."[27] University of Missouri law professor Orrin B. Evans wrote a memo to Registrar S. W. Canada emphasizing the new provision and its potential application to enrollment of other nonwhite students.[28] Canada in turn contacted President Frederick Middlebush to inquire whether this meant for "all the so-called colored races; i.e., yellow, red, brown, and black, a change in the State's policy is indicated."[29]

Missouri's overall educational policy on race was retrenchment.[30] Some quality indicators regarding the education of black children improved in Missouri: from 1933 to 1937, the number of high schools increased from 44 to 68, the rates of eighth graders attending high school rose to 76 percent, and the rates of high school graduates attending college to 22 percent; from 1930 to 1945, the number of black children attending school increased from 80.3 percent to 92.5 percent (as the rates for white children declined slightly from 83.0 to 82.9 percent); and average salaries were $1,519 for black teachers and only $1,239 for white teachers.[31] It is important to note that black children were concentrated in urban areas where educational indicators were higher for whites as well as blacks.[32] Division of white and black students deepened, and white schools were clearly more advantaged than black schools. The state constitutional mandate for racial segregation was upheld by the Missouri Supreme Court as late as 1952 and not officially overturned by federal decisions until 1976.[33]

Missouri led segregationist states through the statutory provisions for out-of-state tuition scholarships for blacks in 1921, a policy diffused through southern and border states. In *Gaines,* the Supreme Court ruled definitively that these out-of-state scholarships were a violation of equal protection, although Missouri maintained "voluntary" scholarships in the Taylor Bill. These out-of-state tuition scholarships did provide benefits to some black citizens seeking opportunities for higher education that were otherwise unattainable. In Missouri, the tuition program was never sufficiently funded; however, many black students did take advantage of these scholarships. Those educated through the tuition scholarships included Guion Bluford, the brother of Lucile who would challenge the white-only admission policy; Vivian Dreer, the daughter of Herman who wrote so forcefully on black leadership and history;[34] and Marian O'Fallon Oldham of St. Louis who would later serve on the University of Missouri's Board of Curators from 1978 to 1984 as its first black member.[35] Howard University law student and Kansas City resident John Royston received an out-of-state scholarship and wrote Governor Lloyd Stark after the Hughes Court declared the program unconstitutional. Along with his fellow students, Royston supported the *Gaines* decision and integration, but he asked the governor to maintain the scholarship program for those already studying out of state.[36]

The cost to the NAACP and related organizations to fight racial segregation in education and other areas was enormous. The organization seemed perpetually on the brink of abandoning its legal agenda because it could no longer afford to pursue it. On the eve of its first and arguably most important victory in the *Gaines* decision, NAACP leaders considered abandoning the case because it had no funds to go further. Similarly, the cost to the states to create and maintain separate institutions was also huge. Missouri expenditures for Lincoln University's law and journalism programs were disproportionate, considering that the number of black Missourians who graduated from these programs was comparatively few.[37] State politicians and educational administrators may have defended the costs for segregated institutions publicly, but they were also quick to reduce expenditures whenever possible.

A critical element of the Hughes doctrine in *Gaines* was that the extraordinary cost to set up separate facilities for one group is irrelevant. Constitutional protections are for individuals, so a state that chooses to segregate must be willing and able to pay for segregated, but substantially equal, facilities. This interpretation, that constitutional rights must be guaranteed for individuals, was not new in *Gaines*. Charles Evans Hughes had applied this principal in earlier opinions, in particular, *McCabe v. Atchison*.[38] Nevertheless, the application of the Fourteenth Amendment's equal protection clause for educational institutions was innovative, and this created the opening for other challenges to racial segregation.

The NAACP legal strategy of attacking education segregation by forcing southern and border states to accommodate black citizens was effective, but the states' response to the organization's judicial victories delayed integration for decades. *Gaines* and other related judicial decisions did create acknowledgment of federal rights of equal protection and required states to provide blacks with educational opportunities. But just as Missouri became a leader in education segregation by tuition scholarships before *Gaines*, it led opponents to integration in the post-*Gaines* environment.

The state's response to the loss at the US Supreme Court led to the establishment of a Jim Crow law school, followed by other graduate programs, for blacks only. Other states soon followed Missouri's example by establishing their own separate colleges and graduate and professional programs to counter efforts at integration.[39] Some failed. For instance, North Carolina created a black-only law school at the same time as Lincoln's law school. However, in North Carolina, the institution closed immediately because only one student enrolled.[40] A positive perspective on the more successful programs, such as at Lincoln University, would be that these institutions of segregation did open doors to educational experiences that for many blacks were otherwise unobtainable.[41] A new generation of lawyers, for instance, was trained at Lincoln. Still, politicians and segregationist leaders may have pretended and argued that these institutions provided educational parity, but these black-only institutions could not realistically be considered equal to white-only alternatives.[42]

One effect of the *Gaines* decision was increased willingness to assail segregation in education and other areas. By the late 1940s, federal and state courts were "besieged with similar cases." The courts had increasing difficulty ruling in ways that were consistent with both state law and the *Gaines* decision.[43] Federal courts were not yet prepared to decide that educational segregation was unconstitutional under provisions of the Fourteenth Amendment. As noted within a decade of the *Gaines* decision, "It is equally certain, however, that the economic obstacles which the Supreme Court has placed in the path of segregated education will make it increasingly difficult for a state to maintain this policy in all levels of the educational system."[44] Likewise, it became increasingly difficult for courts to reach a decision that educational segregation was "substantially equal." Ultimately, the US Supreme Court would fully reject the separate but equal doctrine in *Brown v. Board of Education*.

Missouri ex rel. Gaines v. Canada could have proven as influential as *Brown v. Board of Education* and led to more rapid desegregation of education if not for Lloyd Gaines's untimely disappearance. The Hughes Court clearly held that any alternative to white institutions must be "substantially equal" in quality. If the NAACP's challenge of the equality of the law school created for blacks had continued through the judicial system to the Supreme Court, the Hughes

Court might have ruled this action a violation of equal protection, particularly with new members more liberal on this issue. However, less than three years after *Gaines*, the Hughes Court cited its decision as a precedent supporting denial of equality as a fundamental individual right in *Mitchell v. U.S.* (1941). The *Mitchell* case, involving equality of accommodation in a Pullman car, likewise suggests the Hughes Court might have been willing to reconsider *Plessy* as well as the separate but equal doctrine.[45] Some scholars see the *Mitchell* case as evidence of "the beginning of a possible shift in the Court's jurisprudence" regarding equal protection.[46] Observers of the Court were keenly aware that membership changes created a more favorable judicial environment for civil rights cases.[47] Of course, what might have happened had Gaines appealed again is unknown. NAACP attorneys challenging racial segregation in education had to find new test cases to pursue. What is undeniable is that Lloyd Lionel Gaines was a trailblazer and his case was a major first step in dismantling the "separate but equal" doctrine of cases such as *Plessy v. Ferguson*.

No other case on educational discrimination would reach the high court for ten years. This is not to say the NAACP counsel, then led by Thurgood Marshall, did not pursue other cases. Many, like the *Bluford* cases in Missouri, did not advance out of the state or federal district courts. Recruitment of plaintiffs remained difficult. After the unfortunate experience with Lloyd Gaines, Marshall became more selective about potential plaintiffs and cases for NAACP sponsorship. Pauli Murray, for instance, had her application for law school rejected by the University of North Carolina because of race three days after the Supreme Court's decision in *Gaines*. Murray was intelligent, dynamic, and committed but Marshall declined to take a potential lawsuit on her behalf because of questions about state residency.[48] Like Houston, Marshall wanted to sponsor a case that was perfect, or at least a case for which the sole justiciable issue would be equal protection.

Eventually, other Supreme Court decisions regarding postgraduate education involving Ada Sipuel and George McLaurin in Oklahoma and Heman Sweatt in Texas would chip away at "separate but equal."[49] As NAACP attorney Robert Carter wrote in the journal *Social Problems* in 1955:

> [I]n 1938, the United States Supreme Court shocked the South out of its complacency. It held in *Missouri ex rel. Gaines v. Canada* that racial segregation could not be enforced under state law unless equal facilities were actually available to Negroes within the state.

By this decision, the Court served notice that if segregation was to be maintained, more than lip service would have to be given to the "equal" phrase of the formula. While no affirmative order was issued requiring that Gaines be admitted to the University of Missouri, it was clear, by implication at least, that unless a "substantially equal" law school for Negroes was established, Gaines and other Negroes would have to be admitted to the University of Missouri. Although not fully foreseen at the time, this really marked the beginning of the end of segregation in public education pursuant to constitutional sanction.[50]

Carter represented the NAACP in cases such as *Sweatt v. Painter* and delivered the oral arguments before the Supreme Court in *Brown v. Board of Education of Topeka*. He succeeded Thurgood Marshall as the head of the NAACP's Legal Defense Fund and later became a federal judge. Carter notes the unrealized promise of *Gaines*: "Full exploitation of this decision was frustrated by the disappearance of Lloyd Gaines, and for a long period following the *Gaines* case there was a dearth of equal educational opportunities for Negroes."[51] World War II and severe strains on NAACP financial resources limited the organization's legal agenda.

It would be easy to underestimate the importance of *Gaines v. Canada*, but the Supreme Court decision opened the door to *Brown* and the ultimate rejection of the separate but equal doctrine. The impact on constitutional law was understood immediately. As Princeton Professor Morroe Berger wrote in a UNESCO report shortly before the Supreme Court decided *Brown*, "the Court has adopted a progressively stringent interpretation of what 'equal facilities' means, thus making segregation more costly and cumbersome than ever." As a result of *Gaines* and related educational discrimination cases, "there are, today, thousands of Negroes attending unsegregated, state-supported institutions in the South, whereas there were none a decade or so ago."[52] Once the Hughes Court emphasized the need for equality, it could only be a matter of time before the Supreme Court would decide that separation was inconsistent with that goal. For instance, constitutional scholars Albert P. Blaustein and Clarence Clyde Ferguson Jr. wrote, "The Gaines case was the beginning of a revolution in the Supreme Court approach to educational problems. True, separate but equal was not overturned. In fact, the Court was expressly giving content to the 'equal' requirement of the formula."[53]

Despite the fact that Gaines's disappearance interrupted the process of de-segregating the University of Missouri and other institutions of higher ed-ucation, the black press continued to report on the case, what it saw as its importance, and its interpretation of its legacy. The *Gaines* case also may be credited with galvanizing Missouri's African Americans as an electoral force. The 1940 election for the US Senate in Missouri was a three-way contest in-volving the incumbent, Harry S. Truman, Governor Lloyd C. Stark, and US Attorney Maurice M. Milligan. Stark was the reformist governor who had led opposition to the political machine headed by Tom Pendergast, and Milligan was the federal prosecutor who won Pendergast's conviction for income tax evasion. Truman, though generally acknowledged as a fair judge and senator, was a product of the Pendergast machine in Kansas City. Stark and others al-leged that Truman won the 1936 Democratic primary only through electoral fraud.[54] It appeared that the popular Governor Stark could defeat Truman in the primary, but Stark also signed the Taylor Bill and helped restructure Lin-coln University without any attempt to integrate the University of Missouri or other public institutions. Columbia attorney Nick T. Cave, who represent-ed the University of Missouri on the *Gaines* case, served as an advisor for the Stark senatorial election campaign.[55]

The black press strongly opposed Stark's candidacy because of his actions related to the *Gaines* case. In June, for example, the *Chicago Defender* report-ed a declaration of the Lincoln University Alumni Association, "Unrestricted warfare on the candidacies of Governor Lloyd Crow Stark of Missouri and State Representative Taylor of Keytesville, for any office in the power of Mis-souri voters to confer" because of "the stand these officials assumed last year in piloting the way for the State of Missouri to avoid the real intent and purpose of the United States Supreme court in the Lloyd Gaines case."[56]

In August, Truman defeated Stark by only about eight thousand votes, a margin smaller than the number of black Democrats in the primary elec-tion.[57] The *Afro-American* claimed, "Opposition of colored voters, based on his unfavorable stand in the Lloyd Gaines—University of Missouri equal-education case, is credited with the defeat of Governor Lloyd C. Stark for the Democratic nomination for U.S. Senator in last week's primary election."[58] During the campaign, Truman spoke of civil rights. As historian David Mc-Cullough notes, "He also took a stand on civil rights, and while by later stan-dards what he said would seem hardly daring or sufficient, for Missouri in

1940 it was radical. . . . He did not favor social equality for blacks and he said so. But he wanted fairness, equality before the law. . . . Legal equality was the Negro's right, Truman said, 'because he is a human being and a natural born American.'"[59] According to Joseph L. McLemore, the St. Louis attorney, politician, and former Lincoln University curator, credited by the *Afro-American* for leading the fight against Stark, "one of the great troubles of the Governor was his lack of respect for the opinion of people generally and his total unconcern about the opinions of colored people whom he wanted to 'keep in their places.'"[60] Given the record Harry S. Truman would later generate in civil rights as president of the United States, this electoral impact could be seen as an important legacy of *Gaines*. Without his reelection, Truman would not have been in position to become first vice president and then president, where he put the country on the path toward racial equality. As McCullough assesses Truman's record, "He had achieved less in civil rights than he had hoped, but he had created the epoch-making Commission on Civil Rights, ordered the desegregation of the armed services and the federal Civil Service, done more than any President since Lincoln to awaken American conscience to the issues of civil rights."[61]

The black press also publicized stories pertaining to segregation in Missouri higher education. For instance, when the state senate voted against a motion to appropriate additional funds to Lincoln University in 1941, the Baltimore *Afro-American* reported the comments of Senator L. D. Joslyn, who argued during debate, "We'd just as well tell the colored students to go ahead and enroll at Columbia, and if the white students don't object, let them stay there."[62] The paper compared Joslyn to another, unnamed, legislator from 15 years earlier, "This member asked why the State had to appropriate an average of one-half million dollars a year for 'a handful' of colored students at Lincoln as long as the State was spending four million dollars a year for the University of Missouri, 'which had plenty of classrooms and instructors to take care of these colored students.'"[63]

The Lincoln Law School closed temporarily during World War II for lack of students.[64] In 1944, as the state toyed with closing the law and journalism schools at Lincoln permanently, H. J. Blanton, a former University of Missouri curator, published editorials in the *St. Louis Post-Dispatch* and the *Kansas City Star* calling for the desegregation of the University of Missouri. The black press picked up these editorials as an important story, and Blanton was quoted in the *Pittsburgh Courier*.

Sooner or later, it has been apparent for several years, the University of Missouri must take down the bars and make the best of what it considers a bad situation. When that time comes, we predict there will be little or no opposition from the student body or from the general public, and no more attention will be paid to a Negro on the campus than is now paid to a Negro in a bus or railroad coach, particularly if the Negro students strive to adjust themselves to standards incident to university circles.

The same article also quoted a *St. Louis Post-Dispatch* editorial in favor of accepting Edith Massey's application to study journalism:

If the board of curators grants the pending application, it will not be the first time a Negro student has been seen on the campus of the university. Exchange students of color have [been] accepted from other countries and have fitted themselves into the student body without any difficulty. In any case, unless the separate schools are re-opened, the board of curators has no recourse but to grant a right that has been affirmed by the highest court in the land.[65]

The University of Missouri remained segregated through the 1940s, and black newspapers continued to pressure the school. In February 1945, for example, the *Afro-American* reported that

Blame for the racial bar against colored students at the University of Missouri was placed upon the higher-ups last week after a series of tests had revealed that students' polls had favored their admittance. By a mere process of elimination, the administrators and others were blamed following four recent polls which indicated that 59 to 77.5 per cent of the representative student population questioned urged the end of the bar.

The report continued, "The St. Louis Post-Dispatch, in an editorial, criticized the handling of the problem, pointing out that the providing of 'equal facilities is a waste of State funds and a farcical way of evading the court's ruling.'"[66] The *Pittsburgh Courier* reported the results of one of these polls as 362-253 in favor of admitting black students to the University of Missouri. The article reminded readers of Lloyd Gaines's role in the desegregation, "Gaines, who fought for admittance to the university's law school, was upheld

in his contention by the US Supreme Court. But, despite the high court's decision, Gaines' desire was never fulfilled. He disappeared."[67]

By 1946 the state of Missouri was spending an enormous amount of money to maintain separate systems for graduate education. Reporting the results
from an economic impact study, the *Afro-American* noted, "It has cost the
State of Missouri more than $500,000 to graduate one colored student from
the School of Law and 10 from the School of Journalism."[68] In another story
about a month later, the *Afro-American* reported on the research of former
University of Missouri professor R. I. Brigham, who argued that "State efforts to uphold a principle contrary to democratic ideals have cost over one
half million dollars." Brigham further described the costs in this way: "Pointing out that only 150 students have been enrolled and only 11 graduated, 1
in journalism and 10 in law, he terms the inflationary cost of segregation as
'justice to the colored man with a vengeance.'"[69] He added, according to the
Cleveland Call, "'such justice will not appeal to Missouri taxpayers,' since it
is forced on them 'by Missouri's illogical desire to support a separate school
system for a six percent minority with a skin pigmentation which differs from
that of the 94 percent majority.'"[70] The *Afro-American* article reiterated, "That
such an education program is not feasible was stated recently in a St. Louis
Post-Dispatch editorial which declared that impoverished Southern States are
hardly able to or willing to go to the same lengths to maintain this separate
set-up."[71] By 1949, the Lincoln Law School had graduated 55 students; journalism, in operation since 1942, had graduated 37.[72]

In 1947, the *Afro-American* and other papers, such as the *New York Amsterdam News*, made much of the aborted publication of an editorial in a University of Missouri student magazine, *Tower Time*. The student editorial argued
that desegregation of the university was rapidly approaching. When the university learned of the editorial, the *Afro-American* reported, it suspended publication of *Tower Time* in an effort to prevent the editorial's dissemination:
"A student editor's insistence on publishing an article on racial questions in
what would have been the forthcoming issue of the University of Missouri's
Tower-time, led to a faculty banning of the magazine, it was disclosed last
Wednesday by Dr. Frederick A. Middlebush, president."[73] According to the
Afro-American, despite the suspension of publication of the magazine, the editorial was "subsequently mimeographed and distributed on the campus and
throughout the State when local printers refused to print the publication."[74]

The magazine's faculty advisor, Dr. W. H. Peden, defended the university's decision, "the article referred to the institution as a 'jim crow' school and urged interracial dating, dancing and swimming. He said the author ignored the fact that the university is required by statute to deny admittance to minorities."[75] Middlebush established a faculty committee to review all student publications. Although *Tower Time* was not the only focus of the investigation, the committee provided a new plan for faculty supervision.[76]

The *Tower Time* editorial, written by Missouri student Jon Moon, argued that black students would soon be admitted to the University of Missouri and should be afforded equal access to every opportunity offered on campus. Moon predicted, "Within your generation, colored students will be enrolled at the University of Missouri. They will demand equality in social affairs and will win it in scholarship and athletics." Despite some offensive turns of phrase, the black press reprinted large portions of Moon's editorial, such as this prediction about how black students would behave at the University of Missouri: "They will, perhaps, be over-aggressive and often insufferable in their new found freedom. But when they believe and feel that their freedom is permanent, they will settle down to the normal routine of school life." Moon also asserted, "The university must engage outstanding colored educators for the teaching staff, and see that the rights of colored students are protected in the local community. The university must see that all social groups—fraternities and sororities included—must be democratic in their selection of members, and that no person be excluded from any social group because of race, color, or creed."[77] This reporting, about support for integration on campus and the unnecessary cost of maintaining two separate systems of education was prominent in the black press as part of a national communication campaign to bring segregated education to an end.

The promise of the *Gaines* decision, unfulfilled in the wake of Lloyd Gaines's disappearance and the abandonment of Lucile Bluford's case, was poised for fruition, not in Missouri, but in Oklahoma. The case of *Sipuel v. Board of Regents of University of Oklahoma* (1948) paralleled the *Gaines* case. Ada Lois Sipuel was a graduate of the historically black Langston University. In 1946, she applied for admission to the University of Oklahoma law school.[78] Sipuel asked for a writ of mandamus which was denied by both a circuit court and the Oklahoma Supreme Court. Her case was accepted by the US Supreme Court, where it moved rapidly.[79]

The Supreme Court, led by Chief Justice Frederick M. Vinson, decided several key cases, most of which were unanimous, which attacked not only the doctrine of separate but equal, but also the doctrine of state action. The Court's decision in *Shelley v. Kraemer* struck a major blow against the doctrine of state action.[80] The St. Louis case involved restrictive covenants—neighborhood rules that prevented blacks from buying houses in the neighborhood—was resolved by a unanimous Vinson Court with a major redefinition of the meaning of state action. The Court found that "Private agreements to exclude persons of designated race or color from the use or occupancy of real estate for residential purposes do not violate the Fourteenth Amendment; but it is violative of the equal protection clause of the Fourteenth Amendment for state courts to enforce them."[81] Neighborhoods could create restrictive covenants as private organizations, but *Shelley* said the courts would be acting illegally if they tried to enforce them.

Thus, favorable sentiment for civil rights ran strong on the Vinson Court. This was because of the predisposition of the justices, the positive atmosphere for civil rights pressed by President Harry S. Truman, and the adoption of civil rights legislation in several states.[82] The US Supreme Court heard the *Sipuel* case on January 7–8, 1948, and issued its short, unanimous *per curiam* opinion on January 12, 1948.[83] The *Sipuel* opinion cited *Gaines* as precedent and read in part,

> On January 14, 1946, the petitioner, a Negro, concededly qualified to receive the professional legal education offered by the State . . . was denied solely because of her color. . . . The petitioner is entitled to secure legal education afforded by a state institution. To this time, it has been denied her although, during the same period, many white applicants have been afforded legal education by the State. The State must provide it for her in conformity with the equal protection clause of the Fourteenth Amendment, and provide it as soon as it does for applicants of any other group. *Missouri ex rel. Gaines v. Canada*, 305 U.S. 337.[84]

The wording of the decision did not specifically order her admission to the University of Oklahoma's law school; it only required that she be provided a legal education "in conformity with the equal protection clause of the Fourteenth Amendment." Oklahoma took this to mean it did not have to allow her to become a student. Rather, "the state's answer was the establishment of a separate law school in the state capitol building as an adjunct to Langston University." Sipuel applied again to the Oklahoma law school and was again rejected. As she prepared a legal challenge to the equality of the new law school, six other African American students applied for graduate school at the University of Oklahoma, all in programs that were not offered to blacks at Langston or elsewhere in the state. Charles Houston's expectations for state response were fulfilled. Confronting the enormous expense necessary to create several separate graduate programs for blacks, "the state finally gave in," although not for Sipuel.[85] Sipuel, the state insisted, had an option in the newly established law school at Langston. It would be another year and a half before Sipuel would ultimately be admitted to the University of Oklahoma.

The NAACP's Robert Carter perceived the importance of the *Sipuel* case: "The Court held that Negroes were entitled to equal educational facilities and at the same time such facilities were available to white persons. Perhaps, more importantly, the Court made it unmistakably evident in its handling of this case that it would not tolerate a cavalier approach by a state to the constitutional right of Negroes to equal educational opportunities."[86] As more cases made their way to the Supreme Court, the Court continued to make it more difficult for states to hold onto old standards of segregated education. In the immediate aftermath of *Sipuel*, the press reported her victory while applying more pressure on the State of Missouri. For instance, the final paragraphs of one news item in the *Afro-American* about Sipuel were dedicated to an editorial from the *St. Louis Post-Dispatch*: "It would be an embarrassment to Missouri to learn that it was trailing Oklahoma in putting aside racial prejudice in university education."[87]

In mid-1948, in the wake of *Sipuel*, the State of Missouri debated significant expenditures to upgrade the Lincoln University law school to stave off legal challenges in which plaintiffs argued that it was inferior to the University of Missouri's. As the state legislature considered appropriating $400,000 for the construction of a law school building for Lincoln, the black press reported on a split in the black community about whether to support such an appropriation. The president of Lincoln, Dr. Sherman Scruggs, and the new dean of the Lincoln University Law School, Scovel Richardson, supported the appropriation. In testimony before the legislature, Scruggs said that while the legislators might one day vote to abolish segregated education, "Until you do,

I know you will want to provide adequate facilities for the education of our Negro students. We don't want any ugly situations or lawsuits in Missouri."[88] The NAACP and the white St. Louis Bar Association, on the other hand, opposed the appropriation. The president of the St. Louis bar association was quoted repeatedly, saying,

> We feel that it would be virtually impossible for such a school to provide adequate legal education or education equal to that provided by the University of Missouri. The public interest demands that lawyers, white or colored, be adequately trained. We also feel that this money could be used to greater advantage and to the greater benefit of white and colored students alike if it were placed at the disposal of the University of Missouri, rather than to a makeshift separate school.[89]

The financial pressure on Missouri and other states establishing segregated graduate and professional programs grew. In February, the *Afro-American* reported, "Segregation is costly, Missouri is learning. A recent study reveals that it costs the State only $228 a year to train a white law student at the University of Missouri and $807, or nearly $600 more to train a student at the Lincoln University Law School."[90] Another estimate by a legal scholar was that the cost to educate a black law student at Lincoln was ten times that of educating a student at the University of Missouri.[91]

The tide seemed to be turning. A December 1948 editorial in the *Afro-American* asserted,

> One day we will write the history of our educational pioneers and our university martyrs. . . . There will be Donald Murray of the University of Maryland, Lloyd Gaines of the University of Missouri, Herman [sic] Sweatt of the University of Texas and Professor McLaurin and Mrs. Ada Sipuel of the University of Oklahoma, to name a few. A generation from now, even the white people themselves, who are responsible for this situation in these backward schools and even more backward States, will ask themselves how they could have been so utterly debased as to ask persons equal to them in money, culture and intellect to accept segregation on the grounds of color."[92]

The *New York Amsterdam News,* also in December 1948, printed a short article of "typical statements" by University of Missouri students in favor of
integration, such as a young woman who said, "'I went to school in the east
where Negro girls ate at the same table and attended classes with me. I might
not have been graduated had it not been for the help of some of my Negro
friends.'"[93]

As the reality of the Supreme Court's action in Oklahoma set in, the University of Missouri's Board of Curators under President Allen McReynolds
asked the state legislature to clear the way to allow the integration of the university. The *Afro-American* reported, "The curators recommended that the
Equal Rights Committee seek a change in Missouri law to permit enrollment
in the university and the teachers' colleges of colored students, 'in those divisions and curricula where instruction of equivalent character' is not afforded by Lincoln University in Jefferson City."[94] Quoted in the *Cleveland Call,*
McReynolds said, "'It is the board's understanding that the United States Supreme Court and subordinate courts have held that, under the Federal Constitution, it is the duty of the state to supply opportunities and facilities for
education to Negro students which are substantially equivalent to those afforded to white students,'" which meant that the state either had to create duplicate programs at Lincoln, "'or the programs at these [white] colleges must
be opened to Missouri Negro students.'"[95] As the state legislature's Equal
Rights Committee, chaired by St. Louis Republican Howard Elliott, considered the curators' request, the public discussion of the proposal continued.

On January 15, 1949, the *Afro-American* reported, "Only a few signed letters have been received by University of Missouri officials commenting on recent suggestions of admitting colored to certain units of the State school here,
Allen McReynolds, president of the university curators, has announced. The
Carthage lawyer declined to state definite figures but pointed out that the letters were so few in number that 'I would say they are too inconclusive to im-
port any meaning. There is a scarcity of comment,' McReynolds said. 'Two or
three of the letters have been commendatories,' while others have expressed
varying forms of doubt regarding the proposals.'" While there was no ground-
swell of support for the desegregation of the school, there was also no ground-
swell of opposition to it. The report concluded, "McReynolds said that while
he has received few letters on the matter, he has read many editorials, chiefly in
the metropolitan papers, all backing the step suggested by the board."[96]

The black press continued the public relations campaign in favor of desegregation with reporting about two private Missouri schools: St. Louis University and Washington University, both in St. Louis. The *Afro-American*
reported, "The integration of students at St. Louis University and in three
departments at Washington University was pronounced a success last week by
the two schools."[97] The *Los Angeles Sentinel* reported the news of the vote by
the Bar Association of St. Louis, an all-white organization, in support of de-
segregating the University of Missouri Law School and of Sidney Redmond's
application to join the association. The application of Redmond, who was
then serving as a St. Louis alderman, the *Sentinel* reported, had been pending
for six months.[98]

Between February 14 and 16, the faculty and student body of the University of Missouri were polled for their opinions about the possible admission
of black students. The survey asked, "Do you support the proposed change in
the Missouri law as proposed by the Board of Curators of the University?"[99]
The results of the poll were overwhelmingly in favor of their admission.[100] As
Afro-American columnist Cardell W. McVickers wrote, "A total of 4,156 students at the University of Missouri in Columbia are tired of seeing only white
faces on the campus. They out-voted 1,847 who wanted to keep the classes
lilywhite. The majority contend that colored students should be admitted to
graduate courses not offered at Lincoln University in Jefferson City."[101] In
response to these survey results, "the student council decided to request the
Missouri General Assembly to amend State laws to allow colored persons to
enroll not only at the university but at other State colleges."[102] The *Cleveland
Call* reported the survey results as evidence that, "Of all places, the 'backward'
South is daily demonstrating that America is conditioned to the acceptance of
Civil rights for all of its citizens."[103]

In mid-March 1947, the chairman of the Equal Rights Committee of the
Missouri House of Representatives, Howard Elliott, introduced legislation to
allow blacks to attend graduate school in state schools if there were no comparable courses available at Lincoln University. As the *Afro-American* reported, the bill had the chance to do much more than that: "Elliott said that after
the bill has been referred to a standing committee of the House for consideration, he will offer an amendment to permit colored students to enroll in
the State university and colleges without any limitation."[104] The House passed
the bill as amended by Elliott on May 4, 1949, by a margin of 100 to 8. As

the *Afro-American* reported, "The voting marks the first major attempt to relax the State's long-standing policy of segregated schools." It did point out, "It does not apply to public elementary and high schools, where the policy of separate schools is to be continued." After so many years of fighting integration, "The bill passed with virtually no discussion."[105]

The Missouri State Senate, with a Democratic majority, was not yet ready to cooperate. An amendment was offered to make the admission of blacks to state schools apply only in cases where there were no courses available at Lincoln University. However, the Senate Education Committee failed to report the bill to the full Senate. The *Afro-American* reported that the bill's sponsor, Representative Elliott, delivered "A severe attack on the State Senate and its Democratic majority leadership for failure to act on the bill."[106] The *Cleveland Call*, meanwhile, reported that Senator Gilmore, the chairman of the Education Committee, blamed the failure to report the bill on "three committee members, who had agreed to vote to drop the racial bars at the University of Missouri," but had changed their minds when racial violence broke out in St. Louis between white and black youth when the city attempted to desegregate city swimming pools.[107]

In June 1950, the US Supreme Court decided a pair of cases concerning equal protection and postgraduate education. On the same day, June 5, 1950, the Supreme Court announced its unanimous decisions in two cases—*Sweatt v. Painter* and *McLaurin v. Oklahoma State Regents*. In his introduction to the opinion in *Sweatt v. Painter*, Chief Justice Vinson summarized twenty plus years of effort that the NAACP began with *Murray v. Maryland* and *Missouri ex rel. Gaines v. Canada*.[108]

The first of these cases, *Sweatt v. Painter*, was a direct descendant of *Missouri ex rel. Gaines v. Canada*. In this case, Heman Marion Sweatt sought admission to the law school at the University of Texas. Texas maintained a program much like Missouri had prior to the *Gaines* decision to provide scholarships for black students to study out of state, despite the fact that *Gaines* clearly found such a practice unconstitutional. Sweatt was denied admission and told by university president Theophilus Painter that the state would create a separate law school for black students.[109] As historian Gary LaVergne writes, when Sweatt applied to the law school in Austin, he "set in motion events that appear surreal today. . . . While trying to prevent Sweatt from enrolling in UT Austin, a panicked Texas political establishment spent more money on

what was called 'Negro higher education' than it had during the entire previous history of the state."[110]

The Vinson Court was reluctant to overturn the precedent of separate but
equal entirely. Thus, *Sweatt* offered no sweeping pronouncement overturning the 1896 *Plessy v. Ferguson* decision, but the Court made it more difficult
for states to maintain segregated institutions that were allegedly "separate but
equal." It found the newly formed Texas State University for Negroes was not
substantially equal to University of Texas Law School. For the Court, the issue
was not whether the black law school was an adequate alternative: "we cannot
find substantial equality in the educational opportunities offered white and
Negro law students by the State. In terms of number of the faculty, variety of
courses and opportunity for specialization, size of the student body, scope of
the library, availability of law review and similar activities, the University of
Texas Law School is superior."[111] This is what Houston and Redmond would
have pursued, had *Gaines* continued toward a second hearing before the Supreme Court. Vinson cited *Gaines* and *Sipuel* as precedents that the equal
protection clause required Sweatt's admission to the Texas Law School. The
Court's decision remained cautious. It did not overturn the separate but equal
standard, but it did raise the bar for states justifying segregated education.

In *McLaurin v. Oklahoma State Regents*, the US Supreme Court raised the
bar higher. George W. McLaurin was in his sixties and a professor at Langston
University. He applied to a doctoral program in education at the University
of Oklahoma, along with five other African Americans seeking graduate education in various programs that were not offered in black schools in Oklahoma. They were admitted to the University of Oklahoma, but were segregated.
"McLaurin was required to sit in a classroom alcove labeled 'Reserved for
Colored.' McLaurin also had a segregated desk in the library behind a stack
of newspapers where white students could not see him. He ate alone in the
university cafeteria."[112]

The Vinson Court found that the restrictions imposed on McLaurin violated his Fourteenth Amendment rights, but, again, the US Supreme Court
resisted a sweeping decision. It did not use language overturning the principle of separate but equal. By making it impossible for the University of Oklahoma to segregate students of color while still allowing them to study at the
institution, the Court made it that much more difficult for states to segregate
students of color. As the NAACP's Robert Carter put it, "Taken together

these decisions meant that for all practical purposes legally enforced segregation in graduate and professional schools was now impossible. In short order all of the state universities in the South, with the exception of state universities in South Carolina, Georgia, Alabama, Mississippi and Florida, and many private universities opened their doors to Negroes."[113] Carter also noted that, at the time of his writing, cases were pending against Alabama and Florida.

These decisions were built on the foundation of *Gaines*. After the Supreme Court's pronouncement of the *McLaurin* and *Sweatt* decisions, the *New York Times* observed,

> Back of both of these decisions is the one handed down on Dec. 12, 1937 [*sic*], in the case of Lloyd Gaines, who sought admission to the University of Missouri. . . . The Supreme Court held the state was bound to provide for Gaines, under the separate-but-equal doctrine, the same educational facilities and opportunities that it offered to white students. That "within-the-state" phrase has dogged the South ever since. It means that if a course is offered to white students, it must be offered to Negroes and under the same circumstances.[114]

One week later, the *New York Times* reported briefly on the story of Gregory Swanson, an African American lawyer who applied for admission to the University of Virginia law school for graduate courses. The law school admitted him but the University of Virginia's governing body, the Board of Visitors, rejected his application in July of 1950, because he was black. This was a decision that the university was destined to reverse, in part because the school had already admitted a black student, Walter Ridley, for a doctorate in education.[115] Swanson sued the university and won an appeal in the federal circuit court in September 1950, on the heels of the Supreme Court's decisions in *McLaurin* and *Sweatt*. The *Times* attributed this appeal and others to the NAACP's success in *Gaines*.[116] The legal importance and popular attribution of the *Gaines* decision as an influence on desegregation was, if delayed, profound.

In the meantime, the University of Missouri continued to refuse all black applicants. After the *Gaines* and *Bluford* cases, Registrar S. W. Canada continued to receive a number of applications from black Missouri residents. They inquired about a broad range of postgraduate or special programs—Reserved

Officers' Training Corps (ROTC), medicine, speech, education, summer school. The university developed a standard operating procedure to handle these requests from black students. The inquiries or applications would be received by Canada, as university registrar. Once a correspondent was identified as black, Canada would forward the application to University of Missouri President Frederick Middlebush. Middlebush would return the inquiry to Canada asking him to consult Attorney William Hogsett for an appropriate response. Hogsett would write Canada back with a "suggested" reply, which Canada would copy directly and return to the potential applicant. Copies of the correspondence would typically be sent to other university attorneys, including Joseph Teasdale in St. Louis and Ruby Hulen in Columbia along with board of curators secretary Leslie Cowan. Hulen would sometimes confirm that a correspondent was indeed a Missouri resident/taxpayer.

The response from Canada would not reject an application but encourage the applicant to contact Lincoln University. For instance, a standard recommendation from Hogsett, which Canada would adopt, read:

> Referring to your application for admission to the University of Missouri, I am without authority to admit you. The laws of Missouri require the Board of Curators of Lincoln University to afford to the Negro people of the state opportunity for higher education in all branches equal to that available at the University of Missouri (Sections 10773–10781), *Revised Statutes of Missouri*, 1939); and any application for enrollment should therefore be made by you to Lincoln University at Jefferson City.[117]

Only once, in September 1942, did Hogsett shows signs of concern. Hogsett consulted with Teasdale requiring the inquiry of Bennie William Gordon, Jr., about the ROTC program, He was concerned that, in the middle of a world war, "a court fight to keep a negro from attempting to equip himself to serve his country as a soldier, by training at the University is *unwise from the University's standpoint*, and we should be very sure of our ground before we advise the University to reject him." In this case, Hogsett had Canada write Gordon, "the establishment of R. O. T. C. is a federal matter within the province of the President of the United States and the Secretary of War, I suggest that you address your inquiry to the War Department at Washington."[118]

Under this procedure, no one took responsibility for refusing to consider a black applicant. Middlebush, in particular, resisted putting decisions or rationale in writing. He kept informed, but for the most part, he let Canada and Hogsett coordinate the policy. One occasion, regarding the letter to Bennie Gordon, is unusual because it gives a hint of Middlebush's involvement. A letter from Canada to Hogsett notes that "President Middlebush has indicated his approval orally."[119] Information was shared beyond the University of Missouri group. Hogsett, for instance, wrote a letter to attorney and former Texas Senator Ben G. Oneal regarding the *Gaines* and *Bluford* cases, presumably for information pertaining to the *Sweatt* case.[120]

Canada was the first of the group to retire, in August 1946. Canada had been named as a party in the mandamus suits of Lloyd Gaines and Lucile Bluford, as well as the defendant in Bluford's 1939 civil suit before the federal district court. Canada's views on segregation are largely unknown, although he clearly did not push to admit Gaines, Bluford, or the other black applicants. Lucile Bluford remembered Canada as polite and friendly even as he read her a prepared statement refusing to allow her to register.[121] Lucile Bluford once looked up Canada in 1984, long after his retirement. She visited him at home and, during their conversation, asked him why he refused to admit her. Canada replied that to do otherwise would have cost him his job.[122]

Charles W. McLane became director of admissions, replacing Canada in the cycle of application refusals, in August 1946. With minor adjustments, the process of dealing with applications from black students remained the same as under Canada. McLane, for instance, sent the following notice to Gus Tolvar Ridgel, an applicant for graduate study in economics from Poplar Bluff:

> I am returning herewith your application for admission to the University of Missouri. The laws of Missouri provide that Negroes residing in the state may receive higher education at Lincoln University and require its Board of Curators to provide in that institution education up to the standard provided in the University of Missouri. Your application for enrollment should, therefore, be presented to Lincoln University in Jefferson City.[123]

Noel Hubbard, the registrar at the Missouri School of Mines, located in the small town of Rolla, also began receiving inquiries and applications from African Americans interested in study at the white-only engineering school. A similar procedure was followed, for instance, on January 19 when Hubbard rejected the application of Elmer Bell Jr.[124] The Missouri School of Mines was an affiliated campus operated through the University of Missouri Board of Curators.

Two of the applicants to the Missouri School of Mines, however, did something that many other black students did not. Elmer Bell Jr. and George Everett Horne contacted the black attorneys in St. Louis and asked for legal representation. On February 7, 1950, attorneys Sidney R. Redmond, Henry D. Espy, and Robert Witherspoon petitioned the circuit court in Boone County for admission to the Missouri School of Mines. Former state senator Allen McReynolds, then-president of the University of Missouri Board of Curators, wrote to William Hogsett about the lawsuit. "As you doubtless know from the public press, we have a suit brought on behalf of two negroes to enter Rolla. There has been a good deal of discussion by the board covering the whole problem. I expect to be back in your office again with the view to having you give this your usual excellent attention."[125] The university requested several delays in the case, in part, because they were preparing to lose, if not capitulate. Gus Ridgel, the student applying for the master's program in economics, was added to the lawsuit with Bell and Horne, so the action affected both the School of Mines and the University of Missouri.

University attorney Lee Carl Overstreet, who replaced Hulen, wrote to McReynolds, Hogsett, attorney Roscoe Anderson, and President Middlebush. Overstreet mentions that Hogsett had the idea to simply admit that Lincoln University did not offer equivalent courses in engineering. Overstreet continues, "It may be that the decisions of the Supreme Court in the Henderson, Sweatt and McLaurin cases will settle this aspect of the case for us but, whether they do or not, I do not think that isolated courses in Lincoln would be held to be the equivalent of the freshman course of study at Rolla if the matter were presented in court."[126] He discusses moving the suit to St. Louis, which he assumes Redmond prefers, but suggests instead that the suit be moved to Cole County, the home of the capital of Jefferson City. "From the legal standpoint, I can find no objection to the bringing of the suit in St. Louis, but I wonder if the Board might not stand in a better light with the out-state citizens of Missouri if the suit were brought in Cole County. Judge Blair is as good a Circuit Judge as any in the state and any decision by him would not be the subject to the possible objection that 'big city' ideologies were being forced down the throats of the good people in out-state Missouri solely as a result of our having filed the case in St. Louis."[127] The case was refiled in the circuit court of Judge Sam C. Blair.

Bell, Horne, and Ridgel won a declaratory judgment in the case against the University of Missouri. Judge Sam C. Blair of the Cole County Circuit Court ordered their admission. McLane confirmed that Ridgel's transcript was satisfactory for admission to the University. On July 26, 1950, McLane wrote Ridgel granting him permission to enroll. Ridgel became the first black student at the University of Missouri. Trumpeting the news, the Baltimore *Afro-American* did something which had become common in the black press—drawing attention to support for desegregation in the white community by reprinting material from white newspapers. "The St. Louis Post-Dispatch, in an editorial entitled 'It was Time,' which hailed Judge Blair's decision, pointing out that: 'Missouri's segregation policy in schools of higher learning was unjust to many residents and costly to all. Lincoln University for colored students could not possibly duplicate the educational advantages of the University of Missouri. Missouri has waited long for action assuring all its citizens of equal rights to higher education. It is not a revolutionary step, but only a proper one.'"[128] The *Los Angeles Sentinel's* headline declared, "Mo. U. Must Admit Negroes, Court Rules," and reported, "This is the first state decision favoring admissions of Negroes to state schools of higher education ever given out here since schools were segregated in 1865."[129]

The fight to desegregate the University of Missouri in Columbia was finally over when Gus Ridgel matriculated as the school's first enrolled African American student in August of 1950. Elmer Bell and George Horne were likewise admitted to the Missouri School of Mines and Metallurgy in Rolla, then a part of the University of Missouri and under Middlebush's authority. The university began to plan for the admission of black students in 1949, in response to proposed legislation in the state House of Representatives. House Bill 182 provided for "admission of qualified Negroes to state institutions of higher learning for graduate and professional training not offered at Lincoln University." The legislation did not pass, but university administrators foresaw integration in the future.[130]

By June 1950, the university's attorneys suggested that "some thought be given to some of the problems which will arise whenever negroes are admitted" since "we, apparently may soon see negro students enrolling in the University, both in Columbia and Rolla." The potential problems, administrators and lawyers expected, were in housing, seating in classrooms, libraries, and cafeterias, participation in extra-curricular activities, and athletics.[131] On July 14, William Hogsett, the university's lead attorney since *Gaines*, wrote

Middlebush regarding "Admission and treatment of Negro students." Although Cole County Circuit Court Judge Blair ruled in favor of the admission of three students, the university's position remained that it would not admit any black applicant who was not a Missouri resident and that it would not admit any black applicant if "substantially equivalent" courses were available at Lincoln University.[132] Hogsett warned Middlebush that "you cannot 'assume' that instruction in Journalism, Law, Education and certain academic subjects offered at Lincoln University is substantially equivalent to instruction offered at the University."[133] He also drafted a resolution on the admission of black students for President Middlebush to sign and release. The resolution codified the limitations on admission of black applicants, though it also mandated treatment of admitted black students "on the same basis of other races."[134]

The admission of Ridgel and the others also raised the question of whether the program for out-of-state tuition scholarships, central to the *Gaines* case—now strictly voluntary under revised statutes after the US Supreme Court decision, would continue. Lincoln University president Sherman Scruggs asked the state attorney general for an opinion on the scholarship program. Assistant Attorney General Aubrey R. Hammett Jr. issued an equivocating opinion on the out-of-state scholarship on July 31, 1950.[135] According to the university attorneys, "Lincoln has gotten an opinion from the Attorney General on the matter of whether or not, under the existing circumstances, they shall continue to pay the out of state tuition of resident Missouri Negroes who seek a course of study which is offered by Missouri University but it is not offered by Lincoln. [MU Vice President Thomas] Brady stated that he has been informed that Lincoln University could not make heads or tails out of the opinion."[136]

Nationwide, the struggle that began with Lloyd Gaines's victory was still featured prominently in the press. In an update on the current state of the fight against segregation in other states, the *Afro-American* argued,

> Good legal work, sound foundations, has smashed the white schools' stronghold, and liberal folk in these states see nothing to do but comply with the inevitable. It all started back in 1937 with the Gaines case in Missouri when on Dec. 12, 1937, a Federal court ruled in favor of Lloyd Gaines, who was seeking admission to the University of Missouri. The court said Missouri had to provide

equal facilities for colored applicants "within the State." This phrase
has provided the key to future decisions in similar cases.[137]

In October 1950, the *Afro-American* reported triumphantly, "White Su-
premacists are taking a real beating on the educational front. . . . Last week,
nine colored students were accepted without question at the University of
Missouri. The previously all-white student body gave them a warm welcome."[138] In November, the *Afro-American* reported, "Nine students have
received a cordial reception at the University of Missouri. The University announced that colored students will be admitted to all its departments at Columbia, and to the School of Mines and Metallurgy at Rolla. 'We agreed,' said
the board, 'that every colored student admitted to the University of Missouri
is entitled to receive and shall receive the same treatment accorded to students
of other races. This shall apply to the seating of students in the classroom,
library, cafeteria, athletic events and concerts.' Colored people not living in
Missouri, however, will not be admitted."[139]

Epilogue

Despite Gaines's disappearance and the unfulfilled promise of his specific case, the decision by the Supreme Court in 1938 was, for many years, the most significant victory of the movement. The black press referred to it repeatedly in stories about other cases in which plaintiffs were fighting segregation, from the *Bluford* case to *Sipuel*, *Sweatt*, *McLaurin*, and others. In a 1948 editorial commemorating Negro History Week, the *Atlanta Daily World* observed that "the Lloyd Gaines decision making it obligatory upon the state to provide equal education for all, has as much significance for our times as the Dred Scott decision."[1] Two years later, in an editorial regarding criticism of African Americans in Georgia for taking too much credit for the advances in civil rights, the editors of the *Daily World* responded with reflection,

> This statement bothered us as we began to think through its implications. We thought of the three victories won before the United States Supreme Court against the White Primaries, and we remembered that all of them were started and won by Texas Negroes. The Segregation Ordinances were won by New Orleans Negroes. The Restrictive Covenants decisions were won by Negroes in Detroit, Washington and St. Louis. The equalization of educational opportunities decision was won by Missouri Negroes, who backed Lloyd Gaines in his fight to study law.[2]

Gaines was a disappointment in its day for failed potential, but as time wore on, it was recognized in the black press as the foundation on which a house of desegregated education was built.

265

The efforts in higher education were prelude to the far broader goal of desegregating all educational institutions, and this achievement came, at least on paper, in the decision of the Supreme Court in *Brown v. Board of Education of Topeka, Kansas* in 1954. In that decision, the US Supreme Court finally did what the NAACP had sought for nearly fifty years—it overturned the principle of separate but equal in education. In the unanimous opinion, Chief Justice Earl Warren cited the important cases which came before: *Missouri ex rel. Gaines v. Canada, Sipuel v. Oklahoma, Sweatt v. Painter,* and *McLaurin v. Oklahoma*. In this case, Warren indicated, the Court was ready to move further.[3] The inevitable conclusion, after decades of legal wrangling and the slow process of chipping away at *Plessy v. Ferguson*, was this: "in the field of public education, the doctrine of 'separate but equal' has no place. Separate educational facilities are inherently unequal."[4]

There was still much to be done after the Supreme Court issued this decision. In fact, it was not possible for the Court to agree, unanimously as Warren wished, on how to instruct states and school districts to proceed in enforcing the decision. A second hearing was called, and a year later, the Supreme Court issued a second decision on the issue of enforcement. Even with the benefit of an additional year of debate, the Court's order with regard to enforcement was vague, relying on the phrase "with all deliberate speed," ordering, "the courts will require that the defendants make a prompt and reasonable start toward full compliance with our May 17, 1954, ruling. Once such a start has been made, the courts may find that additional time is necessary to carry out the ruling in an effective manner."[5] The momentous nature of the Supreme Court's decision in *Brown*, the overturning of the legality of separate but equal as it applied to education and, eventually, to other aspects of life, cannot be overstated. And it all began with the Supreme Court's decision in *Missouri ex rel. Gaines v. Canada*.

While the ruling in *Gaines* did not directly result in the desegregation of the University of Missouri, it is rightly viewed as a first step of major importance. The black press noted the case's importance as other important victories were won and so, too, did the white press. In 2009, the *New York Times* revisited the story of Lloyd Gaines and his case against the University of Missouri, on the occasion of the one-hundredth anniversary celebration of the NAACP. The article noted, "Had he not vanished at 28, Lloyd Gaines might be in the pantheon of civil rights history with the Rev. Dr. Martin Luther

King, Jr., Thurgood Marshall and other giants. . . . Instead, Mr. Gaines has been consigned to one of history's side rooms, his name recalled mainly by legal scholars and relatives." The article concludes, "Lloyd Gaines is now revered at the university, which awarded him an honorary law degree in 2006. That year, the state bar awarded him a law license, posthumously."[6] Lloyd Gaines and his legal counsel had the courage to file and win the first—and in many ways most crucial—battle in the US Supreme Court to desegregate education in the United States. The *Gaines* case was foundational in the process of undoing racial segregation.

Redmond, Espy, Witherspoon and other African American attorneys continued to press for racial equality in St. Louis on behalf of the NAACP, and they were joined by other younger lawyers, including David Grant and Frankie Muse Freeman.[7] Redmond was refused membership on account of race by the St. Louis Bar Association as late as 1949. He served as the president of the National Bar Association and implemented a full agenda to help African Americans in the legal profession and among the public. Some of his reforms included creating the *National Bar Journal*, edited initially by his friend and colleague Charlie Houston, and establishing free legal assistance centers. Espy and Redmond remained active in the local NAACP chapter, and Redmond served as president through 1945. He clashed with David Grant and other local NAACP leaders over the future of the St. Louis branch and its legal agenda. The younger leadership became stalwarts within the Democratic Party and wrested control of the St. Louis NAACP from the Redmond coalition. Under Redmond's leadership, the St. Louis branch focused more on and supported a legal agenda. Under Grant, a greater emphasis was placed on mass protest and demonstration. Grant's administration was also considerably less frugal than Redmond's.[8] Redmond also pressed for renewal of the state NAACP organization, which essentially had been dormant since a state conference in Kansas City in 1931.[9]

Redmond and Espy served as leaders within the Republican Party through the 1940s. Redmond was selected as a delegate to the Republican National Convention in 1940 and supported the nomination of Wendell Willkie. Espy served as a delegate to the Republican National Convention in 1948. Although the state Republican Party "never gave us a break," Redmond refused to abandon the party because of the poor treatment in Mississippi and elsewhere in the South. But, Redmond noted, "if the party doesn't wake up it will…lose the backing of Negroes all over the country."[10] Redmond was appointed to the municipal office of associate city counselor and was elected as the first black St. Louis alderman in 1944. He served as an alderman through the mid-1950s. He was appointed to the state board of education in Missouri, a near reversal of roles from the 1930s.

Henry Espy would also continue his legal practice and pursue a number of civil rights cases. In 1942, he entered the US Army as a private during World War II, disrupting his legal career. In the same year, the US Navy acquired his family's property in Vero Beach, Florida, through eminent domain to build an airfield. After the war, the property was transferred to the city rather than to the Espy family, which had requested its return. Espy engaged in a protracted lawsuit to reclaim the land.[11] Sidney Redmond became a fictionalized hero, with his sidekick Henry Espy, in a novel on race relations in Missouri, *Gone by Sundown*.[12] Unfortunately, the novel's historical context and its description of the *Gaines* case in particular is pure fiction. Generally, the local leadership of the NAACP legal agenda, who did much of the backbreaking work preparing litigation, is largely unremembered or relegated to a footnote. The national leadership attracts most of the attention, yet the local attorneys were critical in the development of the civil rights cases.

Walter White would continue as executive secretary of the NAACP until his death in 1955; his replacement at the helm was Roy Wilkins. Sidney Redmond was asked for his opinion of the notable national civil rights leaders of 1930s and 1940s. Redmond ranked the NAACP secretary highest. "Well, Walter White I would think would certainly be the outstanding one. He spoke in a loud voice, and he had the respect of most people. I don't know anyone who was his equal unless it is Dr. King. The NAACP hasn't been the same since he left. Not that it isn't continuing to do a good job." Asked about Roy Wilkins, another key figure during the period of the *Gaines* case, and Walter White's successor, Redmond described him as "very good" but went on to say, "I wonder if Roy is letting things get out of hand, like when they wanted to discharge one of the lawyers up there for making a statement. They should not have interfered with that. They lost a lot of good lawyers. Everybody in the department resigned. All of the staff." Redmond commented on his membership on the board of education positively. "Well, I'm just pleased with the fact that since I have been here I have done all I could to make St. Louis a better city and to enlarge opportunities of Negroes. That has been a tremendous undertaking. It has hurt me with a lot of white people. But that's a price you have to pay for progress." [13]

Thurgood Marshall replaced Charles Hamilton Houston as NAACP special counsel during the *Gaines* litigation. Houston devoted more time to his Washington law firm, but he also continued to work diligently in civil rights cases. Although Marshall's role in *Gaines* was largely advisory, he took over the NAACP legal agenda established by Houston. The national organization divided, giving the NAACP Legal Defense and Education more autonomy. Marshall served as the head of the organization through the *Sipuel, Sweatt,* and *McLaurin* lawsuits. He also carried the day in the *Brown v. Board of Education* decisions and saw the US Supreme Court reject educational segregation and the separate but equal doctrine in the early 1950s. Although the struggle for civil rights would continue, the primary objectives in education, set out by Nathan Margold and Charles Houston, were accomplished.

Marshall led the legal troops to victory in *Brown*, but Houston was not there. Charles Houston died from a heart ailment on April 22, 1950, before the US Supreme Court ruling that declared segregation inherently unequal and ended racial segregation in education. His colleague and cousin, William Henry Hastie, Jr., was confirmed as the first African American judge of the US Court of Appeals on July 19. Hastie compared Houston to another leader: "He guided us through the legal wilderness of second-class citizenship. He was truly the Moses of that journey. He lived to see us close to the promised land of full equality under the law, closer than he ever dared hope when he set out on that journey, and so much closer than would have been possible without his genius and his leadership." [14] Charles Houston blazed the trail from segregation to the threshold of equality. The case for Lloyd Gaines was the last mountain before the promised land of justice and equality.

Notes

Introduction

1. *Simple Justice: The History of Brown v. Board of Education and Black America's Struggle for Equality*, 213.

2. Robert L. Jack, *History of the National Association for the Advancement of Colored People*, 74.

3. "The Supreme Court faced squarely for the first time the issue of racial segregation in education in the 1938 case of *Missouri ex rel. Gaines v. Canada.*" Although other education cases reached the Court, it never considered the constitutionality of racial segregation. Dennis J. Hutchinson, "Unanimity and Desegregation: Decisionmaking in the Supreme Court, 1948–1958," 4.

4. John Hope Franklin, *From Slavery to Freedom: A History of Negro Americans*, 3rd ed., 553.

5. Leon A. Ransom, "Education and the Law: Gaines v. The University of Missouri," 111. Within a month of the Supreme Court's decision, this journal published the full text of the opinion. Ransom served as co-counsel for *Gaines* at the final stage of litigation.

6. Morroe Berger, *Equality by Statute: The Revolution in Civil Rights*, 133; Richard Bardolph, *The Civil Rights Record: Black Americans and the Law, 1849–1970*, 271.

7. Quoted by Carl T. Rowan, *Dream Makers, Dream Breakers: The World of Justice Thurgood Marshall*, 78.

8. Gaines described himself alternatively as Negro and colored. Language can be powerful, and descriptions can define individual and group identity. Currently, African American or black are popular terms to describe Americans who trace lineage to Sub-Saharan Africa. We use these sociopolitical terms interchangeably. However, usage of these terms was at best rare during the 1930s and the era of the *Gaines v. Canada* litigation. In this book, we also use the words that were spoken or written frequently by participants of this time, such as African descent, Afro-American, colored, and Negro. The dominant term during the latter nineteenth century was colored. Indeed, the NAACP, founded in 1900, is an organization to promote the interests of "Colored People." By the early twentieth

century, the word Negro, capitalized by proponents such as Booker T. Washington and W.E.B. DuBois, became customary terminology. Use of the word Black to describe African Americans was not standard until the 1960s, long after *Gaines* and its aftermath. See Tom W. Smith, "Changing Racial Labels: From "Colored" to "Negro" to "Black" to "African American"; and Lee Sigelman, Steven A. Tuch, and Jack K. Martin, "What's in a Name? Preference for "Black" versus "African American" among Americans of African Descent." The US Census Bureau used the term "Negro" as an ethnic designation until announcing an end to the practice on February 25, 2013. We capitalize Negro and African American but not colored, black, or white unless appropriate for the context.

9. According to census data, African Americans in St. Louis made up 6.4 percent of the population in 1900, 6.4 percent in 1910, 9.0 percent in 1920 and 11.4 percent in 1930, and 13.3 percent in 1940. For Kansas City, the comparable percentages are 10.7, 9.5, 9.5, 9.6, and 10.4. The percentage of African Americans in Independence and St. Joseph, two western Missouri municipalities near Kansas City actually declined over these decades. See Campbell Gibson and Kay Jung, "Historical Census Statistics on Population Totals By Race, 1790 to 1990, and By Hispanic Origin, 1970 to 1990, for Large Cities And Other Urban Places In The United States," 2005, Population Division, Working Paper, No. 76 (February). The NAACP and its allies were tracking these trends, see L.S. Curtis, Report of the Statistician, Missouri State Association of Negro Teachers, "Changes in the Distribution of the Negro Population of Missouri during the Last Fifty Years," November 7, 8, & 9, 1935, in NAACP Archives.

10. State population rose from 3.1 million to 3.7 million. Percentage of African American population for the state from 1900 to 1940 by decade was 5.2, 4.8, 5.2, 6.2, and 6.5 percent. See Campbell Gibson and Kay Jung, "Historical Census Statistics on Population Totals by Race, 1790 to 1990, and by Hispanic Origin, 1970 to 1990, for the United States, Regions, Divisions, and States," 2002, US Bureau of the Census, Population Division, Working Paper, No. 56 (September).

11. Mark V. Tushnet, *The NAACP's Legal Strategy against Segregated Education, 1925–1950,* 29–31. Many historical narratives of civil rights cases limit discussion to national NAACP counsel such as Charles Houston and, later, Thurgood Marshall. For instance, one otherwise fine account credits no contribution to local counsel in the *Gaines* case until after the appeal to the Supreme Court. See Gilbert Jonas, *Freedom's Sword: The NAACP and the Struggle against Racism in America,* 44. While Houston's impact cannot be underestimated, he depended on local co-counsel, particularly at the earlier stages of the litigation.

12. Jack Greenberg, *Crusaders in the Courts: How a Dedicated Bank of Lawyers Fought for the Civil Rights Revolution,* 37. Greenberg offers two English proverbs "no writ, no right" and "no lawyer, no law" to emphasize that local, black practicing attorneys were necessary for pressing for civil rights in the South.

13. See, for instance, white attorneys were in charge following the strike in nearby East St. Louis. Mark Robert Schneider, *We Return Fighting: The Civil Rights Movement in the Jazz Age,* 137.

14. Richard Kluger, *Simple Justice: The History of Brown v. Board of Education and Black America's Struggle for Equality;* Genna McNeil, *Groundwork: Charles Hamilton Houston and the Struggle for Civil Rights;* Mark Tushnet, *The NAACP's Legal Strategy against Segregated Education, 1925–1950.* See also, Geraldine Segal, *In Every Fight Some Fall,* for a biography of Houston.

15. William H. Hastie, "Charles Hamilton Houston (1895–1950)," 365.

16. Charles H. Houston to Sidney R. Redmond, September 24, 1936, 2.

17. Greenberg, *Crusaders,* 6. When Marshall left his office, he repeated Houston's words to his replacement, Greenberg, 8.

18. Genna Rae McNeil, "Charles Hamilton Houston," in John Hope Franklin and August Meier, eds., *Black Leaders of the Twentieth Century,* 229.

19. See, for instance, Houston to Redmond, April 30, 1936. Later in the case, Thurgood Marshall also contributed information for press releases. Memorandum from White to Marshall, May 25, 1938.

20. Notes for telegrams, December 12, 1938. "Copies of decision sent to 1 S.R. Redmond—for St. Louis Argus 2 *Kansas City Call* 3 [Baltimore] Afro American 4 [Pittsburgh] Courier, 5 Walter White 6 Leon Ransom."

21. Telegram from Wilkins to Houston and Redmond, July 11, 1936, Houston to Wilkins, July 12, 1936.

22. Lucile H. Bluford, Oral History, May 15, 1989, Women in Journalism, Washington Press Club Foundation, 69.

23. Frank F. Stephens, *A History of the University of Missouri,* 605. According to James Olson and Vera Olson, *The University of Missouri: An Illustrated History,* 83, after the Supreme Court decision, Gaines "left the state and did not pursue the matter."

24. *Plessy v. Ferguson (1896),* 163 U.S. 537.

25. Charles Lofgren, *The Plessy Case: A Legal-Historical Interpretation,* 5.

26. *Missouri ex rel Gaines v. Canada,* 337.

27. *Brown v. Board of Education of Topeka* 347 U.S. 483 (1954), 495.

28. *Brown v. Board of Education of Topeka* 349 U.S. 294 (1955), 301.

29. *Gaines v. Canada,* 305 U.S. 337 (1938), 345.

30. Ibid., 351.

31. Ibid., 351, 352.

1 Lloyd Gaines and the Missouri Mileau

1. Most of this personal history comes from two versions of Lloyd Gaines's autobiography, which he prepared for Charles Houston and the NAACP entitled "Lloyd Lionel Gaines." Lucile Bluford, who knew Gaines personally, says he was the youngest son of five children. "The Lloyd Gaines Story," 242.

2. Gaines recalls, "even then, we were aware of many of our shortcomings and could not help but envy our more fortunate white friends, who received free transportation to and from a modern consolidated school of longer duration, better equipment, and offering a greater variety of subject matter." Gaines autobiography, 2, in NAACP archives.

3. Oscar Minor Waring was the first black principal (1879–1909) of Sumner High School, originally called High School for Colored Students, established in 1875 as the first high school for blacks west of the Mississippi. A graduate of Oberlin, Waring was a noted educator but at least one source remembers him as a lawyer as well, see John A. Wright, *Discovering African American St. Louis,* 2nd ed., 33; Michael Fultz, "City Normal Schools and Municipal Colleges in the Upward Expansion of Higher Education for African Americans," 25.

4. Within two years, Gaines finished eighth grade; three years later he completed the four years of high school.

5. Both high schools, Sumner and Vashon, remain as part of the integrated St. Louis public school system; however, both have changed locations. The Vashon High School building of Gaines's day is now part of the Harris-Stowe State University campus.

6. Gaines autobiography, 4. He spoke with several black lawyers in St. Louis, including, according to Dwyane Smith, Homer G. Phillips, mentioned below. *We Have Not Had Such Luck: A Lloyd Gaines Case Study,* 77.

7. Gaines mentions St. Louis University and the University of Iowa as other attractive alternatives. SLU was a private school that had admitted African Americans but ceased the practice.

8. Bluford, "Lloyd Gaines Story," 243, notes only "he wanted to study law in his own state university which the taxes of his family helped support."

9. *Dred Scott v. Sandford* 60 U.S. 393 (1857).

10. Herman Dreer, *Negro Leadership in St. Louis,* 7.

11. The segregation ordinance was the first use of the initiative in St. Louis. Although Baltimore in 1910 and other cities approved ordinances for residential segregation, the St. Louis initiative was the first in which the public voted for residential segregation.

12. James Neal Primm, *Lion of the Valley: St. Louis Missouri, 1764–1980,* 3rd ed., 410–414; Lana Stein, *St. Louis Politics: The Triumph of Tradition,* 15. Though nearly all commentators describe the special election as one ballot measure, there were actually two initiative provisions, one for segregation for blocks with all members of one race and a second for blocks with 75 percent of one race. See *St. Louis Globe-Democrat,* February 28, 1916. They passed with similar margins, 52,318–17,841 and 52,025–17,823. The unanimous Supreme Court decision was *Buchanan v. Warley,* 245 U.S. 60 (1917).

13. See, for instance, Nathan B. Young, *Your St. Louis and Mine;* Priscilla A. Dowden-White, *Groping toward Democracy: African American Social Welfare Reform in St. Louis, 1910–1949.*

14. See Elliott M. Rudwick, *Race Riot at East St. Louis, July 2, 1917,* Charles Flint Kellogg, *NAACP: A History of the National Association of Colored People,* 221–227, and Daniel T. Kelleher, *The History of the St. Louis NAACP, 1914–1955,* 36–41. The quote is from the oral history of St. Louis attorney and local NAACP leader David E. Grant.

15. Alexander John Peter Garesché was a leading St. Louis attorney who challenged loyalty oaths in the 1865 Missouri Constitution in his and in a successful companion case before the US Supreme Court, *Cummings v. Missouri* (1867). J. Clay Smith, Jr., *Emancipation: The Making of the Black Lawyer 1844–1944,* 331, quotes Garesche: "But while I

will maintain ever the distinction between political and social equality, I shall necessarily deny that they are synonymous terms, but the law has granted to people of color political equality and however I may depreciate the manner in which it has been brought about, still it is an accomplishment."

16. Smith, *Emancipation,* 332–333.

17. In their discussion of the "Problems of Population and Race," Paul W. Paustian and J. John Oppenheimer wrote, "It is generally recognized that the Negro finds it very hard to obtain justice in the courts, either in criminal actions or in civil suits in which the adverse party is a white man. The Negro defendant seems to be subject to an almost irrebuttable presumption of his guilt, and the difficulty of obtaining competent counsel, together with the practice of excluding Negroes from jury service, makes justice difficult to obtain." *Problems of Modern Society: An Introduction to the Social Sciences,* 231. Paustian was on the faculty at Stephens College in Columbia.

18. Even by late 1939, Charles Houston needed books and information on court rules in Missouri in order to file an NAACP-sponsored civil case for damages in a federal court. He complained to Thurgood Marshall, "I could not get the books and court rules. None of our lawyers had them either in St. Louis or Kansas City." Asymmetric information gave advantage to white establishment interests, particularly in civil rights cases. Houston to Marshall, October 18, 1939.

19. Smith, *Emancipation,* 333, 352; Arthur D. Shores, "The Negro at the Bar: The South"; From "Missouri Court Frees Negroes Convicted by Unfair Trial," *Philadelphia Intelligencer,* September 19, 1934, quoted in full by Fitzhugh Lee Styles, *The Negro and the Law,* 49–50.

20. Doug Hunt, "A Course in Applied Lynching," 130–137.

21. Vaughn lost the 1920 Republican primary to the incumbent, Leonidas Dyer, 7,373-1,406. Howard University Law School graduate Joseph McLemore won the 1922 Democratic primary to become the state's first African American party nominee for the US Congress, but he also would lose to Dyer in the general election. *Official Manual 1921–1922,* 314; *Official Manual 1927–1928,* 410, 445; Smith, *Emancipation,* 333; William F. Nowlin, *The Negro in American National Politics,* 1931, 101–102.

22. *Shelley v. Kraemer* 334 U.S. 1 (1948). Vaughn represented the J. D. Shelley family who purchased a house located at 4600 Labadie Avenue in St. Louis in violation of the restrictive covenant governing the sale. Another owner in the neighborhood, Louis D. Kraemer and his wife, opposed the sale and sued for enforcement of the covenant preventing blacks from owning property there. In 1945, the trial court ruled on behalf of the Shelleys, but the Missouri Supreme Court reversed the decision in 1946. The US Supreme Court decision was 6–0 in favor of the Shelleys.

23. Clement E. Vose (*Caucasians Only: The Supreme Court, the NAACP, and the Restrictive Covenants,* 159–160) discusses how Thurgood Marshall and Charles Houston thought that Vaughn was premature in filing for a writ of certiorari. In addition, they believed Vaughn was an inexperienced appellate attorney and that he chose the wrong constitutional grounds—the Thirteenth Amendment's prohibition of slavery rather than the Fourteenth Amendment's equal protection clause—to argue the case. Vose also notes

the role of white St. Louis attorney Herman Miller in oral argument of *Shelley.* Richard Kluger (*Simple Justice,* 311–312) concurs with the observation about Vaughn's competence at the federal level. Genna McNeil (*Groundwork: Charles Hamilton Houston and the Struggle for Civil Rights,* 181–182) comments on the support provided by the national NAACP and Vaughn's co-counsel Herman Miller. Some argue the Supreme Court's rationale remains difficult to sustain as time has passed, for instance, see Mark D. Rosen, "Was *Shelley v. Kraemer* Incorrectly Decided? Some New Answers," 451–512.

24. August Meier and Elliott Rudwick, *Along the Color Line,* 138.

25. "Principles of the Citizens Liberty League," *St. Louis Argus,* December 26, 1919, 1; "Citizens Liberty League Approved by the Party Leaders in Conference," *St. Louis Argus,* February 6, 1920, 1.

26. Phillips received 1,848 votes, Vaughn 2,104, and incumbent Congressman Leonidas Dyer 8,030. Dyer would go on to win the general election. *Official Manual 1929–1930,* 303.

27. Smith, *Emancipation,* 558–559, quote at 559.

28. John A. Wright, *Discovering African-American St. Louis,* 66–67.

29. Edward T. Clayton, "The Strange Murder of Homer G. Phillips," 48; H. Phillip Venable, "History of the Homer G. Phillips Hospital," 542.

30. Other suggestions were that the murder resulted from evidence given in a perjury charge against fellow lawyer George Vaughn or a dispute with a janitors' union local. See Clayton, "The Strange Murder," 49–50.

31. Smith, *Emancipation,* 333.

32. Styles, *Negroes and the Law,* 232.

33. Ibid., 234. According to Smith, *Emancipation,* 334, by 1939, the year following the *Gaines* decision, there were only 51 lawyers in Missouri.

34. Charles H. Houston, "The Need for Negro Lawyers," 49.

35. Smith, *Emancipation,* 11; Sidney Redmond, oral history.

36. Houston, "The Need for Negro Lawyers," 52.

37. After his term in the senate, Redmond's grandfather Hiram Revels became president of Alcorn Agricultural and Mechanical College and edited the *Southwestern Christian Advocate.* Redmond's aunt, Susan Revels Clayton, and her husband, Horace, edited and published the *Seattle Republican.* Another aunt, Maggie, married Perry W. Howard, attorney and influential leader of the Black and Tan Republicans. See George Alexander Sewell and Margaret L. Dwight, *Mississippi Black History Makers,* 14–16, 355–360; Willard B. Gatewood, *Aristocrats of Color: The Black Elite, 1880–1920,* 133–135.

38. Redmond was "one of the top ten graduates from Harvard," Sewell and Dwight, *Mississippi,* 271.

39. Walter J. Leonard, *Black Lawyers,* 142–143. Redmond did attend Harvard Law School with Houston's cousin William Henry Hastie (LL.B. 1930, S.J.D. 1932).

40. For instance, see Charles H. Houston (Reno, NV) to Sidney Redmond (St. Louis), September 1, 1936. Houston also knew Redmond's father, Houston to Redmond, August 27, 1936.

41. Redmond, oral history. Houston likewise had returned to work with his father, a Howard Law School graduate and practicing attorney in Washington, DC.

42. African Americans led the Mississippi Republican Party from about 1924 through the late 1940s. For many years, S.D. Redmond was chairman of the state executive committee. His law partner and son-in-law, Perry Howard, was the national committeeman and Mary Booze, daughter of civil rights leader Isaiah T. Montgomery, was the national committeewoman. See V. O. Key Jr., *Southern Politics in State and Nation,* 286.

43. Smith, *Emancipation,* 298–299, 319–320, quote at 298; Schneider, *We Return,* 98–100. Smith notes that "evidence points to mistreatment of S.D. Redmond" (320), but also notes of continued legal difficulties including federal charges against Redmond and Perry W. Howard. Both attorneys eventually left Mississippi and set up a partnership in Washington, DC. Redmond, however, continued his practice in Mississippi, as he was co-counsel in a case before the state Supreme Court in 1932. Political scientist V. O. Key (*Southern Politics,* 286) quotes the *Birmingham Age-Herald* (August 13, 1948) that at his death, Sidney D. Redmond, "believed to have been the wealthiest Negro in Mississippi history, left an estate of $604,801.09." Charles Houston also identifies S.D. Redmond as one of three "notable exceptions" among older black lawyers in the South who challenged the establishment. See "The Need for Negro Lawyers," 52.

44. "New Auditorium Jim Crow Causes St. Louis Suit," *Afro-American,* October 20, 1934, quoted in full by Styles, *Negroes and the Law,* 35–36; Kelleher, *History,* 69–72. Judge Ryan had previously served as Dean of the St. Louis University School of Law. An oft-repeated exchange between City Counselor Charles M. Hay and the future plaintiff Joseph Harris went: "Joe, I don't know why you want to attend the opera. All I do at the opera is sleep." "Well Mr. Hay, I have as much right to sleep there as you do." (Kelleher quoting David M. Grant, an influential African American attorney and Democratic operative, 70, although newspapers also reported the anecdote.)

45. Herman Dreer, *Negro Leadership in St. Louis: A Study of Race Relations,* 1955, 85. Physicians and politicians comprised other important but smaller categories in Dreer's list. He also notes that acknowledged leaders tended to have higher levels of education and to come from more upper-class individuals, 86, 114.

46. Ibid., 80–81, 109–113

47. Ibid., 109. Earlier, in 1934, Dreer surveyed high school students and decried the limited knowledge of black leaders. "This study clearly shows that the educational background of the Negro is rich in the experiences of white people and meager in the experiences of his own." Ibid., 50.

48. Kelleher, *History,* 61. Kelleher had the opportunity to conduct interviews with Redmond, Espy, Witherspoon, and contemporaries. Transcripts of those interviews, unfortunately, seem not to have survived.

49. Kelleher, *History,* 61–65.

50. Ibid., 68, quoting Robert L. Witherspoon.

51. Ibid., 66.

52. R.P. Watts, "St. Louis welcomes N.A.A.C.P. Conference," *The Crisis,* May 1935, 151.

53. Sullivan, *Lift Every Voice and Sing,* 221.

54. "St. Louis Host to 26th Annual Conference," August 1935, 248. Evening mass meetings, including the commendation of the Spingarn Medal to educator Mary McLeod Bethune, occurred in the Vashon High School auditorium.

55. Sullivan, *Lift Every Voice and Sing,* 221–222.

56. Edwina W. Mitchell, *The Crusading Black Journalist Joseph Everett Mitchell,* 2, 10. "He wielded his editorial pen against the University of Missouri for refusing to admit Negro students." 22.

57. Dreer, *Negro Leadership,* 97–100. Kelleher (*History,* 61) says Mitchell "organized a Negro political machine and became a power behind the scene in local Republican politics."

58. Kelleher, *History,* 7–8, 62. While the Gaines case was under appeal, Mitchell wrote "the *Argus* has been the local Branch of the NAACP during the past twenty-five years" (*St. Louis Argus,* May 7, 1937, quoted by Kelleher, 62).

59. Mitchell, *Crusading Black Journalist,* 43–44. Mitchell was elected President for 1933–1934.

60. "Little by little, the Negro press, and its allies such as the National Association for the Advancement of Colored People, the Urban League and other organizations working in the interest of the Negro, have improved the Negro's lot in American a hundred fold. Without the Negro newspapers to work in cooperation with these great organizations, we are not too modest to say that the Negro would not have advanced as far toward the first-class citizenship as he has." Mitchell, *Crusading Black Journalist,* 28.

61. "The St. Louis American—A Local Institution," http://www.stlamerican.com/site/about/history/.

62. Nathan B. Young Jr., Oral History.

63. Antonio F. Holland, *Nathan B. Young and the Struggle over Black Higher Education,* 191–195, 203.

64. In his oral history, Sweets would describe meeting Joseph Pulitzer, O.K. Bovard, and Joe Holland of the *St. Louis Post-Dispatch* shortly after his arrival in St. Louis. Pulitzer provided inspiration encouraging Sweets to remain in St. Louis and dedicate his efforts to a successful newspaper business. See also Wright, *Discovering,* 49–50.

65. Bennie G. Rodgers in Doris A. Wesley, Wiley Price, and Ann Morris, *Lift Every Voice and Sing,* 21.

66. Peoples Finance Corporation was established in 1923 to provide banking services to African Americans in St. Louis. Other attorneys, including Nathan B. Young Jr., owner of the *St. Louis American,* Joseph McLemore, and Robert Witherspoon, as well as other professionals and businesses had offices in the Peoples Finance Building. See *St. Louis City Directory* 1931, 1938, 1940, and Wright, *Discovering,* 25.

67. For instance, attorney Robert Vann was co-owner and editor of the *Pittsburgh Courier.* Marjorie McKenzie Lawson maintained a law practice with her husband Belford while

a feature writer for the *Courier* from 1941–1955. (Belford Lawson was counsel in the Maryland case of *Murray v. Pearson,* before Charles Houston and Thurgood Marshall took over the case.) Percy Greene, the future editor of the *Jackson Advocate,* apprenticed law under the elder Sidney D. Redmond in Mississippi. Greene relates that they reviewed Sidney R. Redmond's Harvard notes. Both Redmond and Greene took the Mississippi bar exam at the same time, but only Redmond passed. See Charles A. Simmons, *The African American Press,* 43–47, 64–65; Sewell and Dwight, *Mississippi,* 270–273; Greene, Oral History, 7–9. Much later, Redmond would tutor Jack Harvey Young, Sr., and Carsie Hall. Both would become attorneys and litigate civil rights cases for the NAACP (Sewell and Dwight, *Mississippi,* 115–116). Young took over the senior Redmond's law office in Jackson.

68. During the 1930s, the era of the *Gaines* case, the *Argus* and the *Call* were the larger black newspapers in Missouri; the circulation of the *American* was comparatively small. From the mid-1950's, the *American* grew to a much larger readership than the *Argus* and the *St. Louis Sentinel,* a newer weekly formed in 1968.

69. Franklin married Ada Crogman, the daughter of Dr. William H. Crogman, a professor and subsequently President of Clark University in Atlanta. Ada Crogman Franklin had taught at Alabama State College and Tennessee State University and was influential in attracting black talent into drama. See Charles E. Coulter, *Take Up the Black Man's Burden: Kansas City's African American Communities, 1865–1939,* 99–117; Sherry Lamb Schirmer, *A City Divided: The Racial Landscape of Kansas City, 1900–1960,* 149–150.

70. Wilkins was born in St. Louis but raised by family in St. Paul, Minnesota. He received a degree in Journalism from the University of Minnesota. "Throughout the 1920s and 1930s, Franklin, Wilkins, and the Call stood out as champions for Kansas City's African American communities" (Coulter, *Take Up,* 112).

71. Felix Payne published a rival black newspaper, the *Kansas City American,* from 1928. Payne was a colorful and influential figure. He operated gambling operations, supported jazz musicians, and owned nightclubs and other businesses, including the Kansas City (KS) Giants, an independent Negro baseball team. Payne was associated with the Pendergast machine in the city and was active in Democratic politics; Chester A. Franklin was Republican. However, the *Kansas City American,* cofounded with physician William J. Thompkins, began to decline in terms of readership and profitability when Thompkins left in 1934. The influence of the *Kansas City American* was limited during the period of the *Gaines* case. See Coulter, *Take Up,* 114–115.

72. "Columbia Missourian Adopts Capital N," *New York Amsterdam News,* September 24, 1930, 20. As noted earlier, leaders such as Booker T. Washington and W.E.B. DuBois pushed for use. One interesting difference among the African American newspapers covering the *Gaines* case was how *they* referred to black students. In the *Afro-American,* for instance, the term most frequently used was "colored." In the *Defender,* the preferred term was "Race student," such as in this story about the difficulties of scheduling the initial *Gaines* trial and the NAACP's legal arguments: "The answer also denied that the maintenance of a scholarship fund for out-of-state study by Race students is equality in education as under the terms of the constitution." ("No Date Fixed for Hearing of U. Of Mo.

Case," *Chicago Defender,* June 20, 1936, 23.) The *New York Amsterdam News* and the *Los Angeles Sentinel* both used "Negro." The word "Negro" was an important part of Lloyd Gaines's case against the University of Missouri from which Gaines had, the *New York Amsterdam News* reported "been rejected solely because he was a Negro." ("Court Ruling on Ban Nears," *New York Amsterdam News,* July 18, 1936, 3.)

73. Journalism School founder Walter Williams, who developed an ethical creed for journalists, became University President in 1930 and remained in office until his death in 1935, about the time Lloyd Gaines began contacts with Registrar S.W. Canada about admission.

74. Simmons, 6.

75. Rodgers interview in Vanessa Shelton, *Interpretive Community and the Black Press,* 187–191.

76. The 62nd raised $6,000 and the 65th added $1,400 at a time when a black private earned only $13 a month. Arnold G. Parks, *Lincoln University, 1920–1970,* 7. Both regiments originally mustered in St. Louis, Missouri, and the intent was to establish a college there.

77. Baxter Foster, in Brazos Santiago, Texas (near Brownsville) to Lucy Foster, March 30, 1865. In March 8, 1865, Baxter writes Lucy of teaching junior officers in "Arithmetic, History, Geography, Grammar & Algebra." The regimental commander, Lt. Col. David Branson, on July 3, 1864, required all non-commissioned officers to learn to read and sergeants to write or be replaced by another who could. Considering it was illegal to educate Negros in Southern states were the regiment was posted, the order was extraordinary for its time (General Order No. 31, HD. Qrs. 62d Cold. Infty., 3rd July 1864, Orders, 62nd USCI, Regimental Books &Papers USCT, RG 94 {G-235}). Antonio F. Holland indicates that the Western Sanitary commission organized classes in reading and writing at Benton Barracks, St. Louis, as black soldiers were mustered in to the infantry. *Nathan B. Young and the Development of Black Higher Education,* 145; *Young and the Struggle,* 115–116.

78. The school system for the city of St. Louis established a normal school for the training of black teachers in 1890. The school became Stowe Teachers College in 1929, but it remained part of the city's public school system. Losing its name, it was merged with the white-only Harris Teachers College in 1954, after the *Brown* decision. Although, with Lincoln, this educational institution is now considered one of Missouri's two Historically Black Colleges, it did not become a state institution until 1979, when the General Assembly took control to create Harris-Stowe State College. See Fultz, "City Normal Schools," 25–28.

79. *Revised Statutes of Missouri* (1929), § 9622. The approved bill on April 15, 1921, was actually Senate Bill 435, "Lincoln University: Providing for organization and scope for higher education of negro race."

80. Rufus E. Clement, "The Impact of the War Upon Negro Graduate and Professional Schools," 145.

81. Some black Missourians, of course, did receive advanced education through the out-of-state tuition program. For instance, David M. Grant, a St. Louis attorney, civil rights leader, and president of the St. Louis Branch of the NAACP in the 1940s, was a

recipient of out-of-state tuition for his education at Howard University School of Law, since he could not attend the white-only University of Missouri. However, Grant was ineligible for financial assistance for his undergraduate liberal arts education at the University of Michigan since there were similar courses at Lincoln University in Jefferson City. David M. Grant oral history.

82. Ibid., 1.

83. Holland, *Young and the Development,* 161–62; Holland, *Young and the Struggle,* 126–127.

84. Holland, *Young and the Development,* chapter 5, cites several examples.

85. Parks, *Lincoln University,* 2007, 22.

86. Dr. John Edward Perry of Kansas City was appointed as a member of the Board of Curators from 1921 to 1924 and again from 1931 to 1935. Perry cites several examples. He mentions that the Board, or more often the Board President, made faculty hiring decisions when "such procedure is absolutely improper and foreign to the regulations" for accreditation by the North Central Association. One (unidentified) Board President hired teachers and then sold them stock, and his wife sold the teachers articles of clothing. Perry also cites an instance of the employment of a man aged 65 years with only an eighth grade education who received $200 monthly "equal to that of some of the assistant professors" who was hired by the President with directions, presumably from an influential politician, "To find something for the employee to do." J. Edward Perry, *Forty Cords of Wood,* 430, 448.

87. Holland, *Nathan B. Young,* 1984, 2006; Parks, *Lincoln University,* 27.

88. Emphasis in the original. See *Crisis,* 26 (September 1923), 226.

89. Columbia was home to two other schools for women's higher education: Stephens Female College and Christian College (now Columbia College).

90. Founded earlier were the University of Michigan in 1817 and the University of Indiana in 1819. Missouri entered the Union in 1821.

91. See for instance, C. Terence Pihlblad, "Mental Tests and Social Problems," 237–243. He received his Ph.D. from the University of Missouri in 1924 (*Possible Applications of Mental Tests to Social Theory and Practice*) and joined the faculty in 1930. He supervised several theses of master's students researching social and economic aspects of the local black community.

92. W. E. Burghardt Du Bois and August Granville Dill, *The College-Bred Negro American,* 24–25.

93. See Audrey Nell Kittel, *The Negro Community of Columbia, Missouri,* chapter 1, Alvin C. Boyd, *An Occupational Study of the Negro Citizens of Columbia, Missouri,* 56–57. Both Kittel and William Wilson Elwang, *The Negroes of Columbia, Missouri: A Concrete Study of the Race Problem,* note that the black population may be underestimated, as it appears not all births (or deaths) in the community were recorded and not all residents enumerated.

94. Columbia had a weekly black newspaper, *The Advocate,* edited by Robert Freedy, but apparently no issues survive. No references to Freedy or the paper appear in NAACP correspondence or related materials, but see Kittel, *Negro Community,* 8.

95. Boyd (*An Occupational Study*) supervised an extensive survey of 1,416 African Americans in Columbia in 1941 as part of a National Youths Administration Project. The surveys were conducted by ten recent graduates of the "Fred Douglass" high school, the segregated, black school in Columbia. In the 1930s, black Columbians, if employed, tended to have low paying jobs in the service sector or as unskilled labor. See Dorothy Martin, *Survey of Juvenile Delinquency in Columbia*, 90–92, 97–108; Elizabeth Cossum Grant, *Some Colored Working Mothers in Columbia*, 41–53; Kittel, *Negro Community*, 21–38. Economic conditions for African Americans nationally, in the North, and in urban areas such as St. Louis and Kansas City were much better than in Columbia. Economic surveys of the time indicate that opportunities for blacks lagged in this Midwestern college town.

96. J. Edward Perry, the black physician who would become a Lincoln University Curator in 1921, had lived and worked in Columbia as its only black doctor before and after the turn of the century. Perry estimated that a quarter of Columbia residents were colored. He also describes how local culture was simultaneously racist and segregationist, yet the depth of these attitudes was rather thin. Some whites would come to him for health care, and medical students from the University of Missouri interned in his office to learn more about practicing medicine (at this time, the School of Medicine had no hospital). University medical faculty, however, refused to interact or even speak with him during his time in central Missouri. See Perry, 159–160, 163–173, 201–203. In 1903, Perry relocated to Kansas City and established medical facilities specifically for blacks, the Perry Sanitarium and, later, the Wheatley-Provident Hospital.

97. Hunt, "A Course"; Douglas Hunt, *Summary Justice: The Lynching of James Scott and the Trial of George Barkwell in Columbia, Missouri, 1923*.

98. *An American Dilemma: The Negro Problem and Modern Democracy*, volume 2, 562. Myrdal also refers to lynching as "a local community affair."

99. *Rope and Faggot: A Biography of Judge Lynch*, chapter 2.

100. Sidney Redmond to Charles Houston, July 18, 1935. The correspondence mentions *two* lynchings in Columbia. The other may be the 1921 lynching of teenager Roy Hammond in Bowling Green, Missouri, as George Vaughn and others had used the incident to lobby the Governor before the Scott lynching. However, the location of the Hammond lynching is not much closer to Columbia than St. Louis, so the letter may refer to an early Columbia lynching of George Burke on September 17, 1889, or another incident. Ralph Ginzburg, *100 Years of Lynchings*, 265.

101. Houston, "Don't Shout Too Soon," 91. Houston expressed the concern that "there must be no violence when Lloyd Gaines arrives at the School of Law in the 1936 or 1937." There is correspondence between NAACP executive Walter White, Houston, and contacts at the University of Missouri such as student Charles M. Spencer on how to increase acceptance of Negroes among the student population. In his "Further memorandum re Lloy [*sic*] L. Gaines vs. Canada," January 24, 1936, Houston gives a somewhat different account of the case and mentions a confession and sentence of another individual. He identifies Nathaniel Sweets and Nathan B. Young as sources of information. The press release was "University of Missouri is Sued over Color Bar," St. Louis, January 31, 1936, 2.

102. Judge David Patterson Dyer, who issued the injunction against the residential segregation ordinance, was his uncle. On anti-lynching crusade and the NAACP's legislative agenda to promote the anti-lynching bill see White, *Rope and Faggot;* Jack, *History,* 26–47; Kellogg, *NAACP,* 209–246; and Megan Ming Francis, *Civil Rights and the Making of the Modern American State.*

103. Hunt, "A Course," 156–159, suggests that some members of the trial jury may have been part of the lynch mob.

104. Although private universities such as St. Louis University and Washington University in St. Louis had once admitted African Americans, they ceased doing so. Teacher, author, and columnist Herman H. Dreer, who graduated magna cum laude from Bowdoin College, applied for graduate admission to both. He received no reply from SLU but, in November 1934, the registrar at Washington University wrote Dreer, "We recognize your high attainment as a scholar and believe you would be a credit to our institution; however, since the University of Missouri, our state institution, does not admit Negroes, Washington University pursues the same policy." Dreer was admitted to and received a Ph.D. in sociology from the University of Chicago in 1955. Dreer, taken from a series in the *St. Louis Argus,* in Gerald Early, ed., *"Ain't But a Place": An Anthology of African American Writings about St. Louis,* 307–315 (quote at 314).

105. The separation between whites and blacks was complete even when artificial. For instance, attorney Sidney Redmond observed: "I found that Negroes are trained through correspondence by the extension department of the University of Missouri but that they get their credits for the work done through Lincoln University." Redmond to Houston, September 24, 1935.

106. The full statutory provision read: "Pending the full development of the Lincoln university, the board of curators shall have the authority to arrange for the attendance of negro residents of the state of Missouri at the university of any adjacent state to take any course or to study any subjects provided for at the state university of Missouri, and which are not taught at the Lincoln university and to pay the reasonable tuition fees for such attendance; provided that whenever the board of curators deem it advisable they shall have the power to open any necessary school or department." *Revised Statutes of Missouri* (1929), section 9622.

107. In addition to Missouri, these states were Maryland (1935)—the focus of the *Murray* case—Kentucky (1936), Oklahoma (1935), Tennessee (1937), Virginia (1936), and West Virginia (1927). Texas had established some graduate programs at the State College at Prairie View and was considering out of state scholarships for other disciplines at the time of the *Gaines* case. See Clement, "The Impact of the War," 147. Fred McCuistion, *Graduate Instruction for Negroes in the United States,* 60–70.

108. From Sidney Redmond interviews, Kelleher, 82.

109. From Henry Espy interview, Kelleher, 83.

110. The literature on *Plessy v. Ferguson* is voluminous. Excellent sources include Otto H. Olsen, *The Thin Disguise;* Charles Lofgren, *The Plessy Case: A Legal-Historical Interpretation;* Harvey Fireside, *Plessy v. Ferguson: Separate But Equal?;* Michael J. Klarman, "The Plessy Era"; Mark Elliott, "Race, Color Blindness, and the Democratic Public: Albion

W. Tourgee's Radical Principles in *Plessy v. Ferguson;*" Keith Weldon Medley, *We as Free-men:* Plessy v. Ferguson; Harvey Fireside, *Separate and Unequal: Homer Plessy and the Supreme Court Decision That Legalized Racism;* Mark Elliott, *Color-Blind Justice: Albion Tourgee and the Quest for Racial Equality from the Civil War to* Plessy v. Ferguson; and Williamjames Hull Hoffer, Plessy v. Ferguson: *Race and Inequality in Jim Crow America.* Re Justice Brown's later comment that the decision was in error, see H.B. Brown, "The Dissenting Opinions of Mr. Justice Harlan," 338, and Mark A. Graber, "Judicial Recantation," 809–810.

111. Legal scholar John Howard notes "*Plessy's* historical significance was not immediately grasped. As late as the 1940s *Plessy* was not included in anthologies of the most important Supreme Court cases." *The Shifting Wind,* 142.

112. State regulation was necessary to ensure segregation because private organizations may not find such policy cost effective. Jennifer Roback details how rules requiring segregation on streetcars replaced a norm of blacks and whites sitting wherever they wanted rather than institutionalizing an existing social practice. Moreover, streetcar companies generally resisted laws for segregation but enforced them once passed. "The Political Economy of Segregation: The Case of Segregated Streetcars."

113. *Joseph W. Cumming, James S. Harper, and John C. Ladaveze v. The County Board of Education of Richmond County, State of Georgia* 175 U.S. 528 (1899).

114. For background and insightful commentary on the *Cumming* case, see J. Morgan Kousser, "Separate but *Not* Equal: The Supreme Court's First Decision on Discrimination in Schools." However, as C. Ellen Connally notes, "A careful analysis of the ruling in Cumming demonstrates that the decision did not deal directly with the issue of racial segregation in public schools." In "Justice Harlan's 'Great Betrayal'? A Reconsideration of *Cumming v. Richmond County Board of Education,*" 73.

115. *Cumming v. Richmond County,* 175 U.S. 528, 545.

116. *Berea College v. Commonwealth of Kentucky,* 211 U.S. 45.

117. 211 U.S. 45, 67. He was joined by Justice William R. Day in dissent. Justice Day wrote the Supreme Court opinion for *Buchanan v. Warley,* 245 U.S. 60 (1917), discussed in Chapter 2 that found the Louisville ordinance requiring residential segregation unconstitutional.

118. The original Kentucky law required a 25 mile separation between educational facilities for blacks and whites. Although the state court overruled that section of the law as "unreasonable and oppressive," Berea College founded the Lincoln Institute in Louisville (about 90 miles distant) for the education of African Americans. The Day Law remained in effect until 1950 when amended by the Kentucky legislature.

119. See, for instance, Connally who observes that *Cumming* and similar decisions were "misread and misinterpreted" to justify practice of segregation, 73. Civil rights activist and California Judge Loren Miller notes "that lower federal and state courts fashioned a separate-but-equal formula for schools out of the Plessy, Cummings, and Berea cases, and in time the fiction grew that the Supreme Court had considered and determined this issue with finality, whereas the truth was that it had only skirted around the question and had spoken only by evasions and indirections. Lower courts were then

faced with the question of what constituted equality within the confines of the doctrine they expounded." *The Petitioners—The Story of the Supreme Court of the United States and the Negro,* 214.

2 Charles Houston and the NAACP's Legal Strategy

1. Clement Vose, *Caucasians Only,* 39–40.

2. Walter White, *A Man Called White,* 142.

3. Geraldine R. Segal, *In Every Fight Some Fall,* 22–24.

4. In his youth, Houston was described as "spoiled, self-centered, reclusive, comfortable, and undisturbed by racism." Gilbert Ware, *William Hastie: Grace Under Pressure,* 143. Bill Hastie describes his cousin, Charlie Houston as "reared in middle class comfort sheltered from many of the harsh realities that most Negroes experienced." Houston was, he adds, "not very acutely or painfully disturbed by American racism. If he was not pleased with the status of the Negro, he was not greatly moved by it and had no passionate concern to change it." William H. Hastie, Foreword to Segal, *In Any Fight Some Fail,* 5, 6. See also McNeil, *Groundwork.* McNeil notes Houston's early uncertainty about entering the legal profession, 34.

5. Rawn James Jr., *Root and Branch: Charles Hamilton Houston, Thurgood Marshall, and the Struggle to End Segregation,* 38–46, McNeil, *Groundwork,* 36–45, and Segal, *In Any Fight,* 25–28.

6. Referring to Harvard, Yale, and Princeton: "As for blacks and other racial minorities, a handful were tolerated as long as they remained inconspicuous; too many blacks, it was feared might change the 'complexion' of campus." Marcia G. Synnott, "The Half-Opened Door," 177. See also McNeil, *Groundwork,* 49–51.

7. Sullivan, *Lift Every Voice,* 168.

8. James, 30–31 and Gilbert Ware, *William Hastie.*

9. Sullivan, *Lift Every Voice,* 168–169. Although an advocate for black higher education and the founder of NCCN, Shepard publicly opposed desegregation in higher education, articulating the view that "Negroes could do their best work only in their own schools." See Pauli Murray, *Song in a Weary Throat: An American Pilgrimage,* chapter 11, and Lenwood G. Davis, *Selected Writings and Speeches of James E. Shepard, 1896–1946, Founder of North Carolina Central University,* 14. On the critical nature of the clearance of transcripts from NCCN, see Charles H. Houston, Memorandum to Hastie, White, and Margold, April 20, 1933, 1–2.

10. See Gilbert Ware, *"Hocutt:* Genesis of *Brown,"* 227–233, and Jerry Gershenhorn, *"Hocutt v. Wilson* and Race Relations in Durham, North Carolina, During the 1930s," 275–308. Hocutt also proved not to be a particularly good student, Tushnet, *NAACP's Legal Strategy,* 53.

11. White, *A Man Called,* 142. Margold was born a Romanian Jew; he later worked on behalf of Native American rights.

12. Tushnet, *NAACP's Legal Strategy,* 28. Tushnet also notes that Margold found producing the 218 page report difficult, and Margold was behind schedule. Many other

responsibilities for the NAACP, including successfully arguing the Supreme Court case of *Nixon v. Condrun* (286 U.S. 73 [1932] re the Texas white primary) before the Hughes Court, and private practice impeded on his work. Tushnet, *NAACP's Legal Strategy,* 25–29; Kluger, *Simple Justice,* 166–173. Kluger evaluates the Margold Report as "a remarkable document. Not that its reasoning was without flaw or that its suggestions were all followed. What it did do was open up vistas, especially at places like Howard Law School. It stood back from the flow of litigation and projected a counter-flow. It did not restrict itself to narrow or obscure arguments. It stayed very close to the Court's own precedents but tried to find some that the Court had not chosen to recall—or had chosen to ignore—in sustaining segregation practices." 169.

13. Houston was one year senior of Margold at Harvard Law, and, for one year, both served on the editorial board of the *Review.* Tushnet, *NAACP's Legal Strategy,* 15; McNeil, *Groundwork,* 115–116.

14. Kluger, *Simple Justice,* 164–165; Tushnet, *NAACP's Legal Strategy,* 13–20; McNeil, *Groundwork,* 114–115; Jonas, *Freedom's Sword,* 41–42. See The American Fund for Public Service, Inc., *Report for Four Years, 1930–1934, Summary of Twelve Years,* November 1934, in NAACP Archives.

15. Nathan R. Margold, *Preliminary Report to the Joint Committee Supervising the Expenditure of 1930 Appropriation by the American Fund for Public Service to the N.A.A.C.P.,* 1930, i–v.

16. Ibid., 94.
17. Ibid., 94-95.
18. Ibid., 15.
19. *Gong Lum, et al., v. Rice, et al.,* 275 U.S. 78 (1927).
20. Ibid., 78, 84–85.
21. Ibid., 275 U.S. 78, 86.
22. Margold, *Preliminary Report,* 18.
23. Ibid., 19.
24. Ibid., 26.
25. Ibid., 22.
26. *Cumming v. Richmond Board of Education,* 175 U.S. 545 (1899).
27. Ibid.
28. Margold, *Preliminary Report,* 27.
29. Ibid., 93.
30. Ibid., 28.
31. Ibid., 29.
32. Ibid., 30.
33. Ibid., 30–31.
34. Ibid., 31.
35. *Yick Wo v. Hopkins,* 118 U.S. 356 (1886).
36. Ibid., 373–374.
37. 118 U.S. 374.
38. Margold, *Preliminary Report,* 32.

39. Ibid., 35.

40. Ibid., 37.

41. Ibid., 41

42. Ibid., 64, 82, and 87.

43. Ibid., 100.

44. Ibid., 101.

45. Ibid., 38.

46. Ibid., 93.

47. Ibid., 93.

48. Ibid., 93–94.

49. Ibid., 95–96.

50. Ibid., 97.

51. Ibid., 98.

52. McNeil, *Groundwork*, 115–116.

53. Hastie's words come from his eulogy at Houston's funeral. See "Charles Hamilton Houston (1895–1950)," *The Crisis*, 365, and "Charles Hamilton Houston," *Negro History Bulletin*, 207.

54. McNeil, *Groundwork*, 133.

55. http://www.loc.gov/exhibits/brown/brown-segregation.html

56. Tushnet, *NAACP's Legal Strategy*, 36.

57. Charles H. Houston, "Educational Inequalities Must Go!" 300.

58. Ibid., 300.

59. Margold, *Preliminary Report*, 2.

60. Houston, "Educational," 300.

61. Charles Hamilton Houston, "Cracking Closed University Doors," 370.

62. Fred McCuistion found that postgraduate education in southern and border states began at Howard University (in the District of Columbia) in 1921. Writing during the year of the *Gaines* decision, he discovered "there are 7 Negro institutions offering graduate instruction—3 public, 3 private, and 1 church-affiliated. No Negro institution offers instruction beyond the master's degree." *Graduate Instruction for Negroes in the United States*, 102. In addition to Howard, the institutions were Atlanta University (GA), Fisk University (TN), Hampton Institute (VA), Prairie View State College (TX), Virginia State College, and Xavier University (LA). Most of the master's level degrees were in education for teaching in segregated schools.

63. By the academic year 1938–1939, 665 black students were enrolled in graduate programs in universities outside the South. Approximately half of those students, 319, were from the southern and border regions. Only 1,069 black students were enrolled from 1930–1938, so the number of students was increasing dramatically. McCuistion, *Graduate Instruction*, 56–57.

64. Houston, "Educational," 301.

65. In addition to the six states offering out-of-state tuition scholarships, others had no opportunities at all. "Nine southern states have no provisions for the education of Negroes on the graduate and professional level." These were Alabama, Arkansas, Delaware,

Florida, Georgia, Louisiana, Mississippi, North Carolina, and South Carolina. McCuistion, 70.

66. Houston to Marshall, December 19, 1939.

67. Houston to Marshall, October 18, 1939, 3.

68. James Jr., *Root and Branch,* 30.

69. http://www.virginia.edu/woodson/projects/kenan/jackson/jackson.html

70. Like Houston, Murray graduated from Amherst College (in 1934). Houston and his lieutenant Thurgood Marshall served as lead counsel. Donald Gaines Murray has no familial relation to Lloyd Gaines. His grandfather was Bishop Wesley John Gaines of the African Methodist Episcopal Church (Houston, Memorandum, "What is the aim of the educational campaign?" March 5, 1936, 5).

71. *Pearson, et al. v. Murray,* 182 A. 590, 169 Md. 478 (1936), 103 A.L.R. 706 (1936), opinion by Chief Justice Carroll T. Bond. The Court of Appeals is the supreme court of the state of Maryland. See also Editorial Comment, "The University of Maryland Versus Donald Gaines Murray," *Journal of Negro Education,* 166–174.

72. Houston, "Cracking," 364.

73. Ibid., 370–372.

74. Margold, *Preliminary Report,* 94.

75. Ibid., 95.

76. Houston, "Educational," 316.

77. Ibid., 316.

78. Houston, "Cracking," 370.

79. Charles H. Houston, "Don't Shout Too Soon," *The Crisis,* March 1936, 91.

80. Houston, "Educational," 316.

81. Houston, "Cracking," 370.

82. Houston, "Educational," 316.

3 Gaines and Losses

1. Following Missouri (1929) were Maryland (1935), Kentucky (1936), Oklahoma (1935), Tennessee (1937), Virginia (1936), and West Virginia (1927). See Rufus E. Clement, "The Impact of the War," 147. As Michael J. Klarman (*From Jim Crow to Civil Rights: The Supreme Court and the Struggle for Racial Equality,* 204) notes, providing blacks with no access to graduate and professional education was "a seemingly flagrant violation of separate but equal" so the Missouri law became the precedent on which other southern and border states could appear to offer postgraduate education for African Americans without actually doing so. In reality, a list of scholarship recipients of the underfunded tuition scholarship program were mostly black teachers seeking summer education rather than college degrees. Sidney R. Redmond to Charles H. Houston, October 24, 1935.

2. Juan Williams, *Thurgood Marshall: American Revolutionary,* 96–97.

3. Mark V. Tushnet, *NAACP's Legal Strategy,* 70–71, points out that Houston had contacted Redmond in mid-July, just after the *Murray* trial case was decided. However, NAACP records clearly indicate that the organization already was seeking information on higher education practices in Missouri in January, and Houston met with Redmond, Espy

and others prior to July 2, 1935. Edward Lovett to (Missouri) Secretary of State Dwight H. Brown, January 15, 1935, January 19, 1935, Sidney Redmond to Charles Houston, July 2, 1935, Houston to Redmond, July 11, 1935, July 15, 1935. Lovett was a Howard University law school graduate who had worked with the firm Houston and Houston and then worked for the NAACP legal team.

4. Houston to Redmond, July 11, 1935.

5. Houston to Redmond, July 15, 1935, "Memorandum for Preliminary Investigation into Exclusion of Negroes from the University of Missouri."

6. Description from Houston to Walter White, May 22, 1939, 6.

7. He added, "The University fights have lagged because new students have not come forward in numbers and asked aid to obtain graduate and professional education." Charles H. Houston, "The University of Missouri Case and the Educational Campaign," December 15, 1937, 1.

8. Memorandum for Preliminary Investigation; Houston to Redmond, July 15, 1935.

9. Redmond to Houston, July 18, 1935 (under Espy's letterhead). Redmond notes here that two Negroes were lynched in Columbia.

10. Redmond to Houston, August 17, 1935.

11. Redmond, Oral History, 5.

12. According to Daniel T. Kelleher, "The lawyers for the University of Missouri took statements trying to prove Espy and Redmond were soliciting business. If this charge had been proved, they would have stood in peril of disbarment. Despite this disquieting threat, Redmond and Espy persevered and there was never a formal charge." *The History of the St. Louis NAACP*, 88.

13. Redmond, Oral History, 5.

14. Redmond to Houston, December 24 (?), 1935. By mid-November, Redmond had "succeeded in getting about eight persons to file applications with the University of Missouri." Redmond to Houston, November 13, 1935.

15. Houston to Redmond, December 26, 1935.

16. Houston to Redmond, July 15, 1935.

17. For instance, the *St. Louis American* and Redmond, Espy, Witherspoon and other lawyers had offices in the People's Finance Building at 11 North Jefferson Avenue.

18. Houston to J. E. Mitchell and Houston to M. B. Young [*sic*], July 12, 1935.

19. Nathaniel Sweets, Oral History, University of Missouri—St. Louis, July 20, 1970. Gaines "was one boy that I paid his way up to Jefferson City. I sent him up there to play football. But Lloyd got up there and chickened out and didn't play football. But he did stay and finish and was a very good student." Sweets claims "the Gaines case had its conception right in our little office" (5).

20. Lucile H. Bluford, "The Lloyd Gaines Story," 242–43. A review of his grades reminds of the magnitude of contemporary grade inflation. Most of the grades on Gaines's transcript were Bs with a few As and Cs. Gaines earned a C+ in the history course on "The Negro in America." Nevertheless, Gaines was considered by all decision-makers as academically strong. UA.

21. Gaines to Walter White, March 6, 1937, 3.

22. Williams, *Thurgood Marshall*, 97.

23. Redmond to Houston, August 27, 1935. Like Redmond and Gaines, Lenoir was born in Mississippi, in Yazoo City in 1890.

24. Sweets Oral History.

25. Redmond Oral History, 5.

26. Houston to Redmond, September 26, 1935.

27. Canada requested transcripts on August 24, and Gaines responded that transcripts were on the way. Lloyd L. Gaines to Registrar, postcard, August 27, 1935, September 10, 1935, UA.

28. Likewise, for undergraduate admission, a transcript from Sumner, Vashon, or other high school signaled the race of the applicant.

29. Depositions in *MO ex rel Gaines v. Canada*, No. 34,337, 15–16.

30. See, for instance, Patricia Sullivan, *Lift Every Voice*, 168–169 and Tushnet, *NAACP's Legal Strategy*, 53.

31. Redmond to Houston, August 27, 1935.

32. Parks, 28.

33. Florence (1938) notes that many states, including Missouri, did not distribute federal funds for vocational education to land-grant schools under the Morrill Act fairly. His article was written after Florence left Lincoln in 1937, during postgraduate studies at Harvard University and before moving to Virginia Union University.

34. Gaines had followed with a registered letter to the Registrar on September 10, 1935 requesting a prompt decision regarding admission (UA). University of Missouri Registrar S. W. Canada sent the following telegram to Lloyd L. Gaines on September 18, 1935: "Regarding your admission to law school President Florence and member board Lincoln University will confer this afternoon in Jefferson City about the matter. Suggest you communicate with President Florence regarding possible arrangements and for further advice."

35. Redmond to Houston, September 24, 1935. St. Louis attorney George C. Willson, a member of the Board of Curators, responded by directing Gaines to the University President and to Board of Curators President and state Senator F. M. McDavid. Willson to Gaines, September 26, 1935. Gaines's letter to the president was addressed to Walter Williams who had recently died and been replaced by Middlebush on July 1.

36. Florence to Gaines, September 23, 1935. Florence met and referred Gaines to Lincoln University Board of Curators President Dr. Joseph Dolliver (J.D.) Elliff, former Joplin educator and then University of Missouri Education professor, a state and regional school inspector.

37. Gaines to Houston, September 27, 1935, 1–2.

38. Houston to Redmond, November 1. It is only through Gaines's short autobiography that we know much about his early life. See Charles H. Houston, "Don't Shout Too Soon," 79, 91.

39. Houston to Redmond, October 2, 1935.

40. Canada was born in Albany, Missouri, and later lived in nearby Stanberry.

41. During the events culminating in the *Gaines* decision, Canada lived at 821 Virginia Avenue in Columbia, near political scientist (and future dean of school of business and public administration) William L. Bradshaw, Circuit Court Reporter Howard B. Lang, football coach Gwinn Henry, and, at 813 Virginia, William Lester Nelson, Representative to US Congress, 1919–1921, 1925–1933 and 1935–1943. The housing neighborhood is long gone and now part of the MU campus, but the latter address is the current location of the University's Gaines Oldham Black Culture Center. The Center is named in part after Lloyd Gaines, the plaintiff in the lawsuit against Canada.

42. Frederick A. Middlebush and Chesney Hill, *Elements of International Relations.* One contemporary book reviewer acknowledges the authors are "thorough, comprehensive, and fair" although also considers the text "dull" and "deplorable," J. Hamden Jackson, *International Affairs Review Supplement,* 19 (June 1941), 268–269. Another reviewer considers the "valuable" work as better than its competitors and "concise and systematic, distinguished throughout by careful statement and sober judgment," John B. Whitton, *American Journal of International Law,* 35, (April 1941), 405–406.

43. David A. Leuthold, *Biographical Directory of the Political Science Department, University of Missouri (Columbia): Faculty, Masters, and Doctors, 1902–1965,* 10. Charles C. Clayton, *Frederick Arnold Middlebush, President, University of Missouri, 1935–1954: Appreciation Banquet, June 10, 1954, at Columbia. Columbia, MO: University of Missouri,* 4, 6.

44. Coincidentally, the year of *Brown v. Board of Education.* The Supreme Court handed down the *Brown* decision in May; Middlebush's planned resignation was effective at the end of June. His influence continued for several more years as President emeritus, a title created uniquely for Middlebush, until his retirement in 1960.

45. Gaines addressed his letter to President Walter Williams, who had recently died. See "Depositions on behalf of respondents," *State ex rel. Gaines v. Canada, Circuit Court of Boone County,* No. 34,337, 32–33. Redmond to Houston, December 8?, 1935 enclosing copy of Frederick A. Middlebush to N.A. Sweets, December 6, 1935, with handwritten note that the letter was "the first letter the president has sent to one of our group."

46. Clayton, 5, in the caption of a photo of Middlebush with the Board of Curators taken in 1938.

47. McDavid was in the Missouri Senate from 1902 to 1910 and a member of the Board of Curators from 1921 and President of the Board from 1933 to his death in 1943. He served as President pro tem of the Senate in 1907.

48. Gaines told Redmond that he had written the previous week in September. Redmond to Houston, October 1, 1935, Gaines to McDavid, November 24, 1935, where he quotes an October 5 response from McDavid that "At first convenience I will talk with the President of the University on this subject," McDavid to Gaines, November (31?), 1935. McDavid claims meetings of the Board of Curators are informal and irregular.

49. Section 9657, R. S. Mo. 1929.

50. Houston to Redmond, November 13, 1935, January 3, 1936.

51. December 30, 1935, S.W. Canada to Arnett G. Lindsey, December 27, 1935.

52. Houston to Redmond, January 3, 1936.

53. Memo re Gaines vs. Canada, Registrar, January 24, 1936.

54. On that "terribly snowy day," the trip to Columbia took two hours and forty-five minutes and three hours and thirty minutes to return. Carl T. Rowan, *Dream Makers*, 71–72.

55. Houston, Memo re Gaines vs. Canada, Registrar, January 24, 1936.

56. Redmond to Houston, February 14, 1936.

57. Houston, Memorandum re Lloyd L. Gaines vs. S.W. Canada, U. Mo., January 24, 1936. Houston added that "Judge [Dinwiddie] ushered us out side door courteously, but obvious that he wanted to be rid of us and was very much disturbed."

58. Houston, "Further memorandum re Lloyd L. Gaines vs. Canada," January 24, 1936. See also Rowan, 72.

59. Houston to Wilkins, January 25, 1936.

60. At the time, George Samuel Schuyler produced a serial for the *Courier*, and he would later work as a business manager for the NAACP. Throughout his career, Schuyler's writing was provocative and he shifted from socialism to support for the John Birch Society. See, for instance, *Black and Conservative: The Autobiography of George S. Schuyler*, 1966.

61. Wilkins to Schuyler, January 28, 1936.

62. Houston to Redmond, January 31, 1936.

63. Houston to N.B. Young and to J.E. Mitchell, February 8, 1936.

64. Houston to Wilkins, July 13, 1936.

65. Houston to Wilkins, July 17, 1936.

66. "Negro Files Suit For Admission to Missouri School," *Salt Lake Tribune*, January 26, 1936, 3A.

67. "Sues to Enter the University of Missouri: N.A.A.C.P. Backing Student," *St. Louis Argus*, January 31, 1936, 1.

68. "Sues to Enter the University of Missouri," 8.

69. "Lloyd Gaines of St. Louis Is Applicant," *The Call*, January 31, 1936, 3.

70. "'Instead of acting on and appraising petitioner's certificate or passing same on to the officers (of the university) having jurisdiction over the same, as he was legally bound to do, Canada referred petitioner to the president of Lincoln university and the president of the board of curators of Lincoln university. This action on Canada's part was unauthorized, illegal: was not taken in good faith in the course of appraising petitioner's (Gaines') scholastic attainments and mental and moral character with a view of determining his fitness to be admitted into the law school, but was wrongfully and arbitrarily done pursuant to a conspiracy between Canada and others, to petitioner unknown, with the unlawful purpose of excluding petitioner (Gaines), a qualified resident of the state of Missouri, from said school of law." "Lloyd Gaines of St. Louis Is Applicant," *Kansas City Call*, January 31, 1936, 1.

71. "NAACP Planning New Drive on Lily-Whitism," *Afro-American*, September 14, 1935, 4.

72. "Univ. of Missouri Color Bar Attacked by NAACP Lawyers," *Philadelphia Tribune,* February 6, 1936, 3; Univ. Missouri Sued By Colored Student: School Officials Stunned When Writ Is Filed," *Cleveland Call and Post,* February 6, 1936, 1; "War Against Jim Crow: NAACP Attorneys File Petition for Mandamus," *Afro-American,* February 8, 1936, 8.

73. Walter Williams, University of Missouri President preceding Frederick Middlebush, established the University Missourian, as means to train student journalists.

74. "Attempt Made to Let Negro Enroll In M.U.: St. Louisan Demands That Registrar Rule on Application," *Columbia Missourian,* January 24, 1936.

75. Edwin Moss Watson, "editor and proprietor" of the *Tribune* owned the newspaper since 1905. A former journalist and lawyer, Col. Watson's views on race relations were complicated. For instance, in 1923, his editorials had opposed entry of the Ku Klux Klan into the area, but he also had incited actions leading to the James Scott lynching (Hunt, "A Course," 128–130, 142–143). See also Chuck Adamson, "Early Tribune publisher was 'a colorful writer,'" *Columbia Daily Tribune,* July 2, 2005.

76. "Negroes Apply for Entrance to MO. U," *Columbia Daily Tribune,* January 24, 1936, 1.

77. See press release, "University of Missouri is Sued over Color Bar," St. Louis, Missouri, January 31.

78. Redmond to Houston, March 3, 1936. McLemore maintained political connections within the state Democratic Party. Given subsequent events, this rumor seems unlikely to be correct, however, it does suggest that university officials felt the need to act quickly in order to control future decisions.

79. According to Redmond, Hulen "informed me that the Board of Curators of the University of Missouri will meet one day this month and pass on the application of our client. Judge Dinwiddie told him to tell me that he would print the writ if we wanted it. However, in view of the fact that our petition sought action on the application I see nothing would be gained for(?) the issuance." Redmond to Houston, March 24 (?), 1935. See also N.T. Cave to S. R. Redmond, March 31, 1936.

80. In addition to Gaines's application to the School of Law, the applications mentioned at this time were for the College of Engineering, the School of Medicine, and the School of Journalism. Minutes of the Meetings of the University of Missouri Board of Curators, February 8, 1936, 1595–1596 (quote at 1595), UA.

81. Ibid, 1596.

82. Minutes of the Meetings of the University of Missouri Board of Curators, March 27, 1936, 1623a–1625 (quote at 1624).

83. Ibid, 1624–1625. Emphasis in the original. See also "Official Notice(?) of Board Action," Leslie Cowan, Board Secretary, to S. W. Canada, Registrar, March 30, 1936.

84. "The notes I made during the meeting show that you made the motion to adopt the resolution regarding the admission of negroes to the University. Of course it is possible that I made a mistake in making my original notes but these notes indicate clearly that you made the motion. According to Roberts' Rules of Order on parliamentary procedure

the chairman of a meeting should not make a motion. Therefore, you will note in the minutes (page 1624) that I have used the general form stating 'Upon motion, properly seconded.' I hope that this will be satisfactory to you." Leslie Cowan, Secretary, to Senator F.M. McDavid, April 8, 1936, UA.

85. "M.U. Board to Decide Today on Negro Case," *Jefferson City Post-Tribune*, March 27, 1936, 6.

86. "Application of Negro Rejected: Entrance of Gaines to University Refused by Curators," *Columbia Missourian*, March 28, 1936, 1.

87. "University of Missouri Refuses Negro Students," *Circleville Herald*, March 28, 1936, 1.

88. A similar case involving J. Reuben Sheeler who wanted to attend law school in Tennessee ended with the prospective plaintiff backing out. Another on behalf of the application of William B. Redmond II (no relation to Sidney) for the University of Tennessee School of Pharmacy ultimately faltered following William Redmond's poor academic performance at Fisk University. Tushnet, *NAACP's Legal Strategy*, 53–55, McNeil, *Groundwork*, 143.

89. For instance, Houston and the St. Louis NAACP branch were distracted by the indictment of Earl Conner Williams for a brutal murder and beating in Spotsylvania National Military Park. Williams, a Missouri resident, claimed to be in St. Louis during the attack, so Houston wanted to hold a branch meeting to seek funds to defray travel expenses of St. Louis witnesses to the federal trial court in Richmond in order to establish his alibi. Williams was represented by court appointed white attorney Callom B. Jones who is (p.2) "a very high class lawyer who spent twelve years in the district attorney's office in Richmond. His interest in the Williams case seems to be based on his conviction that Williams is innocent and that a frame-up is threatened." Williams had been arrested in Mississippi, but he recanted a confession. Houston to Redmond, April 2, 1936. See also "Jurymen at Scene of Lovers' Lane Murder" and "City Furnishes Trial Witnesses," (Fredericksburg, VA) *Free Lance-Star*, June 23, 1936, 1. According to one report, "Approximately a hundred witnesses have been called." "Williams Trial Set For Monday," *Free Lance-Star*, June 20, 1936, 1.

90. Genna Rae McNeil, *Groundwork*, 142–43. Rowan, *Dream Makers*, 70.

91. Rowan, *Dream Makers*, 70.

92. Kelleher, *History*, 88–90.

93. The correspondence between Houston and Redmond from the NAACP archives contains numerous references to travel, filing, and other expenses paid (eventually) in sums of $50 or less. Much later, in the only exception, Houston would cover two days per diem for Espy and attorney Robert Witherspoon during the Boone County hearing for Gaines (Houston, "Office Memorandum re Gaines vs. U. Missouri, tried Columbia, Mo. 7–10–36," July 11, 1936 4).

94. Marshall to Wilkins, Memorandum, "Inaccuracies in press releases," October 24, 1939.

95. Minutes of the University of Missouri Board of Curators, December 18, 1936, 1688–1689, February 12, 1938, 2028–2029, UA.

96. Rowan, *Dream Makers,* 73.

97. *The State of Missouri at the relation of Lloyd L. Gaines, Relator, vs. S. W. Canada, Registrar of the University of Missouri, and the Curators of the University of Missouri, a body corporate, Respondents,* April 1936, No. 34,337.

98. Houston to Redmond, April 4, 1936.

99. Press release, "New Suit Filed Against University of Missouri to Aid Negro Applicant," April 17, 1936.

100. "Missouri Varsity Bars Lloyd Gaines," *Afro-American,* April 4, 1936, 22.

101. "Missouri U. Curators Say 'No' to Gaines," *The Call,* April 3, 1936, 2. "New mandamus suit is necessary as original suit in Boone county court was designed to force action by Registrar Canada on Gaines' application. The action of curators makes continuance of present mandamus suit unnecessary.... When Gaines filed his petition, he had received no answer from either Canada, the registrar, nor from the board of curators relative to his application for admittance to the law school. His application was neither accepted nor denied."

102. "Negro Fails to Gain Admittance to Missouri U," *Cleveland Call,* April 16, 1936, 3.

103. "MO. U. Challenges Merit of Lincoln," *Afro-American,* June 6, 1936, 6; "University of Missouri Denies Lincoln University (Mo.) is Accredited," Columbia, Mo., May 23, 1936.

104. "Univ. of Missouri Denies Rating of Race University," *Chicago Defender,* June 6, 1936, 1; "University of Missouri Denies Lincoln University (Mo.) is Accredited."

105. Houston was involved in the trial for William Redmond in Nashville while Redmond worked to schedule the Boone County trial.

106. Houston to Redmond, April 30, 1936. The University's lawyers were university attorney Nick T. Cave and former county prosecutor Ruby Hulen (Columbia), former Judge Fred L. Williams and Board member George C. Willson (St. Louis), former Senator and Board President Frank M. McDavid (Springfield), and lead attorney William S. Hogsett (Kansas City). McDavid and Willson were added to the counsel listed earlier. Gaines had addressed one of his original letters to Willson; McDavid was the sitting Board President.

107. Press release, "State Asks Delay in U. of Missouri Suit," May 22, 1936.

108. "William S. Hogsett," obituary, *Kansas City Times,* April 25, 1960. His reputation was earned "because of his legal experience and the variety of cases he had handled. Many lawyers went to him over the years for advice in complicated legal matters."

109. "William S. Hogsett."

110. Wm. S. Hogsett to Ken Teasdale (St. Louis attorney), August 23, 1942. This is an inquiry from Hogsett to a colleague in St. Louis. Canada's inquiry involved a letter from Bennie William Gordon Jr., of Webster Groves, a St. Louis suburb (Canada to Hogsett, August 19, 1942). FAM.

111. The three other applicants, also deposed, were Arnett G. Lindsay (Law), John A. Boyd (Mathematics), and Nathaniel A. Sweets (Journalism). A substantial majority of the time was focused on Gaines's deposition. The applicants graduated from Lincoln, except

for Lindsay, who graduated from Howard University and knew Charles Houston. "Depositions on behalf of respondents," *State ex rel. Gaines v. Canada, Circuit Court of Boone County,* No. 34,337. Sweets later said he was admitted to the University but was rejected when he arrived. "When I got over there, the registrar saw me, he said, 'You must be at the wrong place.'" Sweets, Oral History.

112. Houston to Redmond, May 23, 1936.

113. Houston did not attend, and Sidney Redmond represented the plaintiff. Henry Espy attended but did not speak. Houston Memorandum to the office, June 8, 1936, 1.

114. George McKeever and Francis McNeily were arrested for shooting and killing of Boone County Sheriff Roger I. Wilson and State Trooper Sergeant Ben O. Booth on June 14, 1933. Dinwiddie knew Sheriff Wilson personally. He presided over the criminal trials during January and June 1936 in nearby Fulton in Callaway County, and both suspects were convicted. McNeily turned state's evidence and was sentenced to 10 years in prison; McKeever was sentenced to death. McKeever's was the last legal hanging in Missouri on December 18, 1936. The sheriff's grandson, Roger B. Wilson, would be a Lieutenant Governor and, briefly, Governor of the state.

115. Charles H. Houston, Memorandum to Office, St. Louis, June 5, 1936.

116. White to Houston, June 8, 1936.

117. Houston Memorandum to the office, June 8, 1936.

118. Redmond to Houston, September 14, 1935. Redmond had met with Gaines, but he had not yet requested legal assistance from the national NAACP.

119. On the same day, Thurgood Marshall and Leon (Andy) Ransom argued the Baltimore County case on school equality. Baltimore County had eleven high schools for whites and none for blacks, see Press Release, "School Equality Before Courts in Two States," New York, July 10.

120. Houston, "Office memorandum re Gaines v. U. Missouri, tried Columbia, Mo. 7–10–36," Jul 11, 1936, 1.

121. O.R. Rogers, "The Weather," *Columbia Daily Tribune,* July 10, 1936; *Columbia Daily Tribune,* July 11, 1936.

122. Paul Paustian, Ursula Genung, and Dorothy Miller, "Introduction" to untitled work, attached with Ursula Genung to Charles H. Houston, February 7, 1938, 1.

123. As chief counsel, Hogsett's role was equivalent to Houston's. Fred Williams would handle much of the procedural work, as Redmond would continue to do. Nick Cave, initially, was the primary local contact for University officials. Frank McDavid was very involved in the early stages of the case, but like George Willson, as a Board member, he was also a party to the lawsuit.

124. "Gaines Case Heard Today," *Columbia Daily Tribune,* July 10, 1936, 1.

125. Houston, Office Memorandum, 2.

126. "Gaines Case Heard Today," *Columbia Daily Tribune,* July 10, 1936, 1.

127. "Gaines Case Opens Today in Columbia: Fight for Admission of Young Man to Missouri University to Be Hot," *The Call,* July 10, 1936, 3

128. Charles H. Houston, "Confidential Office Memorandum re Gaines Vs. U. Missouri, tried Columbia, Mo. 7–10–36," July 11, 2013.

129. Ibid., 2.

130. Ibid., 1.

131. Ibid., 2.

132. Ibid., 2.

133. The *St. Louis Post-Dispatch* printed much of Hogsett's opening statement. Ibid., 1.

134. Ibid., 1. Paustian, Genung, and Miller, 2. Redmond to Houston, March 8, 1938.

135. Houston, Office Memorandum., 2.

136. Ibid.

137. Paustian, Genung, and Miller, 2. Houston forwarded Genung's confidential letter to Redmond as evidence "which proves how the dean of the Missouri law school perjured himseld [*sic*] on the witness stand in the Gaines case." Houston to Redmond, February 28, 1938.

138. Transcript of *State ex rel. Gaines v. Canada,* Circuit Court of the County of Boone, June 1936, v. 34 337, 58–59.

139. Transcript, 62–64.

140. Transcript, 76–77. Elliott estimated that 85 percent of all those who take the state bar exam pass, but 90 percent of Missouri Law School graduates pass. As Houston notes, he admitted the percentages were only a guess, but he did not back down from this assessment.

141. Transcript, 114.

142. Transcript, 74. Former University of Missouri Professor J.D. Elliff had opposed many of the earlier efforts of President Nathan B. Young to improve Lincoln University. According to Antonio Holland, Elliff "had a rather limited vision in regard to education for blacks" (*Young and the Struggle,* 173) and supported racial segregation in education. Holland notes that "In the 1930s Elliff told [historian] Dr. Lorenzo J. Greene that 'cows would be grazing on the moon before a Negro was admitted to the University of Missouri'" (n. 40, 174).

143. Transcript, 74. In 1935, the legislature reduced the appropriation for scholarships to the differential between in-state and out-of-state tuition. E.R. Adams, the Assistant State Superintendent of Public Schools, described the financial situation and disbursement of funds for out of state tuition scholarships. He noted limited and decrease in funds, also noting that the law required Lincoln University officials to handle the program. The State Superintendent took over the program because it was not implemented. Houston's NAACP press release provocatively says the Superintendent's Office "has illegally been administering the scholarships from 1921," "U. Missouri Case Before Court," Columbia, July 10. Admitting a current controversy with the Lincoln Board of Curators over control of the scholarship program, Adams concluded his testimony by stating "And I hope they take that out of our hands and administer it." 89–93 (quote at 93).

144. Transcript, 99.

145. Ibid., 99–100.

146. Ibid., 101.

147. Paustian, Genung, and Miller, 3.

148. Transcript, 101–102 (quotes at 102). Of course, the decision to reject Gaines's application was not made by elected representatives in the legislature, but by a resolution of the unelected Board of Curators.

149. Transcript, 108.

150. Office Memorandum, 2.

151. Houston's perception was that Dinwiddie's views had changed. "When Redmond and I first went to see him last January, he indicated that the people in Columbia had discussed the matter and were of opinion that a Negro could force his way into the U.Mo. if he insisted on it; and he wanted us to take the case direct to the State Supreme Court on the ground it would be an authoritative decision and would be accepted by the entire state, rather than force him to rule. Between January and June he had begun to see just the opposite."

152. "U. Missouri Case Before Court," Columbia, Mo., July 10, 1936, 3

153. "U. of Mo. Officers Say all Foreigners Are Welcome," *Afro-American*, July 18, 1936, 3; "U. Missouri Case Before Court," Columbia, Mo., July 10, 2.

154. "St. Louis Court's Decision Is Expected July 27ᵗʰ," *Afro-American*, July 18, 1936, 3; "U. Missouri Case Before Court," 1 (quoting Redmond). Houston (and/or Wilkins?) appeared to prefer quotations of local counsel, so it is unclear whether these (and others) words attributed to Redmond are actually his or Houston's. The *St. Louis Argus* agreed that a long legal fight was in the offing: "Both parties, according to reports, have indicated that they will not be content with the state supreme court's ruling in the case and that eventually if will be carried to the United States Supreme Court." Elizabeth Cobb. "MO. U. Ban is Upheld," *St. Louis Argus*, July 31, 1936, 1.

155. "Missouri U. Case Under Advisement," *Kansas City Call*, July 17, 1936, 2.

156. "Judge Dinwiddie Hears 4 Cases: Suit of Lloyd Gaines Vs. University Curators Set for Friday," *Columbia Missourian*, July 7, 1936, 1.

157. "Gaines Case Heard Today," *Columbia Daily Tribune*, July 10, 1936, 1.

158. "Missouri U. Files Answer to Negro," *Joplin Globe*, May 24, 1936, 10.

159. "Missouri U. Files."

160. "To Submit Briefs in University Case: Action of Negro for Entrance to school to Go to Higher Courts." *Columbia Tribune*, July 11, 1936, 1.

161. "To Submit Briefs in University Case," 2. North Todd Gentry was a former Circuit Court Judge, State Attorney General, and Missouri Supreme Court Judge and Curtis B. Rollins was a former President of the Missouri Board of Curators and the son of James S. Rollins, the "father of the University of Missouri," slaveholder, and Congressman who switched his stance and helped pass the Thirteenth Amendment in the US House of Representatives.

162. "Educational Equality Exists Without Admitting Negroes," *Columbia Missourian*, July 10, 1936, 1.

163. Ibid.

164. "Gaines Case Taken Under Advisement," *Columbia Missourian*, July 11, 1936, 1.

165. "Gaines Mandamus Suit Heard By Court," *Joplin Globe*, July 11, 1936, 13.

166. Ibid.

167. "Court Ponders Suit Against Missouri U," *St. Louis Globe-Democrat,* July 11, 1936, 4a.

168. *State ex rel. Gaines v. Canada,* July 24, 1936.

169. Houston, Redmond, Espy, and Witherspoon discussed filing a separate lawsuit against Lincoln University to establish a law school "knowing full well it would be lost" but depriving the University of Missouri of a defense and persuading African Americans of the need to go against the University of Missouri. "No definite decision on this as yet. If brought, Redmond and I would be out of it so that there would be no confusion about our position. It would be handled by counsel unconnected with Gaines' case."

170. The *Columbia Daily Tribune* reported "It has been previously agreed among the attorneys for both sides that an appeal would be taken, whichever side lost the case." "Dinwiddie Rules Against Gaines," July 24, 1936, 1. The day after the trial, the newspaper predicted the case involves "an issue that is apparently headed for the United States Supreme Court regardless of decisions in Missouri state courts...." "To Submit Briefs in University Case," *Columbia Daily Tribune,* July 11, 1936, 1.

171. "Long Battle Expected in Gaines Case," *Call,* July 31, 1936, 2.

172. Houston (Reno, NV) to Redmond, August 25, 1936, 1–2.

173. The decision, according to the newspaper, concerned "Lloyd L. Gaines, St. Louis Negro, who is attempting to force his entrance into the University of Missouri which has never accepted Negro students refusing to permit the negro to enter the university." "Dinwiddie Rules Against Gaines," *Columbia Daily Tribune,* July 24, 1936, 1.

174. "Lloyd Gaines Loses Suit in Circuit Court," *Columbia Missourian,* July 24, 1936, 1. The primary comparison was with the *Murray* case in Maryland. The two cases, as observed in the *Missourian,* were very similar: "Practically the only difference in the case in Maryland and the one here is that Maryland had provided $10,000 for fifty scholarships of $200 each for the years 1935–37. Requests totaling 383 were received for these scholarships and 113 applications were filed. The state court held that Pearson's chance at obtaining one of these scholarships was 'slender' and decided he did not equal educational opportunity. They did not, however, rule on whether a chance to attend a college outside the state constituted equal protection." Of course, Raymond Pearson was President of the University of Maryland, and it was Donald Gaines Murray would have been eligible for a scholarship.

175. Roy Wilkins to Sidney R. Redmond, July 28, 1936, 2. "It may be that the Maryland case was so sudden and was won so quickly that wide public interest did not have a chance to be aroused. You are reaping the benefit of attention missed by the Maryland."

176. An NAACP memo indicates that Houston's account was forwarded to "Miss Morgen of Time Magazine on July 13 in accordance with her request for a story." V. Warmsley, July 13, 1936.

177. "White Missouri," *Time,* August 3, 1936, 32.

178. Wilkins "had a tough time with them because they wanted so much exact information that we did not have. They particularly wanted to know the precise ground on

which Judge Dinwiddie ruled for the university. I could not gather this from the Post-Dispatch clipping which you sent us. I read them what the Post-Dispatch said but they said that was not sufficient." Wilkins to Sidney R. Redmond, July 28, 1936, 1. He also asked for more: "People will be interested in the grounds upon which Judge Dinwiddie acted and in the next steps to be taken by us, together with a pep statement by the lawyers." The reporters were interested in the personal impact as well. "*Time* made the pertinent comment that if the case will take two years in the supreme court, Gaines will be cheated out of his law course. That is true. What have you to say on that, if anything?" Wilkins to Redmond, 1–2.

179. Rowan, *Dream Makers,* 74.

180. Elizabeth Cobb. "MO. U. Ban is Upheld," *St. Louis Argus,* July 31, 1936, 1.

181. "Appeal in U Of MO. Case Set for Nov," *Cleveland Call,* August 6, 1936, 7.

182. "May 18 Set As Date for Case Of Univ. Of Mo," *Chicago Defender,* April 3, 1937, 1.

183. "University of Missouri Case Hearing May 18," Jefferson City, Mo., March 27, 1937.

184. "Appeal in Mo. U. Case to get Early Hearing," 1936.

185. Calloway was also active in the National Bar Association and the Kansas City Urban League, see Charles E. Coulter, *Take Up,* 98.

186. The anti-lynching bill sponsored by Rep. Joseph A. Gavagan was a legislative priority of the NAACP and Walter White in particular. The House Education Committee had held hearings on an anti-lynching bill beginning on March 30.

187. Houston to C.A. Franklin, April 29, 1937, Houston to C. H. Calloway, April 29, 1937. Houston to Franklin.

4 Substantially Equal If Separate

1. Roy Wilkins to Sidney R. Redmond, July 28, 1936, 2.

2. Houston noted that Howard B. Lang, the official Court Reporter at the Boone County courthouse, was helpful. Houston to Redmond, August 1936 and September 1, 1936. Houston and Lang visited and discussed paintings displayed in the courthouse, Lang to Houston, August 27, 1936.

3. Redmond to Wilkins, July 30, 1936.

4. Gaines identified work experience including service station help, hotel service, and domestic service, in addition to playground and community center supervision and one year as a high school and adult teacher for English and social studies. Gaines to White, March 6, 1937, 2–3.

5. Redmond to Wilkins, July 30, 1936, Houston to Redmond, August 25, 1936, 2.

6. Gaines to Houston, August 5, 1936.

7. Houston to Redmond, August 25, 1936, 2. Coincidentally, Houston, Redmond, and Gaines had all been members of the Alpha Phi Alpha fraternity.

8. Houston, "Memorandum for Mr. White and Mr. Spingarn—re Joint Committee advancing scholarships to Lloyd L. Gaines and William L. Redmond II."

9. Houston to Redmond, September 24, 1936, 1.

10. Gaines to "Brother Houston," September 1936 (probably the 6th or 7th). Gaines notes that Michigan charged $75 a semester and Missouri about $50 a semester (tuition based on credit hours rather than a flat semester fee). The state tuition scholarship was then around $25 a semester. Although Gaines does not mention it explicitly, the obvious implication is that the state would eagerly cover this cost in order to win the lawsuit and maintain legally segregated schools. "In addition to the $150 tuition at Michigan for the academic year, I have an estimated expense of $335, including 35 for books, 75 for incidentals, 90 for room, and 135 for board. I have made arrangements to cover this amount" through other sources.

11. Houston to Redmond, September 27, 1936.

12. Gaines to White, September 6, 1935.

13. Houston, "Memorandum for Mr. White and Mr. Spingarn—re Joint Committee advancing scholarships to Lloyd L. Gaines and William L. Redmond, II," September 4, 1936.

14. Houston, Memorandum to White and Spingarn. A similar procedure had been followed in the Maryland case.

15. White to Gaines, September 10, 1936. The person portraying the role of the friend was Arthur B. Spingarn. He wrote checks for tuition from personal funds and was reimbursed by the NAACP and the American Fund for Public Service (the Garland fund).

16. Gaines to White, September 12, 1936.

17. White to Gaines, September 15, 1936.

18. Cashier, University of Michigan to NAACP, October 5, 1936. "Mr. Gaines has informed us that his tuition would be paid by your organization, and we allowed him to register with that understanding."

19. Houston had stated this in his memorandum, and his handwritten response to White confirmed "I want the fraternity to take care of Gaines the second semester. If it doesn't we will have to arrange the loan." White to Houston, October 7, 1936.

20. Requisition, March 3, 1937; Houston to Arthur B. Spingarn, March 5, 1937; Gaines to White, March 6, 1937; Arthur B. Spingarn to Houston, March 6, 1937.

21. Gaines to White, March 6, 1937, 1–2; Gaines to "Brother Redmond," March 14, 1937.

22. April 12, 1937.

23. Houston to Gaines, September 28, 1936.

24. Gaines to Houston, September 1936.

25. Gaines to Houston, November 28, 1936. Gaines has some trouble with a seminar in economic theory and withdrew from the course. Generally, Gaines believed "things are working out nicely so far. The academic pace is terrific, but I am still in the running—may not be first, but don't intend to be among the last either." Gaines also had a full-time job "as a teacher and principal of adult classes at the Jones School," the one majority school in Ann Arbor.

26. Houston to Gaines, September 15, 1936.

27. Houston to "Dear Gaines," March 16, 1937. Gaines wrote to Walter White that "I received a "B" average for the semester's work just completed. My program consisted of economic statistics, labor market and a cognate in political science—political parties and electoral problems; my present one, economic theory, statistics, accounting, consumption, and labor problems—all in the department of economics." Gaines to White, March 6, 1937, 1.

28. Redmond to Hogsett, September 4, 1936; to Houston, September 4, 1936; to Hogsett, September 22, 1936; to Houston, September 25, 1936.

29. Houston to Redmond, September 15, 1936.

30. Houston to Redmond, September 24, 1936, 1.

31. Ibid., 1–2.

32. Ibid., 2. Moore, of course, sponsored the legislation creating Lincoln University and the out-of-state tuition scholarships. A former mathematics instructor, Tull "continued to hold this important post [as Lincoln's Business Manager] over a long period of years in spite of frequent changes of administration resulting from upheavals in State politics." A Lincoln alum who had taught at Tuskegee Institution, Tull was brought in by Nathan B. Young and he would outlast Florence. See untitled item, *Lincoln University Bulletin,* February–May 1940, v. 45 (nos. 1–2), 10.

33. Ibid., 3.

34. Redmond to Houston, September 25, 1936.

35. Redmond to Houston, October 13, 1936. Not much has changed since then.

36. Redmond to Houston (New York), January 5,1937.

37. Houston to "Dear Aunt Sidney" Redmond, March 5, 1937. Redmond had complained about lack of reimbursement for printing costs. Charlie wrote Sidney back that he had omitted to provide a bill, and "If you weren't such a swell guy I would kick your pants…." Redmond's humorless response noted his original February letter included the printer's bill.

38. Redmond to Houston, March 26, 1937.

39. If the briefs were not filed in a timely manner, either University counsel could request a dismissal or the Supreme Court judges could choose to dismiss.

40. Houston to Redmond, March 30, 1937; Redmond to Houston, telegram, April 3, 1937; Houston to Ralph E. Murray, et al., April 11, 1937; Houston to Redmond, April 11, 1937.

41. Redmond to Houston, April 14, 1937.

42. Houston to Redmond, May 25, 1938, 1. He made this statement at the time of filing the petition for a writ of certiorari before the US Supreme Court. The day before, Houston forwarded the petition to Walter White with the handwritten note indicating "Completely exhausted." Houston to White, May 24, 1938.

43. 303 U.S. 613 (1938). The Hughes Court ruled to overturn the murder conviction of Joe Hale as courts in McCracken County had systematically excluded eligible blacks from jury pools for several decades. The decision was made on the basis of the Fourteenth Amendment's equal protection clause. At the time Houston, Leon A. Ransom, and

Thurgood Marshall argued the case before the Supreme Court, Houston was also working on the petition for a writ of certiorari in the *Gaines* case.

44. James, *Root and Branch,* 105.

45. Rowan, *Dream Makers*, 75.

46. Redmond to Marshall, October 19, 1936.

47. Rowan, *Dream Makers,* 70, 76.

48. Redmond to Houston, April 15, 1937.

49. Ibid., Redmond to Houston, April 17, 1937.

50. Redmond to Houston, April 15, 1937.

51. Houston to Redmond, April 20, 1937.

52. Missouri was then on its third constitution; the first, in 1820, was from statehood. The general structure of the Supreme Court came from the state's 1865 Constitution and was maintained in the reconstructionist 1875 Constitution. A constitutional amendment in 1890 gave the judges fixed, ten-year terms. Gubernatorial appointment, followed by election for the remainder of the term, was used to fill vacancies. The structure of the judicial system would be reorganized, and Missouri would get a new Constitution in 1945, several years after the resolution of the *Gaines* case. A member of the state Supreme Court was called Judge, though the presiding officer, a position that rotated through members, was called the Chief Justice. See State of Missouri, *Official Manual, 1937–1938,* 137. These titles remain today.

53. Ernest S. Gantt had attended MU, and Ernest M. Tipton graduated from the MU Law School. George Robb Ellison attended the Missouri Law School for a year, but had no law degree. James Marsh Douglas received a law degree from Washington University and C. A. Leedy Jr., earned a law degree from St. Joseph's Law School, although his education seems to be largely independent study while clerking for a circuit court judge. Contemporary profiles list no legal degree for Chief Justice Charles Thomas Hays, William F. Frank, or Ernest S. Gantt.

54. Houston to Charles Florence, May 15, 1937. Espy continued to be listed as cocounsel, but he apparently neither attended the Supreme Court appeal nor contributed directly to the brief.

55. "Gaines Case to Be Heard Tomorrow," *Columbia Missourian,* May 17, 1937, 1. The headlines may be interpreted as evoking some sympathy for Gaines: "Gaines Case to Be Heard Tomorrow: Negro Denied Admission to M.U. Gets Appeal," and "Asked Entrance in 1935."

56. Fred L. Williams, Nick T. Cave, William S. Hogsett, and Ralph E. Murray, "Respondents' Brief," Missouri Supreme Court; May Term 1937, LLG.

57. They again noted that the state, when it granted a scholarship, covered only the tuition differential and covered no additional expenses for out-of-state colleges.

58. Press release, "Decision in Missouri U. Case Expected in 6 Weeks," Jefferson City, Missouri, May 21.

59. Quotes from "Decision in Missouri U. Case;" see also "Respondents' Brief."

60. "The Supreme Court Hears MO. U. Case: Racial Line Is Attacked," *St. Louis Argus,* May 21, 1937, 1.

61. "Attorneys Oppose Negro Entering M.U.: Supreme Court Told Efforts of St. Louis Black Is Contrary to 'Unvarying' Policy of State," *Joplin Globe,* May 9, 1937, 7.

62. Ibid.

63. Redmond to Houston (Reno, NV), August 3, 1937.

64. See Conrad G. Harper, "Houston, Charles Hamilton," in Raymond W. Logan and Michael R. Winston, *Dictionary of American Negro Biography,* 329–330; McNeil, *Groundwork,* 146–147; Williams, *Thurgood Marshall,* 99; James, *Root and Branch,* 84–85, 106.

65. Historian W. Sherman Savage cited "differences between the Board of Curators and President Florence" as the reason for dismissal. Missouri Professor and Lincoln University Curator J.D. Elliff "charged that politics was the underlying cause for the dismissal of President Florence." *The History of Lincoln University,* 271; Antonio Holland, et al., *The Soldiers' Dream Continued,* 21.

66. Redmond to Houston (Reno, NV), August 3, 1937.

67. Elliff "charged that under the present system of playing politics with the school, accreditation was threatened, and that he could have no part of this in good conscience." Albert Marshall, *Soldiers' Dream: A Centennial History of Lincoln University of Missouri,* 21.

68. From the news clipping, "Meddlers Blamed as M.U. Law Dean Resigns: Dr. Masterson Assails Noisy Group of Politically-Minded Lawyers Who Interfere," Redmond sent to Houston on May 28, 1938. Law school histories do not identify the nature of the dissatisfaction leading to Masterson's resignation. Masterson arrived in Missouri in 1934 from the University of Idaho. Under his deanship, the number of full-time faculty grew to eight and the Missouri Law Review began publication. Professor J. Coy Bour, served as acting dean both before and after Masterson's tenure. Percy Anderson Hogan, "History of the University of Missouri Law School," 283, 291; see also Hogan in Jonas Viles, *The University of Missouri,* chap. 17.

69. "The University of Missouri Case," 1.

70. *State ex rel. Gaines v. S. W. Canada, et al,* 113 S.W.2d 783 at 785.

71. Ibid., 785.

72. Ibid. Statutes regarding Lincoln were enacted in 1870, 1887, 1891, and 1921. *State ex rel. Gaines v. S. W. Canada, et al.,* 786–787. Some coverage in the black press in Missouri gave extensive coverage to this legislative history. See "To Appeal on Constitutional Right Ground," *St. Louis Argus,* December 17, 1937, 1.

73. *State ex rel. Gaines v. S. W. Canada, et al.* 113 S.W.2d 783 at 787.

74. 113 S.W.2d 783 at 787. "The provisions of section 9622…make it clear that the Legislature did not intend that negroes and whites should attend the same university in this State."

75. 113 S.W.2d 783, 787–789. In *Lehew v. Brummell* (1890), the Missouri Supreme Court upheld segregation in Grundy County even when there was no black school in the district, authorizing transportation to a different town. The Court used federal decisions of *Plessy v. Ferguson* and *Gong Lum v. Rice* to justify segregation.

76. *State ex rel. Gaines v. S. W. Canada, et al,* 113 S.W.2d 783, 789..

77. 113 S.W.2d 783, 790–791, quote at 791.

78. 113 S.W.2d 783, 787.

79. According to the Missouri Supreme Court opinion, the 1921 act "cannot be repealed or amended except by subsequent general legislation. Legislation of a general character cannot be included in an appropriation bill. To do so would violate Section 28 of Article IV of the Constitution which provides that no bill shall contain more than one subject which shall be clearly expressed in its title. There is no question but what the mere appropriation of money and the amendment of Section 9622, a general statute granting certain authority to the board of curators, are two different and separate subjects." 113 S.W.2d 783, 790. The court's decision in *State ex rel. Gaines v. S. W. Canada, et al.* has been cited subsequently within state courts on this point.

80. Redmond to Houston, December 11, 1937.

81. Redmond to Houston, December 12, 1937.

82. Houston, "The University of Missouri Case," 1.

83. Redmond to Houston, December 12, 1937.

84. "Gaines Loses Missouri U. Case Appeal," *Call,* December 10, 1937, 1.

85. "The court held that Lloyd Gaines' case differed very much from the Gaines Murray case in Maryland, upon which the plaintiff had placed much reliance, in that the State of Maryland had made no provision for higher education for Negroes as the State of Missouri has done; that the provisions made by the State of Maryland for higher education of the Negroes outside of the state were inadequate." "To Appeal on Constitutional Right Ground," *St. Louis Argus,* December 17, 1937, 1.

86. "Attorneys for Gaines, backed by the NAACP, expected a reversal in the Missouri Court and have announced that an appeal will be filed to the United States Supreme Court in due course." "NAACP to Take Missouri U's Color Bar Case to U.S. Court," *Afro-American,* December 18, 1937, 6.

87. "Loses Fight to Enter U Of Missouri," *Chicago Defender,* December 8, 1937, 2.

88. "To Appeal on Constitutional Right Ground."

89. "Negro Students Barred From M.U," *Joplin Globe,* December 10, 1937, 8. The *Globe* reported: "The opinion asserted that the Lincoln university act passed by the state legislature in 1921 'showed a clear intention to separate the white and Negro races for the purposes of higher education,' and added that the advantages for higher education afforded Negroes in the state were 'substantially equal' to those furnished white students."

90. Ibid. The phrase actually was a quotation from the 1890 state Supreme Court decision of *Lehew v. Brummell.*

91. "Negro Loses Fight to Enter State U," *St. Louis Globe-Democrat,* December 10, 1937, 1.

92. "Rules Negro Has No Right in White Schools Of State: Supreme Court Refuses to Order Missouri U. to Admit Lloyd D. [*sic*] Gaines to Law Department," *St. Louis Post-Dispatch,* December 10, 1937, 8a.

93. "Rules Negro Has No Right."

94. Ibid.

95. Redmond to Houston, December 12, 1937.

96. Frances Williams to Houston, May 24[?], 1937. An African American civil rights activist, Williams was from Kentucky, but she was raised in St. Louis.

97. Editor Ed Watson fell ill and died on November 30, before the state Supreme Court issued its opinion. The newspaper's point of view on educational equality did not change.

98. Its headline read, "Court Rules Against Negro in M.U. Case," and included sub-headlines such as, "Sustains Dinwiddie's Decision Denying Writ of Mandamus," "Says Statute Is Clear," and "Holds Gaines Was Not Denied Right of Legal Education." *Columbia Daily Tribune*, December 10, 1937, 1.

99. "Court Rules Against Negro." The assertion, as noted above, is incorrect.

100. Ibid. The quotation in *Gaines* originates from *Lehew v. Brummell*, 103 Mo. 546, 15 S.W. 765 (1890).

101. "Negro Loses Fight to Enter University," *Columbia Missourian*, December 10, 1937, 1.

102. Ibid.

103. "Supreme Court Closes Door of M.U. to Negroes," *Jefferson City Post-Tribune*, December 10, 1937, 6.

104. There were competing newspapers in Jefferson City, but, since 1933, both were owned and operated by the same parent company. The *Daily Capital News* was the morning, Democratic paper and the *Post-Tribune* was the afternoon, Republican paper.

105. "May Go to U.S. Tribunal," *Jefferson City Daily Capital News*, December 10, 1937, 4.

106. "Court Bans Negroes," *Billings Gazette*, December 10, 1937, 3.

107. Houston to Redmond, December 14, 1937; telegram December 16, 1937.

108. "In case of State ex rel. Gaines, app. v. Canada, etc. resp., No.35286. Appellant's motions for rehearing and to modify opinion overruled." Eppa F. Elliott, Clerk, February 25, 1938.

109. Houston to Redmond, February 28, 1938.

110. Houston to Redmond, March 1, March 8, April 14, May 10, 1938, Redmond to Houston, March 9, April 13, April 15, May 14, 1938. See also "Memorandum re preparation of record for the United States Supreme Court in *State ex rel. Gaines* vs. *Canada et al.*," May 10, 1938.

111. Houston to Redmond, April 11, 1938, 1. Any delay might strengthen the University's position. In addition, Judge Fred Williams had already requested a delay from Redmond because William Hogsett was occupied with other legal matters. Redmond to Houston, April 7, 1938.

112. Houston to Redmond, May 25, 1938, 1. Limited copies of the petition were available, even co-counsel Henry Espy did not receive one.

113. On October 29, 1938, wrote to editors at the *Argus, Afro-American, Call, Chicago Defender, Norfolk Journal and Guide, Pittsburgh Courier*, and *Washington Tribune*. For example, he would "appreciate your publishing notice next two issues urging Negroes

from states having scholarship laws who have been denied scholarship because appropriations exhausted or because tuition at outstate University lower than tuition at home state university to send official letters rejecting their scholarship applications to Charles Houston…." Houston to Robert L. Vann (*Pittsburgh Courier*), October 29, 1938.

114. "N.A.A.C.P. Appeals to High Court," *St. Louis Argus,* June 3, 1938, 8; "M.U. Case Appeal to U.S. Court," *The Call,* June 3, 1938, 2.

115. B.C. Stephens to Houston, June 1, 1938.

116. Houston to Redmond, June 4, 1938.

117. Redmond to Houston, June 9, 1938.

118. Redmond to Houston, July 13, 1938. See also Howard, *The Shifting Wind,* 262; however, Howard's conclusion about this disappearance is unsupported.

119. He acknowledged Redmond's letter and responded, "If there is anything we can do toward helping to clear up this matter, please let us know." Houston to Redmond, July 15, 1938.

120. "Gaines New Civil Service Employee of State of Michigan." *St. Louis Post-Dispatch,* December 12, 1938, 6; Bluford, "The Lloyd Gaines Story," 243.

121. White to Redmond, March 25, 1938, 1–2.

122. Houston to Redmond, April 1938.

123. Roger Baldwin also served as the Director of the American Civil Liberties Union. He also lived in St. Louis from 1906–1917 where he began his career as a social worker and developed an interest in liberal reforms. Tushnet, *NAACP's Legal Strategy,* 2–4.

124. As noted in an obituary for White, "His skin was fair, his hair blond, his eyes blue and his features Caucasian. He could easily have joined the 12,000 Negroes who pass the color-line and disappear into the white majority every year in this country. But he deliberately sacrificed his comfort to publicize himself as a Negro and to devote his entire adult life to completing the emancipation of his people." "Walter White, 61, Dies in Home Here," *New York Times,* March 23, 1955, 30. See also August Meier and Elliott Rudwick, "White, Walter (Francis)," in Logan and Winston, *Dictionary of American Negro Biography,* 646–650.

125. This research would lead to Fred McCuistion, *Graduate Instruction.* See George Murphy to White, telegram, January 5, 1938.

126. White to Redmond, March 25, 1938, 1.

127. Ibid., 2.

128. Memo, White to Houston, March 24, 1938.

129. Redmond to Houston, March 22, 1938.

130. Redmond to White, April 19, 1938.

131. The St. Louis Branch also covered $32.54 of Redmond's unpaid expense for the Gaines case. Redmond to White, April 19, 1938, Redmond to Houston, April 19, 1938, Houston to Redmond, April 21, 1938.

132. Houston to S. W. Moore, April 21, 1938. Moore was secretary of the St. Louis Branch, and Espy was President. Redmond wrote to the NAACP Board of Directors, of which he was a member, on December 7, 1938: "May I suggest that the national office

take a different attitude towards the branches? The only time we (the St. Louis branch) ever get a letter is when an appeal is made for funds or we are requested to send telegrams and then the letter is a stereotyped one. With all the help in the national office, branches that are doing something might occasionally receive a letter of commendation or a request for advice on proposed policies. Most people are just tired of being used." He had other complaints about the national office as well. White chastised his "friend" Redmond, criticized those who are "constantly harping on why things are not done differently, and defended the work of the national office. White concluded, "let me say one thing with complete frankness: We have no objection to criticism and, in fact, welcome it. But it does not help us carry a load which at times is back-breaking to have to answer petty criticisms of things we cannot handle with our present machinery." White to Redmond, December 20, 1938, 2. See also, White to Redmond, December 30, 1938.

133. In a "personal" note to Houston, White wrote, "Is it necessary that Sidney be paid a fee in the University of Missouri case? Have you made any definite commitment to him as to the amount? Sidney is in financial position not to need a fee and his activity in this case will mean, as it already has meant, an enormous prestige which he otherwise would not have gotten. In any event, if he gets a fee it should be a most modest one." White to Houston, November 7, 1938.

134. Houston to Osmond K. Faenkel, July 13, 1938, 2.

135. Houston to Nathan Margold, June 22, 1938.

136. Nathan R. Margold to Houston, August 15, 1938. When Margold's acknowledgement arrived, Houston was in Knoxville, Tennessee, on a fact-finding trip from a congressional committee investigation of the T.V.A. Secretary to Mr. Houston to Margold, August 17, 1938.

137. Houston to Fraenkel, July 13, 1938, 1. In 1954, Fraenkel would become general counsel for the ACLU. *Norris v. Alabama* 294 U.S. 587 (1935).

138. Houston to Fraenkel, July 13, 1938, 2.

139. Houston to Fraenkel, July 24[?], 1938.

140. Houston to White, October 10, 1938.

141. White to Board of Directors of the American Fund for Public Service, Attention: Mr. Roger N. Baldwin, October 12, 1938.

142. Houston to Redmond, October 29, 1938.

143. Houston, "Press Release" draft, November 11, 1938, 2.

144. The afternoon of October 10, 1938, Wilkins sent telegrams to the Baltimore *Afro-American,* the *St. Louis Argus,* the *Black Dispatch,* the *Chicago Defender,* the *Call,* the *Norfolk Journal and Guide,* and the *Pittsburgh Courier.* He wrote letters for the *New York Age,* the *Amsterdam News,* and the *Philadelphia Tribune.*

145. "High Court to Review Missouri U. Exclusion," October 14, 1938.

146. "U.S. Will Rule in Gaines Case," *Afro-American,* October 15, 1938, 8.

147. E. Washington Rhodes to Roy Wilkins, October 12, 1938.

148. Houston to Supreme Court, November 4, 1938.

149. Leon A. Ransom contributed to the brief for Gaines. Fred L. English (St. Louis), Nick T. Cave, and Ralph E. Murray also are listed as counsel on "Respondents' Brief in Opposition to Petition for Certiorari," LLG.

150. This illustrative account comes from the staff correspondent of the *St. Louis Post-Dispatch,* Richard L. Stokes, printed in "Decision of the Missouri Supreme Court on the Admission of Negroes to State Universities," 726. The NAACP press release reports that all Justices participated in questions with the exception of Justice Stanley Reed. Moreover, the NAACP added that "Most of the questions were directed to counsel for the university, who were frequently forced to correct overstatements which they were making to show how exceedingly generous Missouri had been in supporting Negro education." "Missouri University "Belongs to Whites Only," State's Lawyers Tell Supreme Court," November 11, 1938.

151. Stokes, "Decision," 726.

152. Ibid., 727.

153. Ibid. These exchanges were also highlighted in the black press. See, for example, "Supreme Court Hears Facts in U. Of Mo. Jim Crow Case," *Chicago Defender,* November 19, 1938, 1.

154. Stokes, "Decision," 727.

155. See, for example, Rawn James Jr., *Root and Branch,* 116–117, and Jeffery Lord, "Two Presidents and the Court: When Bigotry Takes the Bench."

156. Carter would become Thurgood Marshall's assistant in 1945. "The Long Road to Equality," *The Nation* (April 15, 2004). Aside from Carter's account, the anecdote seems unsupported. Of course, Sidney Redmond also addressed the Supreme Court, although the legend only mentions Houston. Houston, his father, and William Hastie, and other black attorneys had argued before the Supreme Court in earlier cases.

157. "Missouri University 'Belongs to Whites Only,' State's Lawyers Tell Supreme Court," November 11, 1938. The comment from the NAACP press release was quoted in papers such as the *Chicago Defender,* "Supreme Court Hears Facts in U. Of Mo. Jim Crow Case," November 19, 1938, 1.

158. James E. Bond, *I Dissent: The Legacy of Chief Justice James Clark McReynolds.* According to Bond, McReynolds's prejudices were legion. He looked down on blacks, Jews, Germans, fascists, liberals, Franklin Roosevelt, Hugo Black, contemporary norms, the direction the country was going, and so forth. Although McReynolds was difficult to get along with, he does not seem so blatantly disrespectful.

159. Stokes, "Decision," 727.

160. "Civil Liberties Union Will Enter Gaines Case," *Pittsburgh Courier,* November 11, 1938, 2.

161. "His Case Argued Before U.S. High Ct," *St. Louis Argus,* November 11, 1938, 1.

162. "Gaines's Case Before U.S. Court," *Afro-American,* November 12, 1938, 1.

163. "Supreme Court Hears Facts in U. Of Mo. Jim Crow Case," *Chicago Defender,* November 19, 1938, 1.

164. "Appeal to High Court," *Jefferson City Post-Tribune,* November 10, 1938, 4.

165. "Gaines Case Taken Under Advisement by High Court," *Jefferson City Daily Capital News,* November 10, 1938, 1.

166. "U.S. Supreme Court Hears Gaines Case," *Columbia Missourian,* November 11, 1938, 1. The staff correspondent for the *Post-Dispatch* was Richard L. Stokes.

167. *Columbia Daily Tribune,* November 10, 1938, 1.

168. *Missouri ex rel. Gaines v. Canada,* 305 U.S. 337 (1938).

169. Ibid., 345.

170. Ibid., 349.

171. Ibid., 349–350.

172. Ibid., 350.

173. In *McCabe v. Atchison, Topeka, and Santa Fe Railway, Co.,* 235 U.S. 151 (1914), the Supreme Court rejected a policy establishing white only railcars because few blacks traveled on the railroad. The majority opinion was written by Associate Justice Hughes during his first term on the Supreme Court.

174. *Gaines v. Canada,* 305 U.S. 337, 351.

175. Ibid., 351–352.

176. Ibid., 352.

177. Ibid., 353.

178. Ibid., 354.

179. "Petition of the Respondents for a Rehearing," 3, LLG. Ralph Murray was dropped from the list of counsel.

180. Rehearing Petition, 6.

181. Ibid., 10–11.

182. Ibid., 12.

183. Moreover, since few blacks had applied for graduate programs, counsel complained of the cost of "*idle teaching staffs* and *empty classrooms,*" Ibid., 13.

184. Ibid., 14.

185. Press release, "State Asks High Court to Re-hear University of Missouri Case," St. Louis, December 30, 1–2.

186. Murray, *Song in a Weary Throat,* 115.

187. Franklin, *From Slavery to Freedom,* 3rd ed., 553.

188. "Supreme Court Spurs Drive for Better Education in South," December 16, 1938, 1.

189. *Gaines v. Canada,* 305 U.S. 337, 338.

190. "Supreme Court Spurs Drive for Better Education in South," December 16, 1938, 1–2.

191. Ibid., 2.

192. See McNeil, *Groundwork,* 151: "The NAACP victory in *Gaines* provided an essential precedent on which a subsequent determination regarding the unconstitutionality of a state to require separation of the races in tax-supported educational institutions could be based. The *Gaines* decision denied the state's unconditional right to exclude a black applicant from a state supported white law school. Thus, based on *Gaines,* a state must either admit black applicants to the established institutions supported by the state or provide equal facilities for their professional or graduate training. The implications were enormous."

193. Ibid., 3.

194. "Damnify Both Races," *Time* 32 (26), December 26, 1938, 22. White's statement would later be quoted in a brief by the University of Missouri counsel as evidence that the

NAACP wanted to destroy establish legal tradition (segregation) and replace it with social equality (rejected in Plessy and other decisions. "Respondent's Brief," *State ex rel. Gaines v. Canada,* May 1939, 52–53.

195. "Statement by Walter White, Secretary of the National Association for the Advancement of Colored People, on Decision of the United States Supreme Court in the University of Missouri Case," December 13, 1938, 1. White's statement used the legal victory as a basis to plea for additional funding (p.2): "The fight for educational equality has in the main been possible by a grant of $10,000 a year from the American Fund for Public Service. That Fund is unable to renew its grant because its money has all been spent. Whether we are able to carry forward the fight so magnificently advanced by the University of Missouri decision depends wholly upon whether or not the people of the country, particularly Negroes, who are the direct beneficiaries, are willing to give of their means to pay the necessary minimum costs."

196. Lucile Bluford to Roy Wilkins, December 12, 1938.

197. Villard, "Issues and Men: Missouri Law School Case," *The Nation* (December 24, 1938), 693.

5 *Gaines* in the Press

1. "Gaines Wins in Supreme Court: Decision Has Far-Reaching Effect in So," December 16, 1938, 1.

2. "Supreme Court Smashes Color Line in Southern Universities," *Pittsburgh Courier,* December 17, 1938, 1.

3. "Kills Dixie Color Line," *Pittsburgh Courier,* December 24, 1938, 24.

4. "Missouri University Graduate Lauds Gaines Court Decision," *Pittsburgh Courier,* December 24, 1938, 24.

5. "Court Hits Dixie Death Blow," *New York Amsterdam News,* December 17, 1938, 1.

6. "Lloyd Gaines Case," *New York Amsterdam News,* December 17, 1938, 10.

7. "Court Opens School," *Afro-American,* December 17, 1938, 1.

8. "The High Court Speaks," *Afro-American,* December 17, 1938, 18. The article repeats the view that "Chief Justice Hughes, speaking for the majority, including Alabama's Mr. Justice Black, decreed that Missouri's State university and its courts erred in barring Lloyd L. Gaines from its law school on account of his color, and will have to admit him."

9. "The High Court Speaks."

10. "Gaines Case New Victory for N.A.A.C.P.," *Call,* December 16, 1938, 1.

11. "The case was won through the diligence of Redmond, Charles H. Houston of Washington and Henry D. Espy of St. Louis in preparing brief and uncovering facts and their 'never-say-die spirit which led them on in face of defeat in Missouri courts." "Helped Win Case," *Call,* December 16, 1938, 1.

12. "The Gaines Decision," *Chicago Defender,* December 24, 1938, 16.

13. "U.S. Supreme Court Rules That State Must Provide Equal Education for Races," *Cleveland Call and Post,* December 15, 1938, 1.

14. "Equality in Education," *Los Angeles Sentinel,* December 15, 1938, 1.

15. Floyd J. Calvin, "The Digest," *Cleveland Call and Post,* December 22, 1938, 6.

16. "The Gaines Case Scores A Victory," *St. Louis Argus,* December 16, 1938, 8.

17. "South's Colleges Comment on High Court Decision," *Afro-American,* December 24, 1938, 16.

18. "Opening of Missouri U. Law School to L. Gaines Called 'Rational, Just.'" *Afro-American,* December 24, 1938, 16.

19. The college was established in 1873 as Branch Normal College, a black educational institution within what is now the University of Arkansas. In 1927, Arkansas Agricultural, Mechanical and Normal College separated from the University of Arkansas in order to provide an independent, black-only college in the state. Today, the institution is known as the University of Arkansas at Pine Bluff.

20. "Watson An 'Uncle Tom' Says N.A.A.C.P. Head," *Chicago Defender,* March 11, 1939, 5.

21. "Poor Leadership," *Chicago Defender,* March 25, 1939, 16.

22. "Black Leadership," *Chicago Defender,* April 8, 1939, 14.

23. "Follow The Law, Not College Presidents," *Chicago Defender,* March 11, 1939, 16.

24. "South's Colleges Comment on High Court Decision," *Afro-American,* December 24, 1938, 16.

25. Moses Gritt, "Missouri Has Figured in Two Greatest Cases," *Afro-American,* December 24, 1938, 16.

26. "Missouri U. Denied High Court Rehearing," *Afro-American,* January 7, 1939, 3.

27. "Discriminatory Practices of Hospitals Hit by Committee," *Afro-American,* December 13, 1947, 5.

28. "Home Grown Hitlers," *Los Angeles Sentinel,* November 17, 1938, 1.

29. "Nazi Bans May Help Us Here," *Afro-American,* January 7, 1939, 1.

30. "Jim Crow Educational Appeasement," *Afro-American,* January 21, 1939, 4.

31. Walter White to Carl Murphy, January 22, 1939. He encouraged Murphy to "Keep up the good work." At the bottom, in a separate section, the *Afro American* reprinted a passage from an editorial published in the University of Missouri's campus newspaper, *The Missouri Student,* favoring campus integration.

32. "NAACP Appeals for Funds to Press Equal Education Fight," *Cleveland Call and Post,* December 29, 1938, 12.

33. "Covering The News Headlines of 1938," *Cleveland Call and Post,* December 29, 1938, 8.

34. "State Seeks New Trial School Case," *Los Angeles Sentinel,* January 5, 1939, 1.

35. "Pushes Fight to Bar Gaines," *New York Amsterdam News,* January 7, 1939, 11.

36. "Asks Supreme Court to Re-Hear Gaines Case," *Chicago Defender,* January 7, 1939, 1.

37. "Missouri U. Protests Decision: Gaines' Opponents Want Rehearing of History-Making Case," *The Call,* December 30, 1938, 1.

38. "M.U. Plans New Legal Move to Bar Negroes," *The Call,* January 6, 1939, 1. "The Missouri state supreme court has ruled several times that mandamus is a discretionary

remedy and may be rejected if not in the interest of public good. The university attorneys are basing their action on the dissenting opinion of Justices McReynolds and
Butler who said that doubtless the state supreme court would be called upon to rule
on this point."

39. "U.S. Supreme Court Reaffirms Missouri Decision: Refuses University's Plea for
Rehearing—Law School Surprised At Quick Rebuff," *Cleveland Call and Post,* January
12, 1939, 3.

40. "The World This Week," *Pittsburgh Courier,* January 14, 1939, 1.

41. "Supreme Court Upholds Gaines Case Decision," January 6, 1939, 1.

42. "The Globe Trotter: Facing a Dilemma," *Atlanta Daily World,* January 15, 1939, 4.

43. "High Court Orders Missouri University to Admit Negroes," *Chicago Tribune,*
December 13, 1938, 17.

44. "George Burns Pleads Guilty to Two Smuggling Indictments," *Louisville Courier-
Journal,* December 13, 1938, 1.

45. "Labor Board Loses Plea for 'Mutiny' Crew," *Washington Post,* December 13, 1938,
1.

46. "Virginia Seen Forced to Aid Colored Students," *Washington Star,* December 13,
1938, 2.

47. "Court Rules School Must Admit Negro," *Louisville Courier-Journal,* December
13, 1938, 1.

48. Ibid., 6.

49. "High Court Gives NLRB New Setback: Also Rules Missouri Law School Must
Admit Negro As Student," *Atlanta Constitution,* December 13, 1938, 9.

50. "NLRB Decision Reversed Again By High Court," *Dallas Morning News,* December 13, 1938, 11.

51. "NLRB Decision Again Hit in Decision By Supreme Court," *Arkansas Gazette,*
December 13, 1938, 5.

52. "The Negroes Win Their Case," *The State,* December 14, 1938 (NAACP archives).

53. Ibid. The section on physical violence is under a separate heading, "The Worst Possible Course," After its discussion of policy alternatives, the editor of the *State* writes, "In
all of this The State is merely presenting a problem, and discussing it, without any present
intention of urging dogmatic proposals for its solution. The issue, which has slept from
Reconstruction days, is now awake again, and the United States of America, outside those
states in the South, probably will not allow it to be re-anesthetized."

54. Walter White to Sidney Redmond, December 30, 1938, 1–2; White to Editor, *The
State,* February 3, 1939.

55. "Court Upholds Negro, Again Sets Back NLRB," *Daily Times-News,* December
12, 1938, 1.

56. "School Must Admit Negro," *Middletown Times Herald,* December 12, 1938, 6.

57. "Missouri U. Loses Action," *Iowa City Press-Citizen,* December 12, 1938, 1.

58. "Supreme Court Decrees Negroes Must Be Admitted to Missouri Law School,"
Denton Record-Chronicle, December 12, 1938, 1.

59. "'Equality for Negro Ordered By High Court," *Kingsport Times,* December 12, 1938, 1.

60. "U.S. Supreme Court Rules Missouri University Must Admit Negro Student," *Miami Daily News-Record,* December 12, 1938, 2.

61. "Court Upholds Negro's Right," *Lima News,* December 12, 1938, 1.

62. "State Must Give Negro Equality in Education Court Rules," *Reno Evening Gazette,* December 12, 1938, 1.

63. "Court Orders Negroes Given Equal Educational Rights," *Wisconsin Rapids Daily Tribune,* December 12, 1938, 3.

64. J. Fred Essary, "Negro's Right to Attend Law School Upheld," *Baltimore Sun,* December 13, 1938, 2.

65. *Murray* was cited in the *Gaines* decision, but it only reached the Maryland Court of Appeals, the state's highest court. For Houston and the NAACP, despite the important symbolic value of the Murray victory, it was necessary to pursue the *Gaines* case, in the hope of setting a precedent enforceable throughout the nation.

66. Essary, "Negro's Right," 2.

67. "Race Tolerance Begins At Home," *Christian Science Monitor,* December 13, 1938, 22.

68. "Best Editorial of the Day," *Helena Daily Independent,* December 18, 1938, 4.

69. "Negroes Upheld in College Case: Right to Attend Missouri University Affirmed by Court," *Los Angeles Times,* December 13, 1938, 3.

70. "Supreme Court Again Rebuffs NLRB in Ruling on Seamen," *San Francisco Chronicle,* December 13, 1938, 4.

71. "Court Backs Negro on Full Education," *New York Times,* December 13, 1938, 1, 10.

72. "Policy of 16 States Affected," *New York Times,* December 13, 1938, 10.

73. "Court Holds M.U. Must Admit Negro," *Joplin News Herald,* December 12, 1938, 1. The sub-headline contained a word rarely used in contemporary news reports, save for Joplin newspapers: "U.S. Supreme Court Tribunal Reverses Decision in Case of St. Louis Black Seeking Admittance to Law School." The term *black* was not common usage as a synonym for African American during this era.

74. "Would Be First Negro to Attend University," *Joplin News Herald,* December 12, 1938, 1.

75. "State University May Open Doors to Negro Student," *Joplin Globe,* December 13, 1938, 1. The *Globe* was the morning paper and the *News Herald* the afternoon paper. The *Globe* operated both papers since 1922; the News Herald ceased publication in 1970.

76. "Must Give Equality to Negro," *Moberly Monitor-Index and Democrat,* December 12, 1938, 1.

77. "No Comment Made By Lloyd Gaines," *Moberly Monitor-Index and Democrat,* December 12, 1938, 4.

78. "Missouri University Must Admit Negro Student," *Sikeston Herald,* December 15, 1938, 11.

79. "Negro Into M.U.," *Kansas City Star,* December 12, 1938, 1. . The newspaper's editors chose this statement from an AP story to lead: "The Supreme court ruled today a

state must give 'equality' to white and Negro law students. It gave this opinion in holding the University of Missouri law school must admit Lloyd L. Gaines, a St. Louis Negro, as a student."

80. "Head of M.U. is Silent," *Kansas City Star,* December 12, 1938, 2.

81. "Rules For A Negro: Equality in Education Defined for Missouri," *Kansas City Star,* December 14, 1938, 3.

82. "May Add Law At Lincoln," *Kansas City Star,* December 14, 1938, 3.

83. "Negro Wins Fight on Missouri U. in Supreme Court." *St. Louis Post-Dispatch,* December 12, 1938, 1.

84. "The Gaines Decision," *St. Louis Post-Dispatch,* December 13, 1938, 2C.

85. "Current Opinion: What Other Editors Are Saying: The Gaines Decision," *Joplin Globe,* December 18, 1938, 8B.

86. "Missouri U. Opened to Negro," *St. Louis Daily Globe-Democrat,* December 13, 1938, 2.

87. "Lincoln U. Board to Take Up Negro Law School Need," *St. Louis Post-Dispatch,* December 13, 1938, 2.

88. "Missouri U. Opened to Negro."

89. "Public Schools Not Affected, Carter Says," *St. Louis Daily Globe-Democrat,* December 13, 1938, 2.

90. "Class in Law May Be Added At Lincoln U," *Daily Capital News,* December 13, 1938, 1.

91. "Court Rules M.U. Should Admit Negro," *Columbia Daily Tribune,* December 12, 1938, 1.

92. "M.U. Silent on Decision in Gaines Case," *Columbia Daily Tribune,* December 12, 1938, 1. The other applicant was Lucile Bluford.

93. Ibid.

94. "Lincoln U. Law School Plan to Fore," *Columbia Daily Tribune,* December 13, 1938, 1.

95. "Ruth Etting Tells Jury How Ex-Husband Shot Pianist in Musician's Hollywood Home," *Columbia Tribune,* December 13, 1938, 1.

96. "Discuss Lincoln U. Law School," *Columbia Daily Tribune,* December 17, 1938, 1.

97. "Sordid Note in Snyder Trial," *Columbia Daily Tribune,* December 17, 1938, 1.

98. "U.S. Supreme Court Rules M.U. Must Admit Negro Till Lincoln U. Gets Law School," *Columbia Missourian,* December 12, 1938, 1; "Dissenting Opinion on Gaines Decision," *Columbia Missourian,* December 12, 1938, 1.

99. "Gaines Refused Admission in 1936," *Columbia Missourian,* December 12, 1938, 1.

100. "Jefferson City, Dec. 12," *Columbia Missourian,* December 12, 1938, 1.

101. The *Detroit News* reported the decision only in its Blue Star edition distributed in northern Michigan, but not in its home edition for the city. "Winner in Court Fight for Equal Education for Negroes, Now Employed on WPA Project," *Detroit News,* December 12, 1938, 2, Michigan State Archives.

6 Public Reaction and Legislative Response

1. In a competitive market, newspapers have economic and ideological incentives to appeal the median news consumer, so news content may reflect the center of the readership for the newspapers. Market segmentation (for instance between mainstream and black press or between Democrat and Republican readers of partisan papers) leads only to search for the median news consumer within the intended market. See Ekaterina Ognianova and James W. Endersby, "Objectivity Revisited: A Spatial Model of Political Ideology and Mass Communication," and James W. Endersby and Ekaterina Ognianova, "A Spatial Model of Ideology and Political Communication: Voter Perceptions of News Reporting."

2. See, for instance, Redmond to Houston, February 9, 1939; "Act for Negro U.: Bill Proposes Reorganization of Lincoln University to Meet Supreme Court Ruling," *Kansas City Star*, February 3, 1939; "Gaines Case is Delayed." *Kansas City Star*, February 7, 1939, 10.

3. In 1955, the *Missouri Student* would be reorganized as the *Maneater*, a reference to the Tiger mascot of the University of Missouri.

4. The case was filed, heard by Circuit Court Judge Walter Dinwiddie, and heard by the Missouri State Supreme Court during the summer. But even when the paper was not on hiatus, there was little coverage.

5. *Missouri Student*, October 26, 1938, 1.

6. The annual selection of a new editor influenced the content of news coverage in the following year. See "Macklin Named to Edit 38–39 Student," *Missouri Student*, April 13, 1938, 1; Aimee Edmondson and Earnest L. Perry, "'To the Detriment of the Institution': The Missouri Student's Fight to Desegregate the University of Missouri," 116–117.

7. One strange aspect of the story is this passage: "He is backed in his fight for admission to the Law School by the Society for Advancement of the Negro Race." There was no such organization and it is clear the student reporter meant the NAACP. Notably, William Hogsett also had stumbled over the organization's name during depositions and had to be corrected by Sidney Redmond. *Missouri Student*, October 26, 1938, 1.

8. William Edward Macklin, "The Inevitable Mr. Gaines," *Missouri Student*, December 14, 1938, 2. Edmondson and Perry, "To the Detriment," do not mention that this editorial was written by Macklin.

9. George Cech, "Spotlight on Missouri," *Intercollegian and Far Horizons*, March 1939, 111.

10. White to Redmond, December 30, 1938, 1. White asked for copies of the paper with "The Inevitable Mr. Gaines" editorial from the *Missouri Student* on February 3, 1939.

11. "Jim Crow Educational Appeasement," *Afro-American*, January 21, 1939, 4; "Missouri U Student Paper Sends Welcome to Lloyd Gaines," *New York Amsterdam News*, December 31, 1938, 3. The Afro-American printed the editorial near criticism of plans to create regional black graduate and professional programs.

12. "N.A.A.C.P. Lawyers in Brilliant Plea Before State Court," *Call*, May 26, 1939, 4.

13. Student Government Association.

14. Glenn Van Horne, "'Try No Half-way Solution to Gaines Case,' Says M.U. Student," *Missouri Student,* January 11, 1939, 2.

15. "Coed Advises Gaines Not to Enter M.U.," *Missouri Student,* March 22, 1939, 3. Edmondson and Perry, "To the Detriment of the Institution," observe that the student editors' willingness to stand by their principles and the editorial creed established by the newspaper was remarkable for the time.

16. White to Redmond and White to Houston, August 1, 1935. Spencer was originally from Oklahoma. He finished his studies at the University of Missouri before the case reached the Supreme Court.

17. Houston to Charles M. Spencer, November 2, 1935. Houston also sought him out as an activist: "You can serve the cause by writing letters to your college papers and by having the question of the admission of Negroes to the University of Missouri discussed before the liberal clubs on the campus. In that way you will be able to get us some authentic information as to the state of campus feeling and will make the student body as one of the phases of educational discrimination against Negroes. Particularly I should like you to raise the question on the campus as to why Negroes should be excluded from a state-supported university and what real harm would result if they were admitted."

18. Spencer to Redmond, February 12, 1936. White seems to have over-estimated Spencer's enthusiasm. Spencer mentions student suggestions to circulate "a petition stating our resolution to accept the new situation without prejudice in our hearts," but he rejected such a "fervent display of absolutism."

19. Cech, "Spotlight on Missouri," 111.

20. Ibid., 112.

21. White to Redmond, December 30, 1938, 1–2.

22. Scholars Aimee Edmondson and Ernest Perry noted this student backlash "appeared to be indicative of the national scene on college campuses." Edmondson and Peary, "To the Detriment," 114.

23. "White Student Gives Views on Gaines Case," *New York Amsterdam News,* January 27, 1940, 4. The paper printed portions of the editorial in earlier coverage, see "Missouri U Student Paper Sends Welcome to Lloyd Gaines," *New York Amsterdam News,* December 31, 1938, 3.

24. "Jim Crow Educational Appeasement," *Afro American,* January 21, 1939, 4.

25. "Missouri U. Student Paper Invites Gaines to 'Come On.'" *Pittsburgh Courier,* December 31, 1938, 2.

26. Bill Macklin (William E. Macklin III) went on to become a reporter for the Associated Press in St. Louis, London, and Kansas City. He was the editor of the *New Ulm* (MN) *Daily Journal* from 1951 to 1980. See Associated Press News Archive, June 11, 1999, and "William 'Bill' E. Macklin III," *Brainerd Dispatch,* June 10, 1999.

27. "Gaines in St. Louis," *Kansas City Call,* January 6, 1939, 1.

28. "Supreme Court Upholds Gaines Case Decision: Missouri Must Now Admit Gaines or Build Law School at Lincoln," *St. Louis Argus,* January 6, 1939, 1.

29. "Gaines May Enter M.U. Law School," *St. Louis Globe-Democrat,* January 10, 1939, 1.

30. Ibid.

31. "St. Louis Negro Plans to Enter M.U. Next Fall," *Joplin News Herald,* January 9, 1939, 10.

32. "Gaines Didn't Say It!" *Pittsburgh Courier,* January 21, 1939, 13.

33. "Gaines Speaks At Local NAACP," *St. Louis Argus,* January 13, 1939, 1.

34. Rufus, "'Farmer' to Appear Minus Gaines Student Poll Results," *Missouri Student,* January 11, 1939, 1.

35. Ibid. It is unclear how editors misreported initials of their agriculture college dean. Miller became dean in August after the mandatory retirement of Frederick B. Mumford. Miller had worked at Missouri since 1904. Frederick B. Mumford, *History of the Missouri College of Agriculture* (Agricultural Experiment Station, University of Missouri, Columbia, MO) 1944, 102, 140.

36. "'Farmer' to Appear Minus Gaines Student Poll Results," 1. Following military service, Harry Barger had a respected career in advertising and public relations for Ralston Purina, Wilson Foods and Sporting Goods, and other firms. He later entered the oil business and was president of Barger Petroleum.

37. "With the Editor…" *College Farmer,* 32 (January 1939), 26.

38. "Refrain for a Purpose," *College Farmer,* January 1939, 20.

39. Edmondson and Perry, "To the Detriment," and Aimee Edmondson and Ernest L. Perry Jr., "Objectivity and the Journalists Creed: Local Coverage of Lucile Bluford's attempt to Desegregate the University of Missouri."

40. Press release, "U. Missouri Case Before Court," Columbia, MO, July 10, 1936, 3.

41. Kittel, *The Negro Community,* 111.

42. Kittel discounted local press coverage but notes black Columbians were knowledgeable. "The local newspapers carried very sketchy accounts of the trial so that no real knowledge of the court proceedings could be obtained from reading their columns. Nevertheless, only a few of the persons interviewed knew nothing of the case or had no opinion about it." 111. Charles Spencer also observed, "Not much play is being made by the local newspapers concerning the event. All that I have read has been regular articles announcing the event—no editorial comment." Spencer also confesses to ignorance since "I am usually so busy that I do not get to read all of the papers." Spencer to Redmond, February 12, 1936.

43. Kittel, *The Negro Community,* 111–112.

44. Ibid., 114–118.

45. Virginius Dabney, "Education of Negroes Tested By New Ruling," *New York Times,* December 18, 1938, 84.

46. Mel Gussow, "Virginius Dabney, 94, Southern Write Who Fought Segregation," *New York Times,* December 29, 1995, A 31; Brooke C. Stoddard, "Words Read 'Round the World," *Virginia Living,* April 2009. Gussow notes that his Pulitzer was for editorials opposing integrated public buses in Richmond and defense of the poll tax that disenfranchised voters. However, Stoddard characterizes Dabney as a southern liberal who opposed the poll tax and other social injustice. Dabney was a member of a group of liberal Southerners who supported racial segregation.

47. "Ruling Brings Out Problem of South," *Baltimore Sun,* December 13, 1938, 2.

48. Ibid.

49. "State Expected to Act," *New York Times,* December 18, 1938, 84. "Lincoln University at Jefferson City has the room space facilities for such a course, but the Legislature will doubtless be asked to make appropriations for faculty salaries and an adequate law library. This would mean an outlay of at least $10,000 annually for salaries, and most estimates are that $50,000 will be required for a library. Young Gaines is a graduate of Lincoln, on which the State has spent some $3,500,000 since 1921."

50. Ibid.

51. "High Court Stands Firm for Gaines," *Columbia Daily Tribune,* January 3, 1939, 1.

52. "Appeal on Negro Student Refused," *Moberly Monitor-Index and Democrat,* January 3, 1939, 1. Wire services and state newspapers had given little coverage to the litigation earlier, but now they covered each step in detail.

53. "Seek Stark's Advice on Gaines Case." *Moberly Monitor-Index and Democrat,* December 17, 1938, 1.

54. Taylor was "honorary alumnus of the University of Missouri," "Proposed Bill Puts Lincoln, M.U. on A Par." *Columbia Missourian,* February 3, 1939, 1.An attorney in Keytesville, the Chariton County seat, he was also a member of the local school board. An NAACP press release claimed Taylor "has not improved the wooden Negro elementary there in the last 25 years, but the white school is a modern brick building." "Missouri Governor Asked to Veto Bill Which Flouts Supreme Court, April 1939, 2.

55. Redmond to Houston, February 8, 1939.

56. "Equality Asked for Lincoln U." *Moberly Monitory-Index,* February 3, 1939, 3; "Suggests Plan for Lincoln U." *Jefferson City Post-Tribune,* February 3, 1939, 3; "Taylor's Bill Asks Lincoln U. Expansion," *Columbia Daily Tribune,* February 3, 1939. The UP story was not quite so blunt. See "Proposed Bill Puts Lincoln, M.U. on A Par." *Columbia Missourian,* February 3, 1939, 1.

57. "Solution of School Dilemma Proposed." *Joplin Globe,* February 4, 1939, 4.

58. Jefferson City Bureau, "Act for Negro U.: Bill Proposes Reorganization of Lincoln University to Meet Supreme Court Ruling," *Kansas City Star,* February 3, 1939. A subsequent article reported on the extended delay for the case of Lloyd Gaines and noted the introduction of the Taylor bill as a response. "Gaines Case is Delayed," *Kansas City Star,* February 7, 1939, 10.

59. "Gaines Case Goes on May Docket of Supreme Court," *Moberly Monitor-Index and Democrat,* February 7, 1939, 3; "Gaines Case Back on High Court Docket," *Columbia Daily Tribune,* February 7, 1939, 1.

60. "Court to Review Gaines Decision," *Columbia Missourian,* February 7, 1939, 1.

61. "Lincoln U. Expansion Is Perfected," *Columbia Daily Tribune,* March 7, 1939, 1.

62. For instance, the *Atlanta Daily World* characterized the bill's passage in the House of Representatives as a battle won by Democrats over GOP opposition, "but only after a brilliant appeal had been made by Rep. O.B. Whitaker, Hickory County GOP stalwart, that qualified Negro students be admitted to the University of Missouri. Declared Stalwart Whitaker: 'Why exclude the children of Negro citizens of the state

when the school is open to the Japanese? I would rather have children of mine associate with those who have made good citizens of Missouri than with Japanese who are being trained to slaughter persons on the battlefield. I do not know of any good reason for this bill. We should answer the United States supreme court's demands by admitting Negroes to our state university." "Pass Equal Education Bill," *Atlanta Daily World,* March 12, 1939, 1.

63. "Lincoln U. Expansion Is Perfected," 1.

64. Ibid.

65. Curtis A. Betts, "Missouri Bill to Evade Gaines Ruling Perfected," *St. Louis Post-Dispatch,* March 7, 1939, 10A. The *Post-Dispatch* reported a milder version of Whitaker's comments too. "Opposition to the bill was led by O.B. Whitaker of Weaubleau and Frank Lowry of Cape Girardeau, Republicans. Whitaker said that he saw no reason to exclude Negroes from the State University, to which were admitted Japanese, Chinese, and students from almost every foreign country. He questioned the sincerity of the language of the bill in directing that equal educational standards would be established, and said that there was no intention of building up Lincoln University to the same standard as the State University. 'The day is past for discriminating against the Negro,' Whitaker said."

66. Joseph L. McLemore to Senator Michael Kinney, March 20, 1939, 1–2.

67. Ibid., 2–3.

68. Ibid., 1.

69. "Negroes: Democrat." *Time,* August 20, 1928, 12 (8), 14.

70. Replacing his brother Senator Thomas "Snake" Kinney after his death in 1912, Kinney served in the Missouri Senate through 1968. His term was longer than US Senator Robert Byrd's, but his record was surpassed by US Congressman John Dingell.

71. McLemore to Kinney, 3.

72. Walter White to Joseph L. McLemore, March 23, 1939. Murphy was the son of *Afro-American* publisher George Murphy. McLemore had sent a copy of the letter to his mentor Charles Houston, March 21, 1939.

73. See, for instance, "Protests Missouri's High Court Dodge," *Afro-American,* April 1, 1939, 21.

74. Walter White to Senator W. B. Whitlow, April 4, 1939. See also White to Marshall, April 3, 1939; Marshall to White, April 4, 1939.

75. Wilkins to White, April 2, 1939; Redmond to Houston, April 10, 1939.

76. Norval B. Barksdale, "The Gaines Case and Its Effect on Negro Education in Missouri," *School and Society,* March 9, 1940, 310.

77. "Curators Ask $900,000 for Lincoln Univ., Get $75,000," *Cleveland Call,* March 30, 1939, 11.

78. Diane E. Loupe, "Storming and Defending the Color Barrier at the University of Missouri School of Journalism: The Lucile Bluford Case," 22.

79. S.W. Canada to Lucile Bluford, January 18, 1939, UA.

80. Loupe, "Storming," 23, and Statement, January 30, 1939, UPP & NAACP A24. The full statement read: "The decision of the Supreme Court of the United States in the

Gaines case has not yet become final but is still pending in the Supreme Court of Missouri for further consideration. When the courts have rendered final judgment in this case, no doubt the officials of Missouri will take such action as seems best to meet the situation. The people of Missouri have established a separate educational system for the races in the State, and any negro desiring university work should apply to Lincoln University which has been established for that purpose. Pending a final decision of this matter, the Board of Curators of the University of Missouri cannot and will not alter the long-established policy of this State."

81. "Equality for Negroes Asked," *Columbia Missourian*, February 11, 1939, LLG. Holmes, minister for 38 years and at Paseo for 18 years, asked blacks in Columbia to "demand their rights, saying that they are taxpayers and deserve equality and equal consideration."

82. Wilkins to White, April 2, 1939.

83. White to Redmond, April 3, 1939; White to Houston, April 3, 1939; White to Whitlow, April 4, 1938; White to Wilkins, April 3, 1939.

84. "Washington is all agog over the Marian Anderson concert," and expects a crowd over 100,000. White to Wilkins, April 3, 1939.

85. News reports estimated the number of attendees as high as 200. "Fight Lincoln U Bill in Missouri," *New York Amsterdam News*, April 22, 1939, 11. See also "Enforcement of Decision Urged," *Los Angeles Sentinel*, May 11, 1939, 1.

86. "Negroes indicated at a Senate University committee hearing that states throughout the nation which have separate schools for the races are looking to the Missouri situation to plan their future school systems." "Measure to Lift Lincoln U. Level Goes to Governor," *Columbia Missourian*, April 19, 1939, 1.

87. W. B. Whitlow to Walter White, April 13, 1939.

88. "Measure to Lift Lincoln U. Level Goes to Governor," *Columbia Missourian*, April 19, 1939, 1.

89. "Bill to Raise L.U. Standards Passes Senate," *Jefferson City Post-Tribune*, April 19, 1939, 1.

90. "Measure to Lift Lincoln U. Level Goes to Governor," 1.

91. "Bill to Raise L.U. Standards Passes Senate," 1.

92. Walter White to Lloyd Stark, telegram, April 20, 1939; letter, April 21, 1939, 1. See also "Ask Veto of Missouri's 'University' Bill," *Chicago Defender*, April 29, 1939, 4.

93. White to Stark, April 21, 1939, 2.

94. Ibid., 3.

95. Ibid., 4.

96. White to Bennett Clark, April 21, 1939.

97. Press release, "Missouri Governor Asked to Veto Bill Which Flouts Supreme Court," April 20, 1939, 2. See also "Missouri Assembly Passes Bill Flouting Court Ruling," *New York Amsterdam News*, April 29, 1939, 7.

98. "Missouri Governor Asked to Veto Bill Which Flouts Supreme Court," 1. The *Pittsburgh Courier* opened the statement with "B-U-L-L-E-T-I-N-!" "Missouri Governor Asked to Veto Taylor Bill," April 29, 1939, 20.

99. White to Redmond (St. Louis), Elmore Williams (Kansas City), Mrs. H.V. Smith (Springfield), and Arthur Williams (Macon), April 20, 1939.

100. Thurgood Marshall, "Memorandum to Branch Officers of Missouri Branches," April 20, 1939.

101. Press release, "Missourians Want Supreme Court Opinion Enforced," Kansas City, MO, May 5, 1939.

102. Stark signed the bill as opposed to letting the bill become law automatically. According to the *Chicago Defender*, rather than "take the easy way out," Stark "chose rather to show his mockery for the court's decision by signing the bill." The *Defender* also referred to bill sponsor Taylor as a "Pendergast henchman." "Missouri Mocks Court's Lloyd Gaines Decision," *Chicago Defender*, May 13, 1939, 3.

103. AP, "Lincoln U. Equality Bill Signed by Stark," *St. Louis Globe-Democrat*, May 4, 1939.

104. Henry D. Espy to Walter White, May 5, 1939.

105. "Oppose Gov. Stark's Federal Appointment," *St. Louis Argus*, May 19, 1939, 1. The resolution began "Be it remembered, that on May 4, 1939, Governor Stark signed the infamous Taylor Bill passed by the Missouri Legislature, which bill purports to afford Negroes educational opportunities equal to those provided for whites at the University of Missouri and which said bill is conceded by the press of the state to be an astute maneuver to circumvent the decision of the United States Supreme Court in the case of Lloyd Gaines vs. The University of Missouri..." and included statements such as "Whereas Governor Stark on numerous occasions has shown avowed hostility to the advancement of the Negro Citizens of the State," 1, 12.

106. White to Redmond, May 22, 1939; Redmond to White, May 24, 1939. Redmond mentions coverage by Harry W. Flannery, the "best commentator" in St. Louis on KMOX. Flannery soon became the foreign correspondent for CBS in Nazi Germany.

107. White to Espy, May 8, 1939. The *Pittsburgh Courier* claimed that signing the law was the end of Stark's "Presidential aspirations." "Finding A Way Out Of A Hole," May 20, 1939, 1. Stark ran for the US Senate in 1940, but lost in the Democratic primary to a rather obscure Jackson County judge, Harry S. Truman. Although his administration is now tarnished by the Taylor Bill, at the time Stark was perceived as a reformer with governmental and civic improvements. He was a fierce opponent of political corruption and, in particular, the Pendergast machine in Kansas City. After losing the Senate election, Stark returned to the family business, the Stark Brothers Nursery.

108. White to Espy, May 8, 1939.

109. Espy to White, May 5, 1939; White to Espy, May 8, 1939, emphasis in the original.

110. "School Man Okeys Plan: NAACP Counsel Says Mo. Gesture Means New Fight," *Afro-American*, July 8, 1939, 2.

111. Charles Howard, "The Observer," *Atlanta Daily World*, July 10, 1939, 2.

112. Louis T. Wright (Chairman of the Board) and Roy Wilkins (Assistant Secretary), NAACP, Minutes of the Meeting of the Board of Directors, May 8, 1939, 3. A press

release publicized the Board's decision, "New Court Fight Over Education Looms in Missouri," New York, May 12, 1939.

113. Press release, "Missouri Governor Asked to Veto Bill Which Flouts Supreme Court," Jefferson City, April 21, 1939, 2.

114. Redmond to Houston, April 15, 1939.

115. Houston to White, April 19, 1939. White agreed: "We, of course, leave to your judgment how much time you need to spend in Missouri." But he also wanted an explanation from Houston in order to "understand the situation more clearly" and to "clear up for us the matter of what hearing it is." White to Houston, April 20, 1939.

116. Houston to Marshall, May 4, 1939.

117. Houston to Marshall, May 9, 1939, 1.

118. Ibid., 2.

119. Redmond to White, May 24, 1939, Houston to White, May 22, 1939, 1.

7 The Case Returns to Missouri

1. Charles H. Houston, "Cracking Closed University Doors," in Fitzhugh Lee Styles, *Negroes and the Law,* 1937, 91.

2. "To Re-Argue Gaines Case Before State Court Next Monday," *The Call,* May 19, 1939, 1. To the publishers of the Kansas City paper, the hearing constituted the "last legal hurdle to be overcome before Lloyd Gaines can enter the University of Missouri...."

3. Houston to White, May 22, 1939, 1.

4. Houston to White, May 22, 1939, 1–2; Fred L. Williams, Nick T. Cave, William S. Hogsett, Ralph E. Murray, "Respondents' Brief," State ex rel. Gaines v. Canada et al., Supreme Court of Missouri, May Term 1939, No. 35286, throughout, esp. 5, 13–15, 18–20, 22–32, 46–48, quote at 31; *Missouri ex. rel. Gaines v. Canada,* 305 U.S. 337, 352 (1938). See also "Gaines Case Is Re-Argued Before Court." *Chicago Defender,* June 3, 1939, 5.

5. Houston to White, May 22, 1939, 1–2.

6. The argument boiled down to this, according to *The Call:* "Charles Houston and Sidney Redmond say [the legislation] does not comply with Supreme Court decision; State, 'Yes.'" Arguing for the inadequacy of the Taylor Bill, Charles Houston told the judges, "'This court can't turn aside the United States supreme court decision, saying that 'we will give you a law school later.' We can't be required to take a mere hope that at some time in the future we will get a law school." When he was asked by Judge Ernest Gantt, "'Isn't the only thing for the state to do now to admit Negroes to the state university until they get good schools of their own,'" the *Call* reported Houston's simple answer: "'Yes, your honor, that is our contention.'" He continued, pressing for the desegregation of the University of Missouri's law school: "'If the state of Missouri wants to spend its money to build a law school for one Negro student, that is Missouri's business,'" but, as the *Call* reported, "...he made it plain that the law school built for this one student must be equal to the one for white students at the University of Missouri." He said that the law school would "...have to meet the requirements of the American Association of Law Schools,

and that in order to be considered for membership in this association, a law school must have operated up to the required standards for two years." "N.A.A.C.P. Lawyers in Brilliant Plea Before Supreme Court," *Call,* May 26, 1939, 1.

7. "The only time the court can consider is the present. Missouri must have a law school in actual operation or else admit Gaines to the University of Missouri law school. In no other way can the United States supreme court mandate be complied with." "Gaines Case Goes Before Missouri Tribunal, 2nd Time," *Cleveland Call,* June 1, 1939, 1.

8. The Kansas City paper reported: "Houston told the court that there was no other remedy for the youth to take in seeking legal training in the state." The *Call* observed, "The N.A.A.C.P. lawyer did not have to argue further because Justice Gantt again interrupted and his remarks showed that he thought Mr. Houston was right. 'When they claim that the Taylor bill fixes things up,' Justice Gantt asked Mr. Houston, 'aren't they admitting that the writ of mandamus was the right remedy?' Mr. Houston replied, 'The attorneys for the state contend that it is all right for the writ of mandamus to be granted against Lincoln university, a Negro school, but not against a white school.'" "N.A.A.C.P. Lawyers in Brilliant Plea Before Supreme Court," *Call,* May 26, 1939, 1, 4.

9. Houston to White, May 22, 1939, 2.

10. Ibid., 2.

11. Ibid., 3.

12. Ibid. Visitors included Lucile Bluford, Elmore Williams, President of the Kansas City Branch of the NAACP, Melba Sweets of the *St. Louis American,* and other representatives from the two metro areas. Houston prefaced this comment by writing, "After the case was over this is what I told them. As I usually go wrong on principles of segregation, I am repeating it to you so if it runs counter to Association policy you can write the St. Louis and Kansas City Branches right away to counteract." Houston had requested that Bluford attend, both as a correspondent for the *Call* and as a potential litigant. Houston to Bluford, May 4, 1939; Bluford to Houston, May 13, 1939.

13. Houston to White, 4. Houston also attacked the "voluntary" out of state tuition scholarships as unconstitutional under the US Supreme Court's *Gaines* decision, 4–5. Houston left Missouri for legal business in Muskogee, Oklahoma, so he would not speak with NAACP leaders for some time.

14. White to Houston, May 26, 1939, 1. White claimed this as the consensus of the NAACP leadership. "I have talked this over with the other fellow[s] in the office here and they all agree. As a matter of fact, the above opinion is a sort of composite of what Thurgood, Roy, George [Murphy] and Arthur [Spingarn] have said."

15. White to Marshall, Memorandum, May 24, 1939.

16. "N.A.A.C.P. Lawyers in Brilliant Plea Before Supreme Court," *Call,* May 26, 1939, 1, 4.

17. Houston to White, 6.

18. "N.A.A.C.P. Lawyers in Brilliant Plea," 1, 4.

19. Ibid., 4.

20. Ibid.

21. Houston to White, May 22, 1939, 14. Strikethrough in Houston's handwritten notes.

22. Minutes, Board of Curators of Lincoln University, June 26, 1939, 52.

23. "Action on Gaines Case Decision Is Further Delayed," *Pittsburgh Courier,* February 18, 1939, 4.

24. "Delegation Opposes New Lincoln Univ. Bill," *Pittsburgh Courier,* March 4, 1939, 2.

25. "Jittery," *Pittsburgh Courier,* March 11, 1939, 8.

26. "Ducking the Issue," *Pittsburgh Courier,* April 1, 1939, 10.

27. "Charles H. Thompson, Ph.D." http://www.journalnegroed.org/editorchief.html.

28. "Drippings From Other Pens: Christian Democracy And The Gaines Decision," *Chicago Defender,* June 24, 1939, 19.

29. Judge William Frank, author of the first opinion and the only Republican, was no longer on the Court. He was replaced by Judge Albert M. Clark. Judge Charles Thomas Hays was absent, otherwise, all judges concurred (again).

30. *State ex rel. Gaines v. Canada et al.* 113 S.W.2d 217, 219.

31. Ibid. *Missouri ex rel. Gaines v. Canada* 305 U. S. 337, 346.

32. *State ex rel. Gaines v. Canada et al.* 113 S.W.2d 217, 220. This includes the Gaines decision under the topic "Equal Protection." William R. Collinson, "The Work of the Missouri Supreme Court for the Year 1939: Constitutional Law," *Missouri Law Review* 5 (November 1940), 391–392. Compare to the previous year's edition where the case is mentioned under the topic "Mandamus," with a footnote that the decision was appealed to the federal Supreme Court and "reversed and remanded on the ground that by the operation of the laws of Missouri a privilege for white law students which is denied to negroes because of their race is contrary to the "equal protection" provision of the Constitution of the United States, and this notwithstanding the fact that there is but a limited demand in Missouri for legal education of negroes." Rush H. Limbaugh, "The Work of the Missouri Supreme Court for the Year 1938: Extraordinary Legal Remedies," *Missouri Law Review* 4 (November 1939), 400–401.

33. "Gaines-Missouri Verdict Reversed: Equality of Lincoln U. Law School in Doubt," *Afro-American,* August 12, 1939, 1.

34. "Missouri Supreme Court Decision Neither Opens Nor Shuts Doors of M.U.: Leaves Them Ajar, So That if Law School at Lincoln U. Does Not Measure Up, Negroes Will Be Admitted," *Call,* August 11, 1939, 1.

35. "Gaines Decision Reversed By Court," *Joplin Globe,* August 2, 1939, 5; "Gaines Case Is Sent Here for Retrial," *Columbia Daily Tribune,* August 1, 1939, 1.

36. "Remand Gaines Suit to Circuit Court," *St. Louis Globe-Democrat,* August 2, 1939, 3.

37. "More Litigation Seen in Lloyd Gaines' Case," *Columbia Missourian,* August 1, 1939, 1.

38. Minutes of the Meetings, Board of Curators, Lincoln University, June 10 1937, 257, LUA.

39. Minutes, June 10 1937, 257–260, LUA.

40. Initially, Florence was given one year's paid leave, however, a week later this was reduced to leave with half-pay, provided that he engaged in post-graduate study, followed by termination. Minutes, June 10 1937, 260, June 18, 1937, 263, LUA. Florence went to Harvard University, and then secured another, permanent position at Virginia Union University.

41. Minutes, April 2, 1938, 282, LUA.

42. In addition to an undergraduate degree from Washburn University, Scruggs earned master's and doctoral degrees at the University of Kansas. Savage, *The History of Lincoln University,* 272.

43. J.D. Elliff to Lloyd C. Stark, June 17, 1937, LCS. See also Holland, et al., *The Soldiers' Dream Continued,* 21.

44. The Governor wrote "I don't want you, under any circumstances, to consider resigning from the Lincoln University Board of Curators." Stark asked for Elliff and State Superintendent of Schools Lloyd King to provide more information. "If you and Superintendent King think things are not going right at any time, please give me the necessary warning. In other words, if there is any trouble about cliques, factions and University politics, I want you to keep me informed." Stark to Elliff, June 18, 1937, LCS.

45. Marshall, *Soldiers' Dream,* 20–21.

46. Elliff to Stark, June 28, 1937; Stark to Elliff, June 29, 1937. Stark entreated him, "I do not want to accept your resignation." He planned to communicate further with Elliff after a trip to Alaska. As late as November, Stark responded, "I have been quietly working on the Lincoln University matter. Please do not insist on my accepting your resignation. I cannot do so at present." Stark to Elliff, November 18, 1937. Stark wanted to wait on the final report of the North Central Association before taking final action. Stark to Elliff, April 27, 1938, May 9, 1938, LCS.

47. Minutes, September 26, 1938, 10, LUA. There were also allegations that Kansas City physician William J. Thompkins, the Curator who had nominated McLemore for the presidency, was ineligible to serve on the Board. President Franklin Roosevelt had appointed Thompkins as Recorder of Deeds for the District of Columbia in April 1934. Opponents to the current Board claimed that Thompkins thus was no longer a Missouri resident, a prerequisite for Board membership. Attorney Henry R. Bracy provided the Board an opinion that Thompkins was indeed a Kansas City resident.

48. Minutes, November 4, 1938, 11, 12, LUA. Lincoln President Sherman Scruggs claimed he alone took action on the allegations of financial impropriety independently of any Board member. Scruggs to Dr. A.J. Brumbaugh, North Central Association of Colleges and Secondary Schools, December 8, 1938, Minutes, 25–26.

49. Sumner High School teacher and Baptist pastor Dreer established the small, private Douglas University in 1935. He was representing the trustees in his appearance before the Lincoln University Board of Curators.

50. Minutes, December 16, 1938, 16.

51. Ibid., 19.

52. See Minutes, March 17, 1939, 33, and May 27, 1939, 42.

53. See Minutes, March 17, 1939, 33; also, see (untitled) nominations in Lloyd C. Stark Papers.

54. His first notice, the appointment letter from Governor Stark, was received on March 10. Perry, *Forty Cords*, 452. Perry had been appointed to the Board of Curators in 1921, when the Missouri Legislature established a public university from the former Lincoln Institute, and a later term through 1935. He worked tirelessly in order to develop Lincoln into a legitimate institution of higher education, 423–448.

55. Minutes, June 26, 1939, 51.

56. Marshall, *Soldier's Dream*, 21.

57. Perry, *Forty Cords*, 452. Perry added that "all subsequent conferences were characterized by harmony and a mutual respect and admiration for all parties concerned." Perry believed that the new "enactment of 1939 took Lincoln University out of politics" and established the Board of Curators as a legitimate "policy making body" with the university president as the chief administrator. Perry, *Forty Cords*, 456.

58. Minutes, June 26, 1939, 54.

59. "Law School At Lincoln Opens in September," *Jefferson City Post-Tribune*, June 30, 1939, 6.

60. "Lincoln U. Will Get Law School," *Joplin Globe*, June 30, 1939, 2A.

61. "Lincoln U. Curators Order Establishment of Law School," *Columbia Daily Tribune*, June 30, 1939, 1.

62. Minutes, Executive Board and Special Committee, July 29, 1939, 58. "Such important factors as future and permanence of the State's intention to continue such a school; the standards to be met in organizing a recognized school; the location of the school at Jefferson City or elsewhere; necessity and availability of space and facilities for housing the school; availability of necessary faculty; probable salaries to be paid; and the like, were discussed at length." Regarding the visit to Columbia, the minutes note: "Very courteous treatment was extended."

63. Deposition, *State ex rel Gaines v. Canada*, No. 34,337, October 10, 1939, 32. According to Taylor, he was ranked number one in his graduating class at the Iowa Law School.

64. Smith, *Emancipation*, 50–51.

65. Houston to Redmond, October 2, 1939.

66. Redmond to Houston, September 30, 1939: "I am doing what I can to comply with your instruction but the dean has refused to let anyone see the student list and those there are reporting everything someone does."

67. Houston to Redmond, October 2, 1939. Houston suggested asking students to provide a list of other students attending each class in order to cross-check who was really enrolled. At the deposition, Redmond was prepared with a motion to inspect records of the law school. William Hogsett, counsel for the University, opened his remarks by noting, "Our position is that the relator or his counsel may inspect any records that he wants.... We have no control over the Lincoln Law School, but I have talked to Dean

Taylor, and that is his attitude also." *State ex rel Gaines v. Canada,* No. 34,337, October 10, 1939, 3.

68. Houston to Thurgood Marshall, October 10, 1939, 2. Another painting was of influential black Philadelphia Raymond Pace Alexander, then on the Board of Directors of the National Bar Association, first organized in 1925. At this time, Sidney Redmond was the President of the National Bar Association and Charles Houston was an editor of the *National Bar Journal.* That they were there to depose Taylor who, in Houston's mind, had turned on the organization's primary goals no doubt inflamed his ire.

69. Houston to Marshall, October 10, 1939, 1. Thurgood Marshall wrote a letter to William Taylor asking for a position at Howard University Law School, but he did not receive it. Thurgood Marshall to William E. Taylor, December 27, 1935, in J. Clay Smith Jr., ed., *Supreme Justice: Speeches and Writings: Thurgood Marshall,* 7–8.

70. In Wesley, Price, and Morris, eds., *Lift Every Voice and Sing,* 129.

71. Minutes, July 29, 1939, 58. The Senate approved an amendment to an appropriation bill (HB 584) to provide an additional $200,000 but the conference committee eliminated the provision.

72. J. Edward Perry, the black physician from Kansas City, articulated the difficulty confronting the Lincoln Curators in this way: "The decision in the Gaines case brought to the board through legislative enactment some serious and difficult problems. The board was mandated to establish schools of journalism and law. Several members of the board did not share the opinion of the Legislature, yet we were under orders and a good soldier or a good citizen always obeys the law. We felt and still feel that as appointees, it is our indispensable duty to do all in our power to direct these departments to the highest degree of efficiency. Our thought was, the number of Missourians desiring to pursue such courses would be limited. The cost would be great and finally regarded as a wanton expenditure of public funds. The thoughts of the majority of the people, as expressed through their representatives in session assembled, were not in accord. The minority in a democratic form of government always yields to the majority. The departments were opened as directed and the best prepared teachers secured as possible to impart information." Perry, *Forty Cords,* 452.

73. Minutes, August 9, 1939, 67. The motion was to "approve the location of the Law School in St. Louis, Missouri; that the President of the University be authorized to rent or lease a building in that city within the next two days to house the Law School and that a law library of 10,000 volumes (which is the minimum under the Association of American Law Schools standards) be purchased immediately." The original trial court argument by University of Missouri attorneys that black law students could use the Supreme Court Library in Jefferson City seems to have either been forgotten or reevaluated.

74. Most contemporary accounts consider these two law schools as white-only, but Hale Giddings Parker graduated from St. Louis University School of Law in 1885, and Walter Moran Farmer graduated from Washington University in 1889. Farmer had difficult experiences with fellow law students, but he went on to be the first black lawyer to argue before the Missouri Supreme Court in 1893. Smith, *Emancipation,* 332. Both universities, however, ceased admitting black students around 1919–1920, as journalist Bennie Rodgers recalled. That unofficial ban continued until around 1947. St. Louis attorneys

George Vaughn, David Grant, and Robert Witherspoon initiated a lawsuit against Washington University as it accepted tax breaks for certain public institution functions but would not admit blacks as students. Vaughn's son was admitted, then others followed. See Rodgers interview by Shelton, *Interpretive Community,* 185; David M. Grant, oral history. In the end, of course, the white, private institutions shared no resources with black, public Lincoln University School of Law.

75. "St. Louis May Get Lincoln Law School," *Atlanta Daily World,* August 16, 1939, 1.

76. Other than the earlier meeting seeking public input on available options, the only time St. Louis or anywhere beyond the capital was discussed officially was on August 9, 1939, when Scruggs was given discretionary authority to locate the new law school in St. Louis. Given the need for Dean Taylor and other faculty members to relocate, and so forth, it is reasonable that this was also discussed earlier.

77. The Taylor Bill authorized construction of additional buildings, but state laws do not allow construction without funds allocated specifically for that purpose. Norval B. Barksdale, "The Gaines Case and Its Effect on Negro Education in Missouri," *School and Society* (March 9, 1940), 310–311. As Appropriations Committee Chair, Representative Taylor presumably understood the limitations inherent in his bill.

78. Dreer, *Negro Leadership,* 80, 109. Regarding Annie Malone, see DeAnna J. Reese, "Domestic Drudges to Dazzling Divas: The Origins of African American Beauty Culture in St. Louis, 1900–1930," in Lee Ann Whites, Mary Neth, and Gary Kremer, *Women in Missouri History: In Search of Power and Influence,* 168–179, and Yussuf J. Simmonds, "Annie Turnbo Pope Malone," *Los Angeles Sentinel,* July 23, 2010. Malone lived modestly, and much of her profits were reinvested in the business and in community service. Her financial support included institutions such as the Howard University School of Medicine, the Tuskegee Institute, and a number of local charities including the St. Louis Colored Orphans Home, later renamed in her honor. Malone's business interests were ultimately eclipsed by a former employee and protégé, Sarah Breedlove, who established her own company under the pseudonym Madame C.J. Walker.

79. "Poro College Moves Plant to Chicago: Entire Block on S. Parkway to House Malone Concern," *Afro-American,* August 2, 1930, 18. Malone is quoted as saying that "…Chicago, in my opinion, is the capital of Negro America." She continued, "St. Louis is a wonderful city. I love my own people in St. Louis. I have tried to serve them. But St. Louis in most of its attitudes is a Southern city. My experience would lead me to doubt that Negro businesses can grow to large magnitude in the South without feeling something of restraint, as well as a certain sense of insecurity."

80. Holland, *Young and the Struggle,* 160. Aaron Malone, President of Poro and a former school principal, served on the Board during the time Nathan B. Young was removed as Lincoln University President.

81. *St. Louis American* publisher Nathaniel Sweets attributes political efforts by former state legislator and National Republican Committeeman Barak T. Mattingly as key for securing Poro College as the law school site. Sweets, Oral History.

82. "Missouri Soon Starts Negro Law Classes," *Dunkirk* (NY) *Evening Observer,* September 13, 1939, 5.

83. For instance, the *Argus* outlined what was necessary: "Within the next 33 days a law school is promised that will meet as set forth by the Association of American Law Schools and the several recognized bar associations around the country. Within the above state time, renovation must be made on the first floor of the Poro College for the housing of the school. Shelves must be installed for the library and ten thousand volumes must be on the shelves when the school officially opens on Sept. 20." "Plan Lincoln Law School: Officials Move Forward With Their Plans," *St. Louis Argus,* August 18, 1939, 13.

84. "Stalling in Missouri," *Pittsburgh Courier,* August 8, 1939, 10.

85. "The Establishment of a School of Law by Lincoln University," *School and Society* 50 (September 9, 1939), 339. Out of state students were charged an additional $40 per year. Tuition to Missouri residents was reported to be free, although the Board of Curators decided only that in-state tuition was equal to that at the Missouri School of Law and that other students be charged an additional $40 per year. Minutes, August 9, 1939, 69.

86. Parks, *Lincoln University,* 89, notes "once established, the school became a member of the American Association of Law Libraries in December 1939, was approved by the Missouri Board of Law Examiners in February 1940, and the American Bar Association in October 1942, and was elected to membership of the American Association of American Law Schools in December 1941."

87. "The Establishment of a School," 339.

88. Minutes, Executive Committee, September 28, 1939, 70. Parks, *Lincoln University,* 89, indicates there were 31 students; Smith, *Emancipation,* 63, 34.

89. David M. Grant Oral History; Dreer, *Negro Leadership,* 43.

90. "Picket Lincoln U's Jim-Crow Law School," *Cleveland Call,* September 28, 1939, 1.

91. Editor Nathan B. Young Jr., called the economic boycott, "buy where you can work." David M. Grant Oral History; Nathaniel Sweets Oral History; Sidney R. Redmond Oral History; Nathan B. Young Oral History, Sidney R. Redmond to Thurgood Marshall, September 22, 1939. The *American* was aggressive in pushing for new employment opportunities, but the *Argus* was less so. Roy Wilkins asserted that Governor Lloyd Stark ordered removal of the picketers. Wilkins to Walter White, September 29, 1939, 1.

92. Redmond to Marshall, September 22, 1939. "The sentiment among the Negroes in St. Louis is almost 100 percent against it."

93. Wilkins to White, September 29, 1939.

94. "Battle Front," *St. Louis Call,* Friday, September 22, 1939.

95. Williams, president of Vashon High School, was one of the Curators who expressed opposition to creation of a Lincoln University law school. Once the decision was made to establish the law school, like other Curators, he supported establishing an effective institution of learning. Minutes, Lincoln University Board of Curators, June 26, 1939, 53.

96. "Why There Should Be No Compromise on The 'Poro' Law School," *St. Louis Call,* September 25, 1939. According to the editorial, "finally, there is the Negro Press, which has been reluctant to denounce the [Lincoln Law School] for what is it. The cause is now known to the public; a sum of money was placed in the hands of the *Kansas City Call* to

handle the advertising and publicity of the law school. It is the first time that any publicity of Lincoln University has been 'farmed out.' This evidently has APPEASED the press."

97. Wilkins to White, September 29, 1939. "I understand that Espey [*sic*] is trying to get Redmond to come out with a statement, but Sidney is silent. That will give you an idea of the division of opinion."

98. Houston to Redmond, September 7, 1939.

99. "Statement of Committee on Administration of N.A.A.C.P. Concerning University of Missouri Cases." October 2, 1939, 1; White to Houston, October 3, 1939; "Memorandum to Mr. Marshall from Mr. White," October 3, 1939; Marshall to Missouri Branches—N. A. A. C. P., October 3, 1939.

100. "Court Must Decide Whether St. Louis Law School Meets Standard, Say N.A.A.C.P.: Move for Rehearing of Gaines Case," New York, October 6, 1939.

101. The *Defender,* for instance, noted "the Colored Clerks Circle, an organization of clerks in various stores, is still picketing the law school, the signs carried by the pickets calling the school a subterfuge.... Publicity releases from the Lincoln university law school say that 30 students are still enrolled in the school, but reports [from the NAACP] are that the number has been reduced to 18 since picketing began." "Principal in The Gaines Case Missing," *Chicago Defender,* October 21, 1939, 1.

102. "St. Louisans Launch Fight to Close Up Jim Crow Law School At Lincoln Univ." *Cleveland Call,* October 29, 1939, 1.

103. "2 Races Picket Mo. Law School," *Afro-American,* January 6, 1940, 3.

104. Elaine Woo, "Harold H. Wilkie, 88; Armless Minister and Advocate for Disabled," *Los Angeles Times,* March 3, 2003; Dallas Bauminger, 2004, "Harold H. Wilkie Fund," February 4, 2009, http://www.uccdm.org/132/harold-h-wilke-fund/.

105. "Whites Join Pickets At Lincoln Law School," *Chicago Defender,* December 30, 1039, 2.

106. Norris Bailey, "Whites Join in Picketing Lincoln's New Law School," *Atlanta Daily World,* January 4, 1940, 1.

107. "Toy Universities," *The Pittsburgh Courier,* January 6, 1940, 8.

108. "Death Removes Anti-Colored U.S. Justice," *Afro-American,* November 25, 1939, 1.

109. "Day by Day: New Deal Supreme Court," *Afro-American,* January 13, 1940, 4.

110. Ibid.

111. Ibid.

112. The early stages of litigation on behalf of Lucile Bluford could have been a distraction. Houston assured Sidney Redmond and Bluford, "Under all circumstances, whether in September, October or November we will go forward with the Gaines case. Confidentially we will be in better position to strike after the new law school has actually got under operation." Houston, however, wanted this strategy to remain confidential: "But don't let any publicity in on this point now." Houston, "Memorandum for Miss Lucile Bluford and Sidney R. Redmond, Esq.: re registration School of Journalism, U. Missouri, September 11, 1939.

113. Depositions, *State ex rel. Gaines v. Canada,* No. 34,337, October 10, 1939. Of the 66 typed pages for the deposition, fully 61 involved examination of Taylor, the remainder were devoted to the other three faculty members. Lincoln University President Sherman Scruggs attended, but no questions were directed toward him.

114. Ernesto Longa, "A History of America's First Jim Crow Law School Library and Staff," 81.

115. Richardson's Chicago law partner, George W. Lawrence, was president of the National Bar Association for 1935–1936. His tenure was followed by Charles Houston's father, William L. Houston, 1937–1938, and his friend and colleague Sidney Redmond, 1939–1940.

116. Depositions, *State ex rel. Gaines v. Canada,* October 10, 1939, 13, 24, 29, 37, 65–68.

117. Depositions, 9, 10. Librarian Barbour and the secretary for Dean Taylor were counted among the employee students.

118. Depositions, 5. Initially, the law school comprised only the first floor and the mezzanine of the one section of the old Poro College. Taylor arranged with the management for space for a student dormitory on the second floor, and claimed additional space would be available upon need. Taylor, however, resisted Houston's suggestion that sharing the building with a pool room and a theatre would interfere with the purposes of the law school. 5–6.

119. According to Longa, "A History of America's," 91–95, Taylor made a dedicated effort for library collection development. Washington University librarian Oscar Orman provided advice about organizing the collection and noted that it exceeded minimal standards of the AALS. To get the collection started, Yale University School of Law donated 6,000 volumes to Lincoln. See also, Depositions, October 10, 1939, 10–11; Minutes, Lincoln University Board of Curators, December 16, 1939.

120. Depositions, 43–45. Taylor read the names and degrees of Missouri faculty from the catalogue, but he could not comment on their abilities.

121. Depositions, 30.

122. Ibid., 34.

123. "New Lincoln Law School Has Passed Its 'First Exam,'" *Afro-American,* October 14, 1939, 3. The newspaper article on ABA certification sat alongside another on the NAACP's plan to pursue final judicial action in the *Gaines* case. "Mo. Law School Legality Assailed," *Afro-American,* October 14, 1939, 3. Taylor did note that Shaforth's review was based on the full 30 students. Depositions, 7–8; Minutes, Lincoln University Board of Curators, December 16, 1939. According to Norval Barksdale, Shafroth's statement said "In respect to the library, the physical equipment, the number of full-time teachers, admission requirements and length of course, the school fully complies with the American Bar Association requirement. Barksdale added, "This did not mean, of course, that the school was being recommended for approval." Barksdale, "The Gaines Case," 311. Shafroth also inspected Howard University for the ABA as its first predominantly black law school when Charles Houston sought accreditation in 1930, see McNeil, *Groundwork,* 74–75.

124. Houston to Marshall, October 10, 1939, 3. Houston thought Taylor's assessment of St. Louis attorney and Lincoln instructor Lucas was harsh. In addition, when applying for the position at Howard, Taylor claimed to have tried 50 murder cases in one year.

125. Houston to Marshall, October 10, 1939, 2.

126. Depositions, 49.

127. Ibid., 64. To Marshall, Houston's version was "I told them I was showing all the respect he was entitled to." Houston to Marshall, October 10, 1939, 3.

128. "Lively Scene As Depositions Are Taken Here," *St. Louis Argus,* October 13, 1939, 1.

129. Ibid., 1, 7.

130. Ibid., 7.

131. Houston to Marshall, October 10, 1939, 3.

8 The Mystery of Lloyd Gaines

1. "…if we locate Gaines and he is willing to go forward with application to University of Missouri we shall proceed in the Circuit Court of Boone County to have a court determination whether the separate law school now being set up in Missouri is a substantial equivalent of the U. Missouri Law School. Sidney Redmond is to make the efforts to locate Gaines by sending registered letters, deliver to addressee only, to all places where Gaines has been recently or where he is likely to be found. If Gaines is not found Sidney is to issue a statement to that effect about September 10–15. Assuming Gaines foundeither [*sic*] thru Sidney or thru others after the word has got abroad that he cannot be located, the next question is the procedure of having him go to the U. Missouri and up to Columbia for hearing." Houston, "Memorandum for Walter, Roy, Thurgood, and Arthur: re University of Missouri and University of Tennessee," August 22, 1939, 1.

2. "I telegraphed you this week asking you to concentrate on efforts to locate Gaines. Please advise me what luck." Houston to Redmond, September 7, 1939.

3. Houston added, "However that is a question of state procedure which you will have to answer for me." Houston to Redmond, September 7, 1939.

4. "So I hope the preliminaries can be carried thru without my presence. We will need lots of money down the line, and the more we can save now the more we will have for a war chest then." "Memorandum for Miss Lucile Bluford and Sidney R. Redmond, Esq.: re registration School of Journalism, U. Missouri," September 11, 1939. See also, Charlie Houston to Sidney R. Redmond, telegram, September 11, 1939. Bluford had been denied admission in February, but her attorneys felt she should attempt to register under the new political environment, after Lincoln University acknowledged it had no graduate program in journalism.

5. White to Redmond, September 12, 1939, White to Prentice [*sic*] Hoffman, September 12, 1939. St. Louis made an additional contribution of $150, Redmond to Marshall, September 22, 1939, Marshall to Redmond, September 23, 1939, Redmond to White, September 29, 1939, and Kansas City also contributed $150, Marshall to Houston, October 3, 1939. White subsequently noted the contributions "will take care of the expenses

of the Gaines case and filing of the Bluford cases. It will, however, be necessary to immediately raise additional funds for the trial of these cases and for further appeals if they be
necessary." White to Redmond, October 10, 1939, 1.

6. Houston, "Memorandum to Sidney R. Redmond, Esq., and Miss Lucile Bluford,"
September 12, 1938, 3.

7. Houston stopped drafting the petition for mandamus in the Bluford case "because
I found myself without information on so many points that the draft looked too much
like a blank piece of paper with lines drawn on it. That situation drilled into my head that
what we needed more than speed was accuracy and completeness. We have had a good record so far in all of our university cases so far as paper work is concerned. We have not had
to amend a single pleading. So it seems to me better from the point of view of history to
be right even if it takes a little longer to get started than to rush off and have to backtrack
almost as soon as we get started." Houston, "Memorandum," September 12, 1938, 1.

8. Redmond to Houston, September 30, 1939.

9. "Second Suit Filed Against U. of Missouri," St. Louis, October 13, 1939.

10. Houston to Marshall, October 10, 1939, 3–4.

11. Lloyd Gaines to George Gaines, November 30, 1937, LLG.

12. Most claims that Gaines earned a master's degree at Michigan can be drawn back
to Lucile Bluford's recollection in "The Lloyd Gaines Story," 243.

13. Personal communication, Office of the Registrar, University of Michigan, January
29, 2014.

14. *Sweatt v. Painter*, 339 U.S. 629 (1950).

15. Gary M. Lavergne, *Before* Brown: *Heman Marion Sweatt, Thurgood Marshall, and
the Long Road to Justice*, 2010, 18–19, 41.

16. Gaines to Houston, November 28, 1936 NAACP; Gaines to George Gaines, October 27, 1936, 2, 4; January 3, 1937, 1, LLG. Lloyd was a teacher and principal for the
evening school.

17. Lloyd L. Gaines to George D. Gaines, October 27, 1936, 4; March 21, 1937; June
14, 1937, 3; September 1937 (with header of March 20, 1937), 1–2, LLG.

18. Lloyd L. Gaines to George D. Gaines, October 27, 1936, 1; April 6, 1937, 3–4;
no date (probably late 1937), 1–3, LLG.

19. Gaines to White, March 6, 1937; Gaines to Redmond, March 14, 1937; Houston
to Gaines, March 16, 1937.

20. He wrote to his brother George, "Excusing college activity, and this doesn't mix
with town life, there is nothing of interest here other than church [and] movies. Anyone
not strictly otherwise busy would soon be bored to death for something to do for variety." April 6, 1937, 3–4. "I am getting kind of tired of Ann Arbor and feel like leaving
any minute—and not later than Sunday. May head home or I may not." Lloyd Gaines to
George Gaines, November 30, 1937.

21. No employment records remain for WPA workers at Civil Service. Gaines mentions contacts with Detroit author and civil rights leader Snow F. Grigsby and plans to
attend the "N.A.C.P. convention" in Detroit in late June in order to "meet some of the
Big Shots and see what they can do about further school finance" for tuition through the

end of the year. He also mentioned the need to vacate his room by June 19, 1937. Lloyd Gaines to George Gaines, June 14, 1937. Bluford, "The Lloyd Gaines Story," 243.

22. Redmond to Houston, July 13, 1938.

23. "Gaines Loses Missouri U. Case Appeal," *Kansas City Call,* December 10, 1937, 1.

24. "Can Enter M.U," *The Call,* December 16, 1938, 1.

25. "NAACP to Help Gaines, Missouri Law Student," *Afro-American,* January 21, 1939, 8.

26. "Gaines Given Job As Business League Head, Shows Desire to Help," *Pittsburgh Courier,* January 28, 1939, 5. Of course, Gaines has taught in Ann Arbor and Lansing, not Detroit.

27. Lloyd Gaines to Callie Gaines, March 3, 1939, 1–2, LLG. For instance, Gaines claimed "There were illegal 'tricks of the trade' being practiced by the company that would certaingly [*sic*] involve me should I have remained there until they were made public. This had to do with the practice of selling a cheap quality gas as 'regular' gas and the selling of the 'regular' gas as 'Ethyl' or the highest priced gasoline. No doubt I was so employed as a 'respected and trusted' man to gyp my unsuspecting friends." See also, Bluford, "The Lloyd Gaines Story," 243–244.

28. Schirmer, *A City Divided,* 2002, 176. Lloyd wrote his mother that he "spoke to a capacity crowd of about fourteen hundred with hundreds being turned away. That is how enthusiastic they were over my coming." Lloyd L. Gaines to Callie Gaines, March 3, 1939, 5–6. All spoke to "overflow audiences" at the Centennial Church at 19th and Woodland. Houston's address in October was backed up by the 105 voice Metropolitan Spiritual Church of Christ choir. Prentis J. Hoffman to Charles H. Houston, October 2, 1939. Houston's estimated audience was over 1,400 with people turned away. Hoffman to Thurgood Marshall, October 16, 1939.

29. Gaines to Callie Gaines, March 3, 1939, (the envelope is postmarked March 4), 1, 7, LLG.

30. Bluford, 1959, writes of all these events occurring at the end of April 1939, but all other evidence suggests this was actually early March. Her oral history notes the confusion of dates. In addition she attributes Gaines's visit as the motivation for her to apply for graduate study in journalism at the University of Missouri. Oral History, May 15, 1989, 54.

31. Edward T. Clayton, "The Strange Disappearance of Lloyd Gaines," 30–32; Daniel T. Kelleher, "The Case of Lloyd Lionel Gaines: The Demise of the Separate but Equal Doctrine," *Journal of Negro History,* 268.

32. Bluford, "The Lloyd Gaines Story," 244. Lloyd had also written his brother George about the first hearing before the state Supreme Court: "My case comes up before the Mo. Supreme Court May 18th," adding, "I won't have to appear at court." Lloyd Gaines to George Gaines, April 6, 1937, 1.

33. "Lively Scene As Depositions Are Taken Here," *St. Louis Argus,* October 13, 1939, 1.

34. "Where Is He?" *St. Louis Argus,* October 13, 1939, 1.

35. Only the four law faculty were called and examined by counsel for Gaines and the University of Missouri. The transcript does not mention a request for Gaines or others

to appear. Likewise, there is no correspondence in the NAACP archives showing an attempt to compel Gaines to attend the deposition. However, Lucile Bluford recalls: "It was during the taking of depositions at St. Louis that Gaines' disappearance fell upon the N.A.A.C.P. attorneys like a bombshell." After the four faculty, she continues, "The deposition of Plaintiff Gaines was next. He was to be asked whether he considered the Lincoln University Law School equal to that at the University of Missouri and whether he would enroll there. When his name was called for questioning, Gaines failed to respond. He was not in the room. He was nowhere to be found. It was not until that moment that his lawyers realized that their client was missing." Bluford, "The Lloyd Gaines Story," 245. The attorneys had been concerned about Gaines' location, but there is no correspondence showing they expected him to attend the depositions in St. Louis on October 7.

36. The questions by University of Missouri counsel regarding the location of Gaines and whether he remained a Missouri resident are consistent with knowledge of stories of bribery for Gaines to leave. However, the position of counsel is likewise consistent with innocent legal action on behalf of their client to see if the litigant intended to pursue the case.

37. See, for instance, press release, "N.A.A.C.P. Still Unable to Find Lloyd Gaines," March 8, 1940.

38. "Where is Lloyd Gaines—Have You Seen Him?" *Call,* October 20, 1939, 1.

39. "Lloyd Gaines Said to Have Vanished," *Afro-American,* October 21, 1939, 1. Presumably the person was Frank Weathers at the Lincoln Law School library.

40. "Family Seeks Lloyd Gaines," *New York Amsterdam News,* October 21, 1939, 1.

41. Ibid.

42. Louis Lautier, "Capitol Spotlight," *Afro-American,* October 21, 1939, 9.

43. "Principal in the Gaines Case Missing," *Chicago Defender,* October 21, 1939, 1.

44. Redmond to Houston, October 20, 1939.

45. Houston to Redmond, October 23, 1939.

46. Redmond to Houston, December 19, 1939.

47. William S. Hogsett to Redmond, December 22, 1939.

48. "The AFRO's Honor Roll," *Afro-American,* January 14, 1939, 4.

49. "Alma Mater of Lloyd Gaines Oldest Land Grant College for Race In U.S," *Chicago Defender,* December 31, 1938, 3.

50. "Gaines' Disappearance," *New York Amsterdam News,* January 20, 1940, 14.

51. Ibid.

52. Lavergne, *Before* Brown, 219, citing Heman Sweatt to Thurgood Marshall, September 19, 1946, and Marshall to Sweatt, September 30, 1947.

53. "Where is Lloyd Gaines?" *Pittsburgh Courier,* October 28, 1939, 10.

54. "Opinion," *Afro-American,* October 28, 1939, 5.

55. Louis Lautier, "Where is Lloyd Gaines?" *Afro-American,* October 28, 1939, 9. See also Williams, *Thurgood Marshall,* 98, 411.

56. Louis Lautier, "Where is Lloyd Gaines?" *Afro-American,* October 28, 1939, 9.

57. "Gaines Missing; May Bring End to Case," *Columbia Missourian,* October 11, 1939, 1.

58. "Law School Case Figure Missing," *St. Louis Globe-Democrat,* October 11, 1939, 3.

59. "Lawyers Can't Find Client Who Won Suit: Report L.C. Gaines, Who Sought to Enter Missouri U. Law School, Missing," *St. Louis Post-Dispatch,* October 11, 1939, 6B.

60. "Negro Seeking MU Admission Long Missing: Gaines Fails to Appear for Deposition Hearing at St. Louis; Case Hits a Snag; M.U. Attorneys Propose to Ask Dismissal of Suit," *Columbia Daily Tribune,* October 11, 1939, 1. The following day, the final paragraph of a *Tribune* report about the mandamus suit of Lucile Bluford reported, "Lloyd Gaines has not been heard from for three months and neither his relatives nor his attorneys seem to know where he is. University attorneys will move for a dismissal of the Gaines case." "Negress Seeks Entrance to U." October 12, 1939.

61. "Negro Seeking Admission to Missouri U. Missing," *Jefferson City Daily Capital News,* October 11, 1939, 2.

62. "Friday, October 13, 1939," *Jefferson City Daily Capital News,* October 13, 1939, 10.

63. "Gaines Files Answer in University Case," *Columbia Missourian,* November 3, 1939, 1.

64. Marshall to Houston, December 22, 1939.

65. Thurgood Marshall to George Murphy, December 28, 1939. The affidavit, however, is no longer attached in NAACP archives. Copies were in high demand. Wilkins wrote to Redmond asking for a copy so he could issue statements to the press. Wilkins to Redmond, January 12, 1940.

66. Houston to Redmond, "In re *State ex rel. Gaines vs. Canada: Affidavit,*" December 27, 1939.

67. Redmond to Wilkins, January 15, 1940.

68. "Gaines Lawyers File New Motion: Set Out That He Won Case and Ask That Cost Be Assessed Against U," *Columbia Daily Tribune,* January 10, 1940, 1.

69. Redmond to Wilkins, January 15, 1940.

70. "Court Dismisses Student's Suit," *Nevada State Journal,* January 2, 1940, 1.

71. "Negro Student's Suit Dismissed," *Wisconsin State Journal,* January 3, 1940, 2.

72. "Negro's Suit to study at Missouri U. Fails," *St. Louis Globe-Democrat,* January 2, 1940, 5A.

73. Ibid.

74. "Gaines Case Dismissed by Circuit Court," *Columbia Missourian,* January 1, 1940, 1.

75. "Gaines Case Is Dismissed by Dinwiddie," *Columbia Daily Tribune,* January 1, 1940, 1.

76. "Problems within the Group," *Atlanta Daily World,* January 19, 1940, 6.

77. Ibid.

78. Gamewell Valentine, "A 'Red' Hot Subject," *Atlanta Daily World,* January 28, 1940, 4.

79. "Defends Lloyd Gaines," *Afro-American,* February 2, 1940, 4.

80. "White Student Gives Views on Gaines Case," *New York Amsterdam News,* January 27, 1940, 4.

81. Houston to Redmond, October 23, 1939. Patterson was a leader of International Labor Defense, a left-wing or communist organization that provided legal representation.

82. Sweets, Oral History.

83. White to Redmond, January 23, 1940.

84. Redmond, Oral History.

85. "Rumor Puts Lloyd Gaines in Mexico," *Afro-American*, February 24, 1940, 2.

86. "Missouri Court Writes 'Finis' to Gaines Case," *Cleveland Call*, January 11, 1940, 3.

87. Press release, "N.A.A.C.P. Still Unable to Find Lloyd Gaines, March 8, 1940; "NAACP Despairs of Finding Elusive Lloyd Gaines," *Afro-American*, March 16, 1940, 6.

88. "Lloyd Gaines Who Causes Law School to Be Started At Lincoln Still Missing," *Philadelphia Tribune*, September 14, 1940, 20.

89. "Gaines Still Missing as MO. U. Case Hangs Fire," *Chicago Defender*, June 14, 1941, 3.

90. "Lloyd Gaines' Disappearance Hampers Bringing Suit to Conclusion," *New York Amsterdam News*, June 14, 1941, 6.

91. "Gaines Still Missing as MO. U. Case Hangs Fire," *Chicago Defender*, June 14, 1941, 3; "Lloyd Gaines' Disappearance Hampers Bringing Suit to Conclusion," *New York Amsterdam News*, June 14, 1941, 6.

92. 321 U.S. 649 (1944).

93. "Pointed Points," *New York Amsterdam News*, April 15, 1944, A7.

94. "Jim Crow Guide to U.S.A.: Separate, BUT Far From Equal," *Afro-American*, January 14, 1950, 13.

95. Gene Hudson and H.B. Webber, *Pittsburgh Courier*, March 6, 1948, 20.

96. Clayton, "The Strange Disappearance," 27.

97. Ibid., 26–27.

98. Ibid., 27–28.

99. Clayton, "The Strange Disappearance," 28. Lucile Bluford visited the Gaines family in St. Louis many times and remained convinced that they never heard from him. Oral History, May 15, 1989, 61.

100. Ibid., 28.

101. Ibid., 32–33.

102. Lloyd Gaines to Callie Gaines, March 3, 1939, 1; Clayton, "The Strange Disappearance," 30. Gaines also writes, "Perhaps I myself am to blame for being unemployed, but not for my sense of independence, responsibilities of manhood, and my fighting spirit that asks no quarter and gives none." 4.

103. Ibid., 4–5; Clayton, "The Strange Disappearance," 30.

104. Ibid., 8.

105. Clayton, "The Strange Disappearance," 31.

106. Ibid., 34.

107. Ibid.

108. Ibid., 31.

109. Redmond, Oral History.

110. Bluford, "The Lloyd Gaines Story," 246.

111. Williams, *Thurgood Marshall*, 411.

112. Chad Garrison, "The Mystery of Lloyd Gaines."

113. Ibid.

114. David Stout, "Quiet Hero of Civil Rights History: A Supreme Triumph, Then Into the Shadow," 19.

115. *The Attorney General's Fourth Annual Report to Congress: Pursuant to the Emmett Till Unsolved Civil Rights Crime Act of 2007*, October 2012. The *Report* lists 125 cases/deaths, but Gaines is not among them, 10–13.

116. Bluford, Oral History, 60.

9 The *Gaines* Legacy

1. "Negro Girl Seeks to Enter College," *Nevada State Journal*, February 10, 1940, 1.

2. Redmond to Houston, September 30, 1939.

3. Press release, "Judge Reserves Decision in Bluford Case: N.A.A.C.P. Attorney Conducts Brilliant Case in Two-Day Trial at Columbia, Missouri," 2. See also "Hogsett Asks Court to Quash Bluford Writ," *Columbia Missourian*, February 10, 1940, 1; "Decision is Reserved in Bluford Suit," *Afro-American*, February 17, 1940, 2; "Missouri Suit Taken under Advisement," *Joplin Globe*, February 11, 1940, 6B; "Suit of Negro to Enter M.U. Studied," *St. Louis Globe-Democrat*, February 11, 1940, 2B.

4. "Court Refuses Writ Filed by Lucile Bluford," *Columbia Missourian*. May 31, 1940, 1.

5. Judge Dinwiddie "also cited the fact that this is the second mandamus suit brought in his court by a Negro seeking admission to the state university and cited the case of Lloyd Gaines, who attempted to enter the school of law. He says that the Gaines case went to the United States supreme court, which held that Gaines was entitled to enter the university and that following this decision the Missouri legislature amended the state laws with reference to the education of Neroes [*sic*] and that Lincoln University established a school of law for Neroes [*sic*] equal to the school of law at the state university. On the second hearing of the Gaines case his attorneys were unable to produce him and the case was dismissed." "Court Denies Mandamus Writ in Negro Case," *Columbia Daily Tribune*, May 31, 1940, 1; see also, 10.

6. "Negro Woman Is Barred from M.U." *Jefferson City Daily Capital News*, June 1, 1940, 4.

7. "Mo. Supreme Court Gets Bluford Appeal," *Afro-American*, April 26, 1941, 8; "Bluford Case Heard by Mo. Supreme Court," *Afro-American*, May 24, 1941, 2; "Bluford Case to Be Heard By Missouri Supreme Court," *Cleveland Call*, May 24, 1941, 1.

8. "Missouri Supreme Court to Review The Bluford Case," *Cleveland Call*, May 31, 1941, 1.

9. "Lincoln U. to Provide Course," *Jefferson City Post-Tribune*, July 8, 1941, 1.

10. Houston and Redmond were joined by Kansas City attorneys Amasa Knox, Charles H. Calloway, James H. Herbert, and Carl R. Johnson. Canada was represented by University of Missouri counsel William S. Hogsett, Nick T. Cave, and Kenneth Teasdale.

"NAACP Plans New Attempt to Pry Open Doors of Missouri U." *Afro-American,* October 14, 1939, 5; "Negro Woman Asks Damages of Missouri U." *Jefferson City Daily Capital News,* November 4, 1939, 4.

11. "Miss Bluford Says She Acting in 'Good Faith,' *Jefferson City Post-Tribune,* October 23, 1940, 1. See also "Dismissal Asked in Bluford Case," *Columbia Missourian,* October 24, 1940, 1.

12. Bluford, Oral History, May 15, 1989, 57.

13. "Miss Bluford Loses Point in Mo. U. Case," *Afro-American,* February 4, 1940, 11. "Bluford Denied Damages in Suit Against Canada," *Columbia Missourian,* October 25, 1940, 1.

14. Collet was a 1937 Roosevelt appointee. Coincidentally, Collet was from Chariton County, Missouri, the home of Representative John Taylor whose bill mandated the creation of black graduate and professional programs at Lincoln University. Collet had been a judge of the Missouri Supreme Court until Senate confirmation in March 1937. The State Court heard the Gaines case in May. President Truman later nominated Collet to the 8th Circuit Court of Appeals in 1947, on which he served until his death in 1955.

15. His opinion continued, "It is safe to assume that the State Court had no intention other than to follow the Gaines case, nor can the good faith of the State in carrying out the mandate of that case can be questioned in view of the prompt establishment of a creditable law school for negroes." *Bluford v. Canada,* 32 F. Supp.707, at 710.

16. Ibid.

17. Ibid. at 711.If a program did not exist, the black Missourian, according to Judge Collet's opinion, would just have to wait until the state created a substantially equivalent black-only alternative. "Furthermore, if plaintiff may maintain this action without alleging previous notice of her desires and opportunity for compliance, will on tomorrow the individual members of the Board of Curators of Lincoln University or the University of Missouri be liable in damages to another negro, if, perchance, late today he or she demands instruction at Lincoln University for which facilities are lacking, and then in the morning demands admittance to the University of Missouri? Yet such would seem to be the result contended for by plaintiff unless the curators should maintain at Lincoln University at all times all departments of instruction, whether used or not, which are available at the University of Missouri. It does not appear that 'a clear and unmistakable disregard of rights secured by the supreme law of the land' would result from a failure on the part of those curators to keep and maintain in idleness and non-use facilities at Lincoln University which no one had requested or indicated a desire to use."

18. Ibid. See also Robert E. Leake Jr., "Constitutional Law—The Fourteenth Amendment and Segregated Education." 591.

19. In a jury trial, Houston encountered complicating factors, for instance no African Americans served on the jury. "New Trial Sought in Missouri Case," *Afro-American,* November 2, 1940, 3, and "Lucille Bluford Loses Missouri U. Damage Suit," *New York Amsterdam News,* November 2, 1940, 1.

20. "Lincoln Journalism Unit Expected in Feb." *Afro-American,* August 16, 1941, 8. According to Lincoln's biennial report, "A splendid faculty and administrative staff was

[*sic*] recruited, and a new building with the latest in equipment was erected on the site of the main campus for its operation." The report continued, "Ten students have indicated their intentions to enter that field and are making their beginning steps to learn the profession of journalism." Bluford, of course, was not among them. "Lincoln University, Jefferson City, Missouri, Biennial Report of the Board of Curators, to His Excellency, Governor Forrest C. Donnell, and the Sixty-Second General Assembly of the State of Missouri," January 1943, 12, LUA.

21. "Drop Journalism Course to Keep Colored Out," *Philadelphia Tribune,* April 4, 1942, 20.

22. "Missouri Versus the U.S.A," *Pittsburgh Courier,* July 19, 1941, 6.

23. Bluford refused because "she found the equipment, faculty and courses are not substantially equal to what the University of Missouri had offered." "U. of Missouri Ends Journalism to Bar Colored," *Afro-American,* April 4, 1942, 24. She also renewed her application for study at Lincoln University for when they created a school that was "equal to the standards for graduate work established at the University of Missouri before the journalism courses were abandoned there." "Bluford Renews Application to Missouri U." *Cleveland Call,* May 9, 1942, 15.

24. Sullivan, *Lift Every Voice,* 253.

25. She applied each semester for several years. Bluford, Oral History, March 19, 1990, 171.

26. This understanding was central to Judge William Frank's opinion in the initial state Supreme Court decision of 1937. The 1875 Constitution of Missouri, Article XI, Section 3, included the provision, "Separate schools shall be established for all children of African descent." States statutes made it "unlawful for any colored child to attend any white school, or for any white child to attend a colored school." *Revised Statutes of Missouri,* 1929, Section 9216.

27. "A general diffusion of knowledge and intelligence being essential to the preservation of rights and liberties of the people, the general assembly shall establish and maintain free public schools for the gratuitous instruction of all persons in this state within the ages not in excess of twenty-one years as prescribed by law. Separate schools shall be provided for white and colored children, except in cases otherwise provided for the law." Article IX Education, Section 1. The Constitution was adopted by referendum at a special election held on February 27, 1945. Political scientist William L. Bradshaw was a delegate to the Constitutional Convention of 1943–1944 and served on the Education Committee. His wife, Doris Bradshaw, worked for educational equality on behalf of the AAUW. See Doris C. Bradshaw to Hubert Wheeler (Commissioner of Education), n.d., DAB.

28. Evans emphasized the distinction between white and "colored." "Would it not appear that a person was either white or he was something else? Since the University of Missouri is designated a white school, have we any authority to receive students of Chinese, Japanese or Malayan descent? I think perhaps you should consider this before next registration." Handwritten at the bottom of the inter-department correspondence is Evan's note "You will note the new const. is quite diff. from the old on this point!" Orrin B. Evans to S.W. Canada, March 5, 1945 FAM.

29. S.W. Canada to Frederick A. Middlebush, March 27, 1945, 1. An application from a Chinese student was held pending a decision, though the decision ultimately made is unclear. From a handwritten note on the correspondence, it appears that the Board opted to check with attorney Hogsett on each relevant application.

30. There was progressivism in some private areas, however. St. Louis University, a Jesuit college, opened admission, reversing a previous policy of white-only admissions, in 1944. The Conservatory of Music of Kansas City also opened admissions around this time.

31. For primary and secondary education, see Lloyd W. King, State Superintendent of Public Schools, *Four Years of Progress with Missouri Public Schools for the Negro,* 22; Sidney J. Reedy, "The Education of Negroes in Missouri," 383. With regard to higher education, see Sidney J. Reedy, "Negro Higher and Professional Education in Missouri," 321–324, and Sidney J. Reedy, "Higher Education Desegregation in Missouri," 284–294.

32. The apparent but erroneous indication that black educational experiences were superior to whites serves as an example of Simpson's paradox, a peril leading to incorrect interpretation of aggregate data. Reedy, "Education of Negroes," 383, notes also that white teachers received an average of 60 hours of training and black teachers 120 hours. The confounding factor is urbanization. There were more educational opportunities in cities than in rural areas.

33. The legal history pertaining to integration of St. Louis public schools is lengthy. As a summary, see footnote one of *Missouri v. Jenkins* (1995), "In related litigation about the schools of St. Louis, the Eighth Circuit has noted that '[b]efore the Civil War, Missouri prohibited the creation of schools to teach reading and writing to blacks. Act of Feb. 16, 1847, §1, 1847 Mo. Laws 103. State mandated segregation was first imposed in the 1865 Constitution, Article IX §2. It was reincorporated in the Missouri Constitution of 1945: Article IX specifically provided that separate schools were to be maintained for 'white and colored children.' In 1952, the Missouri Supreme Court upheld the constitutionality of Article IX under the United States Constitution. Article IX was not repealed until 1976.' Liddell v. Missouri, 731 F. 2d 1294, 1305–1306…"

34. For Bluford and Dreer, see "Lincoln University, Jefferson City, Missouri, Biennial Report of the Board of Curators, to His Excellency, Governor Lloyd C. Stark, and the Sixtieth General Assembly of the State of Missouri," January 1939, LUA. Previous reports did not list scholarship recipients, although the office of the State Superintendent of Education operated the scholarship program (contrary to state statute). Guion Bluford studied mechanical engineering at the University of Kansas. Loupe, "Storming," 22. Bluford's son (Lucile Bluford's nephew), Guion (Guy) Bluford Jr., would become the first African American astronaut.

35. For Oldham, see James and Vera Olson, *The University of Missouri,* 83. Olson incorrectly identifies her as "Marion." Her maiden name is alternatively spelled O'Fallan and O'Fallon, the more common name is given here. The Black Culture Center on the University of Missouri campus was named to honor Lloyd Gaines and Marian Oldham.

36. John Royston to Lloyd "Starks," January 1939 (no date), 1. Royston mentions discussions among students at Howard who assume, like many others, that Missouri would open the state university's graduate and professional programs because of the unrealistic cost of maintaining separate facilities. Royston concludes, "The eyes of the whole field of education are now upon the State of Missouri and it is for you to take the first progressive step which, you will find, is not as hard as some will lead you to believe. I hope you will read a recent issue of the 'Missouri Student' in which the editor discusses this problem very intelligently." 3.

37. It is difficult to establish the extra cost entailed. Although funding for black institutions of higher learning was lower than for white institutions, the number of students served was also lower. One estimate was that in 1946 it cost Lincoln University $500,000 for one law school and ten journalism graduates. Lavergne, *Before* Brown, 83.

38. *McCabe v. Atchison, Topeka, and Santa Fe Railway, Co.* 235 U.S. 151 (1914). See, for instance, Howard, *The Shifting Wind,* for a discussion of Hughes's perspective on civil rights.

39. Several southern states ignored the *Gaines* decision. Beyond Missouri, only two states reacted: North Carolina created the rather unsuccessful North Carolina Center School of Law, and Kentucky allowed "qualified" black students to attend the University of Kentucky Law School. Harold R. Washington, "History and Role of Black Law Schools," 398, 399–400; Smith, *Emancipation,* 63. Other black colleges and professional schools were established by some states following Sweatt and other Supreme Court decisions.

40. The law school at the North Carolina School for Negroes opened on September 25, 1939, but closed by the end of the month. See Murray, *Song in a Weary Throat,* 127.

41. Although dominant black opinion in Missouri opposed the creation of the Lincoln University programs in law and journalism, creation of these programs did leave to greater educations opportunities for some African American individuals. This instrumental argument was made as early as the 1890 Missouri Supreme Court opinion in *Lehew v. Brummell,* claiming that through educational segregation "colored children...have made a rapid stride in the way of education," 103 Mo. 551. Of course, the instrumental argument does not make comparisons between educational advancement for segregation and integrated systems.

42. Pauli Murray notes that in North Carolina, the *Hocutt* case and other decisions by white university administrators were made on the explicit understanding that black colleges did not provide a suitable education for post-graduate study. Murray, *Song in a Weary Throat,* 110.

43. Leake, "Constitutional Law," 591. "The result of these cases was that where the state law placed a mandatory duty upon the proper officials to provide substantially equal facilities for education within the state, the agency responsible for the administration of the legislation was entitled to 'reasonable advance notice of the intention of a negro student to require such facilities.'"

44. Ibid., 593.

45. 313 U.S. 80, 94. The case involving Illinois Representative Arthur Mitchell, the lone black member of Congress, of course, pertained to *interstate* commerce rather than state law. The opinion by Chief Justice Hughes noted "The denial to appellant of equality of accommodations because of his race would be an invasion of a fundamental individual right which is guaranteed against state action by the Fourteenth Amendment" citing *Gaines* and *Mc McCabe v. Atchison, T. & S.F. Rwy. Co.* (1914).

46. Hoffer, *Plessy v. Ferguson,* 162.

47. See, for instance, Scovel Richardson, "Changing Concepts of the Supreme Court as They Affect the Legal Status of the Negro," 129.

48. Murray, *Song in a Weary Throat,* 114–115, 125–127. Murray later received a law degree from Howard University, although she felt discrimination as a woman there. She was a leader in the civil rights movement on issues of race and gender, and she became the first African American ordained as an Episcopal priest.

49. *Sipuel v. Oklahoma State Board of Regents,* 332 U.S. 631 (1948); *McLaurin v. Oklahoma State Board of Regents,* 339 U.S. 637 (1950); *Sweatt v. Painter,* 339 U.S. 629 (1950).

50. Robert L. Carter, "Legal Background and Significance of the May 17th Decision." 216.

51. Ibid.

52. Morroe Berger, *Racial Equality and the Law,* 30.

53. Blaustein and Ferguson, *Desegregation and the Law,* 107.

54. The 1936 Democratic primary was also a close three-way contest and included Milligan's brother, Representative Jacob L. Milligan.

55. Cave, a former state senator, was close to Stark. He was named chairman of the Stark-for-Senator campaign organization but stepped down because he could not leave his law practice in Columbia. Cave was then named chairman of the Stark-for-Senator Advisory Committee. "Memo to the Press," February 17, 1940, March 11, 1940, LCS. Stark subsequently appointed Cave as Judge of the Kansas City Court of Appeals. Governor to Secretary of State, June 1, 1940, LCS.

56. "Turn Thumbs Down on Gov. Lloyd Stark." *Chicago Defender,* June 15, 1940, 4.

57. In the final tally, Truman won with 41 percent of the Democratic votes (268,354), Stark received 40 percent (260,221), and Milligan trailed with 19 percent (127,378). Truman followed this with another close victory in the general election over Republican and former state senator Manvel Davis. Secretary of State, *Official Manual of the State of Missouri, 1941–1942.*

58. "Mo. Voters Cut Stark for Stand on School Case," *Afro-American,* August 17, 1940, 2.

59. David McCullough, *Truman,* 227–28.

60. "Mo. Voters," *Afro-American,* 2.

61. McCullough, *Truman,* 915.

62. "Open U. of Missouri to All, Says Senator," *Afro-American,* August 2, 1941, 24.

63. Ibid.

64. Smith, *Emancipation,* 63.

65. "Whites Favor Mixing Of Races At University Of Missouri," *Pittsburgh Courier,* January 29, 1944, 5.

66. "Missouri U. Bias Laid to Higher-ups," *Afro-American,* February 3, 1945, 10.

67. "Gaines Case Aftermath: Missouri Students Would Admit Race," *Pittsburgh Courier,* January 27, 1945, 23.

68. "Mo. Taxpayers Overburdened by Dual Postgraduate Setup," *Afro-American,* May 18, 1946, 16.

69. "Higher Education Pattern Held Costly to Missouri," *Afro-American,* June 29, 1946, 17.

70. "Missouri Spends $500,000 to Train One Race Lawyer," *Cleveland Call,* June 8, 1946, A1.

71. "Higher Education," *Afro-American,* June 29, 1946, 17.

72. Of the 55 graduates, only 33 passed the bar exam and 12 were in private practice. *Biennial Report of the Board of Curators of Lincoln University, Jefferson City, Missouri, and Dalton Vocational School, Dalton, Missouri, to His Excellency, the Governor, and the Sixty-Second General Assembly of the State of Missouri, for the Period Beginning July 1, 1949 and Ending June 30, 1951,* 4, LUA.

73. "Student Magazine at Univ. of Mo. Banned for Urging End to JC," *Afro-American,* March 8, 1947, 16.

74. "Student Paper Suspended When Editor Refuses to Drop Article on Equality," *Afro-American,* April 5, 1947, 16.

75. "Student Magazine at Univ. of Mo. Banned for Urging End to JC," *Afro-American,* March 8, 1947, 16.

76. Edmondson and Perry, "To the Detriment," 117.

77. Ibid.

78. John T. Hubbell, "The Desegregation of the University of Oklahoma, 1946–1950," 371.

79. "The University of Oklahoma's Slow Path to Racial Integration," *Journal of Blacks in Higher Education,* 2009, No. 63, 64.

80. A small sample of the scholarship which review and critique the legal reasoning of the *Shelley* decision includes Vose, *Caucasians Only;* Louis Henkin, "Shelley v. Kraemer: Notes for a Revised Opinion"; and Rosen, "Was Shelley v. Kraemer Incorrectly Decided?"

81. *Shelley v. Kraemer,* 334. U.S. 1.

82. Whittington B. Johnson, "The Vinson Court and Racial Segregation: 1946–1953," 222.

83. It was the first of "several jolts from the Vinson Court" which were received by "the second cornerstone of racial segregation, the separate-but-equal doctrine." Johnson, "The Vinson Court," 224.

84. *Sipuel v. Board of Regents,* 332 U.S. 631 (1948).

85. Hubbell, "The Desegregation," 373.

86. Carter, "Legal Background," 217.

87. Douglass Hall, "Mrs. Fisher Waiting for University Gates to Open While State Officials Deliberate," *Afro-American,* January 24, 1948, 1.

88. "Taking Cue From Oklahoma Case, Missouri Ups Lincoln's Funds," *Cleveland Call,* February 7, 1948, 2A.

89. Sam Lacy, "St. Louis Debates Over $400,000 for Law School," *Afro-American,* May 15, 1948, A2.

90. "Equal School Fights Rage in 6 States," *Afro-American,* February 7, 1948, 1.

91. Loring B. Moore, "The Due Process of Law in Race Cases," 261.

92. "Our Educational Martyrs," *Afro-American,* December 4, 1948, 2.

93. "Missouri Students Favor End of Bias," *New York Amsterdam News,* December 11, 1948, 5.

94. "Missouri U. Asks Mixed Classes," *Afro-American,* December 11, 1948, 1.

95. "Missouri University Approves Admission of Negro Students," *Cleveland Call,* December 1, 1948, 1A.

96. "Missouri U. 'Open-Door' Proposal Backed by the Press," *Afro-American,* January 15, 1949, 12.

97. "Mixed Colleges Prove Success in St. Louis," *Afro-American,* February 19, 1949, C3. Saint Louis University began readmitting black students in 1944. Moore, "The Due Process," 261.

98. "Voluntary Bar Ass'n Debates Negro's Bid for Membership," *Los Angeles Sentinel,* February 3, 1949, A2.

99. "Univ. of Mo. Students Vote 2–1 to Admit All Applicants," *Afro-American,* February 26, 1949, 2.

100. "Missouri Students Shun Bias," *Los Angeles Sentinel,* March 3, 1949, A3.

101. Cardell W. McVickers, "Signs of Progress," *Afro-American,* February 26, 1949, 4.

102. "Univ. of Mo. Students Vote 2–1 to Admit All Applicants."

103. Nation Is Ready for Civil Rights," *Cleveland Call,* May 4, 1949, 4B.

104. "Bill to Open Mo. Colleges Offered," *Afro-American,* March 19, 1949, C4.

105. "Mo. House Votes 100–8 to Drop Colleges' Race Ban," *Afro-American,* May 7, 1949, C3A.

106. "State Schools Stand of Mo. Democrats Hit," *Afro-American,* December 24, 1949, 20.

107. "Little Chance for Missouri Measure Opening Schools," *Cleveland Call,* July 9, 1949, 2B.

108. *Sweatt v. Painter* 339 U.S. 629.

109. Dwonna Goldstone, "Heman Sweatt and the Racial Integration of the University of Texas School of Law," 88.

110. LaVergne, *Before Brown,* 6. On the swift response, see 118. See also "The Sweatt Family Blazes a New Trail Into Jim Crow," *Journal of Blacks in Higher Education,* Summer 1995, No. 8, 35.

111. *Sweatt v. Painter.*

112. "Separate and Unequal: Two Black Student Pioneers Who Were Treated as Social Pariahs at Predominantly White Universities," 27.

113. Carter, "Legal Background," 217.

114. "Negroes of South Gain in Colleges," *New York Times,* September 3, 1950, 25.

115. University of Virginia. "Breaking Traditions." http://explore.lib.virginia.edu/exhibits/show/hoos/breaking-traditions/gregory-swanson-and-walter-n—

116. The *Times* reported, "The Swanson decision came thirteen years after Lloyd Gaines, a Negro, won the first major battle against the color line in higher education. Mr. Gaines brought action against the University of Missouri when that school rejected his application. In December, 1937 [*sic*], the Supreme Court held that the state had to provide equal opportunities for white and Negro students.""Segregation Test Case in Virginia." *New York Times,* September 10, 1950, 145. For reasons that are unclear, the *Times* frequently reported the date of the Supreme Court decision incorrectly.

117. This letter was sent from Wm. S. Hogsett to S.W. Canada, April 7, 1944. Canada sent these words to Girard T. Bryant and Dora Rose Washington on April 22, 1944, FAM.

118. Canada to Bennie William Gordon Jr., September 21, 1942. See also Smith, *We Have Not Had Such Luck,* chapter 10.

119. Canada to Hogsett, September 21, 1942.

120. William S. Hogsett to Ben G. Oneal (May 1944). What information was shared cannot be fully known. Canada forwarded another copy of the letter from Hogsett to Oneal to Middlebush as late as June 5, 1945, with attached correspondence saying "I await your instructions."

121. Loupe, "Storming," 23.

122. Bluford, Oral History, 63–64. Pam Johnson, "The Unforgettable Miss Bluford," Poynter Institute, February 23, 2004. Bluford was in Columbia to receive a Medal for Distinguished Service in Journalism from the University of Missouri. She received an honorary doctorate from the University in 1989.

123. Charles W. McLane to Gus Tolver Ridgel, February 9, 1950.

124. Noel Hubbard to Elmer Bell Jr., January 19, 1950.

125. Allen McReynolds to William Hogsett, March 13, 1950. McReynolds also expressed concern that the Board should not contradict the legislature. McReynolds to Robert S. Eastin, March 15, 1950.

126. In *Henderson v. U.S.,* 339 U.S. 816 (1950), the Vinson Court ruled that railroads must provide equal dining facilities to black and white passengers, regardless of their numbers, under the federal Interstate Commerce Act. The Court did not address the separate but equal doctrine in its decision.

127. Lee Carl Overstreet to Allen McReynolds, Roscoe Anderson, William Hogsett, and Frederick Middlebush, April 11, 1950. Overstreet later writes Hogsett that "I have just finished reading the opinions of the Supreme Court of the United States in the cases of Sweatt v. Painter and McLaurin v. Oklahoma State Regents and, apart from the citation, with approval of the Gaines, Sipuel and Fisher cases, I find nothing in the which bears directly upon our declaratory judgment suit." Overstreet to Hogsett, June 7, 1950.

128. Missouri U. Open to All," *Afro-American,* July 8, 1950, 3.

129. "Mo. U. Must Admit Negroes, Court Rules," *Los Angeles Sentinel,* July 6, 1950, A3.

130. "Legislation Concerning Admission of Negroes to the University of Missouri," Charles W. McLane to Frederick A. Middlebush, December 21, 1949. The two-page memo from the Director of Admission who replaced Canada describes provisions of the amended bill and makes recommendations about handling applications.

131. Lee-Carl Overstreet to F. A. Middlebush, June 10, 1950.

132. Hogsett to Middlebush, July 14, 1950, 1–2. Hogsett also addressed points from Vice President Thomas A. Brady's memos on "List of difficult situations that may arise" and "Questions Regarding Negro Students—Employment and Housing," 2–4.

133. Ibid., 3.

134. "To All Members of the University Staff," July 18, 1950. Hogsett to Middlebush, July 19, 1950.

135. The opinion concluded that "until amended or repealed…the Curators of Lincoln University may make arrangements" for out-of-state tuition, "however this is discretionary with said Board and not mandatory." Hammett to Lincoln University, Attention Sherman D. Scruggs, July 31, 1950, 3.

136. Overstreet to Hogsett, August 29, 1950.

137. "4 States Still Defy Court on Education," *Afro-American,* September 16, 1950, 20.

138. "The Week's News in Tabloid," *Afro-American,* October 14, 1950, 5.

139. "Total of 233 Students Now in Dixie Colleges," *Afro-American,* November 18, 1950, 20.

Epilogue

1. "Negro History Week," *Atlanta Daily World,* February 8, 1948, 4.

2. "'Don't Crow Too Loud, You Georgians,'" *Atlanta Daily World,* January 26, 1950, 6.

3. *Brown v. Board of Education of Topeka,* 347 U.S. 483 (1954).

4. Ibid., 483, 495.

5. *Brown v. Board of Education of Topeka,* 348 U.S. 294, 301 (1955).

6. Stout, "Quiet Hero," 19.

7. Grant was a graduate of the Howard University School of Law, but he had been a Democrat throughout the 1930s. Freeman would later serve on the U.S. Commission on Civil Rights for sixteen years. See Freeman, in Wesley, Price, and Morris, eds., *Lift Every Voice and Sing,* 153.

8. Kelleher, *The History of the St. Louis NAACP,* 106–110.

9. Ibid., 66–67.

10. Dowden-White, *Groping toward Democracy,* 55.

11. Todd Lewan and Dolores Barclay, "Torn from the Land," part 1, in Arlene Notoro Morgan, Alice Irene Pifer, and Keith Woods, *The Authentic Voice: The Best Reporting on Race and Ethnicity,* 185–210.

12. Peter Leach, *Gone by Sundown* (Arlington, VA: Gival Press, 2011).

13. Redmond, Oral History.

14. Hastie, "Charles Hamilton Houston," 365.

References

Archives

Lincoln University Archives, LUA

Lloyd L. Gaines Collection, University of Missouri, LLG

National Association for the Advancement of Colored People, Reproduced from the Collections of the Manuscript Division, Library of Congress

St. Louis Black Community Leaders Oral History Project, University of Missouri—St. Louis:
> David Grant
> Sidney R. Redmond
> Nathaniel Sweets
> Nathan B. Young (Jr.)

State Historical Society of Missouri:
> Frederick A. Middlebush Papers (FAM)
> Doris Bradshaw Papers (DB)
> Lloyd C. Stark Papers (LCS)
> UM—St. Louis Black History Project (1980–1983), Collection, 1895–1983 (BHP)
> University of Missouri, President's Office, Papers (UMP)

University Archives, University of Missouri—Columbia (UA):
> Bluford
> Gaines

Center for Oral History and Cultural Heritage, University of Southern Mississippi:
> Percy Greene

Women in Journalism (oral history project), Washington Press Club Foundation:
> Lucile H. Bluford

Articles

Bluford, Lucile H. "The Lloyd Gaines Story." *Journal of Educational Sociology* 32 (February 1959): 242–246.

Brown, H. B. "The Dissenting Opinions of Mr. Justice Harlan." *American Law Review* 46 (May–June 1912): 321–352.

Carter, Robert L. "Legal Background and Significance of the May 17ᵗʰ Decision." *Social Problems* 2 (April 1955): 215–219.

Clayton, Edward T. "The Strange Disappearance of Lloyd Gaines." *Ebony* 6 (May 1951): 22–34.

———. "The Strange Murder of Homer G. Phillips." *Ebony* 6 (October 1951): 48–53. Reissued, 32 (September 1977): 160–164.

Clement, Rufus E. "The Impact of the War Upon Negro Graduate and Professional Schools." *Journal of Negro Education* 11 (July 1942): 365–374.

Collins, Lauren. "Brown's Legacy Then and Now: Race and Law School Admissions Debates Continue after Nearly 70 Years." *AALL Spectrum Magazine* 8 (April 2004): 8–11.

Connally, C. Ellen. "Justice Harlan's 'Great Betrayal'? A Reconsideration of Cumming v. Richmond County Board of Education." *Journal of Supreme Court History* 25 (March 2000): 72–92.

Dreer, Herman. "The Education of the Negro with Respect to His Background." *Journal of Negro History* 19 (January 1934): 45–52.

Editorial Comment. "The University of Maryland versus Donald Gaines Murray." *Journal of Negro Education* 5 (April 1936): 166–174.

Editors. "Exclusion of Negroes from State Supported Professional Schools." *Yale Law Journal* 45 (May 1936): 1296–1301.

Editors. "White Missouri." *Time* 28 (August 3 1936): 32.

Editors. "The Mysterious Case of Lloyd Gaines: Pioneer of University Desegregation." *Journal of Blacks in Higher Education* 9 (Autumn 1995): 22.

Editors. "The University of Oklahoma's Slow Path to Racial Integration." *Journal of Blacks in Higher Education* (2009): 64.

Edmondson, Aimee, and Earnest L. Perry Jr. "Objectivity and Journalists' Creed: Local Coverage of Lucile Bluford's Attempt to Desegregate the University of Missouri." *Journalism History* 33 (Winter 2008): 233–240.

———. "'To the Detriment of the Institution': The Missouri Student's Fight to Desegregate the University of Missouri." *American Journalism* 27 (Fall 2010): 105–131.

Elliott, Mark. "Race, Color Blindness, and the Democratic Public: Albion W. Tourgee's Radical Principles in *Plessy v. Ferguson*." *Journal of Southern History* 67 (May 2001): 287–330.

Endersby, James W., and Ekaterina Ognianova. "A Spatial Model of Ideology and Political Communication: Voter Perceptions of News Reporting." *Harvard International Journal of Press/Politics* 2 (Winter 1997), 23–39.

Fultz, Michael. "City Normal Schools and Municipal Colleges in the Upward Expansion of Higher Education for African Americans." *Perspectives on the History of Higher Education* 29 (2012): 17–41. Also published as Marybeth Gasman and Roger L. Geiger, eds., *Higher Education for African Americans before the Civil Rights Era, 1900–1964*. New Brunswick, NJ: Transaction, 2012.

Florence, Charles Wilbur. "The Federally Aided Program of Vocational Teacher-Training in Negro Schools." *Journal of Negro Education* 7 (July 1938): 292–302.

Garrison, Chad. "The Mystery of Lloyd Gaines." *Riverfront Times* (April 4 2007).

Gershenhorn, Jerry. "*Hocutt v. Wilson* and Race Relations in Durham, North Carolina, During the 1930s." *North Carolina Historical Review* 78 (3 July 2001): 275–308.

Goldstone, Dwonna. "Heman Sweatt and the Racial Integration of the University of Texas School of Law." *Journal of Blacks in Higher Education* 54 (Winter 2006/2007): 88–97.

Graber, Mark A. "Judicial Recantation." *Syracuse Law Review* 45 (1994): 807–814.

Grothaus, Larry. "'The Inevitable Mr. Gaines': The Long Struggle to Desegregate the University of Missouri 1936–1950." *Arizona and the West* 26 (Spring 1984): 21–42.

Hastie, William H. "Charles Hamilton Houston (1895–1950)." *The Crisis* 57 (June 1950): 364–365, 405–406.

———. "Charles Hamilton Houston." *Negro History Bulletin* 13 (June 1950): 207–208.

Henkin, Louis. "*Shelley v. Kraemer*: Notes for a Revised Opinion." *University of Pennsylvania Law Review* 110 (1962): 473–505.

Heos, Bridget. "U.S. Supreme Court Decides Cases Based on 13th and 14th Amendments." *Missouri Lawyers Weekly* (February 26, 2007).

Higginbotham, Jr., A. Leon, and William C. Smith. "The Hughes Court and the Beginning of the End of the "Separate but Equal" Doctrine." *Minnesota Law Review* 76 (May 1992): 1099–1131.

Hogan, Percy Anderson. "History of the University of Missouri Law School." *Missouri Law Review* 5 (June 1940): 269–292.

Houston, Charles H. "Cracking Closed University Doors." *The Crisis* 42 (December 1935): 364, 370, 372.

———. "Educational Inequalities Must Go!" *The Crisis* 42 (October 1935): 300–301, 316.

———. "Need for Negro Lawyers." *Journal of Negro Education* 4 (January 1935): 49–52.

———. "Don't Shout Too Soon." *The Crisis* 5 (March 1936): 79, 91.

———. "Future Policies and Practices Which Should Govern the Relationship of the Federal Government to Negro Separate Schools." *Journal of Negro Education* 7 (July 1938): 460–462.

Hubbell, John T. "The Desegregation of the University of Oklahoma, 1946–1950." *Journal of Negro History* 57 (October 1972): 370–384.

Huber, Patrick J. "The Lynching of James T. Scott: The Underside of a College Town." *Gateway Heritage* 12 (Summer 1991).

Hunt, Doug. "A Course in Applied Lynching." *Missouri Review* 27 (Summer 2004): 122–170.

Hutchinson, Dennis J. "Unanimity and Desegregation: Decisionmaking in the Supreme Court, 1948–1958." *Georgetown Law Journal* 68 (October 1979): 1–96.

Johnson, Whittington B. "The Vinson Court and Racial Segregation: 1946–1953." *Journal of Negro History* 63 (1978): 222–224.

Kelleher, Daniel T. "The Case of Lloyd Lionel Gaines: The Demise of the Separate but Equal Doctrine." *Journal of Negro History* 56 (October 1971): 262–271.

Klarman, Michael J. "The Plessy Era." *Supreme Court Review* 1998 (1998): 303–414.

Kousser, J. Morgan. "Separate but *Not* Equal: The Supreme Court's First Decision on Discrimination in Schools." *Journal of Southern History* 46 (February 1980): 17–44.

Kruse, Kevin M. "Personal Rights, Public Wrongs: The *Gaines* Case and the Beginning of the End of Segregation." *Journal of Supreme Court History* 2 (1997): 113–130.

Leake, Robert E., Jr. "Constitutional Law—The Fourteenth Amendment and Segregated Education." *Louisiana Law Review* 8 (May 1948): 588–594.

Levins, Harry. "Segregation, Show-Me Style: *Brown vs. Board* was Almost Arnold vs. Kirkwood." *St. Louis Post-Dispatch* (May 15, 1994): B1.

Longa, Ernesto. "A History of America's First Jim Crow Law School Library and Staff." *Connecticut Public Interest Law Journal* 7 (2007): 77–104.

Lord, Jeffery. "Two Presidents and the Court: When Bigotry Takes the Bench." *American Spectator* (July 14, 2009).

Loupe, Diane E. "Storming and Defending the Color Barrier at the University of Missouri School of Journalism: The Lucile Bluford Case." *Journalism History* 16 (Spring/Summer 1989): 20–31.

Marshall, Thurgood. "An Evaluation of Recent Efforts to Achieve Racial Integration in Education through Resort to the Courts." *Journal of Negro Education* 21 (Summer 1952): 316–327.

McGuinn, Henry J. "The Courts and Equality of Educational Opportunity." *Journal of Negro Education* 8 (April 1939): 150–163.

Moore, Loring B. "The Due Process of Law in Race Cases." *National Bar Journal* 2 (December 1944): 240–262.

Ognianova, Ekaterina, and James W. Endersby. "Objectivity Revisited: A Spatial Model of Political Ideology and Mass Communication." *Journalism and Mass Communication Monographs* 159 (October 1996).

Pihlblad, C. Terence. "Mental Tests and Social Problems." *Social Forces* 5 (December 2, 1926): 237–243.

Ransom, Leon A. "Education and the Law." *Journal of Negro Education* 7 (October 4, 1938): 597–599.

———. "Education and the Law: *Gaines v. The University of Missouri*." *Journal of Negro Education* 8 (January 1939): 111–117.

———. "Legal Status of Negro Education under Separate School Systems." *Journal of Negro Education* 8 (July 1939): 395–405.

Redmond, Sidney R. "National Bar Day." *National Bar Journal* 1 (July 1941): 87–90.

Reedy, Sidney J. "The Education of Negroes in Missouri." *Journal of Negro Education* 16 (Summer 1947): 381–386.

———. "Negro Higher and Professional Education in Missouri." *Journal of Negro Education* 17 (Summer 1948): 321–324.

———. "Higher Education Desegregation in Missouri." *Journal of Negro Education* 27 (Summer 1958): 284–294.

Richardson, Scovel. "Changing Concepts of the Supreme Court as They Affect the Legal Status of the Negro." *National Bar Journal* 1 (October 1941): 113–129.

Roback, Jennifer. "The Political Economy of Segregation: The Case of Segregated Streetcars." *Journal of Economic History* 46 (December 1986): 893–917.

Rosen, Mark D. "Was *Shelley v. Kraemer* Incorrectly Decided? Some New Answers." *California Law Review* 95 (April 2007): 451–512.

Sawyer, R. McLaran. "The Gaines Case: The Human Side." *Negro Educational Review* 38 (January 1987): 4–14.

Shores, Arthur D. "The Negro at the Bar: The South." *National Bar Journal* (December 1944): 266–272.

Sigelman, Lee, Steven A. Tuch, and Jack K. Martin. "What's in a Name? Preference for 'Black' versus 'African-American' among Americans of African Descent." *Public Opinion Quarterly* 69 (Autumn 2005): 429–438.

Smith, Tom W. "Changing Racial Labels: From 'Colored' to 'Negro' to 'Black' to 'African American.'" *Public Opinion Quarterly* 56 (Winter 1992): 496–512.

Stokes, Richard L. "Decision of the Missouri Supreme Court on the Admission of Negroes to State Universities." *School and Society* 48 (December 3, 1938): 726–727,

Stout, David. "Quiet Hero of the Civil Rights History: A Supreme Triumph, Then Into the Shadows." *New York Times* (July 12, 2009): A19.

Synnott, Marcia G. "*The Half-Opened Door:* Research Admissions Discrimination at Harvard, Yale, and Princeton." *American Archivist* 45 (Spring 1989): 175–187.

Tabscott, Robert W. "Unfinished Business in 1938, Lloyd Gaines Was Poised to Become a Major Figure in the Desegregation of America: But Then He Vanished." *Everyday Magazine, St. Louis Post-Dispatch* (February 23, 1992): 1C.

Thompson, Charles H. Editorial Comment. "The Missouri Decision and the Future of Negro Education." *Journal of Negro Education* 8 (April 1939): 131–141.

Venable, H. Phillip. "History of the Homer G. Phillips Hospital." *Journal of the National Medical Association* 53 (November 1961): 541–555.

Ware, Gilbert. "*Hocutt:* Genesis of *Brown.*" *Journal of Negro Education* 52 (Summer 1983): 227–233.

Ware, Leland B. "Setting the Stage for Brown: The Development and Implementation of the NAACP's School Desegregation Campaign, 1930–1950." *Mercer Law Review* 52 (2000–2001): 631–673.

———. "Contributions of Missouri's Black Lawyers to Securing Equal Justice." *Journal of the Missouri Bar* 67 (January–February 2011): 42–50.

Washington, Harold R. "History and Role of Black Law Schools." *Howard Law Journal* 18 (1974): 385–422.

Whitehead, Hope. "Commentary: Mound City Bar Members Have Rich Heritage." *St. Louis Daily Record/St. Louis Countian* (May 1, 2004).

Zagier, Alan Scher. "Black Trailblazer Gets Posthumous Law Degree." *Columbia Daily Tribune* (September 29, 2006).

———. "Disappearance Not Investigated." *Columbia Daily Tribune* (September 21, 2006).

Books

Bardolph, Richard. *The Civil Rights Record: Black Americans and the Law, 1849–1970.* New York: Crowell, 1970.

Berger, Morroe. *Racial Equality and the Law: The Role of the Law in the Reduction of Discrimination in the United States.* Paris, France: United Nations Educational, Scientific and Cultural Organization, 1954.

———. *Equality by Statute: The Revolution in Civil Rights.* Garden City: Doubleday, 1967.

Beth, Loren P. *John Marshall Harlan: The Last Whig Justice.* Lexington: University Press of Kentucky, 1992.

Blaustein, Albert P., and Clarence Clyde Ferguson Jr. *Desegregation and the Law: The Meaning and Effect of the School Segregation Cases.* New Brunswick, NJ: Rutgers University Press, 1957.

Bond, James E. *I Dissent: The Legacy of Chief Justice James Clark McReynolds.* Fairfax, VA: George Mason University Press, 1992.

Christenson, Lawrence O., William E. Foley, Gary R. Kremer, and Kenneth H. Winn. *Dictionary of Missouri Biography.* Columbia: University of Missouri Press, 1999.

Coulter, Charles E. *Take Up the Black Man's Burden: Kansas City's African American Communities, 1865–1939.* Columbia: University of Missouri Press, 2006.

Davis, Lenwood G., ed. *Selected Writings and Speeches of James E. Shepard, 1896–1946, Founder of North Carolina Central University.* Madison, NJ: Fairleigh Dickinson University Press, 2013.

Dowden-White, Priscilla A. *Groping toward Democracy: African American Social Welfare Reform in St. Louis, 1910–1949.* Columbia: University of Missouri Press, 2011.

Du Bois, W. E. Burghardt, and Augustus Granville Dill. *The College-Bred Negro American.* Atlanta: Atlanta University Press, 1910.

Early, Gerald, ed. *"Ain't but a Place": An Anthology of African American Writings about St. Louis.* St. Louis: Missouri Historical Society Press, 1988.

Egerton, John. *Speak Now Against the Day: The Generation Before the Civil Rights Movement in the South.* New York: Knopf, 1994.

Elliott, Mark. *Color-Blind Justice: Albion Tourgee and the Quest for Racial Equality from the Civil War to Plessy v. Ferguson.* London: Oxford University Press, 2006.

Fireside, Harvey. Plessy v. Ferguson: *Separate But Equal?* Springfield, NJ: Enslow Publishers, 1997.

———. *Separate and Unequal: Homer Plessy and the Supreme Court Decision That Legalized Racism.* New York: Carrol & Graf Publishers, 2004.

Francis, Megan Ming. *Civil Rights and the Making of the Modern American State.* New York: Cambridge University Press, 2014.

Franklin, John Hope. *From Slavery to Freedom: A History of Negro Americans,* 3rd ed. New York: Alfred A. Knopf, 1967.

Franklin, John Hope, and August Meier, eds. *Black Leaders of the Twentieth Century.* Urbana: University of Illinois Press, 1982.

Gatewood, Willard B. *Aristocrats of Color: The Black Elite, 1880–1920.* Bloomington: Indiana University Press, 1990.

Ginzberg, Ralph. *100 Years of Lynchings.* New York: Lancer Books, 1969.

Greenberg, Jack. *Race Relations and American Law.* New York: Columbia University Press, 1959.

———. *Crusaders in the Courts: How a Dedicated Band of Lawyers Fought for the Civil Rights Revolution.* New York: Basic Books, 1994.

Greene, Lorenzo J., Gary R. Kremer, and Antonio F. Holland. *Missouri's Black Heritage,* rev. ed. Columbia: University of Missouri Press, 1993.

Heaney, Gerald W., and Susan W Uchitethe. *Unending Struggle: The Long Road to an Equal Education in St. Louis.* St. Louis: Reedy Press, 2004.

Higginbotham, A. Leon, Jr. *Shades of Freedom: Racial Politics and Presumptions of the American Legal Process.* New York: Oxford University Press, 1996.

Hoffer, Williamjames Hull. Plessy v. Ferguson: *Race and Inequality in Jim Crow America.* Lawrence: University of Kansas Press, 2012.

Holland, Antonio Frederick. *Nathan B. Young and the Struggle over Black Higher Education.* Columbia: University of Missouri Press, 2006.

Holland, Antonio Frederick, et al. *The Soldiers' Dream Continued: A Pictorial History of Lincoln University of Missouri.* Jefferson City: Lincoln University Printing Services, 1991.

Howard, John R. *The Shifting Wind: The Supreme Court and Civil Rights from Reconstruction to* Brown. Albany: State University of New York Press, 1999.

Hughes, Charles Evans. *The Supreme Court of the United States: Its Foundation, Methods and Achievements, an Interpretation.* New York: Columbia University Press, 1928.

Hunt, Doug. *Summary Justice: The Lynching of James Scott and the Trial of George Barkwell in Columbia, Missouri, 1923,* 2010.

Jack, Robert L. *History of the National Association for the Advancement of Colored People.* Boston: Meador Publishing, 1943.

James, Jr., Rawn. *Root and Branch: Charles Hamilton Houston, Thurgood Marshall, and the Struggle to End Segregation.* New York: Bloomsbury Press, 2010.

Jonas, Gilbert. *Freedom's Sword: The NAACP and the Struggle Against Racism in America, 1909–1969.* New York: Routledge, 2005.

Johnson, Kimberley. *Reforming Jim Crow: Southern Politics and State in the Age before Brown.* New York: Oxford University Press, 2010.

Kellogg, Charles Flint. *NAACP: A History of the National Association of Colored People. Volume I: 1909–1920.* Baltimore: Johns Hopkins Press, 1967.

Klarman, Michael J. *From Jim Crow to Civil Rights: The Supreme Court and the Struggle for Racial Equality.* New York: Oxford University Press, 2004.

———. *Unfinished Business: Racial Equality in American History.* New York: Oxford University Press, 2007.

Key, V.O., Jr. *Southern Politics in State and Nation.* New York: Knopf, 1949.

Kirkendall, Richard S. *A History of Missouri, 1919 to 1953.* Columbia, MO: University of Missouri Press, 1986.

Kluger, Richard. *Simple Justice: The History of Brown v. Board of Education and Black America's Struggle for Equality.* 2 volumes. New York: Knopf, 1975.

Latham, Frank B. *The Great Dissenter: John Marshall Harlan.* New York: Cowles, 1970.

Lavergne, Gary M. *Before Brown: Heman Marion Sweatt, Thurgood Marshall, and the Long Road to Justice.* Austin: University of Texas Press, 2010.

Leonard, Walter J. *Black Lawyers: Training and Results, Then and Now.* Boston: Senna & Shih, 1977.

Lofgren, Charles. *The Plessy Case: A Legal-Historical Interpretation.* London: Oxford University Press, 1987.

Logan, Rayford W., and Michael R. Winston, eds. *Dictionary of American Negro Biography.* New York: Norton, 1982.

Long, Michael G., ed. *Marshalling Justice: The Early Civil Rights Letters of Thurgood Marshall.* New York: Amistad, 2011.

Marshall, Albert P. *Soldiers' Dream: A Centennial History of Lincoln University of Missouri.* Jefferson City: Lincoln University, 1966.

McCullough, David. *Truman.* New York: Simon & Schuster, 1992.

McCuistion, Fred. *Graduate Instruction for Negroes in the United States.* Nashville, TN: George Peabody College for Teachers, 1939.

McNeil, Genna Rae. *Groundwork: Charles Hamilton Houston and the Struggle for Equal Rights.* Philadelphia: University of Pennsylvania Press, 1983.

Medley, Keith Weldon. *We as Freemen: Plessy v. Ferguson.* Gretna, LA: Pelican Publishing, 2003.

Meier, August, and Elliott Rudwick. *Along the Color Line: Explorations in the Black Experience.* Chicago: University of Illinois Press, 1976.

Middlebush, Frederick A., and Chesney Hill. *Elements of International Relations.* New York: McGraw-Hill, 1940.

Miller, Loren. *The Petitioners—The Story of the Supreme Court of the United States and the Negro.* New York: Pantheon Books, 1966.

Mitchell, Edwina W. *The Crusading Black Journalist: Joseph Everett Mitchell.* St. Louis: Farmer Press, 1972.

Morgan, Arlene Notoro, Alice Irene Pifer, and Keith Woods. *The Authentic Voice: The Best Reporting on Race and Ethnicity.* New York: Columbia University Press, 2006.

Murray, Pauli. *Song in a Weary Throat: An American Pilgrimage.* New York: Harper & Row, 1987.

Myrdal, Gunnar. *The American Dilemma: The Negro Problem and Modern Democracy.* 2 volumes. New York: Harper, 1944.

Nelson, William E. *The Fourteenth Amendment: From Political Principle to Judicial Doctrine.* Cambridge: Harvard University Press, 1988.

Nowlin, William F. *The Negro in American National Politics.* New York: Russell and Russell, 1970 (1931).

Olsen, Otto H. *The Thin Disguise: Turning Point in Negro History:* Plessy v. Ferguson. New York: Humanities Press, 1967.

Olson, James, and Vera Olson. *The University of Missouri: An Illustrated History.* Columbia: University of Missouri Press, 1988.

Parks, Arnold G. *Lincoln University, 1920–1970.* Charleston, SC: Arcadia Publishing, 2007.

Paustian, Paul W., and J. John Oppenheimer. *Problems of Modern Society: An Introduction to the Social Sciences.* New York: McGraw-Hill, 1938.

Perry, J. Edward. *Forty Cords of Wood.* Jefferson City: Lincoln University Press, 1947.

Primm, James Neal. *Lion of the Valley: St. Louis Missouri, 1764–1980,* 3rd ed. St. Louis: Missouri Historical Society Press, 1998.

Rowan, Carl T. *Dream Makers, Dream Breakers: The World of Justice Thurgood Marshall.* Boston: Little, Brown, 1993.

Rudwick, Elliott M. *Race Riot at East St. Louis, July 2, 1917.* Carbondale: Southern Illinois University Press, 1964.

Ryan, Yvonne. *Roy Wilkins: The Quiet Revolutionary and the NAACP.* Lexington: University Press of Kentucky, 2014.

Savage, W. Sherman. *The History of Lincoln University.* Jefferson City, MO: New Day Press, 1939.

Schirmer, Sherry Lamb. *A City Divided: The Racial Landscape of Kansas City, 1900–1960.* Columbia: University of Missouri Press, 2002.

Schneider, Mark Robert. *"We Return Fighting" The Civil Rights Movement in the Jazz Age.* Boston: Northeastern University Press, 2002.

Schuyler, George S. *Black and Conservative: The Autobiography of George S. Schuyler.* New Rochelle: Arlington House, 1966.

Segal, Geraldine R. *In Any Fight Some Fall.* Rockville, MD: Mercury Press, 1975.

Sewell, George Alexander, and Margaret L. Dwight. *Mississippi Black History Makers,* rev. and enl. ed. Jackson: University Press of Mississippi, 1984.

Simmons, Charles A. *The African American Press: A History of News Coverage during National Crisis, with Special Reference to Four Black Newspapers, 1827–1965.* Jefferson, NC: McFarland, 1998.

Smith, Jr., J. Clay. *Emancipation: The Making of the Black Lawyer, 1844–1944.* Philadelphia: University of Pennsylvania Press, 1993.

Smith, Jr., J. Clay, ed. *Supreme Justice: Speeches and Writings: Thurgood Marshall.* Philadelphia: University of Pennsylvania Press, 2003.

Styles, Fitzhugh Lee. *Negroes and the Law.* Boston: Christopher Publishing, 1937.

Stein, Lana. *St. Louis Politics: The Triumph of Tradition.* St. Louis: Missouri Historical Society Press, 2002.

Stephens, Frank F. *A History of the University of Missouri.* Columbia: University of Missouri Press, 1962.

Sullivan, Patricia. *Lift Every Voice: The NAACP and the Making of the Civil Rights Movement.* New York: New Press, 2009.

Telgen, Diane. *Defining Moments:* Brown v. Board of Education. Detroit, MI: Omnigraphics, 2005.

Tushnet, Mark V. *The NAACP's Legal Strategy against Segregated Education, 1925–1950.* Chapel Hill: University of North Carolina Press, 1987.

Tushnet, Mark V., ed. *I Dissent: Great Opposing Opinions in Landmark Supreme Court Cases.* Boston, MA: Beacon Press, 2008.

Viles, Jonas. *The University of Missouri: A Centennial History, 1839–1939.* Columbia: University of Missouri, 1939.

Vose, Clement E. *Caucasians Only: The Supreme Court, the NAACP, and the Restrictive Covenant Cases.* Berkeley: University of California Press, 1959.

Ware, Gilbert. *William Hastie: Grace under Pressure.* New York: Oxford University Press, 1984.

Wesley, Doris A, Wiley Price, and Ann Morris, eds. *Lift Every Voice and Sing: St. Louis African Americans in the Twentieth Century.* Columbia: University of Missouri Press, 1999.

White, Walter. *Rope and Faggot: A Biography of Judge Lynch.* New York: Knopf, 1929.

———. *A Man Called White: The Autobiography of Walter White.* Bloomington: Indiana University Press, 1948 [1970].

Whites, Lee Ann, Mary Neth, and Gary Kremer, eds. *Women in Missouri History: In Search of Power and Influence.* Columbia: University of Missouri Press, 2004.

Wilkins, Roy, and Tom Mathews. *Standing Fast: The Autobiography of Roy Wilkins.* New York: Viking, 1982.

Williams, Juan. *Thurgood Marshall: American Revolutionary.* New York: Times Books, 1998.

Winfield, Betty H., ed. *Journalism 1908: Birth of a Profession.* Columbia: University of Missouri Press, 2008.

Wormser, Richard. *The Rise and Fall of Jim Crow.* New York: St. Martin's, 2003.

Wright, John A. *Discovering African-American St. Louis,* 2nd ed. St. Louis: Missouri Historical Society Press, 2002.

Young, Nathan B. *Your St. Louis and Mine.* St. Louis: N.B. Young, 1937.

Young, William H., and Nathan B. Young. *Your Kansas City and Mine.* Kansas City: W. H. Young, 1950.

Dissertations, Theses, and Reports

Boyd, Alvin C. *An Occupational Study of the Negro Citizens of Columbia, Missouri, 1941.* Columbia: A National Youths Administration Project, 1941.

Brigham, Robert Irving. "The Education of the Negro in Missouri." Ph.D. diss., University of Missouri, 1946.

Clayton, Charles C. *Frederick Arnold Middlebush, President, University of Missouri, 1935–1954: Appreciation Banquet, June 10, 1954, at Columbia.* Columbia: University of Missouri, 1954.

Cook, Delia Crutchfield. "Shadow across the Columns: The Bittersweet Legacy of African-Americans at the University of Missouri." Ph.D. diss., University of Missouri, 1996.

Daniel, Ansley K. "Student Access to Higher Education: A Historical Analysis of Landmark Supreme Court Cases *Missouri ex rel. Gaines v. Canada, Registrar of the University of Missouri*, 1938, and *Grutter v. Bollinger*, 2003." Ph.D. diss., Georgia State University, 2012.

Dreer, Herman. "Negro Leadership in Saint Louis: A Study in Race Relations." Ph.D. thesis, University of Chicago, 1955.

Elwang, William Wilson. "The Negroes of Columbia, Missouri: A Concrete Study of the Race Problem." M.A. thesis, University of Missouri, 1904.

Grant, Elizabeth Cossum. "Some Colored Working Mothers in Columbia." M.A. thesis, University of Missouri, 1935.

Greene, Debra Foster. "Published in the Interest of Colored People: The St. Louis Argus Newspaper in the Twentieth Century." Ph.D. diss., University of Missouri, 2003.

Haynes, Ross Alan. "The Importance of the Black Press in the Desegregation of the University of Missouri." M.A. thesis, University of Missouri—Kansas City, 1994.

Holland, Antonio Frederick. "Nathan B. Young and the Development of Black Higher Education." Ph.D. diss., University of Missouri, 1984.

Kelleher, Daniel T. "The History of the St. Louis NAACP 1914–1955." M.A. thesis, Southern Illinois University Edwardsville, 1969.

King, Lloyd W. *Four Years of Progress with Missouri Public Schools for the Negro.* Jefferson City: State Superintendent of Public Schools, 1939.

Kittel, Audrey Nell. "The Negro Community of Columbia, Missouri." M.A. thesis, University of Missouri, 1938.

Leuthold, David A. *Biographical Directory of the Political Science Department, University of Missouri (Columbia): Faculty, Masters, and Doctors, 1902–1965.* Columbia: Department of Political Science, University of Missouri, 1966.

Margold, Nathan R. *Preliminary Report to the Joint Committee Supervising the Expenditure of 1930 Appropriation by the American Fund for Public Service to the N.A.A.C.P.* New York: NAACP, 1930.

Martin, Dorothy. "Survey of Juvenile Delinquency in Columbia." M.A. thesis, University of Missouri, 1934.

Sawyer, Robert McLaran. "The *Gaines* Case: Its Background and Influence on the University of Missouri and Lincoln University, 1936–1950." Ph.D. diss., University of Missouri, 1966.

Shelton, Vanessa. "Interpretive Community and the Black Press: Racial Equality and Politics in the *St. Louis American* and the *St. Louis Argus*," 1928–1956." Ph.D. diss., University of Iowa, 2007.

Slavens, George Everett. "A History of the Missouri Negro Press." Ph.D. diss., University of Missouri, 1969.

Smith, Dwyane. "We Have Not Had Such Luck: A Lloyd Gaines Case Study." Ph.D. diss., University of Missouri, 2000.

Court Cases

Berea College v. Commonwealth of Kentucky, 211 U.S. 45 (1908).

Bluford v. Canada, 32 F. Supp. 707, (W.D. Mo. 1940).

State ex rel. Bluford v. Canada, 153 S.W. 2d 12 (Mo. 1941).

Brown v. Board of Education, 347 U.S. 483 (1954).

Brown v. Board of Education, 349 U.S. 294 (1955).

Buchanan v. Warley, 245 U.S. 60 (1917).

Civil Rights Cases, 109 U.S. 3 (1883).

Cumming v. Richmond Board of Education, 175 U.S. 528 (1899).

Cummings v. Missouri, 71 U.S. 277 (1867).

Dred Scott v. Sandford, 60 U.S. 393 (1857).

Hale v. Kentucky, 303 U.S. 613 (1938).

Henderson v. U.S., 339 U.S. 816 (1950).

Thomas R. Hocutt v. Thomas J. Wilson, Jr., Dean of Admissions and Registrar, and the University of North Carolina, Superior Court, Durham County, North Carolina (March 28, 1933).

Lehew v. Brummell, 103 Mo. 546, 15 S.W. 765 (1890).

Gong Lum v. Rice, 275 U.S. 78 (1927).

McCabe v. Atchison, Topeka, and Santa Fe Railway, Co., 235 U.S. 151 (1914).

McLaurin v. Oklahoma State Board of Regents for Higher Education, 339 U.S. 637 (1950).

State of Missouri ex rel. Lucile Bluford v. S. W. Canada, Registrar of the University of Missouri, No. 35754, 348 Mo. 298, 153 S.W.2d. 12.

Missouri ex. rel. Gaines v. Canada, 305 U.S. 337 (1938).

Missouri v. Jenkins, 515 U.S. 70 (1995).

Mitchell v. U.S., 313 U.S. 80 (1941).

Donald G. Murray v. Raymond A. Pearson, et al., (1935).

Nixon v. Condrun, 286 U.S. 73 (1932).

Norris v. Alabama, 294 U.S. 587 (1935).

Raymond A. Pearson, et al. v. Donald G. Murray, 182 A. 590, 169 Md. 478, 103 A.L.R. 706 (1936).

People ex rel. King v. Gallagher, 93 N.Y. 438 (1883).

Plessy v. Ferguson, 163 U.S. 537 (1896).

Shelley v. Kraemer, 334 U.S. 1 (1948).

Slaughterhouse Cases, 83 U.S. 36 (1873).

Sipuel v. Oklahoma State Board of Regents, 332 U.S. 631 (1948).

Smith v. Allwright, 321 U.S. 649 (1944).

State ex rel. Gaines v. Canada, Circuit Court of Boone County, No. 34,337 (1936).

State ex rel. Gaines v. Canada, No. 35286, 342 Mo. 121, 113 S.W.2d 783 (1937).

State ex rel. Gaines v. Canada, No. 35286 344 Mo. 1238, 131 S.W.2d 217 (1939).

Strauder v. West Virginia, 100 U.S. 303 (1879).

Sweatt v. Painter, 339 U.S. 629 (1950).

U.S. v. Cruikshank, 92 U.S. 542 (1875).

University of Maryland v. Donald G. Murray, 169 Md. 478 (1936).

Yick Wo v. Hopkins, 118 U.S. 356 (1886).

Index

Throughout this index the abbreviation "Gaines" is used to indicate references to "Missouri ex rel. Gaines v. Canada." Page numbers appearing in italics refer to illustrations.

Missouri Student, 147–52, 153–57, 188, 316n3, 316n7
Mitchell, Joseph E., 15, 18, 19, 57, 154, 278nn56–60
Mitchell, N. A., 14
Mitchell, William, 19
Mitchell v. U.S., 243, 344n45
Moberly Monitor-Index and Democrat, 140, 160
Moon, Jon, 249
Moore, Walthall M., 22, 26, 94, 302n32
Moran, Margaret Gladys, 99
Morrill Act, 23, 290n33
Mound City Bar Association, 14, 17, 79, 201
Murphy, Frank, 204, 225
Murphy, George, 70, 164
Murray, Donald Gaines, 49–50, 66, 89, 102, *172,* 252, 288n70, 299n174
See also *Pearson, et al v. Murray*
Murray, Pauli, 226, 243, 343n42, 344n48
Murray, Ralph E., 76, 205, 308n149, 310n179
Myrdal, Gunner, 25, 282n98

NAACP (National Association for the Advancement of Colored People)
about, 31
background and overview of *Gaines* and, 3–9
Bluford cases and, 239
financing litigation and, 33, 241, 244
Gaines and, 12, 227, 228, 229–30, 232, 234
Kansas City Branch of, 88, 165–66, 171
Legal Defense and Education, 269
on Lincoln University Law School, 202
litigation strategy of (*See* litigation strategy of NAACP)

national convention of 1935, 18–19, 278n54
Plessy v. Ferguson and, 27
press releases (*See* press releases, NAACP)
segregation tolerance and, 159
St. Louis branch of (*See* St. Louis branch of NAACP)
Taylor Bill and, 170
name of *Gaines* case, 72
National Bar Association, 15, 196, 267, 328n68, 332n115
National Bar Journal, 267, 328n68
National Labor Relations Board (NLRB), 133, 138, 139–40
Nazi antisemitism compared to US racial discrimination, 121, 129–30, 139, 149, 154, 164
"Negro," term of, 21, 83, 99, 280n72
Nevada State Journal, 223–24
News Herald, 99, 140, 155, 314n73
New York Age, 20, 66
New York Amsterdam News
on *Bluford* case, 226–27
on campus attitude towards blacks, 253
on *Gaines,* 124, 131, 150, 154, 217–18
on Gaines disappearance, 215, 218, 229–30
use of "Negro," 21, 280n72
New York Times, 140, 159–60, 235, 257, 266–67, 319n49, 347n116
NLRB (National Labor Relations Board), 133, 138, 139–40
North Carolina, 136, 242, 343n39
North Central Association of Colleges and Secondary Schools, 60, 74, 192, 195, 281n86

O'Dunne, Eugene, 49
Oklahoma, 144, 249–51, 256
Oldham, Marian O'Fallon, 241, 342n35

tuition programs, out-of-state. *See* out-
of-state tuition programs
Tull, Irvin C., 94, 302n32
Turpin, Charles, 14
Tushnet, Mark, 3–4, 5, 44,
286–87n12

unequal school funding, 33–43
United Press, 105, 162, 166–67, 191,
199
University of Arkansas, 213n19
University of Maryland, 49, 50, 65, 100
University of Michigan
about, 281n90
Gaines at, 90–93, 211, 212, 301n25,
302n27
University of Missouri
about, 2–3, 12, 24, 247
admission practices of, 55, 59–
61, 63–72, 257–59, 260–63,
293–94n84
defense in *Gaines,* 70–71, 73–75
desegregation of, 253–54
journalism school of, 239
Lincoln University Act of 1921 and,
26–27
reaction to *Gaines* Supreme Court decision, 160
term "Negro" and, 21
See also Board of Curators, University
of Missouri; *Missouri ex rel. Gaines
v. Canada*
University of North Carolina, 32, 60,
243
University of Oklahoma, 249–51, 256
University of Texas, 255–56
University of Virginia, 48, 51–52, 62,
257

Valentine, Gamewell, 226
Van Horne, Glenn, 151–52
Vashon High School, 11, 15, 19,
275n5, 278n54

Vaughn, George L., 14–15, 17, 18, 25,
275–76nn21–23, 276n26
Villard, Oswald Garrison, 121
Vinson, Frederick M., 250, 255–56
Vose, Clement E., 275–76n23

Waring, Oscar Minor, 274n3
Warren, Earl, 266
Washington Post, 133
Washington Star, 134
Washington University, 197, 199, 254,
283n104, 328–29n74
Watson, Edwin Moss, 293n75, 306n97
Watson, John Brown, 128
Webber, Harry B., 230
Weathers, Frank, 211, 227, 336n39
Whitaker, O. B., 162, 319–20n62,
320n65
White, Walter, *174*
about, 5, 108, 268, 307n124
financial aid to Gaines and, 90–92
funding *Gaines* and, 130–31, 210,
333–34n5
Gaines circuit court trial and, 75–76
Gaines disappearance and, 228, 233
Gaines federal appeal and, 108–
9, 111, 121, 307nn132–33,
310–11nn194–95
Gaines remand trial to state and, 171,
186–87, 323n171, 324n14
garnering student support, 150, 152,
153, 316n10
lynchings and, 25, 95
on Margold, 32
press and, 130, 136, 150, 312n31,
316n10
Stark and, 169
Taylor Bill and, 164, 166, 167–68
Whitlow, George, 165, 166–67
Wilke, Harold, 203
Wilkins, Roy
about, 5, 6–7, 20, 268, 279n70
Gaines and, 171, 229–30